# Ships of Discovery and Exploration

# Ships of Discovery and Exploration

## Lincoln P. Paine

*A Mariner Original*
HOUGHTON MIFFLIN COMPANY
BOSTON · NEW YORK
2000

BOOKS BY LINCOLN P. PAINE

SHIPS OF THE WORLD: AN HISTORICAL ENCYCLOPEDIA

WARSHIPS OF THE WORLD TO 1900

SHIPS OF DISCOVERY AND EXPLORATION

Visit our Web site: www.houghtonmifflinbooks.com.

*Library of Congress Cataloging-in-Publication Data*
Paine, Lincoln P.
Ships of discovery and exploration / Lincoln P. Paine
p.    cm.
"A Mariner original."
Includes bibliographical references (p.   ).
ISBN 0-395-98415-7
1. Discoveries in geography.  2. Ships.  I. Title.
G80.P28 2000
910'.9—dc21    00-040802

Printed in the United States of America

Book design by Robert Overholtzer

QUM 10 9 8 7 6 5 4 3 2 1

To Hal Fessenden

*A Sinbad in his own right*

# Contents

# Illustrations

# Preface

Ships of Discovery and Exploration is based in large part on *Ships of the World: An Historical Encyclopedia,* published in 1997. Seventeen new articles help fill in the gaps in the exploratory tradition as presented in the earlier book. Several entries have been rewritten or corrected in light of new scholarship and suggestions made by reviewers and other readers of *Ships of the World.*

A great number of people contributed to this effort in various ways. For help in pulling together information, illustrations and maps from a variety of disparate sources, and for reading some of the new material, I would like to thank Norman Brouwer, curator of ships at South Street Seaport Museum Library; Lars Bruzelius; Nick Burningham, Duyfken Project; Jim Delgado, Vancouver Maritime Museum; Francisco C. Domingues; Martin Evans and Janet West; Jackie Field; Joseph Jackson, New York Yacht Club; Steve McLaughlin; Frances McSherry; Rosemary Mosher; Colin Starkey, National Maritime Museum, Greenwich. The administrators of the Maritime History Information Exchange Group (MARHST-L) and Queens University, Toronto, are to be commended for maintaining a lively international forum for the discussion of maritime history; MARHST's many subscribers have helped answer countless questions and turned light to dark corners.

No research project of this scope can be undertaken without consulting a wide variety of sources, and I would be remiss were I not to acknowledge those librarians upon whom I have relied at the University of Southern Maine, Portland; the New York Public Library; the National Maritime Museum, Greenwich, England; and South Street Seaport Museum, New York.

On a personal note, I am grateful to Elizabeth Mitchell and Alex Krieckhaus, and Chris Graves and JoAnn Ward, and their children, for their hospitality when I was far from home. I must also thank John Wright, my agent (*provocateur*) and friend; my collaborators on *Ships of the World,* Jim Terry, Eric Berryman, and, especially, Hal Fessenden to whom I dedicate this volume; and above all my wife, Allison, and our daughters, Kai and Madeleine.

Lincoln P. Paine
Portland, Maine
April 2000

# Introduction

**S**hips of Discovery and Exploration recounts the stories of more than 130 ships that sailed in exploratory voyages in all parts of the world and for all sorts of reasons. Until the nineteenth century, all kinds of ships were used for exploration. Only in the mid-1800s were ships built for specific exploratory assignments, so it is not possible to speak of the evolution of discovery ships as a distinct type before about 150 years ago. It is equally difficult to treat the history of maritime discovery as a continuous process, for until the European "age of discovery," which started in about the fifteenth century, exploration was a regional phenomenon in which limited horizons were gradually expanded. Some of these regions were small, almost local, but others — Europe itself, the Indian Ocean and East Asia, and Oceania — were vast areas comprising a multiplicity of heterogeneous networks. Europe's overriding contribution to maritime discovery was to connect these regions and to create a more or less unified global network for the transportation of goods, peoples, and ideas. This development occurred only in the last 500 years, but much of the groundwork that made it possible was laid over the course of thousands of years before that.

The focus of maritime exploration prior to the late eighteenth century had a geographic orientation. By that time, the outlines of the world's oceans had been well defined and described. In the Age of Enlightenment, toward the end of the eighteenth century, the mission of voyages of exploration came to embrace the study of ethnography, zoology, and botany, and increasingly, specialists in these fields signed on for long voyages. Advances in technology — the need to lay submarine cables, for instance — and lines of inquiry related to the economics of fisheries and environmental and navigational sciences introduced a new dimension into the work of maritime discovery. This resulted in the construction of a wide variety of purpose-built vessels designed to examine the waters of the world beneath the surface in new ways.

For much of the early period of discovery the names of the vessels used in exploration, if indeed they had names, are unknown. To tell the story of maritime discovery with reference only to a handful of specific named ships would be to overlook some of the most daring and decisive of our forebears' achievements. In recent years, a number of early voyages of discovery have been re-created in vessels, and along routes, of greater or lesser authenticity. These vessels — Polynesian voyaging canoes, Mesopotamian reed boats, Greek galleys, Irish curraghs, Arabian dhows — have drawn attention to what was possible. Even if the results of some of these modern voyages are inconclusive, they almost invariably throw new light on our understanding of the past.

The South Pacific is the locus of one of the oldest and most sustained efforts of exploration by any maritime people. The islands of Oceania are divided into three main groups, reflecting both geographic and ethnographic characteristics. Farthest to the west, and settled first, are the islands of Melanesia,* which lie within a broad band between

---

* *Neisos* is Greek for "island": Melanesia = "black islands" (for the relative color of the inhabitants' skin); Micronesia = "small islands"; Polynesia = "many islands."

New Guinea and the Fiji Islands. To the east is Polynesia, a huge triangle whose sides are described by a line drawn between Easter Island (Rapa Nui) in the east, New Zealand in the southwest, and Hawaii to the north. Micronesia, north of Melanesia, spans the Pacific from Palau to Kiribati and embraces the Marshall, Caroline, and Mariana island groups. Although many specifics remain unknown, one widely accepted theory is that the distant ancestors of the islanders encountered by Europeans from the sixteenth century on originated in the Solomon Islands just east of New Guinea, that the pattern of settlement was generally from west to east, and that the process began about 3,500 years ago.

The first push brought these seafaring settlers to the island groups of Santa Cruz, Vanuatu, New Caledonia, and Fiji in about 1,500 BCE. Within another 500 years — that is to say, around the time of Homer, or a little before — they had settled Samoa and Tonga. The Society Islands (Tahiti) were colonized by about 500 BCE, and within another 1,000 years Polynesians had spread out to reach Pitcairn Island and Easter Island to the south and east and Hawaii to the north. Among the last and largest islands to be reached were those of New Zealand, between 1,000 and 1,300 years ago. The chronology of the settlement of Micronesia is less well understood, although it appears that certain islands were settled from Melanesia and others from Polynesia.

The vessels in which the Polynesians sailed were large double canoes, probably about 60 or 70 feet (18 to 21 meters) long (though vessels of 100 feet [31 meters] are not unknown today), capable of carrying the people, supplies, and material goods necessary for establishing sustainable communities on uninhabited islands. These catamarans* had a deck spanning the distance between the two hulls and they were rigged with V-shaped (or wishbone) sails. As important as their boatbuilding skills, the Polynesians evolved a sophisticated set of naviga-

tional skills known as wayfinding, which incorporated many of the elements of navigation used today but without recourse to mechanical or electronic instruments. Astronomy and latitude sailing were of particular importance, as was the ability to read and interpret the patterns of waves and swells, the location of fish and sea mammals, the flight paths of birds, prevailing and shifting wind patterns, and other meteorological conditions.

Although the prevailing winds in Polynesia blow from east to west, there are periodic shifts. It is believed that the Polynesian explorers took advantage of these changes to sail downwind to the east on a west wind fully confident that if they did not find new lands, the wind would shift to the east and allow them to run downwind back to their point of origin. Thus exploration was for the most part the product of two-way intentional voyaging; only occasionally were new islands discovered as a result of accidental drift voyaging. One such voyage may have brought Melanesian canoes from Fiji to New Zealand before the arrival of the Polynesian ancestors of the Maori, who probably arrived from Tahiti in about 1000 CE. But New Zealand lies south of Polynesia, in a high latitude on the far side of a belt of variable winds across which it is very difficult to return. This may explain why it was discovered about 500 years later than Easter Island, even though the latter is 3,000 miles farther from the Solomons, and why the Maoris eventually abandoned the sea road to the heart of Polynesia. Adverse winds and currents also help explain why Melanesian and Polynesian contact with northern Australia was only sporadic and did not result in any apparent attempt to establish permanent settlements.

As the dating of settlement in individual island groups suggests, the progress of exploration in Oceania was punctuated by lulls of considerable duration. By the time Europeans reached the Pacific, long-distance voyaging within Polynesia seems to have abated somewhat. In the eighteenth century, there was more voyaging within central Polynesia than to the extremes, and the English sailors on Captain James Cook's expedition in HMS *Endeavour* in the early 1770s were impressed

---

* The word "catamaran" refers to a vessel comprising two parallel hulls with a raised deck spanning the distance between them. The word, which is of Tamil (Sri Lankan) origin, originally meant a vessel of lashed logs—more like a barge or raft than the nimble Polynesian craft.

with the navigational ability of Tupia, a Tahitian who returned to England with them and who related that some islanders undertook voyages lasting as long as twenty days.

The motives underlying these extensive migrations are not known. Population pressures may have played a part, perhaps under threat of ostracism and exile. The search for raw materials for trade was probably incidental to exploration itself, although trade between colonies and homelands, as well as kinship networks, may have sustained two-way communication between distant islands following initial settlement.

For the extent and duration of sea voyages, the discovery and settling of Oceania has no parallel. Prior to the Viking voyages to Iceland in the eighth century and Greenland and North America in the tenth century, most maritime exploration occurred along the shores of continental landmasses, or within relatively dense island groups such as those of Indonesia, the Ryukyus off Japan, the Aleutian chain in Alaska, and the Leeward and Windward islands of the Caribbean. There is also evidence for long-distance waterborne trade between Ecuador and Mexico on the Pacific coast, in the early centuries of the Christian era, and more definitively for trade between Sri Lanka and Indonesia in the Indian Ocean, but how these routes originated is unknown.

Ancient records, both written and archaeological, make it difficult to determine whether the earliest coastal trade routes resulted from purposeful maritime exploration of the unknown or from the realization that ships were a more convenient and efficient means of transportation than land-based caravan routes. Although the overland route from Mesopotamia to the Indus Valley is shorter than the sea route, there is evidence of a sea link between the Harappa states of the Indus Valley and the Sumerian kingdom at the head of the Persian Gulf as early as 2500 BCE. Similarly, Egypt's Queen Hatshepsut mounted a trade expedition from the head of the Red Sea to Punt, on the Somali coast, in 1500 BCE. What seems to distinguish the pioneers of these sea routes from their Polynesian contemporaries is the fact that they were not sailing into the unknown; they sailed in search of new routes between two known and inhabited destinations.

The ancient Greeks produced a great number of adventure stories that seem to explain how they opened sea routes to the world beyond their Aegean. The most famous of these is that of Jason and the Argonauts, who sailed in the *Argo* from the Aegean Sea to the Black Sea and east to Colchis, in present-day Georgia. It is clear from the nature of the account that Colchis was a known, if remote, place; what Jason and his crew discovered, if anything, was not a new place, but a sea route to it. In addition to such legends, there are the fragmentary accounts of several real voyages of exploration. In the late seventh century BCE, Egypt's pharaoh Necho sent a number of Phoenician vessels on a circumnavigation of Africa from the Red Sea to the Mediterranean. According to Herodotus, this voyage took three years, during which the sailors stopped each fall to plant crops for the following year. He also tells, in some disbelief, how in the course of their voyage from east to west, the sailors had the sun on their right, which could have happened only if they were south of the Equator. About 300 years later, a Greek named Pytheas sailed out of the Mediterranean to the British Isles, to a land rich in amber (Denmark or farther east in the Baltic), and to a mysterious place called Thule, variously identified as Iceland, the Faeroe Islands, or Norway. In his journey to the British Isles, anyway, Pytheas was sailing in the wake of the Phoenicians, who had access to the tin mines of Cornwall. But in any case, neither Necho's captains nor Pytheas achieved anything of long-lasting consequence: northern Europe opened gradually from the south, as the Roman Empire expanded, and southern Africa would not be rounded again until the fifteenth century. Yet the possibility that such voyages took place is far from remote.

Of more immediate significance in the ancient world was the discovery by Mediterranean traders of the seasonal monsoons that facilitated navigation between Africa, Arabia, and India. This discovery, credited to the second-century-BCE Eudoxus of Cyzicus, in Asia Minor, was really an intelligence coup; the sailors of the Indian Ocean had sailed to the rhythms of the monsoons for centuries. (Eudoxus is reported to have disappeared attempting to round Africa counterclockwise, from west to east, in an effort to avoid the Ptolemy VIII's confiscatory customs duties after his first two voyages.)

For hundreds of years following the extension of Rome's hegemony over western Europe, such long-distance exploration as took place was confined to the Indian Ocean and western Pacific. Persian and Arab traders established direct trade links to China via Southeast Asia by the seventh century, but these included many ports of call and the route was spliced together from strands of shorter routes.

The next burst of maritime exploration came from the Baltic — Europe's northern inland sea — and was initiated by the Scandinavians. Vikings began by expanding along the east-west corridor of the Baltic. They established themselves in northern Russia, and soon their river-oriented trade networks extended south to the Black Sea and Byzantium and east to the Caspian. West from the Baltic, the Vikings conquered along the coasts and rivers of the British Isles and western Europe as far south as the Mediterranean. Following in the wake of Irish monks — St. Brendan is specifically recognized for this achievement — who reached Iceland around 790, the Norse reached Iceland in about 860. From there, in 982, Eirik (The Red) Thorvaldsson sailed west for Greenland to spend there a three-year term of exile for murder. A quarter century later, his son Leif (The Lucky) sailed farther west, to Newfoundland, called Vinland, where the remains of a Viking encampment have been unearthed at L'Anse aux Meadows. This settlement did not last long. The outpost was too remote, the population available to sustain it too small, and the rewards too few. The abandonment of the Vinland colony prefigured the contraction of the Viking's Atlantic world. The Greenland settlements ended regular communication with Iceland in 1347, and vanished a century later; Iceland's contacts with Europe also entered a long period of decline.

By this time, traders of the Hanseatic League, centered on German cities in the Baltic, had superseded the Vikings as the dominant seafarers in northern Europe, while Mediterranean seafarers had begun their first forays into the Atlantic. The latter initiatives were fueled by the profits from trade and the search for more. Christian Europe first got a taste of the benefits of commerce with the East when the Crusaders gained a foothold in the Levant, in the late eleventh century. By the early thirteenth century, Genoese and Venetian merchants were also active in the Black Sea. The Genoese established themselves in Trebizond, on the north coast of modern Turkey, an entrepôt for overland trade with India. Mediterranean traders were also engaged in an expanding trade with northern Europe. In the early thirteenth century, Genoese merchants entered the Atlantic, and by the 1270s their galleys, as well as those of Majorca and other trading states, regularly plied between Genoa and Bruges, initiating the first sustained navigation by Mediterranean sailors between Mediterranean and Atlantic ports.

The westward shift received additional impetus in 1291, when the Egyptian Mamluks captured Tyre and Acre, the last Christian trading centers on the eastern Mediterranean coast. The Genoese devised a number of schemes by which to circumvent the Muslim middlemen who now controlled the spice trade. One of these was a voyage in 1291 by the brothers Ugolino and Vadino Vivaldi, who fitted out two galleys for a voyage to India via Ceuta, a Moroccan port opposite Gibraltar, the implication being that they would attempt to circumnavigate Africa, just as Eudoxus had — and for much the same reason — fourteen centuries before. The Vivaldis disappeared without a trace, but this voyage is regarded as a milestone in the history of Atlantic exploration. Far from being a quixotic adventure, it was an effort by practical merchants to overcome a serious commercial setback.

In the fourteenth and fifteenth centuries, Genoese seamen increasingly found themselves sailing under foreign flags — especially that of Portugal, for which they discovered or helped settle the Canary Islands (the Islas Fortunatas of antiquity), the Madeiras, and the Azores. Although most of his energy was directed toward the exploitation of his holdings in the Azores and Madeira, Portugal's entrepreneurial Dom Henrique (Prince Henry, 1394–1460) sent ships down the west coast of Africa in search of slaves and gold. By 1434, the Portuguese knew the coast as far as Cape Bojador in Mauritania. Progress southward continued, and the Portuguese reached the Cape Verde Islands in 1445. Three years later they erected a fort on the island of Arguim, off the northern Mauretanian coast, from which they conducted a lucrative trade in slaves, ivory, and gold.

These voyages, originally made in square-rigged *barcas* and *barinels,* and by the 1430s in small lateen-rigged caravels, helped foster navigation in the Atlantic. But there is no indication that Dom Henrique contemplated circumnavigating Africa or finding a shortcut to the Indies. The credit for that effort goes to his grandnephew João (John) II, who ruled Portugal from 1481 to 1495, during which time he fostered a program of maritime exploration to reach India via a sea route around Africa. To ensure the feasibility of this, he dispatched two simultaneous expeditions. Pero da Covilhão went directly east to India, from where he reported on the possible existence of a sea route to the west around southern Africa. At the same time, Bartolomeu Dias rounded the aptly named Cape of Storms — taking a longer view, the King later dubbed it the Cape of Good Hope — from west to east, returning to Lisbon in December 1488 after an absence of more than sixteen months.

All of this exploratory activity attracted any number of ambitious mariners. The Genoa-born Columbus conceived a bold plan to establish a direct route to "the land of India and the great island of Cipango and the realms of the Great Khan . . ." — that is, Japan and China. His estimates of the distances involved — 2,400 miles (3,860 kilometers) from the Canary Islands to Japan and 3,550 miles (5,700 kilometers) to China — were wrong. But with the patronage of Ferdinand and Isabella of Spain, Columbus reached the Caribbean on his first voyage, in 1492–93, and landed in South America and Central America on his fourth and final voyage, in 1502–4. Although he was aware that he had discovered a new world, he was reluc-

tant to admit that he had not found the Orient, and died cherishing the belief that he had been within ten days' sail of the Ganges River.

At the time of Columbus's first voyage, no one could have predicted the benefits to be reaped by Spain — and the world — as a result of his gross underestimation of the distances involved. His object, after all, was the discovery of a route to the Indies, to cut out the middlemen in the lucrative spice trade. (Had Columbus been embarked on a voyage to find something unknown, no one would have backed him; such a scheme by Columbus or any other European of his time would have been inconceivable.) João II was briefly interested in Columbus's plan, but declined his proposal when Dias returned from the Cape of Good Hope. No one can fault the Portuguese king for sticking with his proven round-Africa campaign, and in the short run, his strategy won out. In 1497, João's successor, Manoel, named Vasco da Gama to lead a four-ship expedition, including the 100-ton nao *São Gabriel.* Vasco da Gama sailed around the Cape of Good Hope to East Africa, from where, with the help of Muslim pilots, he sailed to Calicut, on the west coast of India. On the second Portuguese voyage to India, in 1500, Pero Alvares Cabral landed on the coast of Brazil. By 1511, the Portuguese were ensconced in the East Indies and had tapped the source of the spice trade. This they now rerouted directly to Lisbon, which became the chief entrepôt of western Europe.

The voyages of discovery that followed these Spanish and Portuguese breakthroughs east and west were breathtaking in their scope and daring. The most famous voyage of the era was the circumnavigation initiated by Ferdinand Magellan, a Portuguese sailing for the Spanish, and completed after his death in the Philippines under the leadership of Juan Sebastian de Elcano, sailing in *Victoria.* The most important aspect of Magellan's voyage was the transpacific leg, although he sailed north of most of the islands of Oceania. European transpacific navigation remained a one-way — east-to-west — enterprise until 1565, when Andrés de Urdaneta, sailing in the *San Pablo,* discovered a way east across the Pacific by sailing on the prevailing westerlies from the Philippines north of Hawaii to California and south to Mexico. This turned out to be the inaugural voyage of the so-called Manila Galleon, which for 250 years carried the riches of the Americas to Asia, and the precious goods of the Orient to Mexico for transshipment to Spain and Europe.

Magellan had originally sailed to determine whether the Spice Islands (the Moluccas) were Portuguese or Spanish, according to the 1494 Treaty of Tordesillas. This agreement divided the world into two hemispheres, one Spanish, the other Portuguese, by means of a north-south line drawn 370 leagues (about 1,200 miles) west of the Cape Verde Islands. If other European powers declined to challenge the Iberian monopoly over extra-European trade, it was not out of respect for such agreements (Tordesillas remained in force until 1750), but because of the dominance of Iberian maritime power. This had its limits, however. One area that was nominally Spanish but over which Spain exercised no practical control was North America, and it is here that the fledgling maritime powers of northern Europe first turned their attention. As they had for the Portuguese and Spanish, Italian navigators led the way.

The first search for a northern route to the Indies is credited to John Cabot, a "citizen of Venice" who, sailing in the *Mathew* under the auspices of England's Henry VII, reached Newfoundland in 1497. The French sponsored two expeditions to the coast of North America in the sixteenth century. Giovanni da Verrazzano, a Florentine, sailed along the coast from North Carolina to Newfoundland in 1524, and ten years later Jacques Cartier probed the St. Lawrence River as far as present-day Montreal in search of a western route to the Pacific. The voyages resulted in little official settlement, and for the time being the European presence in this part of North America was limited to an assortment of European fishermen who established seasonal camps on the shores of Newfoundland and traded for furs on the side.

The English search for the Northwest Passage began in earnest with Martin Frobisher's voyages in the 1570s; Francis Drake also searched for a western outlet of the Northwest Passage on the Pacific Coast of North America during his circumnavigation in the *Golden Hind* of 1577–80. The effort ended in 1616 when John Bylot returned from his expedition in *Discovery* to Lancaster Sound, north of Baffin Island — which would later prove to be the gateway to the Northwest Passage — and Hudson Bay. These voyages excited some interest, but they required too great an outlay in men and ships for too little return, and the English abandoned their efforts for 200 years, although the sub-Arctic waters of the Davis Strait, between Greenland and Baffin Island, remained profitable whaling grounds. Exploration to the south proved more feasible and profitable. The English established North American colonies that provided an outlet for their expanding population. These, in turn, created overseas markets for domestic industry. Sir Walter Raleigh sponsored a succession of exploratory voyages in the 1570s, but permanent organized settlement only began with the establishment of colonies at Jamestown, Virginia, in 1607 and Plymouth, Massachusetts, in 1621. The Dutch soon followed, at New Orange (Albany, New York) in 1624 and New Amsterdam (New York City) 1625.

Yet the primary source of wealth was still in the East. The Dutch were the first to break the Iberian trade monopoly in the Indies. In the sixteenth century, dynastic marriages brought the Netherlands under Spanish control. This gave Dutch merchants (among others) access to the trading emporia in Spain and Portugal, which were united under one crown from 1580 to 1640. The United Provinces of the Netherlands declared their independence from Spain in 1581, and Philip II retaliated with an embargo on Dutch shipping. Nothing daunted, in 1595 the Dutch sent a fleet of five ships directly to the East Indies; seven years later they founded the United East India Company (Verenigde Oostindische Compagnie, or VOC) and in 1619 they established themselves at present-day Djakarta on the island of Java, in the settlement they called Batavia. Not content to follow the traditional trade routes of the Indian Ocean as the Portuguese had done, the VOC pioneered new, more direct routes. As their wealth grew, so did their need for new markets, and in 1638, the Dutch governor in Batavia ordered the navigator Abel Tasman to explore the little-known Terra Australis "for the improvement, and increase of the [VOC's] general welfare." Tasman's voyages in the *Heemskerck* and *Limmen* brought him to Tasmania, New Zealand, Tonga, and northern Australia, but they proved unfruitful from a mercantile point of view and the search was abandoned; the burghers of the VOC had little time for idle speculation. The English had followed the Dutch to the East, but the merchant navigators of the East India Company focused on establishing a presence in familiar territories.

In the eighteenth century, the wealth created by the fortunes from international trade helped finance a wave of exploratory voyages animated by a spirit of scientific inquiry. Sailing in the North and South Atlantic in HMS *Paramore* between 1698 and 1700, Edmund Halley made a comprehensive study of magnetic variation, an understanding of which is crucial to the proper interpretation of compass readings. On a third voyage he completed a detailed survey of tidal currents in the English Channel. Safe and efficient navigation was also one of the primary concerns underlying Captain James Cook's voyage in *Endeavour* in 1768, a mission sponsored by the Royal Society. This learned body was interested in observing the transit of Venus across the sun, "a phenomenon that must . . . contribute greatly to the improvement of astronomy, on which navigation so much depends." In the course of three voyages, Cook and his crews also circumnavigated Antarctica (although the English never glimpsed the continent), explored the coast of New Zealand, twice visited Hawaii (where Cook was killed), and surveyed the coast of the Pacific Northwest and Alaska in search of the elusive Northwest Passage.

Sailing in 1766, two years before Cook's first voyage, Louis Antoine de Bougainville added a new dimension to the explorer's work. In addition to seeking out new lands, which Bougainville found by sailing through the South Pacific at a higher latitude (that is, farther south from the Equator) than

any of his predecessors, the French also undertook the study of ethnography, zoology, and botany. France sustained an active program of exploration in the Pacific that continued throughout the revolution and the Napoleonic Wars, and in Australian waters (England colonized the continent in 1787), European rivalry was often set aside in the interest of scientific cooperation.

The English and French were not the only nations engaged in voyages of exploration in this period. Russia's eastward expansion across Siberia had raised the prospect of a Russian seaport open to the world. Russia's seaports on the White, Baltic, and Black seas were all of limited use, owing to their peculiar geography. Though nineteenth-century Russian navigators' efforts were oriented primarily toward the northeast corner of Asia and Alaska, they also contributed to the European reconnaissance of Oceania. In the twentieth century, Russian exploration focused especially on the Northeast Passage, the Eurasian counterpart to the Northwest Passage. The English navigator Richard Chancellor had also attempted to find such a route to the Orient in the 1550s, but it was not until 1878–79 that Adolf Nordenskiöld, a Swede, completed the transit in the *Vega*.

In the nineteenth century, Americans also began to show an interest in exploration. The Great United States Exploring Expedition to the South Seas, led by Lieutenant Charles Wilkes in the USS *Vincennes*, was the first such voyage sponsored by the government. The thousands of specimens collected by expedition scientists between 1838 and 1842 formed the nucleus of the Smithsonian Institution's collections. There would be others — to the Dead Sea, the Paraná River in South America, and the North Pacific, for instance — but they were of relatively limited scope in the grand scheme of things.

Animated by the inquisitive spirit of the Enlightenment though these voyages certainly were, trade, evangelism, the urge to spread European culture, and above all improved navigation still played critical roles in European exploration. As world trade grew, so did the need for accurate charts, and most expeditions were geared toward compiling data of use to navigation. France established a Dépôt des Cartes et Plans, a repository for charts and maps, in 1720. In 1779, Alexander Dalrymple was named hydrographer of the East India Company, but it was not until 1795 that the Royal Navy, whose hundreds of ship captains were desperate for accurate charts in their wide-ranging war against France, made a similar appointment. This also fell to Dalrymple, who held the post of Hydrographer of the Navy until 1808. The primary focus of the Admiralty's Hydrographic Office and its counterparts in other maritime countries was the mapping of the world's navigable waters, but there were incidental benefits to these vital yet tedious and unheralded undertakings. It was on one such expedition, to the southern tip of South America and the Pacific, that HMS *Beagle* carried the extraordinary naturalist Charles Darwin, whose observations in the course of the five-year voyage led him to formulate his revolutionary theory of evolution.

The Pax Britannica following the Napoleonic Wars signaled a renewal of the English search for the Northwest Passage. The Scottish explorer Alexander Mackenzie had searched for one on the overland trek he made across Canada in the 1790s, and the Lewis and Clark expedition of 1804–6 demonstrated that there was no watery shortcut to the Pacific through what became the continental United States. Inspired by favorable reports brought back by whalers operating to the west of Greenland, the Royal Navy dispatched an exploratory expedition to search for the Northwest Passage, in HMS *Isabella* and *Alexander* in 1818. This initiated an almost continuous series of expeditions that probed ever farther into the Arctic from east to west. In 1825, Frederick William Beechey sailed in HMS *Blossom* via the Bering Strait to see whether there was any possibility of making the passage from west to east. The search for the Northwest Passage reached its greatest intensity following the disappearance of Sir John Franklin's ships, HMS *Erebus* and *Terror*, in the 1840s. Over the course of the next twelve years, more than a dozen ships from Britain and the United States set out in search of the missing ships, but it was not until 1859 that the crew of Francis M'Clintock's *Fox* learned the grim fate of Franklin and his men. M'Clintock also established the existence of the Northwest Passage, although it remained impassable by ship until the Norwegian explorer Roald Amundsen pioneered the icy route in *Gjøa* in 1906.

Whereas exploration in the eighteenth century had been driven by the desire for economic benefit on the one hand and a spirit of enlightened curiosity on the other, the polar explorations of the nineteenth century seem to be somewhat quixotic ventures motivated by national pride and personal vanity. The economic and political benefits were almost nonexistent, and the scientific gains slight. In this respect they anticipated the race to the moon, and it is an odd coincidence that the first lunar landing and the first transit of the Northwest Passage by a commercial vessel, the oil tanker *Manhattan* (on a voyage of symbolic value only), took place one month apart in 1969.

These Arctic excursions had their counterparts in the Antarctic. The dangers of the Southern Ocean and the ice barrier around the southern continent were well known, and prior to the Franklin expedition, the *Erebus* and *Terror* had narrowly escaped shipwreck amid the ice fields of Antarctica. The first confirmed sighting of Antarctica was made by the American sealer *Hero*, sailing from the South Shetland Islands, southeast of Cape Horn, in 1820. In the wake of the American Robert Peary's claim to have reached the North Pole in 1909, Amundsen, now sailing in the *Fram*, and the Royal Navy's Commander Robert Falcon Scott, in *Terra Nova*, raced for the South Pole. Amundsen arrived on December 16, 1911, followed a month later by Scott and his companions. Unfortunately, the English group froze to death en route back to their ship. These Antarctic expeditions were terrestrial, Antarctica being a continent, whereas the Arctic is a frozen sea, but voyages around the shores of the continent of Antarctica were in all cases remarkable feats of seamanship. Of these perhaps the most astonishing was that of the English explorer Ernest Shackleton following the loss of his ship, *Endurance*, after which he and four companions sailed 800 miles in the 22-foot

*James Caird* to seek help at the remote Norwegian whaling station in the South Shetland Islands.

By now, exploration was entering a new phase of scientific inquiry oriented toward the oceans themselves. Heretofore exploration had chiefly involved the gathering of geographic knowledge useful for trade, navigation, and various aspects of empire building. The ocean depths themselves had received only cursory investigation. The look below was prompted by a variety of factors. Foremost was the development of the telegraph and the need for submarine cables, starting in the 1860s. This made a knowledge of the ocean deeps mandatory and led to inquiries into what lay between the surface and the bottom. In the days before electronics, such elementary tasks as gauging the depth of the ocean were carried out with sounding leads, a difficult but not impossible assignment when the depths to be plumbed exceeded 30,000 feet (9,100 meters), as they did on the *Challenger* expedition of 1872–76. Despite the complexity of the tasks, such expeditions were made in a variety of vessels requisitioned from other branches of the service: screw sloops, steam yachts, and gunboats, for instance.

A dramatic shift in the direction of ocean research was signaled by the launch of the U.S. Commission of Fish and Fisheries research ship, *Albatross,* in 1883. The first purpose-built oceanographic research vessel in the United States and one of the first in the world, it was designed for studying the health and potential of the country's commercial fisheries. In the century that followed, marine science grew to embrace a wide variety of new disciplines, including physical oceanography (an extension of hydrographic surveying), chemical and biological oceanography, submarine geology, and meteorology. Entirely new types and classes of ship were designed for work in such

fields as deep-water search and rescue and nautical archaeology, oil-field research, environmental monitoring, and calibrating navigational and guidance systems for the Navy. The vessels employed include manned submersibles like the *Alvin* and *Trieste,* the floating instrument platform *FLIP,* Jacques Cousteau's *Calypso,* and the deep-sea drilling platform *Glomar Challenger.* New technologies have also been employed in the construction of icebreakers that have opened formerly inaccessible polar regions to the outside world. Designed for service in northern Siberia, the Soviet Union's nuclear-powered *Arktika* was the first surface ship to reach the North Pole, in 1975 — sixteen years after the submarine USS *Skate* surfaced there through the ice.

While technology has been making it possible to explore the oceans in all their dimensions, there has been renewed interest in understanding how mankind first mastered the waters. That there was long-distance navigation in ancient times is an established fact, but we can only begin to understand how it happened, or might have happened, by recreating our ancestors' voyages in vessels and with navigational apparatus similar to what they might have used. Contemporary explorers emulating long-distance Polynesian voyages have used traditional navigational techniques to find their way in modern reproductions of voyaging canoes such as *Hokule'a* and *Hawai'iloa.* Thor Heyerdahl retraced the route of the traders who plied between Mesopotamia and the Indus Valley in antiquity in the reed raft *Tigris,* and Tim Severin's *Brendan* sailed in the wake of the Irish monks who first settled Iceland. Incredible in themselves, these voyages animate our understanding of how people surmounted phenomenal odds to plunge into the unknown to do business on great waters.

# NOTE

Each entry comprises three parts: the vessel's basic specifications, a narrative history, and a source note. Complete publishing information for all works cited in the source notes can be found in the Bibliography.

The basic specifications of the vessel in question include the following information:

*L/B/D:* Length, beam, and draft, or depth in hold (dph), given in feet and meters.

*Tons:* Usually given in gross registered tons (grt), displacement (disp.), old measurement (om), or builder's measurement (bm). For submarines, both surface and submerged tonnages are given.

*Hull:* Hull material, usually wood, iron, or steel. For submarines, dd stands for the design — the maximum depth to which the submarine can submerge.

*Comp.:* Complement, including crew and/or passengers, where known.

*Arm.:* Armament, including the number of guns and caliber or weight of projectile, in either standard or metric measurement.

  *carr.:* carronade
  *pdr.:* pounder
  *TT:* torpedo tube

*Mach.:* Machinery, including type of propulsion, horsepower, number of screws, and speed.

*Des.:* Designer.

*Built:* Builder, place, and year of build.

### FLEET DESIGNATIONS

HMS: Her/His Majesty's Ship
RMS: Royal Mail Ship
USS: United States Ship

# Advance

Brigantine. *L/B/D:* 88' × 21.8' × 8.4' dph (26.8m × 6.6m × 2.6m). *Tons:* 144 tons. *Hull:* wood. *Comp.:* 17. *Built:* New Kent, Md.; 1847.

Originally built as a merchant ship, *Advance* became the flagship of the first U.S. Arctic expedition in 1850 when she was purchased by the New York merchant Henry Grinnell and dispatched with *Rescue* to take part in the search for Sir John Franklin's HMS EREBUS and TERROR. Under command of Lieutenant Edwin J. De Haven, USN, *Advance* departed New York on May 23, 1850, and sailed for Davis Strait and Baffin Bay. From there the ships headed west through Lancaster Sound north of Baffin Island. On August 25, the expedition reached Devon Island, where a shore party found the remains of a campsite as well as a number of British ships also engaged in the search for Franklin. In September 1853 the two ships were caught in pack ice, with which they drifted through Wellington Channel as far as the northern tip of Devon Island, which they named Cape Grinnell. The ice carried the ships south again to Lancaster Sound and then east to Baffin Bay and Dover Strait before releasing its grip on June 7, 1854. The ships returned to New York, and over the next twenty months *Advance* was fitted out for a second expedition, this time under Assistant Surgeon Elisha Kent Kane, a veteran of the first voyage.

The Second Grinnell Expedition sailed through Smith Sound at the head of Baffin Bay and into Kane Basin. There the members of the expedition saw Humboldt Glacier, then the largest known glacier, and attained 78°43'N, farther north than any Europeans before them. During their first winter in Rensellaer Harbor all but six of their sled dogs died and the crew members were laid up with scurvy. In March, two men were killed in an attempt (made too early in the season) to establish a forward depot for overland expeditions. A later expedition reached Cape Constitution, which Kane mistakenly believed led to a warmer Open Polar Sea hypothesized by Commander Edward Inglefield in 1852. The latter had sailed in search of the Franklin expedition in the steam yacht *Isabel,* and confirmation of the existence of the Open Polar Sea was probably the real object of Kane's mission. Faced with the prospect of another winter aboard *Advance,* eight of the crew attempted to make their way overland to Upernavik. They failed, but with the assistance of Eskimos at Etah and other settlements, they returned safely to the ship. The winter was one of horrifying privation, and the expedition's survival was due almost entirely to the Eskimos, from whom the men were able to obtain food. Reduced to cannibalizing *Advance* for fuel, the survivors abandoned ship on May 17 and over the next month hauled their three boats, supplies, and four invalid crew members 80 miles to open water. Sailing south and east along the coast of Greenland, they reached Upernavik on August 6, 1854, and by October they were back in New York.

Berton, *Arctic Grail.* Corner, *Doctor Kane of the Arctic Seas.* Kane, *U.S. Grinnell Expedition in Search of Sir John Franklin.* U.S. Navy, *DANFS.*

# HMS Adventure

(ex-*Raleigh, Marquis of Rockingham*) Bark (3m). *L/B/D:* 97.3' × 28.4' × 13.2' dph (39.7m × 8.7m × 4m). *Tons:* 336 tons. *Hull:* wood. *Comp.:* 81. *Built:* Fishburn, Whitby, Eng.; 1771.

Within a few months of his return from his first voyage to the South Seas in HMS ENDEAVOUR,

James Cook — newly promoted to commander — was assigned to undertake a second voyage to determine the existence of a southern continent, or Terra Australis, long hypothesized by navigators and geographers. As this would entail an extensive survey of the Southern Ocean, he was given two ships, RESOLUTION, the flagship, and *Adventure,* which sailed under command of Commander Tobias Furneaux, a veteran of Captain Samuel Wallis's 1766–68 circumnavigation in HMS DOLPHIN. Like *Endeavour* and *Resolution, Adventure* was originally a North Sea collier rigged as a bark; she was rerigged by the navy following her purchase in 1771.

The two ships departed from Plymouth on July 13, 1772, and remained in company for seven months, stopping at the Azores, the Cape Verde Islands, and Cape Town. In November they departed Cape Town and sailed south. After cruising among the ice fields, the two ships crossed the Antarctic Circle on January 17, 1773, reaching as far south as 67°15′S. On February 8 the two ships were separated in a fog, and by prior arrangement Furneaux turned *Adventure* for New Zealand, about 4,200 miles (6,750 kilometers) away. They called first at Van Diemen's Land (Tasmania) — visited by Abel Tasman in HEEMSKERCK and *Zeehaen* in 1642 — and charted the island's southern coast, although they failed to realize that it was an island and not part of New Holland (Australia). (Adventure Bay takes its name from the ship, and Cook named the Furneaux Islands northeast of Tasmania on his third expedition in *Resolution* and DISCOVERY.)

*Adventure* arrived in Queen Charlotte Sound, New Zealand, on May 7 and was joined ten days later by *Resolution.* The ships' crews traded with the Maori, whom Cook had visited in *Endeavour* in 1769–70. A month later they sailed for Tahiti; en route many of *Adventure's* crew became ill with scurvy and one died. The ships arrived at Tahiti on August 15 and remained there until September 7. Upon their departure, they embarked a man named Omai, of Huaheine, who returned in the *Adventure* to England and spent two years in London under the patronage of Sir Joseph Banks and Lord Sandwich. Sailing west, the ships called at

Tonga (Friendly Islands) before shaping a course for Queen Charlotte Sound.

As they were sailing down the coast of New Zealand at the end of October, the two ships were separated in a storm. Adverse weather prevented *Adventure's* return to Queen Charlotte Sound until November 30, four days after *Resolution* had sailed for England. Furneaux decided to return to England alone, but on December 17, one day before their planned departure, ten of the ship's company were sent to gather fresh vegetables for the voyage and were killed in a fight with some Maoris. Five days later the remainder sailed due east; they rounded Cape Horn on January 10, 1774, and anchored on March 19 at Cape Town, where they stayed one month. After a voyage of two years and three days, *Adventure* anchored at Spithead on July 14. Though the voyage was not the success it might have been, *Adventure* had the distinction of being the first ship to circumnavigate the globe from west to east. The ship was subsequently taken over by the navy for use as a storeship in North America until 1783, when she was broken up.

Brock, "Cook's *Endeavour* and Other Ships." Cook, *Journals of James Cook.* McGowan, "Captain Cook's Ships."

# Aid

Ship. *Tons:* 300. *Hull:* wood. *Comp.:* 115–120. *Arm.:* 2 × 6pdr, 4 × 4pdr, 4 small. *Built:* Deptford Dockyard, Eng.; 1562.

The Queen's ship *Aid* was one of three built in 1562 as war with France threatened. In the fall of the same year *Aid* was assigned to help supply the English garrison at Le Havre until the capture of the Huguenot-held port by loyalist forces in August 1563. *Aid's* next important mission came in 1577, when the Adventurers to the North-West for the Discovery of the North-West Passage, or the Companye of Kathai, was formed to follow up Sir Martin Frobisher's discovery of Frobisher Bay on Baffin Island in GABRIEL the previous year. The inlet promised to be the much sought after Northwest Passage, but more important was his discovery of what was widely believed to be gold. *Aid* sailed as flagship of an expedition that included *Gabriel* and *Michael* and about 150 men. Departing in mid-May, the ships arrived at Baffin Island on July 17. They returned home at the end of the summer with three Eskimos — a man and a woman with her child, all of whom died after a month in England — and 200 tons of ore assayed as yielding a profit of £5 in gold and silver per ton.

On the basis of this hopeful but erroneous assessment, Frobisher sailed at the head of sixteen ships with a view to exploring the Northwest Passage, mining ore, and establishing a manned settlement. After taking possession of Greenland — renamed West England — in the name of the Queen, Frobisher and company continued to the west. In 1578 Frobisher Bay was filled with ice and after losing one ship to a floe, they sailed west into what they called Mistaken Strait, now Hudson Strait. The fleet doubled back to Frobisher Bay, where *Aid* was hulled below the waterline by an ice floe and repaired with a sheet of lead. After mining 1,350 tons of ore and erecting a house for future use (immediate plans for leaving a party to winter there were abandoned), they sailed home. Five years of trying to extract precious metals from the ore brought home on the second and third voyages were fruitless; the Company of Cathay went under and the Baffin Island rocks were "throwne away to repayre the high-wayes."

As tensions between Spain and England worsened, *Aid* was rebuilt and in November 1580 took part in the reduction of Smerwick Fort in Ireland where a combined Spanish-Papal force had taken refuge. Again under Frobisher's command, *Aid* was one of two Queen's ships contributed to Sir Francis Drake's twenty-five-ship expedition to the Spanish West Indies in 1585. In October, the fleet anchored at Bayonne, Spain, where Drake compelled the governor to allow his ships to water and provision before they departed again on October 11. Proceeding to the Cape Verde Islands, Drake burned Santiago, Porto Praya, and Santo Domingo when their inhabitants failed to ransom the towns. The English went on to ransom Santo Domingo and Cartagena, and sacked St. Augustine, Florida. They then sailed for Sir Walter Raleigh's colony at Roa-noke, North Carolina, and returned to England with the colonists in July 1586.

Two years later, *Aid* was one of six ships in Drake's western squadron based at Plymouth to await the arrival of the Spanish Armada. She remained with the English fleet from the day of the first action on July 31 through the final defeat of the Spanish ships at the Battle of Gravelines on August 8. In 1589, *Aid* again sailed with Drake as part of the poorly executed "Counter-Armada." The triple aim of this venture was to destroy the remaining Armada ships in their homeports in Spain and Portugal, restore the pretender Dom Antonio to the Portuguese throne, and seize the Azores as a base from which to attack the Spanish treasure fleets from the West Indies. The overly ambitious plan failed in all its primary objectives and returned to England. In 1590, *Aid* was broken up after a quarter century of service to the Elizabethan navy.

Glasgow, "Navy in the French Wars." Stefansson, *Three Voyages of Martin Frobisher.* Sugden, *Sir Francis Drake.*

## Albatross

Brigantine (1f/2m). *L/B/D:* 299′ × 21.6′ × 16.9′ dph (91.1m × 6.6m × 5.2m). *Tons:* 638 grt. *Hull:* iron. *Comp.:* 79. *Mach.:* 2 screws. *Built:* Pusey & James Shipyard, Wilmington, Del.; 1882.

The first purpose-built research vessel commissioned in the United States was built for the U.S. Commission of Fish and Fisheries, whose first commissioner, S. F. Baird, wanted a platform for the study of the conditions and potential of America's coastal and offshore fisheries. When launched, *Albatross* was the most advanced research ship in the world. Equipped with two large laboratories and a darkroom, she was also the first government-built ship fitted with electric lights, which had been invented by Thomas Edison three years before.

From 1883 to 1888, *Albatross* worked out of the Fish Commission's summer shore station at Woods Hole, Massachusetts, site of today's National Marine Fisheries Service Laboratory and the Woods

▲ The first purpose-built oceanographic research vessel in the United States, **Albatross** was also one of the most technologically sophisticated when she was launched in 1882. *Courtesy Scripps Oceanographic Institute, La Jolla, California.*

Hole Oceanographic Institute. The focus of her investigation was the effect of environmental variables on commercial fish species. In 1886, Baird wrote to *Albatross*'s first and longest-serving captain, Zera L. Tanner:

> as in previous cruises, you will make collections by trawl, dredge, or otherwise, of the marine animals inhabiting the waters, whether vertebrate or invertebrate, and will gather as many data as you can respecting their relationship to each other and to their physical surroundings.

In his twelve-year tenure with the *Albatross*, Tanner oversaw the development of a variety of ocean science instruments, including the dredging quadrant to calculate the depth at which gear was actually set; a neuston net, for gathering microorganisms in the surface layer of the sea, and the Tanner net, by which deep trawls could be closed and raised without contamination by organisms from shallower depths.

In 1887, the vessel was transferred to the West Coast, where she was employed by the U.S. Revenue Service (the forerunner of the Coast Guard) to patrol the Alaskan seal fisheries. In 1891–92, the eminent marine zoologist and oceanographer Alexander Agassiz chartered *Albatross* for the first of three extended cruises for deep-sea research and the study of coral reef formation. Put under Navy command in the 1890s, she was used in conducting surveys of the waters off southern California (1904) and of the Philippines (1907–1910). In the course of the latter expedition, *Albatross*'s researchers made 577 deep-sea dredges, which resulted in the delivery of 400,000 preserved fish to the U.S. National Museum in Washington, D.C., for classification.

Declared unseaworthy, *Albatross* spent the next few years undertaking surveys of the fisheries in San Francisco Bay. In 1914, she emerged from an overhaul with a schooner rig and improved research facilities, but she saw no further work until the United States entered World War I, when she was stationed in the Caribbean on antisubmarine patrols. After the war *Albatross* returned to Woods Hole, where she was decommissioned in 1921. American Nautical Schools, Inc., attempted to use her as a training ship, but this project failed for lack

▲ This photo, by either Thomas Mitchell or George White, shows men from the **Alert** cutting ice blocks during an expedition to Greenland in the 1870s. *Courtesy National Maritime Museum, Greenwich.*

of funds, and *Albatross* was scrapped in Hamburg, Germany, sometime after 1928.

Peterson, *"Albatross."*

# HMS Alert

Screw sloop (1f/3m). *L/B:* 160′ × 32′ (48.8m × 9.8m). *Tons:* 751 bm. *Hull:* wood. *Arm.:* 17 × 32pdr. *Mach.:* steam, 381 ihp, 1 screw. *Built:* Pembroke Dockyard, Wales; 1856.

Following the many attempts to find Sir John Franklin's expedition, lost while searching for the Northwest Passage in the mid-nineteenth century, British interest in Arctic exploration waned. When the British again turned north, it was to conduct research in terrestrial magnetism and the search for the Magnetic North Pole. In 1875, the Admiralty dispatched HMS *Alert* and *Discovery* under

the command of George S. Nares. A veteran of HMS *Resolute* in the last government-sponsored search for Franklin, Captain Nares was reassigned from command of the CHALLENGER expedition specifically to take charge of the British Arctic Expedition.

The two ships left Portsmouth on May 29, 1875, and after taking aboard dogs in Greenland, proceeded up the Davis Strait as far as Ellesmere Island's Lady Franklin Bay. *Discovery* remained there while *Alert* pressed on to Cape Sheridan (82°24′N), 53 miles to the north — a new farthest-north record. She remained icebound from September 1, 1875, to July 31, 1876. In April 1876, separate parties were sent out to explore. Commander Markham and his men reached 83°20′N — 400 miles shy of the North Pole — and Lieutenant Beaumont's expedition to northeast Greenland reached 82°18′N. These parties and the ships' companies were stricken with scurvy, and several men died before the expedition was brought under control. *Alert* began drifting south in July; in August she and *Discovery* got under way again from what was henceforth called Discovery Harbor, reaching

England in October. The expedition proved that Greenland was an island and laid to rest the theory of an ice-free polar sea. (In honor of *Alert*'s achievement, the world's northernmost permanently inhabited settlement, on Ellesmere Island, is named Alert.)

Nares again commanded *Alert* in 1878, on a two-year hydrographic survey of the Strait of Magellan. Laid up at Chatham on her return, the ship was refitted and donated to the United States to sail in Captain Winfield Scott Schley's expedition for the relief of the Adolphus Greely expedition, stranded on Ellesmere Island.

Nares, *Narrative of a Voyage to the Polar Sea.*

# Al-Jagir

*Hull:* wood. *Comp.:* 50 rowers, 50 soldiers. *Built:* India, <1342.

One of the greatest travelers of the Middle Ages was Ibn Battuta. Although he hailed from the Atlantic seaport of Tangier, Morocco, Ibn Battuta began his travels as a reluctant seaman, and he had been on the road for about five years before he embarked on a ship for the first time, on a passage across the Red Sea from Jeddah to a place near modern Port Sudan. Nevertheless, in the course of his travels he grew to be quite knowledgeable about seafaring and became an admirer of the major ports of the world, the most important of which he deemed Alexandria, Egypt, Quilon and Calicut in India, the Genoese Black Sea port of Sudaq in the Crimea, and Zaitun (Ch'üan-chou), China, all of which he wrote about. Ibn Battuta did not bother to describe in detail many of the ships in which he sailed, and his observations were limited to those aspects of each that interested him most.

Ibn Battuta's travels took him first through the Middle East, along the coast of East Africa as far as Mombassa and Kilwa, then through Asia Minor, across the Black Sea, through part of central Asia, and, in 1334, to Delhi, India. There he remained for seven years, serving the court of Sultan Muhammad ibn Tughluq. At the end of this period, the Sultan appointed him to lead an embassy to China with gifts that included one hundred horses

(highly prized in China), cloths and linens, and other goods. After marching overland to a port on the Gulf of Cambay, Ibn Battuta and his entourage embarked in three vessels, *Al-Jagir, Manurt,* and *Al-'Ukairi. Al-Jagir,* in which Ibn Battuta sailed, carried seventy of the horses and was rowed by fifty oarsmen. The complement included fifty Abyssinian soldiers, "the guarantors of safety on this sea; let there be one of them on a ship and it will be avoided by the Indian pirates and idolaters."

The ships made their way down the coast in stages, stopping at more than a dozen ports, including Goa (which first came under Muslim control in 1312), Hinawr, Mangalore, Cannanore, and Calicut. The latter was "visited by men from China, Jawa, Ceylon, the Maldives, al-Yaman and Fars, and in it gather men from all quarters. Its harbour is one of the largest in the world." Here the Sultan's gifts were transshipped to Chinese vessels, three kinds of which are identified: junks (the largest), *zaws,* and *kakams.* Shortly after the ships were loaded, but while Ibn Battuta was still ashore, one of them was wrecked, and the remainder sailed off without him. He attempted to meet up with them at the southern Indian port of Quilon, but without success. Reluctant to confess his failure to the Sultan, Ibn Battuta remained on the coast and took part in an expedition against Goa, fleeing from there when it came under attack from its original ruler. At this point, Ibn Battuta decided to quit India altogether and, evidently more comfortable at sea than he had been, sailed to the Maldive Islands, four hundred miles southwest of Sri Lanka. Marrying into the leading families and serving as a judge, he lived there for about two years before resuming his eastward journey.

Ibn Battuta's travels seldom took him beyond the limits of the Islamic world. All along the Malabar coast of India he encountered Muslim traders, scholars, and soldiers from Arabia, East Africa, and the Persian Gulf area; the Maldivians were "all of them Muslims"; and his account of China describes Muslim communities in Canton and Hangchou. He was, however, the first Muslim traveler to record his observations and impressions of all he saw. In the course of twenty-nine years of travel, he covered some seventy-five thousand miles, and he certainly merits the epithet of "the traveler of this [Muslim] community," bestowed upon him by Ibn Juzayy, who took down Ibn Battuta's *Gift to Those Who Contemplate the Wonders of Cities and the Marvels of Travelling.*

Ibn Battuta, *Travels.*

# Alvin

Submersible. *L/B/D:* 22′ × 8′ × 7′ (7m × 2.4m × 2.1m). *Tons:* 16 disp. *Hull:* steel sphere; aluminum frame. *Comp.:* 3. *Mach.:* lead-acid batteries, 3 screws; 1 kt. *Des.:* Bud Froelich. *Built:* General Mills, Minneapolis, and Hahn & Clay, Houston (sphere); 1964.

Irked by the fact that oceanographers had no way to observe the workings of the ocean depths except through what they could measure or capture from the deck of a surface ship, Allyn Vine proposed the development of a submarine with windows. At a meeting of oceanographers held in Washington, D.C., in 1956, Vine, a Woods Hole Oceanographic Institute ocean engineer, observed that

> a good instrument can measure almost anything better than a person can if you know what you want to measure. . . . But people are so versatile, they can sense things to be done and can investigate problems. I find it difficult to imagine what kind of instrument should have been put on the BEAGLE instead of Charles Darwin.

Six years later, the U.S. Navy's Office of Naval Research and Woods Hole contracted with General Mills/Litton Industries to build the Navy's first Deep Submergence Research Vessel, which was commissioned on June 5, 1964, and given the name *Alvin,* for ALlyn VINe.

Though designed specifically for oceanographic research to be undertaken by Woods Hole, *Alvin* had been paid for by the Navy, for which she has undertaken several search and recovery missions. The first of these was to find a hydrogen bomb lost in the sea about five miles southeast of Palomares, Spain, after a U.S. Air Force B-52 collided with a KC-135 tanker plane during refueling on January 17, 1966. Less than a month later, *Alvin* and the less maneuverable *Aluminaut* began searching for the missing bomb in an area 350 kilometers (135

miles) square and over 790 meters (2,600 feet) deep. On March 15, during the nineteenth dive, Marvin McCamis, Cal Wilson, and Art Bartlett located the bomb, which was finally recovered from a depth of 853 meters (2,800 feet) on April 7.

In 1985, *Alvin* veteran Bob Ballard began planning a search for RMS *Titanic.* On August 31, following initial site research by a French team, cameras on the *Argo,* a remotely operated vehicle (ROV) tethered to the research ship *Knorr,* located the sunken liner at a depth of 3,780 meters (12,400 feet). The following July, Ballard, Dudley Foster, and Ralph Hollis descended in *Alvin,* to which was tethered the ROV *Jason Junior.* After a three-hour, fifty-minute search on their first dive, they became the first people to see the majestic liner since her tragic sinking on April 15, 1912.

These two spectacular investigations are the best known of *Alvin*'s research, but in fact the submersible has been used in more than 2,000 scientific dives since 1967. Operating first from a makeshift pontoon mother ship named *Lulu* (for Vine's mother) and, since 1982, from a variety of other vessels, *Alvin* has served as a vehicle for groundbreaking research of the ocean floor and submarine canyons, examining geological features, and gathering biological specimens — including a swordfish that wedged its sword between *Alvin*'s passenger sphere and the outer frame at a depth of 610 meters (2,000 feet). On October 16, 1968, *Alvin* slipped out of her cradle while being launched and sank in 1,535 meters (5,036 feet); she was recovered on Labor Day, 1969, after being located by *Aluminaut.* In 1974 the original sphere was replaced by a titanium one, and the same year *Alvin* was used to conduct research of the Mid-Atlantic Ridge jointly with the French vessels *Archimede* and *Cyana* in Project Famous. Three years later *Alvin* undertook her first research in the Pacific, off the Galápagos Rift. Later research has taken her as far north as the Strait of Juan de Fuca, in the Pacific, and the Gulf of Maine in the Atlantic.

Kaharl, *Water Baby.*

# Anunciada

Caravel(?) (3m). *Hull:* wood. *Built:* Portugal; <1500.

No sooner had Vasco da Gama's three ships returned from India in 1499 than plans were laid for a second Portuguese expedition to capitalize on the trade of Calicut on India's west coast. Gama declined to serve as *capitão-mor,* and the post fell to the somewhat obscure Pero Álvares Cabral, who sailed at the head of a fleet of thirteen ships. The names of only three of these ships are known: *Anunciada, El Rei,* and *São Pedro.* In all, only five of Cabral's ships completed the voyage to India and home, *Anunciada* among them; two turned back to Portugal while still in the Atlantic, and six were lost.

The fleet departed Lisbon on March 8, 1500, amid great fanfare led by King Manoel. The fleet sailed down the Atlantic in a westward arc that took advantage of the northeast and southeast trade winds. One ship broke off from the fleet off the Cape Verde Islands and returned to Portugal only two weeks out. A month later, on April 21, during Easter week, a landfall was made on the coast of Brazil at a spot named Monte Pascoal ("Easter Mountain"). The ships turned for shore and, after sailing up the coast for about 40 miles, anchored in Porto Seguro (which is today Baía Cabrália) in the land the Portuguese called Santa Cruz. They remained here until May 1, refreshing themselves and trading trinkets with the local Tupi Indians, by whom they were well treated and whom they treated well in return. As was their custom, the Portuguese left two exiles (*degredados*) with the Tupi to learn their customs and language; a supply ship was also dispatched to Lisbon to inform the king of their discovery, the most comprehensive account of the Portuguese findings being a long letter to the king from Pero Vaz de Caminha. They then weighed anchor and turned for the Indian Ocean.

Although the Portuguese are traditionally credited with being the first Europeans to visit Brazil, Vicente Yáñez Pinzón, captain of Christopher Columbus's Niña in 1492, had spent several months on the coast earlier that year. Making a landfall near present-day Recife, or possibly Fortaleza, he had sailed 50 miles up the Amazon River (which he believed to be the Ganges) and continued up the coast to the Gulf of Paria in what is now Venezuela. Much of this area fell on the Portuguese side of the line of demarcation established by the 1494 Treaty of Tordesillas, and the Spanish did not follow up on Pinzón's discovery.

The remainder of the Portuguese voyage was difficult. Even before reaching the Cape of Good Hope, Cabral lost four ships in a storm that lasted three weeks. Among these was one commanded by Bartolomeu Dias, who had led the first European expedition around the Cape in 1488. After landing on the African coast at Sofala, Mozambique, and Kilwa, the Portuguese hired pilots to guide them to Calicut, where they arrived on September 13, 1500. Here the Samudri Raja (the successor to the ruler known to Gama) allowed the Portuguese to establish a trading factory. He also asked the Portuguese to seize a ship at Cochin that was carrying, illegally, one of his war elephants. Relations soured, however, thanks in large part to the high-handedness of the Portuguese and the hostility of the local Muslim merchants, who attacked the factory and killed more than fifty Portuguese. In retaliation, Cabral burned ten Muslim ships, fired on the undefended town, killing several hundred people, and sailed for Cochin. Despite the earlier seizure of one of their ships, the raja of Cochin, Unni Goda Varma, saw an opportunity to best his rivals to the south and allowed the Portuguese to load their remaining ships. The Portuguese sailed in mid-January, bringing with them two of the raja's servants, Idikella Menon and Parangoda Menon, and a Malabar Christian, Joseph of Cranganor. By way of exchange, the Portuguese left behind several of their crew, who established what became the first permanent Portuguese factory in India.

After a further stop at Cannanur, the Portuguese turned for Malindi, where Sancho de Tovar's *El Rei* was wrecked. Although all five surviving ships returned to Portugal, they were separated en route. *Anunciada,* under Nicoláu Coelho, and a ship commanded by Diogo Dias (Bartolomeu's brother) put into a West African harbor at or near

Dakar, Senegal, in early June. Here they met a fleet of four ships that had been dispatched to follow up on Cabral's discovery of Brazil. Accompanying this expedition as a supernumerary was the Florentine merchant banker and ship chandler Amerigo Vespucci, who had helped outfit Columbus's third expedition and whose name would later be given to both continents of the New World.

*Anunciada* and the other ship arrived in Lisbon on June 25, 1501, followed a month later by the other three ships. Although the voyage had been costly in men and ships, the Portuguese presence in India was now established permanently, and the ground had been laid for the settlement of Brazil, which is now the largest Portuguese-speaking country in the world.

Greenlee, *Voyage of Pedro Álvares Cabral to Brazil and India*. Morison, *European Discovery of America: Southern Voyages*. Subrahmanyam, *Legend and Career of Vasco da Gama*.

## Arctic

(ex-*Gauss*) Topsail schooner (1f/3m). *L/B/D:* 165.4′ × 37.2′ × 21.6′. *Tons:* 650 grt. *Hull:* wood. *Comp.:* 32–43. *Mach.:* triple expansion, 275 ihp, 1 screw; 5 kts. *Built:* Howaldt Shipyard, Kiel; 1901.

The German research vessel *Gauss* was built for the German Antarctic Expedition of 1901–3 to determine the location of the South Magnetic Pole. The leader of the expedition was the glaciologist and explorer Erich von Drygalski, and the ship was named in honor of the German mathematician Karl Friedrich Gauss, who first predicted the position of the pole. *Gauss* sailed from Germany on August 11, 1901, and her crew first sighted the Antarctic continent on February 21, 1902. The same day, the ship became trapped in the ice off what the Germans called Kaiser Wilhelm II Land (now Wilhelm II Land), where she would remain for more than a year. Drygalski led a number of overland expeditions, including one to a mountain they named the Gaussberg (Gauss Mountain). The ship was finally freed from the ice on March 31, 1903.

After a stop at Cape Town, *Gauss* returned to Germany on November 24.

At the instigation of Jacques Elzéar Bernier, the Canadian government purchased the ship, which was renamed *Arctic* and fitted out for the Canadian Polar Expedition to the North Pole. At the last minute, the ship was requisitioned for police work in the Northern Territories. In 1904–5, *Arctic* established several Royal North-West Mounted Police posts around Hudson Bay, and wintered at Fullerton. The following year, Bernier sailed on the first of a series of expeditions to assert Canada's claim to the islands of the Arctic Archipelago. These remote territories — from 60°W to 141°W, and as far north as the Pole — most of which had been explored by British explorers, had been ceded to Canada by Britain in 1880, but Canada had made no systematic effort to exercise jurisdiction in the sparsely populated islands.

Departing Quebec in July 1906, *Arctic* sailed to Labrador and from there up the Davis Strait to Lancaster Sound. Bernier hired two Eskimos to accompany their expedition at Bylot Island. They continued through Lancaster Sound, Barrow Strait, Viscount Melville Sound, and Melville Strait, taking possession of islands as far west as Prince Patrick (120°W) before turning back. On many of the islands they found stores, tablets, and records left by earlier explorers, including a marble tablet dedicated "To the Memory of Franklin, Crozier, Fitzjames and all their gallant brothers" of the ERЕBUS and TERROR expedition, which the crew of Francis L. M'Clintock's *Fox* had erected at Beechey Island in 1858. After wintering at Bylot Island from September 1906 to July 1907, the Canadians annexed Ellesmere Island and then turned for home, reaching Quebec in October.

Bernier continued his work of annexation in two further voyages. In 1908–9, *Arctic* was frozen in at Winter Harbor on Melville Island, and various parties crossed McClure Strait to Victoria and Banks Islands, which were duly annexed. Most important, the Canadians erected a plaque at Winter Harbor stating Canada's claim to the entire Arctic Archipelago. The following year they attempted to complete the Northwest Passage via McClure

Sound, but "stopped by a floe from 50 to 60 feet thick with hills on it as high as any berg," they put back to Admiralty Inlet at the top of Baffin Island. Over the winter they explored the Brodeur Peninsula and the frozen Hecla and Fury Strait between the Gulf of Boothia and Foxe Basin.

In 1922, the Canadian government dispatched Bernier in the *Arctic* on the first of a series of annual patrols of the northern islands. Under the auspices of the Department of the Interior, *Arctic*'s crew and passengers were charged with establishing and maintaining a variety of administrative outposts, including quarters for the Mounted Police, customs houses, and post offices. In 1923, *Arctic* embarked legal and judicial personnel to find and try the murderers of Robert James, a trader who had sailed as Bernier's second officer in 1910. *Arctic*'s last voyage was completed in 1925, when she was sold for breaking up at Quebec.

Canada's claims to the islands of the high Arctic have been confirmed in a variety of ways. In 1930, the government purchased from Norway the records pertaining to Otto Sverdrup's FRAM expedition of 1898–1902, during which he had claimed the Sverdrup and Ringnes Islands for Norway. This act served as a quit-claim to Norwegian and Danish rights to the Canadian Arctic. Although Canada's sovereignty over the northern islands is recognized in law, there is considerable debate as to whether the channels and straits — especially those that make up the Northwest Passage — are internal waters (as Canada claims) or international waters (as the United States, among others, argues).

Bernier, Jacques Elzéar. *Cruise of the "Arctic," 1906–7; Cruise of the "Arctic," 1908–9; Master Mariner and Arctic Explorer; Report of the Dominion of Canada Government Expedition.* Drygalski, *German South Polar Expedition 1901–03.*

## Arend

Ship (3m). *L:* 120′ (36.6m). *Hull:* wood. *Comp.:* 110. *Arm.:* 32 guns. *Built:* Netherlands; <1675.

In 1675, Arend Roggeveen applied to the States General of the United Provinces of the Netherlands for a charter to search for unknown or un-

confirmed lands in the South Pacific. Although he died before he could undertake the mission, in 1721 his son Jacob made a similar proposal to the Dutch West India Company. They fitted him out with *Den Arend* ("The Eagle"), *Thienhoven* (100 feet [30.5 meters], twenty-four guns, eighty crew), and *Den Afrikaansche Galei* (92 feet [28 meters], fourteen guns, thirty-three crew). In particular, Roggeveen intended to search for Davis's Land, reputedly seen in latitude 27°S about 1,500 miles (2,400 kilometers) from the coast of South America by the English buccaneer Edward Davis in 1687. The ships sailed from the Texel on July 26, 1721, and after a stop in Brazil rounded Cape Horn. Sailing northwest, Roggeveen's men were the first Europeans to visit the island they christened Easter Island, on April 5 (Easter Sunday), 1722. Thereafter the ships sailed west, following the route of Willem Schouten and Jacob Le Maire in EENDRACHT in 1616. On May 19, the *Afrikaansche Galei* was lost on Takapoto Island in the Tuamotu Archipelago, and five sailors deserted the expedition. Having made no substantial discovery, Roggeveen was bound to return home. Deciding that rounding Cape Horn again would be impossible with a sick and disabled crew, he determined to sail west and then north around New Guinea to Batavia, where they arrived on October 3. There, the Dutch East India Company (VOC) confiscated the ships and property of the rival West India Company crews before sending the men on to the Netherlands.

Roggeveen, *Journal of Jacob Roggeveen.*

## Argo

Galley (1m). *L/B/D:* 54′ × 9.3′ × 2′ (16.5m × 2.8m × 0.6m). *Hull:* wood. *Comp.:* 20. *Des.:* Colin Mudie. *Built:* Vasilis Delimitros, Spetses, Greece; 1984.

In the early 1980s, Tim Severin decided to retrace the voyage of the Greek hero Jason from the Aegean to Colchis on the eastern shores of the Black Sea. The most comprehensive version of the Golden Fleece myth is recorded in the *Argonautica* of Apollonius of Rhodes, written in the third century BCE. According to Apollonius, in order to reclaim the throne from his uncle, Jason was sent by Pelias of Iolcus to capture the Golden Fleece from Colchis. His ship was built by Argos and crewed by fifty Greek heroes, including Argos and Jason. Passing through the northern Aegean, they traversed the Dardanelles, the Sea of Marmara, and the Bosporus and proceeded east along the southern shore of the Black Sea to Colchis, in what is thought to be present-day Georgia. There, King Aeetes told Jason that he could have the Golden Fleece only if he yoked two fire-breathing oxen, plowed a field, sowed it with dragon's teeth, and slew the warriors who would spring from the seed on the same day. Aided by Aeetes' daughter Medea, Jason succeeded in his task. According to Strabo (fifth century BCE), the legend of the Golden Fleece originated in the Colchians' practice of using wool to filter gold dust from the rivers.

Working from pictorial and other evidence, Colin Mudie drew plans for a galley from about 1200 BCE. The new *Argo* departed Volos on May 2, 1984, crossed the Aegean, and entered the Dardanelles nineteen days later. By June 15 the ship was in the Black Sea, where, proceeding under oars alone for most of the time, she made her way slowly eastward. Among the ports of call the crew could identify with Greek myth was Eregli, near the River Acheron, where Herakles descended into the Underworld to capture Hades' watchdog, Cerberus, and where Idmon the soothsayer and Tiphys, Jason's helmsman, died. Once east of Sinope, *Argo* encountered favorable winds, although the storms of the first thirty-six hours tested the mettle of the Bronze Age design and the twentieth-century crew to the utmost. Ten days later they arrived at Giresun Island, known as the Island of Ares; here Jason met four of his Colchian cousins, who had been shipwrecked en route to Greece and who agreed to accompany him back to their home. On July 19, the new *Argo* departed Hopa, Turkey, the first ship to clear the port for the Soviet Union since World War II. Once in Soviet territorial waters, the crew were greeted by the sail-training bark *Tovarishch* and a crew of professional oarsmen and other athletes, who helped row *Argo* the rest of the way to Poti. There the latter-day Argonauts were

welcomed by thousands of Georgians for whom the legend of Jason and the Golden Fleece remains very much a part of the popular culture. After several days of celebration, *Argo* was towed and rowed up the Rhioni River (as the Phasis River is now known) until she ran aground on a mud bank abreast of Jaladdi, the oldest Bronze Age settlement yet found on the Rhioni.

Jason's route home varies in different versions of the myth. Some say he returned the way he came, whereas others have him ascending the Danube or some other rivers and proceeding overland to the Mediterranean. Severin and his crew returned via more conventional means, and *Argo* was eventually taken to the Exeter Maritime Museum in England.

Apollonius Rhodius, *Argonautica*. Severin, *Jason Voyage*.

## Arktika

(ex-*Leonid Brezhnev*) *Arktika*-class icebreaker (1f/2m). *L/B/D:* 435.3′ × 91.9′ × 30.1′ (148m × 28m × 11m). *Tons:* 18,172 grt. *Hull:* steel. *Mach.:* nuclear reactors, steam turbines, 75,000 shp, 3 screws; 18 kts. *Built:* Baltic Shipbuilding & Engineering Works, Leningrad, USSR; 1974.

The second nuclear-powered icebreaker built by the Soviet Union, after LENIN, *Arktika* was the first of five vessels in her class. Originally named for the General Secretary of the USSR, she was designed for the sea routes of the Northeast Passage across the top of the Soviet Union; in 1975 she became the first surface ship to reach the North Pole. Sponsored by T. B. Guzhenko, minister of the merchant fleet of the Soviet Union, the expedition was described simply as a "scientific-practical experimental voyage" intended to test the new icebreaker in more extreme conditions than the ship would ordinarily encounter. Under command of Captain O. G. Pashnin, *Arktika* sailed from Murmansk on August 9, 1975, and reached the North Pole eight days later.

This trip was not to be repeated for another decade, but since the mid-1980s, the voyage to the North Pole has become one of increasing popularity for tourists, who travel in great comfort to the top of the world aboard Russian, Swedish, German, and other ships.

Gardiner, ed., *Shipping Revolution.*

## L'Astrolabe

(ex-*L'Autruche*) Frigate (3m). *Tons:* 450. *Hull:* wood. *Comp.:* 109. *Built:* France; 1781.

*L'Astrolabe* was the second of two ships in Comte Jean-François de La Pérouse's expedition to the Pacific in 1785–88. A former supply vessel, *L'Astrolabe* sailed under command of Paul-Antoine-Marie Fleuriot de Langle. In company with LA BOUS-SOLE, she sailed from Brest on August 1, 1785, calling at Brazil, Chile, Easter Island, and Hawaii before making an extensive survey of the Pacific coast of North America from Mount St. Elias to Monterey. The two ships then crossed to Macao and stayed there for the first two months of 1787 before sailing to the Philippines, the Sea of Japan, Sakhalin Island (where de Langle was honored by having a bay named for him), and along the Kurile Islands to the remote Russian settlement at Petropavlovsk on the Kamchatka Peninsula.

In September, they sailed south and did not make landfall until December 6, when they landed in the Samoan Islands (which the navigator, Louis Antoine de Bougainville, had named the Navigator Islands) and anchored at Tutuila. On December 11, de Langle went ashore to get fresh water and was attacked by more than 1,000 Samoans, who killed him and eleven of his crew, and wounded twenty others. Although the attack seemed unprovoked, the magnanimous La Pérouse refused to allow any reprisals, carrying out to the letter Louis XVI's injunction that "he will have recourse to arms only as a last extremity, only as a means of defense, and in circumstances when any tolerance would inevitably place the ships and the King's subjects in danger."

La Pérouse appointed Robert Sutton de Clonard to command *L'Astrolabe* and the ships sailed for Botany Bay, Australia, where they arrived on January 24, 1788. The French deposited their last dispatches home with the English officers of the "First Fleet," which arrived in Botany Bay the same week. Their letters announced that they intended to visit Tonga, New Caledonia, the Solomon Islands, the Louisiade Archipelago, and the west coast of Australia, before returning to France in June 1789. Nothing was heard from the ships after their departure from Botany Bay in March, and in 1791, the French government dispatched a search expedition under Chevalier d'Entrecasteaux in *La Recherche* and L'ESPÉRANCE. No sign of the La Pérouse expedition was discovered until Captain Peter Dillon recovered artifacts from the ships on the island of Vanikoro in 1826.

La Pérouse, *Journal of Jean-François de Galaup de La Pérouse.* Shelton, *From Hudson's Bay to Botany Bay.*

## L'Astrolabe

(ex-*Coquille*) Corvette (3m). *Tons:* 380. *Hull:* wood. *Comp.:* 70–79. *Built:* France; 1811.

Shortly after returning to France from a three-year circumnavigation as lieutenant in Louis de Frey-

◄ The French frigate **L'Astrolabe** and corvette **La Zélée** aground in the Torres Strait toward the end of **L'Astrolabe**'s third and last circumnavigation, undertaken in 1837–40. The painting is by Louis Le Breton, official artist of the expedition. *Courtesy Peabody Essex Museum, Salem, Massachusetts.*

cinet's L'URANIE, Louis I. Duperrey and his colleague Jules S-C Dumont d'Urville made a proposal for a new circumnavigation to the Minister of Marine, the Marquis de Clermont Tonnerre. The twin aims were scientific — including studies of terrestrial magnetism and meteorology — and geographic, with a view especially to confirming or correcting the position of islands and other landmarks essential to safe navigation. Departing Toulon on August 11, 1822, *Coquille* ("Shell") sailed via Ascension Island, St. Catherine Island (arriving the week that Brazil declared its independence from Portugal), and the Falklands — where the shipwrecked *Uranie* still lay — before rounding Cape Horn. Once in the Pacific, *Coquille* sailed along the coast of South America as far as Paita, Peru, and then headed west through the Tuamotu Islands to Tahiti, arriving on May 3. The expedition continued westward through the Society, Friendly (Tonga), and Fiji Islands. Though the French were bound for Australia, horrendous weather forced them to steer northwest, and they passed the Santa Cruz and Solomon Islands before landing at Louis de Bougainville's Port Praslin, New Britain. From there *Coquille* continued along the northern coast of New Guinea to the Dutch entrepôt at Amboina, where the French spent most of October.

*Coquille* sailed to Port Jackson (Sydney) via the west and south coasts of Australia, and after a two-month layover continued to New Zealand in April 1824. After two weeks visiting with the English missionaries, who had been established there for nine years, the French sailed north through the Ellice and Gilbert Islands and west through the Carolines to New Guinea, where they arrived at the end of July. After a stop at the Dutch settlement of Surabaya, *Coquille* turned for France via the British islands of Mauritius — formerly the French Ile de France — and St. Helena, where the British had imprisoned the French emperor Napoleon Bonaparte from 1815 to his death in 1821. The *Coquille* arrived at Marseilles on March 24, 1825.

Upon returning to France, *Coquille* was renamed *L'Astrolabe,* in honor of one of La Pérouse's ships that had disappeared in 1788. Under Dumont d'Urville, whose interests were more geographic and ethnographic than Duperrey's, *Astrolabe* would undertake two further voyages of discovery. The first, from 1826 to 1829, was concentrated in Australian and western Pacific waters, with a view especially to locating any trace of the La Pérouse expedition. After a survey of Australia's south coast, *Astrolabe* sailed to New Zealand, where her crew made extensive ethnographic and zoological studies. The French continued to Tonga and the Fiji Islands, where they charted 120 islands — many of them previously unknown — before heading west to the waters around New Guinea. After repairs to the ship at Amboina, Dumont d'Urville sailed east through the Torres Strait and south to Tasmania, where he learned that the English captain Peter Dillon in 1826 had found relics of La Pérouse's expedition on Vanikoro. Sailing to the New Hebrides, the French confirmed these findings and gathered artifacts which they brought back to Marseilles on February 24, 1829, after further stops at Guam, in the East Indies, and at Ile de France. (Dillon had returned earlier, and Charles X of France named him to the Legion of Honor.)

Although English and American whalers and sealers had been hunting in the Southern Ocean for the half century since Cook's 1774 voyage into the ice in ENDEAVOUR, and Bellingshausen had sailed near Antarctica in 1820–21 in VOSTOK and *Mirny,* the French had played no active role in the exploration of the South Seas. In 1836, Emperor Louis-Philippe decided to mount an expedition to locate the South Magnetic Pole, with Dumont d'Urville as its leader in *L'Astrolabe.* Unlike the ship's previous two expeditions, she would be accompanied by *La Zélée,* under Charles Hector Jacquinot, a veteran of the previous expedition; between them, the ships embarked seven scientists and naturalists. Departing Toulon on September 7, 1837, the two ships sailed via Tenerife and Rio de Janeiro for the Strait of Magellan, where they remained from December through January 1838, taking aboard a Swiss and an Englishman who had been living among the Patagonians. Turning south, on January 22, the ships were confronted with an impenetrable mass of ice that Dumont d'Urville described as a marvelous spectacle. More severe and grandiose than can be expressed, even as it lifted the imagination it filled the heart with a feeling of involuntary terror; nowhere else is one so sharply convinced of one's impotence. The image of a new world unfolds before us, but it is an inert, lugubrious, and silent world in which everything threatens the destruction of one's faculties.

The ships were unable to make much progress southward, although they sighted the previously named Palmer Peninsula, and sailed for Chile in April 1838, where two men died of scurvy and twenty-two others either deserted or were too ill to continue. From South America the expedition sailed through many of the larger Pacific Island groups — the Marquesas, Tahiti, the Samoas, the Tongas, Fiji, then northwest through the Santa Cruz Islands, the Solomons, and the Carolines before coming to the Spanish island of Guam. *Astrolabe* and *Zélée* continued to the Philippines, the Dutch East Indies, and then westabout to Tasmania, where they arrived in November 1839. The two ships sailed south on the first day of the new year, and on January 19 they saw the part of Antarctica they called Terre Adélie (for d'Urville's wife), though they were unable to land. They also crossed the path of USS *Porpoise*, one of the ships in the expedition led by Captain Charles Wilkes in USS Vincennes.

After determining the approximate position of the South Magnetic Pole, the French ships returned to Tasmania, where they reembarked some of their sick crew before sailing for New Zealand. The French were also chagrined to find that the English had made significant advances in settling the land they had once considered for a French colony. From there the ships made their way back to France, arriving at Toulon on November 7, 1840. Twenty-two crew had died, and another twenty-seven had deserted or left the expedition because of illness, but the ships had brought back the largest quantity of natural history specimens ever garnered in a single expedition. Although Dumont d'Urville died before its publication, his account of *Astrolabe*'s third voyage ran to twenty-three volumes, with five atlases. The ship's previous two voyages resulted in seven volumes and four atlases by Duperrey and fourteen volumes and five atlases by Dumont d'Urville.

Brosse, *Great Voyages of Discovery.* Dumont d'Urville, *Two Voyages to the South Seas by Captain Jules S-C Dumont d'Urville.* Dunmore, *French Explorers in the Pacific.*

# B

## Bathysphere

*L:* 4.8′ diameter (1.4m). *Tons:* 2.5 tons. *Hull:* steel. *Comp.:* 2. *Des.:* Otis Barton and Cox & Stephens. *Built:* Watson-Stillman Hydraulic Machinery Co.; 1930.

In the late 1920s, the New York Zoological Society began a concentrated study of the ocean depths 9 miles (14 kilometers) off the coast of Nonsuch Island, Bermuda, in 32°12′N, 64°36′W. Disappointed with the meager returns from deep-sea trawls, Dr. William Beebe sought to develop a way of observing the deep firsthand. Because pressure increases by 14.7 pounds per square inch for every 10 meters (33 feet) in depth, the observation platform had to be strong, compact, and round, to distribute the pressure evenly. With the help of Otis Barton, a bathysphere (from the Greek for "deep sphere") was built in 1929. It proved too heavy for the tender, *Ready,* and a second was completed in 1930. With a skin 1.5 inches thick and two 8-inch-wide fused-quartz observation windows, the two-man observation ball was attached to a cable and lowered from the tender. A second cable provided electricity and a telephone connection to the surface. Oxygen was supplied by two cylinders, and carbon dioxide and moisture were absorbed by trays of soda lime and calcium chloride, respectively.

The first descent was made on June 6, 1930, to a depth of 244 meters (800 feet). Five days later *Bathysphere* went down to 435 meters (1,426 feet), and on August 15, 1934, reached 923 meters (3,028 feet), the extreme limit of the tether. (The previous record depths were 117 meters [383 feet] for a submarine and 160 meters [525 feet] for an armored suited diver in a Bavarian lake.) However, record depths were only incidental to the work at hand.

"Every descent and ascent of the bathysphere," wrote Beebe, "showed a fauna, rich beyond what the summary of all our 1,500 [sampling] nets would lead us to expect." In addition to discovering and photographing weird and hitherto unknown species of eels, lanternfish, squid, and jellyfish, Beebe was fascinated by the amount of light generated by animals in the deep, especially beyond 518 meters (1,700 feet), the absolute limit to which sunlight penetrated. The last dives in the *Bathysphere* were completed in 1934, and comparable depths were not attained until after World War II, when Auguste Piccard developed the first self-propelled bathyscaph ("deep boat"), TRIESTE.

Beebe, *Half Mile Down.*

## HMS Beagle

Bark (3m). *L/B/D:* 90.3′ × 24.5′ × 12.5′ (27.5m × 7.5m × 3.8m). *Tons:* 235 bm. *Hull:* wood. *Comp.:* 75. *Arm.:* 5 × 6pdr, 2 × 9pdr. *Des.:* Sir Henry Peake. *Built:* Woolwich Dockyard, Eng.; 1820.

HMS *Beagle* was originally launched as one of 115 *Cherokee*-class 10-gun brigs built by the Royal Navy between 1807 and 1830 and was used in a variety of roles, including surveying and antislaver patrols. By the time of her first voyage *Beagle* had been converted to a bark rig. Her first major expedition was from May 1826 to October 1830 with HMS *Adventure,* to chart the straits and passages of the southern tip of South America; it was during this voyage that the Beagle Channel, skirting the southern edge of Tierra del Fuego, was explored and named. Under the stress of arduous conditions in the waters around Tierra del Fuego, Captain Pringle Stokes killed himself in August 1828. Short of provisions and with many of the crew ill, *Beagle* returned to Buenos Aires, where Lieutenant Robert FitzRoy took command for the homeward voyage.

FitzRoy commanded *Beagle* on her subsequent circumnavigation, during which she was to complete the survey of Tierra del Fuego, the Chilean coast, and a number of Pacific islands, and to carry out chronometric observations — she carried twenty-two chronometers. Among the seventy-four crew and passengers were three Fuegians who had been taken to England and were returning home. Also assigned to the ship was a twenty-one-year-old botany student, Charles Darwin, whose professor, J. S. Henslow, considered him not a "*finished* naturalist, but . . . amply qualified for collecting, observing, and noting, anything new to be noted in Natural History." *Beagle* departed Devonport on December 27, 1831, and after stops in the Cape Verde Islands and Bahía arrived at Rio de Janeiro on April 4. After three months of hydrographic surveys of the Brazilian coast (Darwin was occupied in researching the rain forest), *Beagle* proceeded to Bahía Blanca, Argentina. It was there that Darwin first uncovered fossils that led him to question the relationship of living and extinct species.

On January 19, 1833, *Beagle* arrived at Ponsonby Sound, Tierra del Fuego, where Jemmy Buttons, York Minster, and Fuegia Basket returned home. Richard Matthews, a missionary sent to minister to the Fuegians, quickly abandoned his calling to return to the ship. In February, *Beagle* returned to Uruguay, via the Falkland Islands. The conditions at the southern tip of the Americas required the use of a second ship, and FitzRoy took it upon himself to purchase an American vessel, renamed *Adventure;* the Admiralty later made him sell the ship in Chile. Surveys of the Argentine coast resumed from April through July, when the ship reached El Carmen, on the Rio Negro, then the southernmost outpost in Argentina. Darwin returned overland from there to Bahía Blanca, then up the Rio Paraná to Santa Fe and finally to Montevideo, where he rejoined the ship on October 21. *Beagle* returned to Tierra del Fuego to complete her survey work in January, then surveyed the Falkland Islands in March and April. She sailed through the Strait of Magellan into Chilean waters in June 1834, and arrived at Valparaiso on July 23. As before, *Beagle* conducted coastal surveys while Darwin made overland treks in the Chilean Andes. After visiting the Chonos Archipelago in November, *Beagle* returned to the Chilean mainland in February and surveyed there until July. After stops at Iquique and Callao, Peru, *Beagle* sailed for the Galápagos Islands, 600 miles west of Ecuador.

The ship arrived there on September 17, and though the expedition remained only one month, it was here that Darwin made the observations — particularly of the thirteen different species of finches — that proved the foundation for his theory of natural selection. *Beagle* left the Galápagos on October 20 bound for Tahiti. For the remainder of the voyage the expedition's primary mission was to make chronometric observations, though there was much of interest to occupy Darwin at their remaining stops, which included New Zealand, Australia, Tasmania, the Cocos (Keeling) Islands, Mauritius, and Cape Town, and then in the Atlantic, St. Helena, and Bahía, Brazil.

*Beagle* finally returned to Falmouth on October 2, 1836. Although Darwin's *Origin of Species* was not published until 1859, his voyage in *Beagle* (during which he had been badly affected by seasickness) laid the foundation for his theories of evolution and natural selection, and profoundly affected the course of modern scientific thought. As Darwin himself wrote, "The voyage in the *Beagle* has been by far the most important event in my life and has determined the whole of my existence."

Six months after her return, *Beagle* was off to Australia under the command of Captain John Lord Stokes, a veteran of the FitzRoy-Darwin voyage. After surveying the western coast between the Swan River (Perth) and Fitzroy River (named for his former commander), she sailed around to the southeast corner of the continent. There, *Beagle* conducted surveys along both shores of the Bass Strait, and then in May of 1839 sailed northabout to the shores of the Arafura Sea opposite Timor. Her crew named a number of geographical features, including Port Darwin (for their former shipmate) and the Flinders River, after the indomitable surveyor of HMS INVESTIGATOR. In so honoring his predecessor, Stokes reflected that "monuments may crumble, but a name endures as long as the world."

Her work in Australia done, *Beagle* returned to England in 1843, after eighteen years' hard service to her nation and the world. Transferred out of the Royal Navy in 1845, *Beagle* ended her days as the Preventive Service's stationary *Beagle Watch Vessel* (renamed *W.V. 7* in 1863) moored at Pagelsham Pool on the coast of Essex. She was sold and probably broken up in 1870.

Basalla, "Voyage of the *Beagle* without Darwin." Darwin, *Diary of the Voyage of H.M.S. "Beagle."* Darling, "HMS *Beagle.*" FitzRoy and King, *Narrative of the Surveying Voyages of H.M.S. "Adventure" and "Beagle."* Marquardt, *HMS "Beagle."* Thomson, *HMS "Beagle."*

## Bear

Barkentine (3m). *L/B/D:* 198.5′ × 29.8′ × 18.8′ (60.5m × 9.1m × 5.7m). *Tons:* 1,675 disp. *Hull:* wood. *Comp.:* 35–40. *Mach.:* steam, 300 ihp, 1 screw. *Built:* Alexander Stephen & Sons, Ltd., Dundee; 1874.

Built for the ten-day-long sealing season — in 1883, her best year, she brought home more than 30,000 pelts — *Bear* was designed for work amid Arctic ice fields. In 1884, she was sold to the U.S. government and took part in the search for the Greeley Expedition, whose seven survivors were found at Cape Sabine. From 1885 to 1927, *Bear* served as a U.S. Revenue Marine cutter stationed in Alaska, where she looked out for seal poachers, shipwrecked whalers, and illicit trade with native Alaskans, ferried reindeer from Siberia to Alaska, and served as a floating courthouse. Laid up at Oakland, California, in 1926 and transferred to the

▼ A photo by Amory H. Waite, Jr., of the **Bear** at Discovery Inlet, the farthest point south reached by the ship during Rear Admiral Richard Byrd's second Antarctic expedition, 1932. *Courtesy Peabody Essex Museum, Salem, Massachusetts.*

city for use as a museum ship, *Bear* starred as the sealer *Macedonia* in the 1930 film version of Jack London's *Sea Wolf*. Rear Admiral Richard Byrd acquired her for his second Antarctic expedition in 1932, and *Bear* sailed there again with the U.S. Antarctic Service in 1938. From 1941 to 1944, USS *Bear* served in the Northeast Atlantic Patrol. Purchased for the sealing trade in 1948, her refit proved too costly and she was laid up in Halifax. In 1963, while in tow to Philadelphia for use as a floating restaurant, she foundered about 250 miles (400 kilometers) east of New York in 42°40′N, 65°11′W.

Bixby. *Track of the "Bear."* Boroughs, *Great Ice Ship "Bear."* Wead, *Gales, Ice and Men.*

# Belgica

(ex-*Patria*) Screw steamer (1f/3m). *L/B/D:* 118′ × 25′ × 13.4′ (36m × 7.6m × 4.1m). *Tons:* 336 grt. *Hull:* wood. *Comp.:* 20. *Mach.:* compound engine, 30 nhp. *Built:* K. Jacobsen, Svelvig, Norway; 1884.

Built for the Norwegian seal trade, *Belgica* was acquired and renamed for Commandant Adrien de Gerlache's Belgian Antarctic Expedition, the chief object of which was to determine the position of the South Magnetic Pole. Outfitting the ship took longer than intended, and the ship did not arrive off Palmer Land until January 1898, late in the Antarctic summer. By March, the ship was icebound near Alexander Island, and over the course of the next thirteen months she was held fast, drifting 600 miles (965 kilometers) along the Antarctic Peninsula shore of the Bellingshausen Sea toward Peter I Island. Unprepared for such an extensive stay in that climate, most of the crew were stricken with scurvy, and command of the expedition devolved temporarily on *Belgica's* first mate, Roald Amundsen, who was assisted by the ship's doctor, Frederick A. Cook. In April 1899, the crew used explosives to free the ship from the ice, and *Belgica* returned to Belgium. Although the *Belgica* expedition was only a minor success, being the first to winter in Antarctica, it did set the stage for the swift advances in Antarctic exploration that culmi-

nated in Amundsen's ascent to the South Pole from the ship FRAM in 1911.

Acquired by N. C. Halvorsen in 1902, and then by the Duc d'Orléans, who embarked in her for research in the Kara and Greenland Seas in 1905, *Belgica* remained in service through 1913.

Cook, *Through the First Antarctic Night.* de Gerlache, *Voyage of the "Belgica."*

# Belle

Barque longue (2m). *L/B:* 51′ × 14′ (15.5m × 4.3m). *Tons:* 45 tons. *Hull:* wood. *Comp.:* 20–30. *Arm.:* 6 guns. *Built:* Honoré Malet, Rochefort, France; 1684.

Discovered in 1995 in the shallow waters of Matagorda Bay off the Texas coast, *Belle* was the flagship of Robert Cavalier, Sieur de La Salle's ill-fated expedition to establish French colonies at the mouth of the Mississippi. One of the most important French explorers of North America, La Salle prospered as a fur trader on the Great Lakes, and his GRIFFON of 1679 was the first ship built on the Lakes. In 1682, he and Henri de Tonty became the first Europeans to sail down the Mississippi River to its mouth, after which he claimed the territory of Louisiana for France. Returning to France, La Salle received the backing of Louis XIV to secure the claim.

On July 24, 1684, he sailed from La Rochelle at the head of a fleet of four ships — *Belle*, a gift from Louis, *Joly* (36 guns), the ketch *St. François,* and the storeship *Aimable.* After a two-month stay in St. Domingue (Haiti) during which *St. François* was seized by pirates, the fleet sailed into the Gulf of Mexico in November. Guided by inaccurate maps, they landed just west of the Mississippi, but, uncertain of their position, they pressed on, only to reach Matagorda Bay, 400 miles west of the Mississippi, in January of 1685. The inhospitable land was made almost unbearable by the loss of *Aimable* and the bulk of the expedition's supplies as she entered the bay. Shortly thereafter, *Joly* sailed for France, leaving *Belle* and some 180 ailing and disgruntled settlers. La Salle made several overland expeditions in search of the Mississippi — of which he believed Matagorda Bay to be a branch — but the settlers left at Fort St. Louis (near present-day Port Lavaca, Texas) were reduced by disease and in skirmishes with the native inhabitants of the coast.

*Belle* remained moored in the bay with a crew of about twenty. Running low on water, in January 1686 the captain tried to sail for Fort St. Louis. The ship was blown east across the bay, ran aground, and sank; only six of her crew survived. A year later, with no end of their ordeal in sight, the would-be colonists numbered fewer than forty. La Salle and about half the company set out in search of help, but two months later he was murdered by his own men near the Trinity River. Of this group, only five reached France; the fate of those who remained at Fort St. Louis can only be surmised, as no effort was made to find them.

In the 1970s, the Texas Historical Commission began a systematic effort to find *Belle*. In 1995, while sweeping the bay with a magnetometer, archaeologists led by Barto Arnold found the ship lying in about twelve feet (four meters) of water just east of the Matagorda Peninsula. A cofferdam was erected around the site and the water pumped out so that what amounted to a dry-land excavation of the site could be carried out. A variety of human remains — including one complete skeleton — and artifacts have been recovered, among them eighty whole or semiwhole casks containing cargo, gunpowder, lead shot, foodstuffs, and pitch; empty casks that once contained wine and water; several boxes containing muskets and trade goods such as beads, rings, combs, and knife blades; one iron swivel gun, two bronze cannons, and a carriage gun; rigging fittings; cooking implements; and personal effects such as a crucifix, bowls, and pipes.

Following the excavation of the smaller items, the remains of the hull were completely disassembled and removed from the site. After careful conservation ashore, they will be reassembled and open to public view.

LaRoe, "La Salle's Last Voyage."

# HMS Blossom

Sloop-of-war (3m). *L/B:* 108.5' × 30' (33.1m × 9.1m). *Tons:* 427 bm. *Hull:* wood. *Comp.:* 100. *Arm.:* 18 × 18pdr. *Built:* Guillaum, Northam, Eng.; 1806.

Among the most ambitious nineteenth-century plans to discover the Northwest Passage was a three-pronged venture involving John Franklin, Edward Parry, and Commander Frederick William Beechey. While Franklin attempted to complete an overland survey of the Arctic coast from the Mackenzie River to Icy Point (James Cook's farthest north with HMS RESOLUTION and DISCOVERY in 1778), Parry would penetrate the Arctic from the east in HMS HECLA and *Fury*, and Beechey — a veteran of Franklin's *Advance* in 1818 and Parry's *Hecla* in 1819 — would sail through the Bering Strait and eastward to rendezvous with the other parties.

After fitting out for the expedition, Beechey's HMS *Blossom* departed Spithead on May 19, 1825, sailing southwest down the Atlantic with stops at Tenerife, Rio de Janeiro, and the Falklands, rounding Cape Horn via Tierra del Fuego. After calling at Concepción and Valparaiso, Chile, she proceeded west to confirm or correct the existence of various islands reported from previous voyages. After visits to Easter Island and Pitcairn Island, *Blossom* continued through the Society Islands to arrive at Tahiti on April 18, 1826. Turning north, she sailed to Onorooroo, Woahoo (Honolulu, Oahu) on May 20, and left from there for Petropavlovsk on the Kamchatka Peninsula, where the English arrived on June 29. There they learned that Parry's *Fury* had been crushed in the ice but that her crew had returned to England in *Hecla*. Passing through the Bering Strait on July 19, *Blossom* arrived at Chamisso Inlet in Kotzebue Sound on July 25, 1826, only five days later than the date agreed to in England eighteen months before — an astonishing feat of seamanship. There being no sign of Franklin, Beechey proceeded to explore the coast as far as 70°38'N, 36 miles northeast of Icy Cape, where they arrived on August 15. From there, Thomas Elson took the ship's barge to look for Franklin, and on August 23, he reached Point Barrow

(71°23′N, 156°21′W), the farthest into the Arctic anyone except Eskimos had ever penetrated and which he named for Sir John Barrow, the second secretary of the Admiralty. (Perhaps discouraged by "the most dreary, miserable and uninteresting portions of the sea coast that can perhaps be found in any part of the world," Franklin turned back to the Great Bear Lake from Return Point five days before Elson reached Point Barrow, 146 miles to the west.)

Sailing from Kotzebue Bay on October 14, *Blossom* headed for Yerba Buena (now San Francisco), where she arrived on November 7. After six weeks in the tiny Spanish port, which Beechey predicted would one day become "a great naval establishment," the expedition called briefly at Monterey and then crossed the Pacific to Macao, arriving on April 11, 1827. After calling again at Petropavlovsk, they returned to Kotzebue Sound. The ice was worse this season, and there was no news of Franklin. On October 5, Beechey turned for home, calling at Monterey, Yerba Buena, and San Blas, Mexico, en route, and arrived in England on October 12, 1827. In addition to the geographical knowledge gained, the two-year voyage resulted in the publication of two important works on botany and zoology. *Blossom* remained in service as a survey ship until 1833 when she was hulked; she was broken up in 1848.

Beechey, *Narrative of a Voyage to the Pacific and Beering's Strait.* Brock, "Dossier HMS *Blossom* 1806–1848." Peard, *To the Pacific and Arctic with Beechey.*

# La Boudeuse

Frigate (3m). *L/B/D:* 134.5′ × 35.1′ × 17.7′ (41m × 10.7m × 5.4m). *Tons:* 550. *Hull:* wood. *Comp.:* 214. *Arm.:* 26 × 8pdr. *Des.:* Raffeau. *Built:* Nantes, France; 1766.

The French were relative latecomers to global circumnavigation and Pacific exploration, but their first major expedition, led by Louis Antoine de Bougainville with the ships *La Boudeuse* and *L'Etoile,* set a new standard. The purpose of the voyage was not only the increase of geographical knowledge, but the study of astronomy, botany, and zoology. The ship's company included the naturalist Philibert de Commerson and the astronomer C. F. P. Véron. There were diplomatic and commercial aspects to the voyage as well. *Boudeuse* sailed from Brest on December 5, 1766, arriving at Montevideo on January 31, 1767. From there she sailed with the Spanish frigates *Liebre* and *Esmeralda* to the Falkland Islands, where the French colony was formally transferred to Spanish rule. Bougainville had founded the colony in 1764, with a view to establishing a French presence on the Cape Horn route, and the islands were called Les Malouines — corrupted by the Spanish to Malvinas — after the St. Malo merchants who underwrote the enterprise. After rendezvousing with the storeship *Etoile,* which had sailed two months after *Boudeuse,* the ships sailed from Montevideo on November 14. Their passage through the Strait of Magellan took fifty-two days, during which the French charted the waters and studied the inhabitants of lower Patagonia and Tierra del Fuego.

Entering the Pacific on January 26, 1768, the ships headed northwest to 20°S before turning west. The ships' first landfall was in the Tuamotus. Unable to anchor, Bougainville called them collectively the Dangerous Archipelago. Continuing west, on April 6, 1768, they arrived at Tahiti, the second Europeans to do so, only ten months after HMS DOLPHIN. Enchanted with the island and its people — especially the women — Bougainville gave it the name New Cythera, for the birthplace of Aphrodite of Greek myth, and claimed it for France. After only nine days, the ships sailed on, the company now including Ahutoru, the brother of the local chieftain, who volunteered to join the expedition and later lived in Paris. Bougainville neglected to discuss the bleaker aspects of Tahitian life, and his reports of the French experience had a profound influence on Enlightenment thinkers such as Rousseau and his concept of the noble savage.

At this point, as Helen Wallis has written, Bougainville became the first explorer "to resist the lure of the safer routes and bear steadily westward from Tahiti, the first, as he claimed, to maintain a westerly course in 15°S into the little-known seas of the south-western Pacific." This course took the French through the Samoan Islands (which they called the Navigators) and on May 22, to the New Hebrides (Vanuatu). These were last seen by Europeans in 1606, when SAN PEDRO Y SAN PABLO and SAN PEDRO had landed there during Pedro Fernández de Quirós's search for the Solomon Islands. As the islanders were not eager for trade and there were few places to anchor safely, Bougainville claimed the land for France before turning again to the west. Again, unlike any of his known predecessors, Bougainville was intent on determining whether there was a passage between New Guinea and Australia. Although *San Pedro* had sailed through the Torres Strait in 1605, a description of that voyage remained buried in the Spanish archives, and eighteenth-century geographers were ignorant of the fact.

June 4 brought the two ships to the Great Barrier Reef, which in 15°S is about 30 miles from the coast of Australia. Though Bougainville was sure that they were in "the vicinity of a great land . . . nothing less than the eastern coast of New Holland," the danger to his ships was too great to justify the risk of further exploration here: "The sea broke with great violence upon these shoals, and some summits of rocks appeared above water from place to place. This last discovery was the voice of God, and we were obedient to it." They worked to the north and June 10 found them in New Guinea's Gulf of the Louisiade, in which they were embayed for ten days before rounding Cape Deliverance to the east. Another ten days brought them to Choiseul Island, where their reception was far from friendly. Though this was the western Solomons, the elusive islands of Alvaro Mendaña's 1568 voyage in LOS REYES, Bougainville did not realize it, just as Commander Philip Carteret had failed to when he passed the same way in HMS SWALLOW only four months earlier.

Sorely in need of fresh food, the French pressed on to New Britain where they happened to anchor within a few miles of Carteret's camp. Sailing around New Ireland, they shaped a course for the Moluccas and arrived at the Dutch settlement at Boeroe on September 1. By the end of the month they were at Batavia (Djakarta), where Bougainville learned the name of his English predecessor, Carteret, who had departed just twelve days before. Although a secret aim of the expedition had been to obtain spices for transplantation on Ile de France (Mauritius), Batavia was so disease-ridden that Bougainville sailed on October 18 after only a hasty refit. The slower *Etoile* was left to proceed at her own pace. After a more extensive refit at Ile de France, they sailed for the Cape of Good Hope in January. On February 26, *Boudeuse* caught up with Carteret in *Swallow* and Bougainville inquired discreetly into the particulars of *Swallow*'s voyage while dissembling about his own. In exchange for his offer of help, Carteret "presented me with an arrow which he had got in one of the isles he had found on his voyage round the world, a voyage that he was far from suspecting we had likewise made." Leaving *Swallow* in their wake, the French pressed on to St. Malo, where *Boudeuse* arrived on March 16, 1769, having lost only seven men in more than two years at sea. In addition to correcting or adding to charts of the Pacific, the expedition returned with specimens of more than 3,000 species of plants and animals.

Bougainville, *Voyage Round the World.* Brosse, *Great Voyages of Discovery.*

# HMS Bounty

(ex-*Bethia*) Ship (3m). *L/B/D:* 91′ × 24.3′ × 11.3′ dph (27.7m × 7.5m × 3.5m). *Tons:* 220 burthen. *Hull:* wood. *Comp.:* 46. *Arm.:* 4 × 4pdr, 10 swivels. *Built:* Hull, Eng.; 1784.

In 1775, the Society for West India Merchants proposed that breadfruit trees, native to the South Pacific, be transplanted to the West Indies to be grown as a food staple for slaves. Twelve years later the Royal Navy purchased the merchant ship *Bethia* especially for the purpose of sailing to the Society Islands "where, according to the accounts which are given by the late Captain Cook, and Persons who accompanied him during his Voyages, the Bread Fruit Tree is to be found in the most lux-uriant state." After the vessel was approved for the purpose by the botanist Joseph Banks, a veteran of Captain James Cook's first voyage, *Bethia* was pur-chased from Messrs. Wellbank, Sharp, and Brown in May 1787. At Deptford Dockyard the ship was refitted to carry 300 breadfruit trees, its upper deck being rebuilt "to have as many Gratings . . . as con-veniently can be to give air; likewise to have Scut-tles through the side for the same reason." Half the trees were destined for Jamaica, and half for the Royal Botanical Garden at St. Vincent; at his dis-cretion Lieutenant William Bligh could take some trees for Kew Gardens on his return to Britain. The Admiralty also ordered the ship sheathed in cop-per. Three boats were also ordered from naval con-tractor John Burr, a 16-foot jolly boat, a 20-foot cutter, and the 23-foot Bounty launch.

On August 17, Bligh was appointed to com-mand HM Armed Vessel *Bounty,* as the ship was officially designated. A veteran of Cook's third voy-age to the Pacific, during which he served as master of HMS Resolution, Bligh was an accomplished hydrographer. Sailing from Portsmouth on De-cember 23, 1787, *Bounty* went to Tahiti, arriving there on October 26, 1788. After five months in the island paradise, which the crew seem thoroughly to have enjoyed except for Bligh's increasingly harsh discipline, *Bounty* weighed anchor on April 6, 1789, with more than a thousand breadfruit trees. Twenty-two days later, five members of the forty-three-man crew seized the ship in a bloodless mu-tiny. The ringleader was Fletcher Christian, whom Bligh had appointed the ship's second in com-mand. He now put Bligh and nineteen of his sup-porters into the ship's launch, which Bligh sailed to the Dutch entrepôt at Timor.

Christian attempted a landing on Tubuai, about 400 miles south of Tahiti, where *Bounty* arrived on May 28. The crew met with a poor reception and soon returned to Tahiti, where they stayed ten days while they loaded 460 hogs and fifty goats and em-barked twenty-eight Tahitians — nine men, eight boys, ten women, and one girl. A second visit to Tubuai was no better, and after a pitched battle with about 700 Tubuaians, 66 of whom were killed,

the mutineers and their Tahitian shipmates de-parted on September 17. Accompanied by the Tubuaian chief, Taroa, three men, and twelve women, who had befriended them, they arrived back at Tahiti on September 20. Sixteen of the mu-tineers (some of whom seem to have been unwill-ing accessories from the start) remained on the is-land, and the next day Christian sailed with the Tubuaians, a few Tahitians, and eight of the crew. Navigating with a defective chronometer and in search of an uninhabited island whose published position was 200 miles east of its actual position, the mutineers reached Pitcairn Island in January or February of 1790. The next day, they burned their ship and attempted to settle the island. As the Eng-lish promptly divided the island among themselves and relegated the Tahitians to second-class status, relations between the men turned violent and sev-eral were killed. The survivors gradually acclimated themselves to their new situation. Eighteen years later, on February 6, 1808, Pitcairn was visited by the Nantucket sealer *Topaz* under Captain Mat-thew Folger. The sole male survivor of the original band of settlers was Alexander Smith, whom Folger gave the new name John Adams, to lessen his chance of arrest should the island be visited by a British warship. Following the publication of Captain Frederick William Beechey's report of his visit aboard HMS Blossom thirteen years after that, Pitcairn came under the protection of the British Crown in 1825.

Fourteen mutineers were eventually arrested in Tahiti by the men of HMS *Pandora,* which had been dispatched for the purpose. On August 28, 1791, *Pandora* struck the Great Barrier Reef and sank; four of the mutineers were drowned. *Pan-dora's* survivors sailed to Timor and the ten sur-viving mutineers were ultimately brought to trial in England. Thomas Ellison, John Milward, and Thomas Burkitt were hanged. Bligh was also given a second chance to complete his mission, which he did in HMS *Providence* in 1792. (*Providence* was later wrecked, on May 17, 1797, when, under com-mand of Commander William Broughton, she ran aground in the Sakashima Islands east of Taiwan during a surveying voyage of the North Pacific.)

The story of the mutiny on the *Bounty* has inspired countless retellings and fictional accounts. The first of several movies of the mutiny, *The Mutiny on the Bounty*, appeared in 1935, starring Charles Laughton and Clark Gable, and featured the *Lilly* as the *Bounty*. Replicas of *Bounty* were built for the 1962 remake starring Marlon Brando and Trevor Howard and for *Bounty* (1985) with Mel Gibson and Anthony Hopkins.

Barrow, *Mutiny and Piratical Seizure of HMS "Bounty."* Bligh, *Narrative of the Mutiny on the "Bounty."* Knight, "H.M. Armed Vessel *Bounty.*" Smith, "Some Remarks about the Mutiny of the *Bounty.*"

# Bounty launch

Launch (1m). *L/B/D:* 23′ × 6.8′ × 2.8′ dph (7m × 2.1m × 0.8m). *Hull:* wood. *Comp.:* 20. *Built:* John Samuel White, Cowes, Isle of Wight, Eng.; 1787.

When Fletcher Christian rallied his supporters to mutiny aboard HMS BOUNTY on April 28, 1789, there was no thought of killing Lieutenant William Bligh. Instead, they put him and nineteen supporters into the ship's launch, together with 28 gallons of water, 5 bottles of wine, 4 quarts of rum, 150 pounds of biscuit, and 20 pounds of pork. Bligh was also given a sextant and four cutlasses. Fully loaded, the 23-foot-long launch had a freeboard of only 7 inches. The day after the mutiny, the launch landed at the nearby island of Tofoa, in the Fiji Islands, but one of the crew was killed by the inhabitants as they prepared to leave the next day. With rations limited to 1 ounce of bread and 4 ounces of water daily (later reduced to half an ounce of bread and 1 ounce of water), Bligh decided to sail direct for the Dutch settlement at Timor, 3,600 miles to the west. The launch passed through the New Hebrides (May 14–15), along the Great Barrier Reef (May 16–June 4), through the Torres Strait between Australia and New Guinea, and on to Timor, arriving on June 12. Miraculously, in sailing forty-three days through uncharted waters in an open boat overcrowded with desperately ill-provisioned men, Bligh had not lost a single one of his crew. Recognized then and now as an outstanding feat of navigation, the voyage of the *Bounty* launch remains almost without peer in the history of navigation.

Bligh, *Narrative of the Mutiny on the "Bounty."* Fryer, *Voyage of the "Bounty" Launch.*

# La Boussole

(ex-*Le Portefaix*) Ship (3m). *Tons:* 450 tons. *Hull:* wood. *Comp.:* 113. *Built:* France; 1781.

Built as the fishery supply ship *Portefaix*, the refitted *La Boussole* ("Compass") was the flagship of Jean-François de Galaup, comte de La Pérouse, on one of France's most famous eighteenth-century expeditions to the Pacific. The expedition had its origins in the Anglo-French rivalry for dominance in the Pacific following the American Revolution. The French had already sent out several expeditions to the Pacific, including those of Louis Antoine de Bougainville's LA BOUDEUSE and *L'Etoile* in 1766–69 and Jean-François de Surville's ST. JEAN-BAPTISTE in 1769–77. By the 1780s, the French had a two-fold interest in such a voyage: to investigate commercial possibilities, especially in the Pacific Northwest fur trade; and to expand on Captain James Cook's geographic, scientific, and ethnographic discoveries. Planning for the expedition involved both the French Navy and scientists, including the naturalist Leclerc de Buffon, the chemist Antoine-Laurent Lavoisier, and the mathematician the Marquis de Condorcet. The expedition also had the personal endorsement of Louis XVI.

*La Boussole* and L'ASTROLABE sailed from Brest on August 1, 1785, calling at Madeira, Tenerife, and Santa Catarina Island near Rio de Janeiro before a calm rounding of Cape Horn. In February, at Concepción and Talcahuano, Chile, La Pérouse took careful note of the Spanish administration, whose policies he credited with stifling the growth of a country "whose products, if they reached their maximum, could supply half Europe." The ships sailed for Easter Island, where they spent a day, and then sailed on to the island of Maui. Although frequently critical of the habits and traditions of native people, and dismissive of the fashionable idea of the noble savage, La Pérouse was clear in the purpose of his voyage and observed that "modern navigators have no other purpose when they describe the customs of newly discovered people than to complete the story of mankind." Reflecting on his stay in the Hawaiian Islands, he wrote:

> Although the French are the first to have stepped onto the island of *Mowee* in recent times, I did not take possession of it in the King's name. This European practice is too utterly ridiculous, and philosophers must reflect with some sadness that, because one has muskets and canons, one looks upon 60,000 inhabitants as worth nothing, ignoring their rights over a land where for centuries their ancestors have been buried.

After less than two days at Maui, the two ships took their departure from the islands on June 1. Three weeks later they made a landfall off Mount St. Elias, Alaska (first named by Vitus Bering in 1741), and followed the coast east and south about 200 miles to Port des Français (Lituya Bay), where they established a camp on an island they purchased from the Tlingits. On July 13, twenty-one sailors and officers were drowned when their boats overturned at the mouth of the bay.

The expedition sailed south on July 30 and, hugging the coast for much of the way, arrived at the Spanish settlement at Monterey on September 14. Ten days later the ships sailed west, naming French Frigate Shoals and Necker Island and stopping at uninhabited Asuncion Island in the Marianas chain before arriving at Macao on January 2, 1787. They remained there for two months, during which the French sold the furs they had collected in the Pacific Northwest and recruited twelve Chinese seamen. After sailing to the Philippines for a brief stay, in April *La Boussole* and *L'Astrolabe* turned north, passing into the Sea of Japan, previously unexplored by Europeans. Sailing up the Strait of Tartary between the mainland and

Sakhalin Island, they landed at Ternei, Suffren Bay, and Castries Bay on the Asian coast, and De Langle Bay (named for *L'Astrolabe*'s captain) on Sakhalin. The ships then transited the Strait of La Pérouse between that island and Hokkaido, and sailed up the Kurile Islands to Petropavlovsk on the Kamchatka Peninsula, where they were feted by Russian officials for twenty-four days.

At the end of October, the two ships headed for the South Pacific, though it was not until December 6 that they encountered land again, anchoring off the island of Tutuila, one of a group that Bougainville had named the Navigator Islands and that now forms part of American Samoa. Despite reservations about the islanders' intentions, La Pérouse allowed de Langle to get fresh water from an island creek, a decision that cost the lives of de Langle and eleven others in a seemingly unprovoked attack by more than 1,000 islanders on December 11. There were no reprisals, and having confirmed the position of the remaining islands of the group, the expedition sailed for the English settlement at Botany Bay, New Holland (Australia), arriving there on January 26, 1788, just as the British were shifting the outpost to nearby Port Jackson (Sydney).

*La Boussole* and *L'Astrolabe* stayed on the Australian coast for six weeks. As at Macao and Petropavlovsk, copies of the ships' logs and charts of the voyage were sent home, this time via a British ship. On March 10, 1788, the two ships weighed anchor. The plan was for the ships to sail east as far as Tonga, then west past New Caledonia and the Solomon Islands, then along the northern coast of Australia from Cape York counterclockwise as far as Tasmania, and then west again to Réunion at the end of the year before returning to France in 1789.

When they failed to return, a succession of search expeditions were sent out, starting with d'Entrecasteaux in *La Recherche* and L'Espérance in 1791–94. In 1826 Captain Peter Dillon happened on artifacts from the ships on the island of Vanikoro north of New Caledonia. His finds were confirmed by Dumont d'Urville in 1828, and in 1959, a New Zealand diver named Reece Discomb located the remains of the ships in False

(Wreck) Passage near Ambi. The ships apparently had grounded on a submerged coral formation. Local tradition suggests that there were survivors, though their fate is unknown.

La Pérouse, *Journal of Jean-François de la Galaup de La Pérouse.* Shelton, *From Hudson's Bay to Botany Bay.*

## Bowdoin

Gaff schooner (2m). *L/B/D:* 88′ × 21′ × 10′ (26.9m × 6.4m × 3m). *Tons:* 66 grt. *Hull:* wood. *Comp.:* 7–16. *Mach.:* diesel, 190 hp, 1 screw. *Des.:* William Hand. *Built:* Hodgdon Bros. Shipyard, Boothbay Harbor, Me.; 1921.

*Bowdoin* was built to designs worked out by Donald B. MacMillan, a veteran of several voyages to the Arctic, including Robert Peary's effort to reach the North Pole in 1906 and a four-year stay in Greenland in 1913–17. Named for MacMillan's alma mater, *Bowdoin* was stoutly built, with a steel-sheathed bow, simple pole masts, and no bowsprit. On July 16, 1921, she departed Wiscasset on the first of her twenty-six voyages north. Sponsored by the Carnegie Foundation and planned for a study of terrestrial magnetism and atmospheric electricity, the voyage took *Bowdoin* north along Labrador and west through Hudson Strait and into Foxe Basin. There, on September 21, she entered Schooner Harbor on Foxe Peninsula and quickly became the focal point for a small village of nomadic Inuits, who joined her over the winter.

Returning to Maine the following summer, she had a seventeen-month layover before embarking on her first expedition to northern Greenland, under the auspices of the Carnegie Foundation and the National Geographic Society. Crossing the Arctic Circle along the coast of Greenland on August 2, 1923, *Bowdoin* and her crew wintered in Refuge Harbor north of Etah, 685 miles from the North Pole. Frozen in for 320 days, they made short trips away from the ship, again in the company of local Inuits, and in April erected a plaque commemorating the men who had died in the Greeley Expedition of 1881–84.

On her next expedition, sponsored by the U.S. Navy and the National Geographic Society, *Bowdoin* sailed in company with USS *Peary*. Members of the crew performed experiments with radio communications from the far north, tried to confirm or disprove the existence of lands reported by earlier expeditions, studied barometric pressure, and made the first color photographic record of Arctic flora and fauna. Using three amphibious planes carried aboard *Peary*, Lieutenant Commander Richard Byrd also made the first aerial surveys of western Greenland. In 1929, MacMillan and *Bowdoin* carried supplies to the Moravian mission at Nain, in northern Labrador, beginning a relationship that would last another fifteen years. The next year, on what proved to be her only trip to Iceland, *Bowdoin* carried students for the first time, and from 1934 on she always sailed with students who paid for the privilege of sailing with "Mac" to the high north.

A few years later, MacMillan married, and despite his previous insistence that no woman — even his wife — would (or could) sail to the Arctic, in 1938 Miriam MacMillan accompanied her husband as far as Nain and then, at the insistence of the rest of the crew, on to Greenland. (In all, "Lady Mac" would make nine voyages with her husband aboard *Bowdoin*. Her glowing accounts of the voyages tended to gloss over the hardships, and veterans of the northern voyages referred to her book as "Green Seas, White Lies.") The following year, MacMillan sold *Bowdoin* to the U.S. Navy. In 1941, he commanded her on a voyage to Greenland where the Navy was building air bases at Sondrestrom on the Arctic Circle and Narsarssuak. MacMillan joined the Hydrographic Service in 1942, but *Bowdoin* returned to Greenland for survey work through most of 1943, after which she was laid up.

In 1946, MacMillan rejoined his old ship, and they resumed their annual trips to Labrador and Greenland. MacMillan made his last voyage in *Bowdoin* in 1954, at the age of eighty, and *Bowdoin* was sold to Mystic Seaport Museum for use as a museum ship. Nine years later, in sad need of repair, she was sold to the Schooner Bowdoin Association and used for chartering in Maine waters. After a lengthy rebuild from 1980 to 1989, she joined the Maine Maritime Academy at Castine and resumed her original educational mission in the Arctic, visiting Labrador for the first time in a quarter century in 1990.

MacMillan, *Etah and Beyond*. MacMillan, *Green Seas, White Ice*. Thorndike, *Arctic Schooner "Bowdoin."*

## HMS Breadalbane

Bark (3m). *L/B/D:* 125′ × 24′ × 18′ dph (38.1m × 7.3m × 5.5m). *Tons:* 428 bm. *Hull:* wood. *Comp.:* 21. *Built:* Hedderwich & Rowan, Glasgow; 1843.

Originally built for a consortium of Scottish merchants, *Breadalbane* spent ten years trading between England and Calcutta. In 1853, she was hired by the British Admiralty to carry coal and other supplies to the *North Star*, a depot ship for the ships searching the Arctic for Sir John Franklin's HMS Erebus and HMS Terror. On May 19, 1853, *Breadalbane* sailed with Captain Inglefield's HMS *Phoenix* (the first propeller ship in the Arctic) and arrived at Beechey Island on August 8. The two ships were anchored to an ice floe when, at about 0330 on August 21, "The ice from the offing closed, and so effectually crushed the transport as to complete her destruction in the short space of fifteen minutes." She sank in 30 fathoms (290 meters) of water about half a mile south of Beechey Island.

While diving beneath the ice in 1975, Joe MacInnis found a fragment of a ship that research subsequently revealed to be from *Breadalbane*. In 1978 he began searching, though it was not until August 11, 1980, that divers working from the Canadian Coast Guard cutter *John A. Macdonald* found the ship largely intact, two masts still standing and the hull in good condition except where she had been hulled by the ice. Because of the depth and icy conditions on the surface, prolonged work on the site was impossible, although the ship's wheel was recovered and given to Parks Canada for conservation.

MacInnis, *The Land That Devours Ships*.

# Brendan

Sailing curragh (2m). *L/B:* 36' × 0.8' (11m × 2.4m). *Tons:* 2,400 lbs. *Hull:* cowhide on wood frame. *Comp.:* 5. *Des.:* Colin Mudie, based on written evidence. *Built:* Crosshaven Boatyard, Cork, Ireland; 1976.

*Brendan* was a re-creation of a medieval Irish curragh built by Tim Severin to demonstrate that the *Navigatio Sancti Brendan Abbatis* — the Voyage of St. Brendan the Abbot — could be a fact-based account of a transatlantic voyage from Ireland to North America made some time between 500 and 1000 CE. On May 17, 1976, with a crew of five, *Brendan* sailed from Brandon Creek, Ireland. Following the Stepping Stone route, the curragh stopped in the Aran Islands, Tory Island, and Ballyhoorisky before crossing to Iona, Tiree, and Stornoway. From the Isle of Lewis, *Brendan*'s crew sailed across 200 miles (320 kilometers) of open ocean to the Faeroe Islands. They sailed from Thorshavn on July 4 and made the 500-mile (800-kilometer) passage to Reykjavik in thirteen days. *Brendan* was hauled and stored for the winter in an airplane hangar. On May 17, 1977, four of the original crew — George Molony, Arthur Magan, Trondur Patursson (who had joined at Thorshavn), and Severin — sailed from Reykjavik for North America. Crossing the Denmark Strait, they rounded the southern tip of Greenland and sailed into the Davis Strait, where they experienced about ten days of gales. Nearly crushed by ice off the easternmost tip of Labrador, they were able to patch the leather skin and stop the leaking. On June 26, *Brendan* landed on Peckford Island in the Outer Wadham Group, about 150 miles northwest of St. John's, Newfoundland, after a fifty-day, 1,300-mile journey across the North Atlantic.

Severin, "Brendan" Voyage.

# Calypso

(ex-*J-826*) Research ship (1f/1m). *L/B/D:* 139′ × 25′ × 10′ (42.4m × 7.6m × 3m). *Tons:* 402 disp. *Hull:* wood. *Comp.:* 27. *Mach.:* diesels, 580 hp, 2 screws; 10 kts. *Built:* Ballard Marine Railway, Seattle; 1942.

Commissioned in 1942, *J-826* was one of 561 yard motor minesweepers (YMS) built during World War II. Turned over to the British, she operated out of Malta, Taranto, and Naples until the end of the war. In 1947 she reverted to U.S. Navy control, but two years later she was sold for use as a ferry operating between Malta and Gozo. Renamed *Calypso,* she had a capacity for 400 people and eleven cars. The next year, she was purchased by Lieutenant Commander Jacques-Yves Cousteau, who had helped found the French navy's Undersea Research Group in 1945, but who was then on leave to further develop SCUBA (Self-Contained Underwater Breathing Apparatus) diving and other means of underwater investigation.

*Calypso* proved an ideal platform for such work. Cousteau and his crews pioneered a wide variety of techniques with which they explored the "silent kingdom" of the world's oceans, coastal waters, and rivers. Their innumerable discoveries focused world attention on the variety and fragility of the world's ocean environment and that of the surrounding shores. Over the next forty-six years, the ship logged more than 1 million miles, chiefly in the Mediterranean, the coast of Africa, North and South America, Oceania, the East Indies, and Antarctica. The primary vehicle of France's oceanographic effort until 1966, *Calypso* carried state-of-the-art equipment, including one- and two-person minisubs, diving saucers, and underwater scooters. In addition, the ship was fitted with a "false nose"

— an observation chamber 10 feet (3 meters) below the waterline — and she carried helicopters and equipment for monitoring meteorological conditions. Perhaps most significant was the Cousteau Society's dissemination of the results of its research through periodicals, books, and documentaries. The first of these, *The Silent World,* took four years to film, and in 1957 Cousteau and his young codirector, Louis Malle, won the Cannes Film Festival's Golden Palm. This was followed by *Beneath the Frozen World* (about Antarctica), *Rediscovery of the World* (about the islands of the western Pacific), and more than sixty other films, including the 1960s television series, *The Undersea World of Jacques Cousteau.*

On January 8, 1996, a barge to which *Calypso* was moored broke loose and drove the vessel onto a piling in Singapore Harbor. She was raised, but the near loss of the fifty-six-year-old ship led the Cousteau Society to proceed with plans to commission *Calypso II,* specially designed as a platform for oceanographic research and powered by diesel engines and a 26-meter-high (85-foot) Turbovoile® — a type of rotor cylinder similar to that designed by Anton Flettner for his *Baden-Baden* in 1920.

Richards, "Sis and *J-826.*" Traonouïl et al., "Reviving a Legend."

# Carnegie

Brigantine (2m). *L/B/D:* 155′ × 33′ × 14′ (47.2m × 10.1m × 4.3m). *Tons:* 568 disp. *Hull:* wood. *Comp.:* 8 scientists, 17 crew. *Des.:* Henry J. Gielow. *Built:* Tebo Yacht Basin Co., Brooklyn, N.Y.; 1909.

The problems of Earth's magnetism have bedeviled navigators ever since the invention of the compass, because the compass points not to the North Pole, or true north, but to the North Magnetic Pole, the location of which changes over time. (In 1992, the North Magnetic Pole was located at about 78°24′N, 104°18′W, about 1,000 miles (1,600 kilometers) south of the North Pole.) To determine an accurate course with a compass, one needs to know the horizontal angle between true north and magnetic north — known as variation, or declination — which varies according to where one is in relation to the Magnetic Pole and other variables.

One of the first to examine this problem had been Edmund Halley, in HMS PARAMORE, but by the twentieth century, the problem remained to be addressed fully. In 1904, the Carnegie Institution began a massive survey of magnetic variation with the establishment of observatories the world over. From 1903 to 1908, the institution employed the brigantine *Galilee* to conduct magnetic surveys at sea; but as her hull included some magnetic materials, she proved less than perfect for the assignment. Thus was born the idea for a completely iron-free vessel designed solely for magnetic research. Her engines, propeller shaft, anchors, and other fittings were of bronze, her anchor hawser was hemp, and she mounted a wooden fisherman's windlass on her foredeck. (It is a nice irony, and speaks volumes of her benefactor and namesake's humanitarian vision, that Andrew Carnegie made his fortune in steel.)

Between 1909 and 1921, *Carnegie* made six voyages, during which she conducted magnetic surveys across all the oceans of the world from as far north as 80°N and as far south as 60°S. The primary magnetic survey completed in 1922, she was

▼ A wooden ship named for a man of steel, the brigantine **Carnegie** of 1909 was built with the express purpose of investigating variations in Earth's magnetic field. *Courtesy National Maritime Museum, Greenwich.*

laid up at Washington, D.C. Six years later, she was recommissioned for a three-year cruise the purpose of which was both to check previous magnetic readings and to conduct basic oceanographic research. Equipped with instruments for bottom sampling, meteorological measurements, and other observations, she departed Washington on May 1, 1928, under Captain James Percy Ault, who had commanded her on three previous expeditions. After sailing to Hamburg via Plymouth, England, she recrossed the Atlantic via Iceland and Barbados to Panama. Transiting the canal, *Carnegie* entered the Pacific in October and sailed for Easter Island. From there the ship sailed east to Peru, and then west again for Yokohama, via Samoa and Guam. From Japan she returned east to San Francisco and then sailed for Hawaii, American Samoa, and Western Samoa. On November 9, 1929, while drums of gasoline were being loaded in preparation for the departure from Apia, the ship was destroyed in an explosion that killed Captain Ault and the cabin boy.

Paul, *Last Cruise of the "Carnegie."*

# HMS Centurion

4th rate 60 (3m). *L/B:* 144' × 40' (43.9m × 12.2m). *Tons:* 1,005 bm. *Hull:* wood. *Arm.:* 24 × 24pdr, 26 × 9pdr, 10 × 6pdr. *Built:* Portsmouth Dockyard, Eng.; 1732.

At the start of the War of the Austrian Succession in 1739, Commodore George Anson took command of a squadron that was given the task of harassing Spanish shipping on the coast of South America and capturing the Manila galleon, the annual shipment of gold and silver from Mexico to the Philippines. His six ships were HMS *Centurion,* *Severn* (50 guns), *Pearl* (40), WAGER (28), *Tryal* (8), and the supply ship *Anna Pink.* Despite the support of First Lord of the Admiralty Sir Charles Wager, Anson was unable properly to man his ship. Short 300 sailors, Anson was given only 170: 32 from Chatham hospital, and 98 marines, many of them novices. In lieu of a land force of 500 men, he

was given "invalids to be collected from the outpensioners of Chelsea college . . . who from their age, wounds, or other infirmities, are incapable of service in marching regiments." Of these, all but 259 deserted before they were embarked in the ships.

These and other delays postponed the sailing date to September 1740, by which time the Spanish had dispatched to the Pacific a squadron of six ships under Don Joseph Pizarro. After stops at Madeira, Brazil, and Argentina, the British ships were separated in a withering autumn rounding of Cape Horn. Worse, the crews began to suffer from scurvy, and the disease was so virulent that *Centurion*'s lieutenant "could muster no more than two Quarter-masters, and six Fore-mast men capable of working; so that without assistance of the officers, servants and the boys, it might have proved impossible for us to have reached [Juan Fernández] Island, after we had got sight of it" on June 9, 1741. They were joined there by *Tryal, Gloucester* (which had "already thrown over-board two thirds of their complement"), and *Anna Pink.* (*Wager* was lost on the coast of Chile on May 15, though many of her crew survived. *Severn* and *Pearl* turned back from the Horn.) By the time the surviving ships left Juan Fernández, they had lost a staggering 626 of the 961 crew they had sailed with; the remaining 335 men and boys were "a number, greatly insufficient for the manning of *Centurion* alone."

On September 9, *Centurion* left the island and three days later captured the merchantman *Nuestra Señora del Monte Carmelo,* from which Anson learned that Pizarro was still in the Atlantic. Over the next two months, the English took three Spanish merchantmen, one of which, *Nuestra Señora del Arranzazú,* was renamed *Tryal Prize* and used as a replacement for the abandoned *Tryal.* On November 13, they seized Paita, burning the town and sinking five ships and taking one. From there they sailed north to keep watch off Acapulco in the vain hope of capturing the Manila galleon. After destroying their prizes and making what repairs they could manage on the hostile Mexican coast, on May 6, 1742, *Centurion* and *Gloucester* sailed for

China. By August 15, the latter was in such a state of decay that she had to be scuttled; eleven days later *Centurion* landed at Tinian, which was in regular contact with the Spanish garrison at Guam. Half of the crew were ashore, Anson included, when a typhoon struck on September 21. The ship's anchor cables parted and *Centurion* disappeared. Believing they might never see her again, Anson and his 113 crew set about to lengthen a small Spanish "bark" in which they planned to sail to China. Three weeks later *Centurion* returned, and on October 21 the reunited crew sailed for Macao, where they arrived on November 12.

As the Chinese looked on all ships not engaged in trade as pirates, fitting out at Macao proved extremely difficult, and *Centurion* was not ready for sea until April 6. Rather than sail directly for England, Anson intended to intercept the Manila galleon off the Philippines. Keeping station off Cape Espiritu Santo for a month, on June 20 they overhauled *Nuestra Señora de la Covadonga* (36 guns), 6 leagues from the Cape (in about 12°35′N, 125°10′E). The Spanish ship was no match for the determined *Centurion,* and Captain Jerónimo de Montero lost sixty-seven crew killed and eighty-four wounded, compared with only two English killed and seventeen wounded. The two ships arrived at Canton on July 11 and Anson's efforts to provision his ship were again frustrated. *Covadonga* was sold for $6,000 to local merchants and *Centurion* sailed for home on December 15, 1743.

*Centurion*'s nearly four-year circumnavigation ended at Spithead on June 15, 1744. Despite the loss of three ships and more than 1,300 crew (only four to enemy action), Anson's capture of the Manila galleon with 1,313,843 pieces of eight and 35,682 ounces of virgin silver outshone any other achievement of England's ten-year war with Spain and was ranked the equal of Drake's circumnavigation in GOLDEN HIND 160 years before. Anson achieved flag rank the following year, and *Centurion* was in a squadron commanded by him at the Battle of Cape Finisterre in which the English defeated Admiral de la Jonquière on May 3, 1747, and captured seven merchantmen, four ships of the line, and two frigates. During the Seven Years' War, *Centurion* was at the capture of Louisburg in 1758, and of Quebec the next year. In 1762, she participated in the capture of Havana. She was broken up seven years later. In addition to eyewitness accounts of Anson's circumnavigation, Patrick O'Brian's *The Golden Ocean* is a readable and accurate, though fictional, account of the voyage.

Anson, *Voyage round the World.*

## HMS Challenger

Screw corvette (1f/3m). *L/B:* 200′ × 40.5′ (61m × 12.3m). *Tons:* 2,306 disp. *Hull:* wood. *Comp.:* 243. *Arm.:* 20 × 8″, 2 × 68pdr. *Mach.:* compound engine, 1,200 hp, 1 screw. *Built:* Woolwich Dockyard, Eng.; 1858.

In the early 1870s, the Royal Society began pushing for a massive oceanographic expedition to probe all three of the world's major oceans — the Atlantic, Pacific, and Indian. The Royal Navy supplied the screw corvette *Challenger* — the largest vessel used for an oceanographic expedition to date — and a crew under Captain George Strong Nares. The team of six civilian scientists, led by naturalist Charles Wyville Thomson, included H. N. Moseley and John Murray. Fitted with a wide array of equipment for taking soundings of up to 6,000 fathoms (11,000 meters), as well as temperature readings, current measurements, and bottom samples from depths of up to 4,000 fathoms (3,700 meters), she sailed from Sheerness on December 7, 1872.

The first ten months of the voyage were spent in the Atlantic, which the ship crossed three times, visiting the Caribbean, Halifax, Bermuda, Madeira, the Canary Islands, Brazil, and Tristan da Cunha. During this time, the scientists established the routine they would maintain throughout their voyage, dredging for animal specimens, taking soundings, and gauging water temperatures and currents, among other measurements, about once every 200 miles. (In the course of the voyage, they made such observations at 362 stations.) Observations were not limited to oceanographic matters alone, and ashore, extensive findings of flora and fauna were made. After seven weeks at Cape Town, *Challenger* sailed on December 17, 1873, bound for the Southern Ocean.

Nine days later she landed at uninhabited Marion Island, then continued east past the Crozets and on to Kerguelen, roughly midway between South Africa and Australia, in latitude 50°S, and then to Heard Island, 300 miles to the southeast, where she was greeted by some resident sealers. From here *Challenger* sailed south, encountering ice in about 61°S, 80°E, on February 11, 1874. She threaded her way through the ice fields until March 1, when she shaped a course for Melbourne. *Challenger* spent a month in Australia, and another five weeks at Sydney, before crossing the Tasman Sea for Wellington.

From New Zealand the expedition sailed north to Tonga and then headed west to the Cape York Peninsula, Australia. From there scientists and crew made their way north and west through the innumerable archipelagos of the East Indies and Philippines before arriving at Hong Kong. *Challenger*'s stay at the British Crown Colony was marked by the departure of Captain Nares, ordered home to command an Antarctic survey in HMS ALERT and *Discovery,* and the arrival of his replacement, Captain Frank Turle Thomson. After backtracking through the Philippines, they sailed east to Humboldt Bay, on the north coast of New Guinea, and the Admiralty Islands, where they named Nares Harbour in honor of their former commander. Turning north for Japan, on March 23, thirteen days out, they recorded their deepest sounding, 4,475 fathoms (8,184 meters), in position 11°24′N, 143°16′E. The ship and her company spent two months in Japan, where *Challenger* was dry-docked at Yokosuka.

On June 15, the expedition sailed east to conduct observations along latitude 35°N between Japan and Hawaii. On their passage south to Tahiti, the expedition discovered that the Pacific seabed was covered with manganese nodules, the commercial exploitation of which first came under consideration in the 1950s. From Tahiti, with its rich coral finds, *Challenger* headed for Juan Fernández Island and then to Chile, where the ship was readied for the passage through the Strait of Magellan. The passage north through the Atlantic Ocean was interrupted only by brief calls at Port Stanley, Montevideo, Ascension, and Vigo, Spain. She dropped anchor at Spithead on May 24, 1876, after a voyage of 68,890 miles in three and a half years. Facilitated in large part by expedition member John Murray, the publication of the fifty-volume expedition report was completed nineteen years later.

The results of the *Challenger* expedition cannot be briefly summarized, but of most general interest were the discovery of more than 4,000 previously unknown specimens of marine life, the first comprehensive study of ocean currents and of the terrain and composition of the seabed, and the discovery that the average depth of the Pacific Ocean is significantly greater than that of the Atlantic. *Challenger* herself was hulked in 1880, but remained in naval service until sold to J. B. Garnham in 1921.

Buchanan et al., *Narrative of the Voyage.* Linklater, *Voyage of the "Challenger."*

# Ch'ing Ho

*Junk. Built:* Lung chiang Shipyard, Nanjing; 1405–33(?).

Between 1405 and 1433, China's Ming emperors dispatched seven expeditions to India, East Africa, and the Red Sea. These expeditions, under the direction of the Muslim eunuch Zheng He, involved hundreds of ships and tens of thousands of sailors, soldiers, traders, and professionals of all sorts. Despite the enormity of the undertakings, documentation of the voyages is relatively scant, and the names of only a few ships are known. In the early sixteenth century, Chu Yün-ming recorded examples of names of the more than 100 ships in the seventh expedition:

Such kinds of names as *Ch'ing ho* ["Pure Harmony"], *Hui k'ang* ["Kind Repose"], *Ch'ang ning*

["Lasting Tranquility"], *An chi* ["Peaceful Crossing"], and *Ch'ing yüan* ["Pure Durability"]. There were also ships designated by the various series "one," "two," and other [numbers].

None of these names can be associated with specific vessels, but there are general descriptions of the ships, and Ma Huan, a veteran of the fourth, sixth, and seventh voyages, wrote a summary of the voyages, "The Overall Survey of the Ocean's Shores."

The motives of Emperor Zhu Di, who initiated these voyages, apparently combined a desire to seek out the deposed Jianwen emperor, Zhu Yunwen; to increase China's international prestige — thirty states, including Egypt, sent ambassadors to the Ming emperor; and to circumvent the Central Asian silk route, which was blocked by the Turkic conqueror Timur (Tamerlane). The imports from China's tribute trade included such valuable commodities as horses and rice, sulfur, timber, hides, medicinal herbs and spices, and gold, silver, and copper. China's primary exports included porcelain, silk, lacquerware, and fine art objects. The Chinese also brought back with them an Ark-like menagerie of animals that included giraffes, lions, leopards, zebras, rhinoceroses, and exotic birds; but these were only spectacular incidentals of this flourishing overseas commerce.

The imperial commitment to maritime affairs at this time can be seen in the numbers of ships built during the reigns of Zhu Di and Zhu Zhanji: about 2,700 warships and patrol vessels for the more than 400 coast guard stations, 400 armed transports for the all-important grain fleet, and 400 warships stationed near Nanjing, the imperial capital until 1421. China's main shipyard was at Lung chiang, also near Nanjing. The exact dimensions of the vessels built here for Zheng He's fleets are unknown, but the largest were probably between 200 and 300 feet (60 to 90 meters) and carried as many as nine junk-rigged masts. What is perhaps most interesting is the variety of specialized ships. The most important were the "treasure ships" (*baochuan*) so-called because they carried treasure "of untold quantities." In addition, there were purpose-built horse carriers — horses being one of the more valuable imports — supply ships, water carriers, troop transports, and at least three classes of warships.

The size of the expeditions was enormous. On the first voyage there were 317 ships, including 62 treasure ships, with a total complement of 27,870 people. The second expedition (which Zheng He organized but did not accompany) sailed with 249 ships. The third carried 38,000 people in 48 ships, most of which must have been of the largest size, as the average complement was nearly 800 people. The fourth fleet comprised 63 ships and 28,560 men; the sixth, 41 ships; and the last expedition sailed with more than 100 ships. (Figures for the fifth fleet do not survive.)

The first four voyages (1405–7, 1407–9, 1409–11, and 1411–13) took the Chinese as far as India. Outward bound, the treasure fleet sailed from the Yangtze, and after stopping at the mouth of the Min River in Fukien Province, proceeded via Champa (Vietnam), sailed through Indonesia with stops on Java and Sumatra or the Malay Peninsula, and then turned into the Strait of Malacca. Heading west across the Bay of Bengal, the ships would visit Ceylon before heading up the west coast of India to Calicut, the primary market of the Indian Ocean. On the last three voyages (1413–15, 1417–19 and, during the reign of Hsüan-tsung, 1431–33), the Chinese returned various foreign representatives to their homes. From Calicut, the fleet sailed to Hormuz, Aden, and other ports in Arabia, and to the East African ports of Mogadishu and Brava (three times) and Malindi. On the seventh expedition, a number of smaller squadrons were detached to visit areas off the main track, calling at ports in Bengal and the Red Sea.

If the overarching purpose of the voyages was to seek tribute and trade, the missions were a success. The authors of the eighteenth-century Chinese work *Essentials of the Comprehensive Mirror of History* noted that the Chinese

bestowed gifts upon the kings and rulers, and those who refused submission they over-awed by the show of armed might. Every country became obedient to the imperial commands, and when [Zheng He] turned homewards, sent envoys in his train to offer tribute.

The military factor was not insignificant, and Zheng He helped wipe out piracy in Indonesian waters, defeated the king of the Rayigama kingdom on Ceylon (who was pardoned by the emperor at Nanjing), and ousted the pretender to the throne of Sumatra, who was executed in China.

This sudden flowering of China-based maritime commerce ended almost as abruptly as it begun. Thanks to a variety of domestic political changes, by the 1440s the Chinese had withdrawn from participation in the wider world. The sudden termination of China's long-distance maritime trade in 1433 has to be seen as one of the more momentous policy decisions in the history of the world, for only seven decades later, the Portuguese Vasco da Gama sailed his diminutive SAO GA-BRIEL into Calicut all but unopposed. A maxim of the Ming navy of Zheng He's time was "The Wo'k'ou [Japanese pirates] come by sea and should be resisted at sea . . . to check them after they are ashore is hard." How different the history of the world would have been had an expansionist China met Europe in the Indian Ocean rather than reclusively on the shores of the South China Sea.

Jung-pang Lo, "Decline of the Early Ming Navy." Levathes, *When China Ruled the Seas.* Ma Huan, *Overall Survey of the Ocean's Shores.* Needham, *Science and Civilization in China.*

## Columbia Rediviva

Ship (3m). *L/B:* 83.5′ × 24.2′ (25.5m × 7.4m). *Tons:* 212 burthen. *Hull:* wood. *Comp.:* 27–50. *Arm.:* 12 guns. *Built:* Plymouth, Mass.; 1787.

The Pacific Northwest's importance to eastern merchants grew rapidly following the visits to the region by HMS RESOLUTION and DISCOVERY on Captain James Cook's third voyage. Boston merchants quickly saw in the abundance of sea otter pelts a way of breaking into the lucrative China

trade, and in 1787 a consortium of six merchants, ship owners, and captains under Joseph Barrell purchased the ship *Columbia Rediviva* and the sloop *Lady Washington.* With John Kendrick in command of *Columbia* (as she was usually known) and Robert Gray in *Lady Washington,* the vessels departed Boston on September 30, 1787. The ships sailed in company until separated in a gale off Cape Horn. *Lady Washington* was the first to arrive at Nootka Sound — a Spanish settlement on the western side of Vancouver Island and the northern limit of the charted coast — on September 17, 1788. She was followed on the twenty-fourth by *Columbia.* When the Americans arrived they found three ships flying Portuguese colors, although they were actually English ships. The Americans remained there through the winter. In March 1789, Gray sailed in search of skins, meeting with great success, especially at Queen Charlotte Island (which he established was, indeed, an island). Returning to Nootka Sound, Gray found that Kendrick had made no effort to trade for the skins that were the object of the voyage. The two ships sailed to Clayoquot Sound on Vancouver Island, where *Lady Washington's* cargo was transferred to *Columbia,* and Gray and Kendrick traded commands. *Columbia* sailed for Canton, via the Sandwich (Hawaiian) Islands, trading skins for tea. *Columbia* sailed for home on February 12, 1790, via the Cape of Good Hope and on August 9 anchored at Boston, the first ship under the American flag to circumnavigate the globe.

Although Kendrick's desultory command of the expedition ensured it was not a profitable one — to all intents and purposes he commandeered *Lady Washington* and never remitted any profits, if there were any, to the owners — Barrell was sufficiently impressed by Gray to dispatch *Columbia* on a second voyage. Sailing on September 28, 1790 — only six weeks after her return to Boston — *Columbia* returned to Nootka Sound on June 4, 1791, after a passage of only eight months. They traded into the fall before returning to Clayoquot Sound. Over the winter they assembled the sloop *Adventure,* the frames of which they had brought out from Boston. In the spring, while *Adventure* sailed north in search of skins, *Columbia* sailed south. On May 12, 1792, Gray

> saw an appearance of a spacious harbour abreast the Ship, haul'd our wind for it, observ'd two sand bars making off, with a passage between them to a fine river. Out pinnace and sent her in ahead and followed with the ship under short sail, carried in from 1/2 three to 7 fm. And when over the bar had 10 fm. water, quite fresh.

The existence of Columbia's River, as Gray called it, had long been postulated. In 1775, Bruno de Hezeta (sailing in *Santiago*) had established the location of the river mouth. The land, as John Boit wrote,

> with little labour might be made fit to raise such seeds as is nessescary [*sic*] for the sustenance of inhabitants, and in short a factory set up here and another at Hancock's River in the Queen Charlotte Isles, wou'd engross the whole trade of the NW Coast (with the help [of] a few small coasting vessels).

The discovery was especially important because it gave the young United States a claim to a region already contested by the Spanish and British, a clamor to which Russia would soon add its voice.

Returning north, *Columbia* resumed the search for sea otter skins with *Adventure* but narrowly missed being wrecked when she struck a rock in Milbanke Sound. At the end of the season, Gray sold *Adventure* to the Spanish and on October 3 sailed for Hawaii and thence to China. Arriving at Macao on December 8, *Columbia* sailed again up the Pearl River on February 2. So ended her career in the Pacific Northwest fur trade. Her exact movements in subsequent years are unknown, but in October 1801 she was broken up, or, as the official register says, "ript to pieces."

Howay, ed., *Voyages of the "Columbia" to the Northwest Coast.*

# Concord

Bark (3m). *L/B/D:* ca. 39′ (keel) × 17.5′ × 8′ dph (11.9m × 5.3m × 2.4m). *Tons:* 55 tons. *Hull:* wood. *Comp.:* 32. *Arm.:* 4 falconets. *Built:* England; 1590–1600.

In 1602, Bartholomew Gosnold sailed to Norumbega, the land encompassing the area of New England (also known then as the "North Part of Virginia"), to establish an English trading settlement. Apart from *Concord*'s name, her complement — thirty-two men under command of Bartholomew Gosnold of whom twelve were to "remayne there for population" — and the fact that she carried a disassembled shallop capable of carrying twenty-five people, little is known of her dimensions or origins. In 1974, the American naval architect William A. Baker posited a vessel of the dimensions (and armament) given above — a fairly typical vessel of the period, with square foresail, mainsail and main topsail, lateen mizzen, and a spritsail.

*Concord* sailed from Falmouth on March 26, 1602, and after passing the Azores in mid-April made her next landfall near Cape Elizabeth or Cape Neddick, Maine. There the English met eight Micmacs who had had previous contact with Europeans, probably French fishermen from the north. Their leader was dressed

> in a Wastecoate of blacke worke, a paire of Breeches, cloth Stockings, Shooes, Hat, and Bande. . . . [W]ith a piece of Chalke [they] described the Coast thereabouts, and could name Placentia of the New-found-land, they spake divers Christian words and seemed to understand much more than we, for want of Language could comprehend.

Turning south, *Concord* came next to a place the English initially called Shole-hope, but "where we tooke great store of Cod-fish, for which we altered the name, and called it Cape Cod." They made their way south of the Cape and on May 21 came to "a disinhabited Iland which afterwards appeared unto us: we bore with it, and named it Marthaes Vineyard." After building a small fort on Elizabeths

Isle (now Cuttyhunk), they briefly visited the far shore of Buzzards Bay, "the goodliest continent that ever we sawe, promising more by farre then we in any way did expect." Notwithstanding the beauty and bounty of the land, and their friendly dealings with the Indians, the intended settlers re-fused to be left behind, and on June 18, *Concord* sailed from the Elizabeth Islands and arrived at Exmouth on July 23. Of *Concord*'s subsequent history, nothing is known.

Baker, "Gosnold's *Concord* and Her Shallop." Quinn and Quinn, ed., *English New England Voyages, 1602–1608.*

# D

## La Dauphine

Ship (3m). *Tons:* 100 tons. *Comp.:* 50. *Built:* Royal Dockyard, Le Havre, France; 1517.

Named for the French Dauphin, born the year before the ship's launch, *La Dauphine* was a French royal ship sailed by Giovanni da Verrazzano on his westward voyage in search of either Cathay and the extreme eastern coast of Asia, or a passage through any land that might lie in his way. Provisioned for eight months, Verrazzano sailed from Dieppe with *La Dauphine* and *La Normande,* but the latter soon returned to France. Departing from the Madeira Islands on about January 17, 1524, *La Dauphine* sailed straight west to near Cape Fear, North Carolina. The ship then sailed south about 225 miles before turning north again. Landing briefly near Cape Fear, *La Dauphine* then sailed along the barrier islands that enclose Pimlico Sound — which Verrazzano initially believed to be the Pacific Ocean — separated from the Atlantic only by the slender Outer Banks. *La Dauphine* next stopped at Arcadia (possibly Kitty Hawk), before sailing offshore until arriving at what is now southern New Jersey. The next identifiable anchorage was New York Bay, where *La Dauphine* anchored the night of April 17 in the Verrazzano Narrows.

Heading east, the French rounded the tip of Long Island and came into Narragansett Bay, passing Block Island, which Verrazzano compared with the Mediterranean island of Rhodes. (Roger Williams later thought he meant Aquidneck, and in time the name was applied to Rhode Island; Verrazzano had actually named Block Island for the French queen mother, Luisa.) A Wampanoag piloted *La Dauphine* into the future Newport harbor, where Verrazzano anchored for two weeks. After working her way through Vineyard and Nantucket Sounds and rounding Cape Cod, *La Dauphine* next landed near Casco Bay, and worked east from there along the Maine coast. Here, on the Penobscot River, Verrazzano recorded the Abnaki name "Oranbega." Europeans corrupted this to "Norumbega" and used it to refer to the whole region now known as New England. After skirting Nova Scotia and Newfoundland, where the Portuguese and English had preceded him, he sailed for home, arriving at Dieppe on July 8, 1524. *La Dauphine's* expedition is important because it was the first to determine that North America was not an extension of Asia. Verrazzano made two subsequent transatlantic voyages, one to Brazil and his last in 1528, when he was killed and eaten by Caribs on Guadeloupe.

Morison, *European Discovery of America: The Northern Voyages.* Wroth, *Voyages of Giovanni da Verrazzano.*

## Descubierta

Corvette (3m). *L/B/D:* 109.2' × 28.7' × 14.1' dph (33.3m × 8.7m × 4.3m). *Tons:* 306 toneladas. *Hull:* wood. *Comp.:* 104. *Arm.:* 14 × 6pdr, 2 × 4pdr. *Built:* Cadiz, Spain; 1789.

Flagship of the most important voyage of discovery dispatched by Spain in the eighteenth century, *Descubierta* ("Discovery") was one of two ships — the other was *Atrevida* ("Daring") — built for an expedition conceived of and lead by Don Alejandro Malaspina. Much influenced by the voyages of Captain James Cook and his successors, both English and French, the Italian-born Malaspina planned a "Scientific and Political Voyage Around the World," the twofold aim of which was to increase geographic and scientific knowledge, and to check on the status of Spain's far-flung possessions, particularly those on the Pacific coast of North America, where both Russia and England were expanding their spheres of influence.

Sailing from Cadiz on July 30, 1789, *Descubierta* and *Atrevida* (under Don José Bustamente y Guerra) made first for the River Plate, which they surveyed before following the coast of Patagonia south. After calling in the Falkland Islands (then a Spanish territory), they rounded Cape Horn and called at several ports on the Chilean coast and at Juan Fernández Island. The two ships then separated and made their way independently to Mexico at the end of March. Here Malaspina received new orders from Madrid. Rather than go to the Sandwich (Hawaiian) Islands, he was to proceed to southern Alaska and survey the coast from Mount St. Elias south to Nootka Sound. In June 1789, the Spanish commander there had arrested two British ships in the fur trade, precipitating the Nootka Sound crisis between Britain and Spain. Departing Acapulco on May 1, 1791, by the end of June the ships were at Yakutat Bay in the shadow of Mount St. Elias and Malaspina Glacier. The ships remained in the area until July 27, exploring as far north and west as Hinchinbrook Island before turning south to arrive on August 12 at the Spanish settlement at Nootka, on the western side of Vancouver Island. After Malaspina conferred with the local Spanish commander and the Nootkas and dispatched cutters for surveys of the surrounding islands and inlets, the ships sailed south looking for the river called "Entrada de Hezeta," reported by the Spaniard Bruno de Hezeta in 1774. (The mouth of the Columbia River would not be seen or named again until the following year, when Robert Gray crossed the bar in his ship COLUMBIA REDIVIVA.) After two weeks at Monterey, the ships headed south to Acapulco, where they helped prepare the schooners SUTIL and *Mexicana* for a voyage to Nootka before heading west to the Philippines by way of the Mariana Islands.

After continuing their survey work in the Philippines and sailing over to Macao, Malaspina turned southeast, landing at Espiritu Santo, and then went on to southern New Zealand, calling at James Cook's Dusky Sound. From there the ships headed west again to Port Jackson (Sydney), New South Wales, where the Spanish landed in March 1793, five years after the arrival of the first English colonists. The Spanish were welcomed as they set about conducting extensive astronomical, hydrographical, and other experiments and gathering numerous specimens of flora, fauna, and minerals. Malaspina was also thorough in his description of the British settlement, particularly with a view to the potential of its hindering Spanish trade between South America and the Philippines, which had been conducted in the Manila galleons almost free of interference for more than 200 years. In his report to the Spanish navy minister, he declared that the British government had established its presence in the Pacific — in Australia, the Sandwich Islands, and at Nootka — "in the shades of rights usurped . . . from the other European nations" and established as far back as the Treaty of Tordesillas in 1494.

*Descubierta* and *Atrevida* left Port Jackson on April 11, sailing northeast for the Friendly (Tonga) Islands and thence east to Callao, on the Peruvian coast. From there they sailed south to double Cape Horn and after a stop at Montevideo returned home to Cadiz on September 21, 1793, ending a voyage of more than four years. Unfortunately for Malaspina, his liberal ideas were at odds with the extreme conservatism of Carlos IV and his court, and he was arrested, stripped of his rank (he had been promoted to Admiral on his return), and exiled. As a result, both Malaspina and his achievements were neglected and his *Diario de viaje* (Diary of the Voyage) was not published in its entirety until 1885.

Cutter, *Malaspina and Galiano*. King, *Secret History of the Convict Colony*. Malaspina, *Journals of Malaspina*. Vaughan et al., *Voyages of Enlightenment*.

# Diana

Sloop-of-war (3m). *L:* 90′ (27.4m). *Tons:* 300 bm. *Hull:* wood. *Comp.:* 67. *Arm.:* 14 × 6pdr, 4 × 8pdr, 4 falconets. *Built:* Sviritsa, Russia; 1807.

One of the most celebrated escapes by ship ever undertaken took place in 1807, when the Russian sloop *Diana,* commanded by Lieutenant Vasilii M. Golovnin, eluded the British fleet at Simon's Bay, South Africa. Assigned as an escort for the storeship *Neva* in the North Pacific, *Diana* did not sail from Kronstadt until July 25, 1807, nine months after *Neva's* departure for Kamchatka and Russia's American colonies. After attempting unsuccessfully to round Cape Horn, Golovnin decided to run east and turn north once he got past Australia. Unaware that Russia and England had gone to war since his departure from Kronstadt, Golovnin put into Simon's Bay on April 21, 1808. Although Golovnin had documents guaranteeing him safe passage by English ships even in the event of war, Commodore Josias Rowley refused to release *Diana* without authorization from England. With neither money for provisions nor permission to sell anything from the ship to raise funds, Golovnin decided he had no recourse but to break his parole and try to escape. After careful study of tidal and wind conditions, at 1830 on May 19, 1809, with a fresh northwest wind, Golovnin ordered the two anchor cables cut and set the storm staysails. As the British had previously ordered the sails unbent and the topmasts housed, the next few hours were ones of frantic activity. Golovnin recalled,

> The officers, marines, petty officers and men all without exception worked the topmast and yards. With great pleasure I recall that within two hours, notwithstanding the strong wind, rain and dark of the night, they succeeded in bending the fore and main topsails, in setting them up, hoisting the topgallant-masts to their places, lifting the topgallant yards and setting up the top[gallant]sails; lifting the studding sail booms to their places, threading through all the studding sail rigging and preparing the studding-sails so that, should the wind permit, we would be able at once to set all the sails.
>
> By 10 o'clock in the evening we were in the open ocean. And so ended our detention, or rather, arrest in the Cape of Good Hope, which lasted one year and 25 days.

Heading south to 40°S, *Diana* ran her easting down past Tasmania, when she turned northward for the New Hebrides, where she anchored at Reso-lution Harbor (named for Captain James Cook's ship) on Tana Island, on June 25. *Diana* finally arrived at Petropavlovsk on September 25, two years and two months out from Kronstadt. From there the ship made a round-trip to the Russian settlement on Sitka Island, and then spent all of 1810 at Petropavlovsk.

In April 1811, Golovnin was ordered to survey "the Southern Kurile and Shantar Islands, and the coast of Tartary, from latitude 53°38′ north to Okhotsk" between northern Japan and southern Kamchatka. In early July, *Diana* stopped at the island of Kunashir for water and provisions. Despite efforts to establish goodwill with his hosts, on July 11 the xenophobic Japanese arrested the unlucky Golovnin, together with another officer, a midshipman, and four sailors. The Russians remained under arrest in Japan until October 16, 1813, when they embarked in *Diana* — which had escaped from Kunashir following the arrests — after two years, two months, and twenty-six days in captivity. (A keen observer, Golovnin later published detailed descriptions of the people, customs, and history of both the Cape Colony and of Japan.) Golovnin returned to St. Petersburg from Okhotsk seven years to the day after his departure. *Diana* remained in eastern waters and ended her days as a munitions ship at Petropavlovsk.

Golovnin, *Detained in Simon's Bay; Memoirs of a Captivity in Japan.* Ivashintsov, *Russian Round-the-World Voyages.*

## Discovery

Ship (3m). *Tons:* 55–70 tons. *Hull:* wood. *Comp.:* 17. *Built:* England; <1602.

At the beginning of the seventeenth century, England's East India Company was eager to find a sea route to the Indies that was not dominated by the Spanish or the Portuguese. At the time, two of the most promising alternatives were the Northeast Passage, over the top of Russia, and the Northwest Passage, across the top of what became Canada. One of the most hard-worked ships in that exploration was *Discovery*, which made six voyages in quest of the Northwest Passage.

In 1602, *Discovery* was one of two "Fly-boates" of 70 tons (the other being *Godspeed*) that sailed under George Weymouth with a combined complement of thirty-five, provisioned for eighteen months by "the right Worshipfull Merchants of the Moscovie and Turkie Companies." On May 2, they sailed north from the Thames to pass through the Orkneys, then south of Greenland until June 28, when they "descried the land of America, in the latitude of 62. degrees and 30 minutes; which we made to be Warwickes foreland" in the southern part of Baffin Island. Heading south, they approached the entrance to Hudson Strait but were kept out by ice and fog. Turning north, the ships returned to 68°53', where on July 19 the crew mutinied and "bare up the Helme" for England. On the return south they sailed into Frobisher Bay, past the entrance to Hudson Strait (named for *Discovery*'s next master) and Ungava Bay in northern Quebec. *Discovery* returned to England at the beginning of August and Weymouth reported that "truely there is in three severall places great hope of a passage, betweene the latitude of 62. and 54 degrees; if the fogge doe not hinder it, which is all the feare I have."

*Discovery* next appeared in sub-Arctic waters in 1610, sailing for the Northwest Company under command of Henry Hudson. The year before, Hudson had sailed in the Dutch East India Company's ship HALVE MAEN to ascend the Hudson River as far as present-day Albany, New York. Back in the employ of his fellow countrymen, Hudson sailed from Gravesend on April 17, 1610, and *Discovery* was the first ship definitely to enter Hudson Strait. Hudson cruised south along the east coast of the bay that bears his name and into James Bay, where on November 10, he and his crew were frozen in with scant provisions. Over the harsh winter, the near-starving crew became increasingly hostile to Hudson's command and on June 22, 1611, they mutinied. Led by Henry Greene, who "would rather be hanged at home than starved abroad," the mutineers put Hudson, his son, and seven of the infirm crew in *Discovery*'s shallop and

sailed away. Hudson was never heard from again. En route home, four of the remaining crew were killed by Eskimos in Hudson Strait — in a rare clash between Eskimos and Europeans — and one more died of starvation before they returned to England under the command of Robert Bylot. Despite the severity of their crime — the masters of the mariners' guild Trinity House said "they deserved to be hanged" — none of the mutineers was brought to trial until 1616, partly, it is believed, because of their claim that they had indeed found Hudson Strait.

Backed by the Prince of Wales, the Northwest Company next dispatched an expedition in search of the Northwest Passage under Thomas Button in *Resolution*, accompanied by *Discovery* under John Ingram; curiously, Ingram's orders included no mention of a search for Hudson or his crew. The ships sailed from London on April 14, 1612, retracing the now familiar route. Button named Resolution Island at the entrance to Hudson Strait and then sailed southwest across Hudson Bay to the site of present-day Fort Nelson. Several of the crew died over the hard winter, but in June 1613 the survivors resumed their search for the Northwest Passage, visiting Churchill River, Roes Welcome Sound, and Mansel Island. The ship's next voyage, under William Gibbons, was cut short by unusually severe ice that embayed them for ten weeks at Gibbons Hole (possibly Saglek Bay).

In 1615, the ship was acquired by William Baffin, and on March 15

> againe set forth the *Discovery*, a ship of fiftie five tunnes or thereabouts, which ship had beene the three [*sic*] former Voyages on the action. The master was Robert Bileth, a man well acquainted with that way: having been employed in the three former Voyages: my selfe [William Baffin] being his Mate and Associate, with fourteen others and two Boyes.

They reached Resolution Island, sailed along the south coast of Baffin Island and Mill, Salisbury, and Nottingham Islands, Foxe Channel, and Southampton Island. Bylot and Baffin also judged, correctly, that Frozen Strait offered no outlet to the west through Hudson Bay. They returned to England on September 8.

The following year, Bylot and Baffin sailed again under the auspices of the Northwest Company and explored western Greenland as far north as Smith Sound. They passed Cary Island and discovered the entrances to Jones and Lancaster Sounds (the true entrance to the Northwest Passage) and reached a farthest north of 77°45′N. This was *Discovery*'s last voyage in search of the Northwest Passage, though she remained in service until 1620. Despite Baffin's careful charting of all the coasts of Baffin Bay over the course of two separate voyages, geographers decided his discoveries were false and the information was gradually removed from maps, until John Ross, sailing in ISABELLA, rediscovered Baffin Bay in 1819. *Discovery*'s farthest-north would not be exceeded until Sir George Nares's expedition in the ships HMS ALERT and *Discovery* in 1876.

Cooke and Holland, *Exploration of Northern Canada*. Johnson, *Charting the Sea of Darkness*. Purchas, *Hakluytus Posthumus*.

# HMS Discovery

(ex-*Diligence*) Ship (3m). *L/B/D:* 91.4′ × 27.4′ × 11.4′ (27.9m × 8.4m × 3.5m). *Tons:* 299 tons. *Hull:* wood. *Comp.:* 75. *Arm.:* 8 guns, 8 swivels. *Built:* Langbourne, Whitby, Eng.; 1774.

*Discovery* was the fourth and smallest of the ships assigned to Captain James Cook on his three voyages of discovery. Built as a brig-rigged collier, Cook ordered her rerigged as a ship, as HMS ENDEAVOUR, ADVENTURE, and RESOLUTION had been. The purpose of Cook's last voyage was to find a Northwest Passage between the Atlantic and the Pacific from the Pacific end, for the discovery of which the British Parliament had pledged £20,000. Two ships were required: *Resolution*, flagship of Cook's second voyage, and *Discovery*, commanded by Captain Charles Clerke, a veteran of Byron's circumnavigation in DOLPHIN and the first two Cook expeditions. George Vancouver also sailed as a midshipman.

*Discovery* sailed on August 1, 1776, and joined *Resolution* at Cape Town on November 10. The ships continued eastward stopping at Van Diemen's Land (Tasmania) and spent three months in the Friendly (Tonga) Islands and at Tahiti. From there, the expedition sailed north. They were the first European ships to visit the Sandwich (Hawaiian) Islands, where they stayed from January 19 to February 2, 1788. Heading northeast, they arrived on the coast of North America on March 7, cruising north until they came to Nootka Sound on the twenty-ninth, where they stayed a month. The ships sailed northwest along the Alaska coast, anchoring in Prince William Sound on March 17 and exploring Cook Inlet two weeks later. Rounding the Alaska Peninsula, they sailed into the Bering Sea, north past Cape Prince of Wales and then north and west as far as Icy Cape. Heading east, the ships made the coast of the Chukotski Peninsula on August 29, and then spent from October 3 to 26 at the Russian settlement at Unalaska before returning to the Sandwich Islands for the winter. The ships sailed again on February 4, 1779, but a sprung foremast in *Resolution* forced them back a week later. On the fourteenth, an altercation between a group of Hawaiians and a shore party led to a skirmish in which four marines and Cook were killed.

Leadership of the expedition fell to Captain Clerke, who moved to the *Resolution;* John Gore took command of *Discovery.* The ship sailed from Hawaii again on March 22 bound for the Russian outpost at Petropavlovsk on the Kamchatka Peninsula — "a few miserable log-houses and some conical huts." In June they made a second attempt to find the eastern approach to the Northwest Passage, sailing past Icy Cape to 71°56′N before abandoning their effort and heading for home on July 24. *Discovery* had been damaged in the ice, and they turned for Petropavlovsk. Captain Clerke died just before they reached Petropavlovsk and was buried there on August 29. Command of the expedition now fell to Gore, a veteran of two expeditions in *Dolphin* as well as Cook's first, in *Endeavour.* James King assumed command of *Discovery.*

Weighing anchor at Petropavlovsk on October 9, the English sailed along the east coast of the Kurile Islands and Japan, and then made for Macao, where they arrived December 1. During their six weeks there, members of the crew had sold sea otter pelts gathered in Cook Inlet for such profit that far from wanting to return home — after nearly four years — they wanted to return to Alaska for more. Nonetheless, on January 12 the ships sailed for England. After a month in Cape Town, they entered the Atlantic Ocean on May 9. Forced north about Ireland, *Discovery* and *Resolution* landed at Stromness in the Orkneys on August 22, 1780, and were back in The Nore on October 4.

Converted to an interyard navy transport, *Discovery* was broken up at Chatham, in October 1797, shortly after the Nore Mutiny.

Cook, *Journals of James Cook*. McGowan, *"Captain Cook's Ships."*

## HMS Discovery

Ship (3m). *L/B/D:* 99.2′ keel × 28.3′ × 15.5′ (30.2m × 8.6m × 4.7m). *Tons:* 330 tons. *Hull:* wood. *Comp.:* 100. *Arm.:* 10 × 4pdr, 10 swivels. *Built:* Randall & Brents, London; 1789.

In 1789, the Spanish and English were at loggerheads over control of lands in the Pacific Northwest. In anticipation of a favorable resolution of the Nootka Sound controversy, the English prepared an expedition to sail under Captain George Vancouver. The primary aims were to survey "the direction and extent of all such considerable inlets . . . as may be likely to lead to" a northwest passage between Cape Mendocino (30°N) and Cook Inlet (60°N), and especially "the supposed straits of Juan de Fuca." The Admiralty furnished two vessels for the purpose, *Discovery* (named for the vessel in which Vancouver sailed as midshipman on Captain James Cook's last voyage to the Pacific), and *Chatham*.

The ships departed Falmouth on April 1, 1791, and, sailing east, called at Tenerife and Cape Town, making a landfall at Cape Chatham, Australia, on September 28. They then rounded Tasmania and landed at Dusky Bay, New Zealand, on November 2, 1791. From there they proceeded to Tahiti and, in early March 1792, Kealakekua Bay, where Cook had been killed in 1779. After two weeks in the Sandwich (Hawaiian) Islands, the ships sailed for North America, arriving off Cape Cabrillo, 130 miles north of San Francisco Bay, on April 17, 1792.

Sailing north, twelve days later *Chatham* and *Discovery* met with Robert Gray's COLUMBIA REDIVIVA, the first ship they had seen in eight months, and then sailed into the Strait of Juan de Fuca and proceeded to Discovery Bay about 70 miles east of Cape Flattery for repairs. From that base they explored Puget Sound (named for Second Lieutenant Peter Puget, who commanded *Chatham* from November 25, 1792) and the San Juan Islands. Here they encountered the schooners SUTIL and *Mexicana*, which were conducting surveys of the coast in conjunction with Spanish claims to the area; relations between the English and Spanish were friendly.

In October, Vancouver turned south and, leaving *Chatham* to cross the bar at the mouth of the Columbia River, proceeded to Yerba Buena (now San Francisco) where, on November 14, *Discovery* became the first non-Spanish ship to sail into San Francisco Bay. The ships remained on the Spanish coast until January 15, 1793, when they sailed from Mendocino for Hawaii, arriving on February 12. While in Hawaii, Vancouver wanted to punish the murder of two men from the storeship *Daedalus* who had been killed en route to Nootka Sound the previous year. He also wanted to mediate a truce between King Kamehameha and King Kahekili, and to persuade them to accept the protection of the King of England. After *Chatham* sailed for the Northwest, *Discovery* remained in Hawaii making surveys of the islands, including the first of Pearl Harbor.

*Discovery* returned to Nootka, arriving on May 20, two days after Puget had sailed on an independent survey. The ships continued to survey Queen Charlotte Sound, including Elcho Harbour on Dean Channel. It was here, just two months later, that Alexander Mackenzie completed the first crossing of North America north of Mexico, on July 21. By the end of the second season, Vancouver's expedition had charted 1,700 miles (2,700 kilometers) of coast from 29°56′N to about 56°N. During the expedition's third visit to Hawaii, Vancouver completed his survey of all of the major Hawaiian islands and Kamehameha formally put his islands under the protection of Great Britain.

In mid-March 1794, the ships sailed for Cook's Inlet, Alaska, which Vancouver had visited in 1778. *Discovery* and *Chatham* separated shortly after departing Hawaii and did not find each other until May 6. *Discovery* made a landfall on Chirikof Island and proceeded to Cook's Inlet on April 12. After determining it was not a river — it had been thought a likely candidate for the Northwest Passage — Vancouver sailed around the Kenai Peninsula for a survey of Prince William Sound. Farther east, in Yakutat Inlet, they encountered a party of 900 Russian-led Kodiak Islanders employed in the seal trade. The Yakutat resented the Russians, whom they viewed, in the words of the expedition's surgeon-botanist Archibald Menzies, "as intruders in their territories, draining their shores & coasts of Seals Otter & Fish on which their subsistence chiefly Depends & that too without making the least return for their depredations."

In the late summer, Vancouver's group completed charting of the northern end of the Alexander Archipelago, having stopped at Cape Decision at the southern end of Chichagof Island in 1793. The ships sailed for California and finally left Monterey on December 2, 1794. After stops at Maria Magdalena, Cocos Island, the Galápagos, and Valparaiso, they sailed into the Atlantic to arrive at St. Helena on July 3. There they learned that England was at war with the Netherlands, and Vancouver seized the Dutch East Indiaman *Macassar,* which had sailed from Cape Town in ignorance of the outbreak of war. *Chatham* was dispatched to Brazil as an escort. *Discovery* sailed on July 15 and Vancouver arrived at the mouth of the Shannon on September 13, 1795. *Discovery* and *Chatham* both arrived at Deptford in late October.

Though Vancouver hoped that his survey would "remove every doubt, and set aside every opinion of a *north-west passage,* or any water communication navigable for shipping, existing between the North Pacific, and the interior of the American continent within the limits of our researches," the search continued. The expedition gave names to scores of places, many of which are in use today. (The city of Vancouver, British Columbia, was not so named until 1886.) Moreover, in the course of the five-year voyage, only five of *Discovery*'s crew died — only one from disease — and none of *Chatham*'s. Converted to a bomb vessel in 1799, *Discovery* was made a convict ship in 1818 and broken up in 1834 at Deptford.

Fisher, *Vancouver's Charting the Northwest Coast, 1791–1795.* Vancouver, *Voyage of "Discovery" to the North Pacific Ocean.*

## HMS Discovery

Bark (3m). *L/B/D:* 171′ × 33.8′ × 15.8′ (52.1m × 10.3m × 4.8m). *Tons:* 1,570 disp. *Hull:* wood. *Comp.:* 39–43. *Mach.:* triple expansion, 450 ihp, 1 screw; 8 kts. *Des.:* William E. Smith. *Built:* Stevens Yard, Dundee Shipbuilders Co., Dundee, Scotland; 1901.

Despite numerous expeditions to the waters around Antarctica in the 1800s, by the close of the century the continent itself remained all but unknown. To remedy this, Britain's Royal Geographical Society proposed a National Antarctic Expedition to explore the interior by sledge. Private and public funds were raised for the construction of a purpose-built research vessel, which was modeled on the design of the whaleship *Discovery* (ex-*Bloodhound*), which had accompanied the Arctic Expedition of 1875–76. Designed to be marooned in the ice, the new *Discovery* had a massively built wooden hull, and was equipped with a hoisting propeller and hoisting rudder. She was also equipped with scientific laboratories and a magnetic observatory.

On August 6, 1901, she sailed from Cowes and after stops at the Cape of Good Hope and Lyttleton, New Zealand, entered the Ross Sea, where her crew discovered Edward VII Land in January 1902. Commander Robert Falcon Scott established win-

▲ Built in 1901 for Commander Robert Falcon Scott's expedition to Antarctica, the auxiliary bark **HMS Discovery** has had a long and varied career as a research ship, training ship, and now as a floating museum in her homeport of Dundee, Scotland. *Courtesy The Mariners' Museum, Newport News, Virginia.*

ter quarters near Mt. Erebus on Ross Island, McMurdo Sound, in early February, and it was not until the following September 2 that the weather permitted the first sledge journey. Later that Antarctic summer, Scott, Ernest Shackleton, and Edward A. Wilson reached 82°16′S, about 500 miles (800 kilometers) from the South Pole. *Discovery* remained icebound through 1902–3, but she was resupplied from the support ship *Morning.* Among the expedition's other accomplishments were the first flight in Antarctica, via the tethered hydrogen balloon, *Eva,* on February 4, 1902, and the first use of electricity in Antarctica, generated by a windmill. With help from the supply ships *Morning* (which had visited in 1902–3) and TERRA NOVA, *Discovery* finally broke free of the ice in February 1904, and after stops in the Balleny Islands, Mac-

querie Island, New Zealand, and the Falklands, arrived at Portsmouth on September 10, 1904.

The following year she was purchased by the Hudson's Bay Company and converted for use as a merchant ship. Between 1905 and 1911 she made seven voyages to Charlton Island in James Bay at the southern end of Hudson Bay. Laid up from 1912 to 1915, during World War I and into 1920 she traded under charter to European ports from Archangel to the Black Sea, and in 1918–19 she made one last voyage to Hudson Bay. In 1916, the company lent her to the government to rescue Shackleton's party, marooned on Elephant Island after the loss of NIMROD. These men were saved before *Discovery*'s arrival, and she loaded grain in South America for the return passage.

In 1923, she was purchased by the Crown Agents for the Colonies for an expedition to undertake "scientific research in the South Sea." Designated a "Royal Research Ship," between 1925 and 1927 she cruised 37,000 miles (60,000 kilometers) between Cape Town, Antarctica, and Drake Strait, conducting research on whaling grounds and oceanographic surveys. Two years later, she was employed in the British, Australian, and New Zealand Antarctic Research Expedition (BANZARE), during which Sir Douglas Mawson and Hjalmar Riiser-Larsen agreed on 45°E as the boundary between Norwegian and British claims in Antarctica, and the British claimed sovereignty over all lands between 73°E and 47°E.

Discovery was laid up from 1931 to 1936, when she was acquired by the Boy Scouts Association for use as a stationary training ship and hostel at London. During World War II she was similarly employed by the Admiralty and her engines were scrapped. She reverted to the Sea Scouts in 1946, and from 1955 to 1979 was used jointly by them and the Royal Naval Reserve. Transferred to the Maritime Trust and restored to her 1925 appearance, in 1986 Discovery was opened to the public as a museum ship in Dundee.

Brouwer, *International Register of Historic Ships.* Savours, *Voyages of the "Discovery."* Scott, *Scott's Last Expedition.*

# HMS Dolphin

6th rate 24 (3m). *L/B/D:* 113′ × 32′ × 11′ (34.4m × 9.8m × 3.4m). *Tons:* 508 burden. *Hull:* wood. *Comp.:* 160. *Arm.:* 22 × 9pdr, 2 × 3pdr. *Built:* Fellowes, Woolwich Dockyard, Eng.; 1751.

The ninth ship of the Royal Navy to bear the name, HMS *Dolphin* saw duty throughout the Seven Years' War and was part of Admiral John Byng's fleet at the Battle of Minorca. (The Admiral's conduct in the battle led to his court-martial and execution.) The year after the war ended, she was made the flagship of an expedition under Commodore John Byron (a veteran of HMS WAGER). The voyage had several purposes — all redounding to "the advancement of the Trade and Navigation" of Great Britain. Chief among them was to establish a base in the South Atlantic from which Britain might monitor traffic bound for the Pacific.

On June 21, 1764, *Dolphin* and the sloop HMS *Tamar* sailed from Portsmouth and made their way down the Atlantic, stopping at the Cape Verdes and at Madeira before crossing to Rio de Janeiro and down to Port Desire. After provisioning at bountiful Port Famine in the Strait of Magellan, Byron sailed back to the Falkland Islands, which he claimed in the name of George III, not realizing that the French had established a colony there the year before. Returning to Port Famine for provisions, Byron was next to have searched for other islands in the South Atlantic. Instead, he sailed through the Strait of Magellan and into the Pacific, from where he had orders to "proceed to New Albion [Francis Drake's name for California], on the Western Coast of North America" and thereafter to search for a Northwest Passage or return to England via the East Indies.

Byron chose to search for the Solomon Islands, discovered by Alvaro Mendaña in LOS REYES in 1568. This course took *Dolphin* first to the island of Más Afuera in the Juan Fernández group, 400 miles (640 kilometers) off the coast of Chile. Continuing north, in the latitude of the Tropic of Capricorn, Byron turned west-northwest and on June 10 came to the island of Takaroa (14°30′S, 143°W) in the Tuamotus. Desperate for fresh provisions, Byron and his crew forced a landing against the inhospitable natives. Here the English found "the carved Head of a Dutch Long boats Rudder," from Roggeveen's *Afrikaansche Galei,* which had been wrecked in 1721. From here Byron sailed west, jogging to the north just before he hit Tahiti, and continuing until he was in the Tokelaus. On June 28, "Finding there is no such Land as laid down in the [chart by] Neptune François for Solomon's Islands," he hauled to the northward for the Mariana Islands. Sailing through the Gilbert Islands, he turned west again to land at Tinian on July 30, where he spent nine weeks. Now in relatively well known waters, the expedition sailed to the north of the Philippines, through the South China Sea to Batavia (Djakarta) and from there, via the Cape of Good Hope, to The Downs, where *Dolphin* arrived on May 9, 1766.

*Dolphin* was in excellent condition, owing mostly to the fact that before her sailing, her hull was sheathed in copper "to cause some further experiments to be made of the efficacy of Copper-Sheathing" against teredo worms. Byron had written from Port Famine, "My Opinion of Copper Bottoms is that it is the finest Invention in the World," and this was confirmed by the master shipwright at Deptford, who declared her "fit for further Service." *Dolphin* was the second Royal Navy ship fitted with copper (the first was HMS *Alarm,* in 1761), but despite the benefits, copper cladding was not widespread until after 1783.

Almost immediately, *Dolphin* was fitted out for a second voyage, under Captain Samuel Wallis. As *Tamar* had sailed to the West Indies with a damaged rudder, *Dolphin*'s consort this voyage would be HMS SWALLOW, under Lieutenant Samuel Carteret. If Byron had accomplished little else, he had forced a redirection in the Admiralty's exploratory focus to the South Pacific, and when the two ships sailed on August 21, 1766, it was to find "Land or Islands of Great extent . . . in the Southern Hemisphere between Cape Horn and New Zeeland . . . in Climates adapted to the produce of Commodities useful in Commerce."

While the lack of any such lands made this unnecessary, the westerlies that predominate in the Southern Ocean made it impossible for the ships to sail 100° to 120° of longitude from the Cape "losing as little Southing as possible." Sailing from Plymouth on August 22, 1766, the two ships made a slow passage down the Atlantic and arrived at the Strait of Magellan on December 17. There followed, in the words of J. C. Beaglehole, "one of the longest and most unpleasant passages of the strait of which there is a record . . . four months in almost perpetual danger of shipwreck." No sooner had they entered the Pacific on April 11, 1767, than Wallis lost sight of *Swallow;* and the two ships carried on alone. Forced to the northwest, by June 10 *Dolphin* was in the Tuamotus, and on June 18 she arrived at Tahiti, the first European vessel to do so. Wallis established excellent relations with the queen, Oborea, and the crews spent six idyllic weeks recovering from scurvy and marveling at the people and climate of Tahiti. When they sailed on July 26, it was with promises to return. The European discovery of Tahiti had a profound effect not only on the subsequent exploration of the Pacific

— by coincidence, Louis Antoine de Bougainville's LA BOUDEUSE and *L'Etoile* arrived at Tahiti only a few months after *Dolphin* — but also on the European imagination. In his introduction to *The Journals of Captain James Cook,* Beaglehole explains:

> Sailors . . . may well be forgiven for thinking themselves imparadised. So almost suddenly, so overwhelmingly, was the idea of the Pacific at last to enter into the consciousness, not of seamen alone but of literate Europe. . . . For Wallis had not merely found a convenient port of call. He had stumbled on a foundation stone of the Romantic movement.

The remainder of the voyage paralleled Byron's, although the westward leg was farther to the south, passing through the Society Islands, then between Tonga and Samoa, before heading north for Tinian. From there, *Dolphin* sailed on to Batavia, then to the Cape of Good Hope and so to The Downs, where she arrived on May 20, 1768. *Dolphin* remained in service as a surveying ship until broken up in 1777.

Byron, *Journal of His Circumnavigation.* Robertson, *Discovery of Tahiti.*

# Duyfken

*Jacht* (3m). *L/B/D:* 63' × 17' × 7' (19m × 5m × 2m). *Tons:* 30 lasts/60 tons. *Hull:* wood. *Comp.:* 20. *Arm.:* 10 guns. *Built:* Netherlands; <1600.

When the United Provinces of the Netherlands declared their independence from Spain in 1581, Philip II retaliated by closing to Dutch merchants the port of Lisbon with its rich trade in oriental spices. The Dutch decided to trade directly with the East, and in 1595 the ships *Hollandia* (400 tons), *Mauritius* (400 tons), *Amsterdam* (200 tons), and *Duyfken* (60 tons) sailed for Java. Although only 80 of the 249 crew survived and *Amsterdam* was lost, the venture was considered successful. In December 1603, another ship called *Duyfken* left the Netherlands under Willem Jansz as part of a fleet of twelve ships. Once in the Indies, Jansz was

▲ A replica of the early-seventeenth-century Dutch jaght **Duyfken,** the first European vessel to visit the coast of Australia, seen here shortly after her launch at Fremantle in 1999. The yards are not yet in place. *Courtesy Nick Burningham, Duyfken Foundation.*

sent to search out other outlets for trade, particularly in "the great land of Nova Guinea and other East- and Southlands." On November 18, 1605, *Duyfken* sailed from Bantam to Banda and then through the Kai Islands and on to Tanjung Deyong, New Guinea. *Duyfken* rounded False Cape and then crossed the Arafura Sea into the Gulf of Carpentaria (thereby missing Torres Strait) and charted 200 miles of the Australian coast, which Jansz considered part of New Guinea. This is the first recorded visit to Australia by Europeans. Finding the land barren and the people inhospitable (ten of his men were killed on various shore expeditions), at Cape Keerveer ("Turnabout") south of Albatross Bay, Jansz headed home and arrived at Bantam in June 1606, two months before SAN PEDRO transited Torres Strait, thereby establishing that New Guinea was not part of a larger southern continent.

Murdoch, *"Duyfken" and the First Discoveries of Australia.* Sigmond and Zuiderbaan, *Dutch Discoveries of Australia.*

# Edward Bonaventure

Ship (3m). *Tons:* 160 tons. *Hull:* wood. *Comp.:* 36. *Built:* <1553.

In 1553, the Mysterie (guild) and Companie of the Marchants Aduenturers for the Discoverie of Regions, Dominions, Iland and Places Unknown, headed by Sebastian Cabot, dispatched an expedition under Sir Hugh Willoughby to sail around the top of Norway in search of a Northeast Passage to China. The three ships were Richard Chancellor's *Edward Bonaventure,* under master Stephen Burroughs, Willoughby's 120-ton *Bona Esperanza,* under William Gefferson, and the 90-ton *Bona Confidentia* under Cornelis Durfoort. The ships put to sea in mid-June and at the end of July became separated in a storm off the Lofoten Islands in northern Norway. *Edward Bonaventure* sailed for Wardhouse (Värdo) and, despite warnings from Scottish merchants, pressed on alone into the White Sea at the beginning of August. The other ships made it to the Lapland coast, where their crews died.

At the mouth of the Dvina River, where the port of Archangel is now situated, Chancellor met with the local governor and through him was invited to the court of Ivan the Terrible at Moscow, 1,500 miles to the south. Cordial relations were established between the czar and Mary Tudor, and, though "robbed homewards by Flemings," Chancellor returned home in the summer of 1554 with a favorable report of his mission, which promised to give the English a firm hold on the valuable fur trade.

In 1555, Chancellor returned to Moscow via the White Sea under a charter from Mary, and English merchants established themselves in Moscow. The following year, Chancellor made a third expedition conveying the first English ambassador to the Russian court, while Burroughs attempted to sail eastward across the Kara Sea in the diminutive *Searchthrift.* In the meantime, Willoughby's two ships had been recovered and Chancellor sailed for England with a total of four ships, conveying the Russian ambassador aboard his own *Edward Bonaventure.* Willoughby's ships sank en route, and *Edward Bonaventure* was wrecked on the coast of Scotland with the loss of Chancellor and his son. The Russian ambassador survived. The elusive Northeast Passage would not be conquered until the voyage of Adolf Nordenskiöld in Vega in 1878–79.

Purchas, *Hakluytus Posthumus.*

# Eendracht

*Hull:* wood. *Built:* Amsterdam, Netherlands; <1616.

The second Dutch ship to reach Australia following Duyfken's voyage of 1605–6, *Eendracht* ("Unity," a popular name for Dutch ships) was en route from the Netherlands to Batavia (Djakarta) under the command of Dirck Hartog when she became separated from the rest of the fleet. Tracing the route pioneered by Hendrik Brouwer in 1610, *Eendracht* sailed east across the Indian Ocean from Cape Town before turning north for Java. On October 25, 1615, Hartog arrived at "various islands, which were, however, found uninhabited." These proved to be Dirck Hartog's Island, off Inscription Point near Shark Bay, Western Australia. The point takes its name from the fact that Hartog erected a post and nailed to it a pewter plate commemorating his visit:

> 1616 On 25 October arrived the ship *Eendracht,* of Amsterdam: Supercargo Gilles Miebais of Liege, skipper Dirch Hatichs of Amsterdam. on 27 d[itt]o. she set sail again for Bantam. Deputy supercargo Jan Stins, upper steersman Pieter Doores of Bil. In the year 1616.

Hartog continued north along the coast that now bears his name and eventually reached the Dutch settlement at Batavia. The plate is now at the Rijksmuseum in Amsterdam, having been rescued from Inscription Point by Willem de Vlamingh, who, in command of *Geelvinck, Nyptangh,* and *Het Weeseltje,* visited the area (which the Dutch called Eendracht's Land) on February 4, 1697, and replaced Hartog's plate with one of his own. This in turn was found by Louis de Freycinet of L'URANIE in 1801, who in 1820 returned in *Le Naturaliste* and took Vlamingh's plate to France. It is now in the Western Australian Maritime Museum in Perth.

Sigmond and Zuiderbaan, *Dutch Discoveries of Australia.*

# Eendracht

*Tons:* 360. *Hull:* wood. *Comp.:* 87. *Arm.:* 19 guns; 12 swivels. *Built:* Netherlands; <1615.

In the early seventeenth century, the United East India Company (Verenigde Oostindische Compagnie, or VOC) had exclusive rights, among Dutch ships, to sail via the Strait of Magellan and Cape of Good Hope. The merchant Isaac Le Maire established the Compagnie Australe to trade in the South Seas, the still unexplored Southland (Australia), Japan, and northern Asia, but his ships could do so only if they found an alternative route to the East. This route, Le Maire believed, lay to the south of the Strait of Magellan, and to prove it he fitted out *Eendracht,* under his son, Jacob, and *Hoorn,* under Willem Cornelisz. Schouten. The

ships left The Texel on June 14, 1615, made a stop in Sierra Leone, and then sailed for Port Desire, where they arrived in early December. While the ships were being careened to clean the bottom growth, *Hoorn* caught fire and was destroyed. Embarking the smaller ship's twenty-two crew, *Eendracht* put to sea again on January 13, 1616. Eleven days later she passed through the Strait of Le Maire between the eastern end of Tierra del Fuego and Staten Island (which the crew named), and on the twenty-ninth doubled Cape Horn — named for their hometown — and entered the Pacific.

After calling at Juan Fernández Island in early March 1616, *Eendracht* headed west in about latitude 15°S. The first landfall was in the northern Tuamotus in April, and from there the track passed through the Tongas and on to the Tabat Islands, near New Ireland and New Guinea. When *Eendracht* arrived at Bantam, Java, in October the VOC representative did not believe that Schouten and Le Maire had found an alternative to the Strait of Magellan, and he confiscated *Eendracht* and her cargo before sending the crew on to the Netherlands. Perhaps most remarkable in this pioneering voyage around what later centuries would call "Cape Stiff" is that in more than sixteen months at sea, only three sailors died.

Beaglehole, *Exploration of the Pacific.* Villiers, ed., *East and West Indian Mirror.*

# Emma Dean

Rowboat. *L:* 16′. *Hull:* wood. *Comp.:* 4. *Built:* Chicago; 1869.

In 1867, Union Army veteran and geologist John Wesley Powell began to explore the Colorado Territory, which was just then being opened to settlement. Powell's undertaking evolved into "a comprehensive survey of the geography, geology, ethnography, and natural history of the country," and especially the deep river canyons etched across the Colorado Plateau. With modest financial support from the Illinois Natural History Society and the Illinois Industrial University, Powell assembled a team of ten men and purchased four boats from a builder in Chicago. The three largest boats, *Kitty Clyde's Sister, No Name,* and *Maid of the Canyon,* were 21 feet (6.5 meters) long and constructed of oak. *Emma Dean,* which Powell used to reconnoiter the rapids, was 16 feet and fashioned in pine. All were powered by oars, not paddles, and were constructed with watertight compartments fore and aft with an open cockpit amidships.

The expedition started out from Green River, Wyoming, on May 24. A week later they entered Flaming Gorge, the walls of which rise in places 2,500 feet (760 meters). Although they were able to manhandle the boats over the sandy shallows, where the rapids were too precipitous they either let the boats down by a line, or portaged them. Frequently they would have to crisscross the river at the head of rapids to find a foothold from which to walk their boats down. In the swift water, without rocks, they could make as much as 12 miles (19 kilometers) in an hour, including stops to bail out the boats.

On June 9, the *No Name* was destroyed in the 50-foot (15-meter) Disaster Falls in the Canyon of Lodore. Though most of the boat's stores — apart from some barometers and a 3-gallon keg of whiskey — were lost, the men were not hurt. Just below this they came to a stretch of river they called Hell's Half Mile, in the course of which the river falls about 100 feet (30 meters). Camping just below this, they lost much of their mess kit when a fire spread through their camp.

The party halted for a few days at the mouth of the Uinta River, and some of the men walked 20 miles (32 kilometers) to the Uinta Reservation for supplies. Explaining that "he has seen danger enough," Frank Goodman left the expedition — which made the remaining three boats less crowded. On July 24 they had to make three portages and covered only three quarters of a mile, their worst day in terms of mileage, but by the end of the month they were well into Glen Canyon, and they reached the mouth of the San Juan River on the last day of June.

Two weeks later they cleared Marble Canyon and came to the confluence of the Little Colorado River at the head of the Grand Canyon. Three quarters of a mile deep in the earth, they were on the brink of what Powell called "the Great Unknown." Entering the canyon they came to a stretch of river that dropped 80 feet (24 meters) in a third of a mile and was surrounded by canyon walls a mile high. "There is no hesitation," wrote Powell.

> We step into our boats, push off, and away we go, first on smooth but swift water, then we strike a glassy wave and ride to its top, down again into the trough, up again on a higher wave, and down and up on waves higher and still higher until we strike one just as it curls back, and a breaker rolls over our little boat.

Despite the initial difficulties, the canyon was full of long, relatively smooth stretches of river that run for 20 miles (32 kilometers) or more without serious obstructions. On August 25, they covered 35 miles (56 kilometers).

Three days later, the canyon turned south at Iceberg Canyon. Fearing that the route was impassable, Captain O. G. Howland informed Powell that he, his brother, Seneca, and William Dunn had decided to leave the expedition and try their luck on foot, across the desert. Powell decided to abandon the *Emma Dean,* and before parting, the remaining crew gave Howland letters, personal effects to be sent on to family members in the event of their deaths, and a duplicate copy of the expedition logs. The Howlands and Dunn were never heard from again. After a day of running furious rapids, Powell's party was clear of the Grand Canyon, and the next day they reached the mouth of the Virgin River. They had traversed the 217 miles (350 kilometers) of the Grand Canyon in sixteen days. So ended what Wallace Stegner has described as "the last great exploration within the continental United States."

Powell, *Exploration of the Colorado River.*

# HMS Endeavour

(ex-*Earl of Pembroke,* later *La Liberté*) Cat-bark (3m). *L/B/D:* 97.6' × 29.3' × 11.3' dph (29.7m × 8.9m × 3.4m). *Tons:* 369 tons. *Hull:* wood. *Comp.:* 85–94. *Arm.:* 6 × 4pdr, 8 swivels. *Built:* Fishburn, Whitby, Eng.; 1764.

In 1768 Lieutenant James Cook was invited to command an expedition to the South Seas sponsored by the Royal Society. (The Society sought the appointment of the hydrographer Alexander Dalrymple, but the Admiralty preferred Cook.) The voyage had a twofold mission. The first was to visit Tahiti to observe (on June 3, 1769) the transit of Venus across the sun, "a phenomenon that must . . . contribute greatly to the improvement of astronomy, on which navigation so much depends." The second mission was to determine whether there was, as suggested by earlier Portuguese and Dutch navigators, a great southern continent, or Terra Australis. The Admiralty's choice of ship for what would turn out to be the first of Captain James Cook's three expeditions to the Pacific Ocean was a bluff-bowed North Sea "cat-built bark" — the name identifies the hull model; the vessel was ship-rigged — which was built originally as a collier. Although the Navy Board had earlier considered HMS *Rose* and *Tryal,* the cat-bark type was well known to Cook, who had first gone to sea in just such ships. "From the knowledge and experience that I have had of these sort [*sic*] of vessels," he later wrote, "I shall always be of the opinion that only such are proper to be sent on discoveries to distant parts."

Renamed *Endeavour* and rerigged as a ship (although she was referred to as "H.M. Bark," to distinguish her from another navy ship of the same name), *Endeavour* sailed from Plymouth on August 25, 1768. Her distinguished company included the naturalists Joseph Banks and Daniel Solander, as well as Second Lieutenants John Gore and Charles Clerke, both veterans of HMS DOLPHIN. After calling at Madeira (September 12), Rio de Janeiro (November 14), and the Bay of Good Success in Le Maire Strait (January 15, 1769), she entered the Pacific and arrived at Tahiti on April 13. Cook's crew established good relations with the Tahitians — who had entertained the crews of Bougainville's LA BOUDEUSE and *L'Etoile* the year before — and remained on the island for three full months. When they finally sailed, the ship's company had been augmented by a Tahitian named Tupaia and his servant, Taiata. After calling elsewhere in the Society Islands (so named because they lay contiguous to one another), they sailed south and then west, and landed on the North Island of New Zealand on October 9. In the course of six months, *Endeavour* established that New Zealand consisted of two main islands — both of which were circumnavigated — separated by Cook Strait, a name suggested by Banks. Abandoning his search for Terra Australis, on March 31, 1770, Cook weighed anchor and sailed due west across the Tasman Sea, hoping to sail into the Indian Ocean via Van Diemen's Land (now called Tasmania, for Abel Tasman whose HEEMSKERCK and *Zeehaen* called there in 1642).

The onset of winter drove *Endeavour* off course, and on April 19, the ship arrived off New Holland (Australia). Nine days later, *Endeavour* entered Botany Bay (just south of modern Sydney), which they named "for the great quantity of New Plants & ca" collected there over the next week. *Endeavour* sailed again on May 6, skirting the coast of Australia until June 10, when the ship was holed on the Great Barrier Reef near Cape Tribulation (15°47'S, 145°34'E). "This was," wrote Cook, "an alarming and I may say terrible Circumstance and threatend immidiate destruction to us as soon as the Ship was afloat." It took two days to free the ship, and the leak was only stopped by fothering, that is, drawing a sail impregnated with oakum under the ship's bottom to stop the leak. Nine days later, Cook landed at what is now Cooktown. Repairs to the ship lasted six weeks, during which Lieutenant Gore shot and stuffed a kangaroo. After claiming New Holland for the British Crown, Cook sailed *Endeavour* through the Torres Strait, stopping at Savu Island (west of Timor), and then sailing on to the Dutch entrepôt at Batavia (now Dakarta). There, thanks to an "electrical chain" Cook ordered

set up for the purpose, *Endeavour* survived a bolt of lightning that did serious damage to a Dutch East Indiaman. The rest of the stay was plagued with difficulty. Further repairs to *Endeavour*'s hull and raging fever and dysentery among the ship's company — seven of whom died, including Tupaia and Taiata — kept the ship at Batavia until December 26, 1770. The voyage across the Indian Ocean saw the death of twenty-three of the crew from disease contracted in the East Indies. *Endeavour* anchored at Cape Town from March 15 to April 14, 1771, sailed for St. Helena (May 1– 4), and anchored in The Downs on July 12, 1771, after a circumnavigation lasting two years, nine months, and fourteen days. Cook was not long at home. Having deposited the "curiosities" gathered in his first epic voyage with Joseph Banks, who later left them to the British Museum, he was promoted to the rank of commander, and in July 1772 he sailed again for the Pacific with RESOLUTION and ADVENTURE. His last, ill-fated voyage, with *Resolution* and DISCOVERY, began in 1776.

Following a refit at Woolwich, *Endeavour* made three voyages to the Falkland Islands and was paid off in September 1774. Sold out of the navy on March 7, 1775, *Endeavour* sailed once again as a North Sea collier for fifteen years. She was purchased by French interests in 1790 and as *La Liberté* entered the whale trade. In 1793, she ran aground off Newport, Rhode Island, and was later broken up by James Cahoon. A replica of the ship was commissioned at Fremantle in 1994.

Cook, *Journals of James Cook.* Knight, "H.M. Bark *Endeavour*." McGowan, "Captain Cook's Ships." Marquardt, *Captain Cook's Endeavour.* O'Brian, *Joseph Banks.*

---

◀ A replica of Captain James Cook's ship **Endeavour,** in which he circumnavigated the globe on the first of three voyages of exploration in the Pacific Ocean between 1768 and 1779. *Photo by Steven Wenban, H.M. Bark Endeavour Foundation.*

# Endurance

Barkentine (1f/2m). *L/B/D:* 144′ × 25′ × 15.5′ dph (43.9m × 7.5m × 4.7m). *Tons:* 300 grt. *Hull:* wood. *Comp.:* 28. *Mach.:* steam, 350 hp, 1 screw; 10.2 kts. *Des.:* Aanderud Larsen. *Built:* Framnaes Mek Verstad, Sandefjord, Norway; 1912.

## James Caird

Whaleboat (2m). *L/B/D:* 22.6′ × 6′ × 3.5 dph (6.9m × 1.8m × 1.1m). *Hull:* wood. *Comp.:* 6–28. *Des.:* Frank Worsley. *Built:* London; 1914.

Shortly after Roald Amundsen led the first expedition to the South Pole in 1911–12, Sir Ernest Henry Shackleton started planning the Imperial Trans-Antarctic Expedition, which he referred to as "the last great Antarctic adventure." A veteran of Robert Falcon Scott's HMS DISCOVERY, and leader of the 1908 British Imperial Antarctic Expedition in NIMROD, Shackleton chose as his ship *Endurance,* a new barkentine built for tourist cruises in the Arctic. (One of her original owners was Adrien de Gerlache, captain of BELGICA, the first ship to winter in Antarctica.) Shackleton intended to land with six men at Vahsel Bay on the Weddell Sea, and from there to march via the South Pole to McMurdo Sound, to be picked up by the ship *Aurora.* To help minimize the amount of supplies to be carried by his own team, crew from *Aurora* were to deposit caches of supplies between McMurdo Sound and the Pole.

Shackleton's venture attracted a great deal of attention. Among the visitors to the ship while she lay at the Isle of Dogs in London was Queen Alexandra, who presented the ship with a Bible inscribed:

> For the Crew of the *Endurance*
> From Alexandra, May 31, 1914

> May the Lord help you to do your duty & guide you through all dangers by land and sea. "May you see the Works of the Lord & all His wonders in the Deep."

The ship had just departed London when World War I started, and Shackleton offered to turn the ship over to the navy. The Admiralty telegraphed a one-word reply: "Proceed." On August 8,

▲ Sir Ernest Shackleton, who is leaning over the side of his ship **Endurance** only days before she sank, captioned this photograph by expedition photographer Frank Hurley "The Beginning of the End." *Courtesy, National Maritime Museum, Greenwich.*

1914, three days after Britain entered World War I, *Endurance* sailed from Plymouth via Madeira to Buenos Aires, where the gifted and tenacious expedition photographer, James Francis Hurley, joined the ship. William Blakewell signed on for the voyage; his friend Perce Blackborow was turned down but stowed away and was eventually enrolled as a steward. Of the twenty-eight men aboard *Endurance,* seven had previous experience in Antarctica and six had been there more than once. Alfred Cheetham had sailed on four expeditions, Frank Wild on three, and the other four on two; six had previously sailed with Shackleton in either *Nim-*

*rod* or *Discovery. Endurance* next called at the Norwegian whaling station at Grytviken on South Georgia Island. Here Shackleton learned that the ice conditions were unusually severe and that the pack ice extended farther north than any of the whalers could remember. After a month at Grytviken, Shackleton decided he could wait no longer.

On December 11, *Endurance* entered the pack ice at the unexpectedly low parallel of 59°S. They maneuvered through the ice for about 1,000 miles until January 19, 1915, when *Endurance* stuck fast in 76°30′S, 31°30′W, only 85 miles from her intended destination. At the mercy of the ice, the ship drifted for nine months, first west along the Luitpold Coast and then north again, parallel to the Antarctic Peninsula. The ice began to relax its grip during July, but over the next few months, *Endurance* was so battered by the ice pack that, as Shackleton wrote, on October 27, 1915, "She was

doomed: no ship built by human hands could have withstood the strain. I ordered all hands out on the floe."

The crew abandoned ship in 69°5′S, 51°30′W, taking off stores and supplies. The men were limited to two pounds of personal gear apiece. A major exception was made for Hurley's glass plate negatives, of which he kept 100 black and white and 20 Paget color transparencies, and an album of previously printed photographs. "Homeless & adrift on the sea ice," as Hurley put it, they were 350 miles from land. The party established a base they called Ocean Camp about a mile and a half from the ruined ship. On November 21, as the ice began to thaw, *Endurance* sank. "At 5 P.M. she went down by the head: the stern the cause of all the trouble was the last to go under water. I cannot write about it." An attempt to walk toward open water a month later was abandoned after a week in

▲ The 22-foot-long **James Caird,** in which Sir Ernest Shackleton and five picked men sailed by dead reckoning through 800 miles of the most inhospitable waters on earth, from Elephant Island to the South Georgia Islands: "Not a life lost and we have been through hell." *Courtesy Dulwich College, London.*

which they covered only eight miles. They dubbed their new site Patience Camp.

The ice began to break up at the beginning of April 1916 and on the ninth Shackleton ordered his men into the boats, which were named for the expedition's benefactors: *James Caird, Dudley Docker,* and *Stancomb Wills.* They were at sea again for the first time in fifteen months, but the following week was one of terror. By day, they were at the mercy of the wind and currents and shifting ice and they spent their nights either on bobbing ice floes or in their half-swamped boats. It was small wonder that many of the men were temporarily deranged when they staggered ashore on Elephant Island on April 15.

Thus far, not a single one of *Endurance*'s crew had died from any cause. Yet Elephant Island's isolation all but assured that they would never be rescued; they would have to help themselves first. Although South America and the Falkland Islands were closer, their best hope was to sail for South Georgia Island, 800 miles away, and bring a rescue vessel from the whaling station. Measuring 22 feet long by 6 feet 6 inches beam, *James Caird* was the biggest of the three boats at Elephant Island, and Henry McNeish, the ship's carpenter, had built up her sides. Now he strengthened the keel, erected a framework for a canvas cover to keep the seas out, and stepped a second mast. She emerged from his ministrations as a lug-rigged ketch and with more than a ton of ballast; her freeboard was 2 feet 2 inches (0.7 meters).

*James Caird* was launched on April 24, and after supplies had been ferried out to her, she stood out from the land at the start of an 800-mile passage through some of the worst seas in the world at one of the worst times of the year. Shackleton had chosen five men for the voyage: McNeish; Frank Worsely, the captain of *Endurance* and an exceptional navigator; Second Officer Tom Crean; Tim McCarthy; and Bosun Vincent. Sailing by dead reckoning, *James Caird* weathered six gales, a hurricane, and a swamping before Shackleton brought his frail boat into King Haakon Bay on the south side of South Georgia Island on May 10. It was an unparalleled piece of seamanship; Worsley had been able to make only four sun sights on the passage, and these under the worst possible conditions. After nine days of rest and waiting for good weather, Shackleton, Worsley, and Crean set out for Stromness, 40 miles (63 kilometers) away on the other side of 5,000-foot (1,500-meter) mountains, glaciers, and snow fields. Marching for thirty-six hours without sleep, they reached Stromness on May 20. Hairy, soot-stained, and dressed in threadbare filthy clothes, the three men presented themselves to the station manager, Thoralf Sørlle. A Norwegian whaler later described the interview:

Manager say: "Who the *hell* are you?" and terrible bearded man in the centre of the three say quietly: "My name is Shackleton." Me — I turn away and weep.

The next day, the whale catcher *Samson* sailed around to rescue the three men left at King Haakon Bay with *James Caird.* On May 22, Shackleton took the whaler *Southern Sky* to rescue the men on Elephant Island, but the pack ice was too thick and he was forced back to the Falkland Islands. The Admiralty could spare no ships for the rescue effort, but the Foreign Office prevailed on South American governments to lend assistance. On June 10, Shackleton embarked in the Uruguayan government ship *Instituto da Pesca No. 1,* but she, too, was unable to penetrate the ice, and Shackleton proceeded to Punta Arenas, Chile. Here he chartered the schooner *Emma,* with the same result; he returned to the Falklands. At the end of August, Shackleton was back in Punta Arenas, where the Chilean government lent him the lighthouse tender *Yelcho.* Shackleton, Worsley, and Crean departed the Straits of Magellan on August 25, and 5 days later they arrived at Elephant Island, 128 days after their departure for South Georgia. All those left behind were alive and well. As Shackleton wrote to his wife on their return, "I have done it. . . . Not a life lost and we have been through Hell."

Though he had failed in his purpose, Shackleton's determination and ingenuity on the *Endurance* expedition earned him a unique place in the history of exploration. In the words of Sir Edmund Hillary, "For scientific discovery give me Scott; for speed and efficiency give me Amundsen; but when disaster strikes and all hope is gone, get down on your knees and pray for Shackleton." *James Caird* is preserved at Dulwich College, Shackleton's alma mater, and Hurley's photographic record of the *Endurance* expedition is invaluable.

Alexander, *Endurance.* Dunnett, *Shackleton's Boat.* Huntford, *Shackleton.* Shackleton, *South.* Worsley, *Endurance: Great Antarctic Rescue.*

# Enhjørning

Frigate (3m). *Hull:* wood. *Comp.:* 49. *Built:* Bremerholm Navy Yard, Copenhagen; 1605.

One of the finest frigates in the navy of Christian IV (r. 1588–1648), *Enhjørning* (in Danish, "Unicorn") appears to have been so named because earlier in the year of her launch all Denmark had been excited by the sale, for 40,000 rix-dollars, of the 6-foot-long horn of a narwhal caught off Iceland. The ship had an active career during Christian IV's campaigns in the Baltic, but she is most celebrated for her connection with Jens Munk's expedition in search of the Northwest Passage. Munk, a veteran of ocean voyaging from Brazil to Novaya Zemlya, was first associated with *Enhjørning* in 1616. At that time, the ship was one of six in a failed expedition against pirates operating in the waters between Denmark, the North Cape, Iceland, and the Faeroe Islands. (In 1615, Munk had sailed as second in command of a two-ship expedition that captured the Spanish pirate Mendoza in the Kara Sea.) Three years later, *Enhjørning* was made flagship of Munk's expedition in search of the Northwest Passage, one of two expeditions bound for China dispatched that year by Christian IV. Among her sixty-five crew were two English veterans of northern voyages: John Watson, who probably sailed with Thomas Button in DISCOVERY in 1613, and William Gordon, whose salary, advance, and bonus (were the passage found) would have equaled about half the cost of the entire expedition.

On May 9, 1619, *Enhjørning* and *Lamprey* sailed from Copenhagen with the personal blessing of Christian IV, but soon after their departure, one man threw himself overboard in the Kattegat, and the ships were forced into harbor in Norway for repairs to *Lamprey*. Putting to sea again on May 30, the ships passed the Shetlands and the Faeroes and by the end of June were off Cape Farewell, Greenland. They crossed the ice-strewn Davis Strait and fetched up in Frobisher Bay at the southern end of Baffin Island. Working their way out of the bay, the ships rounded Resolution Island on July 11, only to drift in the ice for two days before resuming their westward course. Actual transit of Hudson Strait took nearly six weeks, as the ships were caught in drifting ice or came to anchor at various points along the southern shore of Baffin Island. They also lost ten days sailing through Ungava Bay in northern Quebec, which Gordon mistook for Hudson Bay. Finally, after passing The Sisters (Digges Islands), the ships turned southwest at the beginning of September. *Lamprey* and *Enhjørning* were separated in a storm, and on September 7, Munk conned *Enhjørning* through the shoal water at the mouth of the Churchill River in northern Manitoba, where they were joined two days later by *Lamprey*.

The unexpectedly cold weather left Munk no choice but to winter at Munk Haven. The ships were hauled over the shallows to be out of the way of the ice, which was already building up around the hulls. Although well provisioned, the men had no winter clothing, and as the weather tightened its grip it became increasingly difficult to hunt or gather fuel. The first death of a crewman came on November 21, followed two weeks later by a second. By February 20, 1620, twenty-one men were dead, and by June 4, when Munk had given himself up for dead, there were sixty-one dead. Munk wrote in his log, "Since I no longer have any hopes of living, . . . I say good-bye to the world and give my soul to God's keeping."

Five days later, he learned that two of his men were still alive ashore, in a destitute state: "we crept all about, wherever we saw the slightest green growing and coming out of the earth which we digged up and sucked the very root thereof . . . and thereafter we began to feel well." By June 18, they could fish a little, and a week later they began preparations for leaving Munk Haven in *Lamprey*. Having unloaded the vessel, hauled her over the rocks to deeper water, and reloaded her, the three men sailed on July 16, leaving *Enhjørning* and their dead comrades behind. Miraculously, *Lamprey* and her enfeebled crew made the hazardous eastward crossing of the Atlantic to fetch up in Sognefjord, Norway, on September 20. Munk recovered well enough to remain in the king's service until 1628, two years after *Lamprey* sank after Christian IV's disastrous defeat at Lutter am Barenberge in August 1626 during the Thirty Years' War.

Hansen, *Northwest to Hudson Bay.*

# HMS Erebus

*Hecla*-class bomb vessel (3m). *L/B/D:* 105' × 28.5' × 13.8' (32m × 8.7m × 4.2m). *Tons:* 372 bm. *Hull:* wood. *Comp.:* 67. *Arm.:* 1 × 13" mortar, 1 × 10" mortar, 2 × 6pdr, 8 × 24pdr. *Des.:* Sir Henry Peake. *Built:* Pembroke Dockyard, Wales; 1826.

Named for the entrance to Hades in Greek myth, *Erebus* was a bark-rigged vessel with a primary armament of two mortars weighing three tons each. After two years in the Mediterranean, she was adapted for work in polar waters and sailed to the Antarctic under a Mr. Rice. In 1839 she came under command of James Clark Ross, a veteran of Arctic expeditions in ISABELLA, HMS HECLA, and VICTORY. Ross's primary mission was to study terrestrial magnetism and locate the South Magnetic Pole, as well as to undertake oceanographic, botanical, and zoological observations.

*Erebus* and HMS TERROR (under Francis R. M. Crozier) sailed from Chatham on September 30, 1839, and after stops at ports of call in the Atlantic and Indian oceans — notably Simon's Bay, South Africa, and Kerguelen Island — they arrived at Hobart, Tasmania, in August 1840. The ships departed for Antarctica on November 12 and encountered ice two days after Christmas. On New Year's Day, 1841, they crossed the Antarctic Circle south of New Zealand. The ships forced their way southward through the pack ice until January 9, when they reached open water — now known as the Ross Sea — in 68°28'S, 176°31'E. Roald Amundsen, who led the first group to reach the South Pole, wrote:

> Few people of the present day [1912] are capable of rightly appreciating this heroic deed, this brilliant proof of human courage and energy. With two ponderous craft — regular "tubs" according to our ideas — these men sailed right into the heart of the pack, which all previous explorers had regarded as certain death. . . . These men were heroes — heroes in the highest sense of the word.

A few days later, the crew landed on Victoria Land, which they claimed for Great Britain and whose landscape they showered with the names of political figures, scientists, acquaintances, and ships, including Mt. Erebus (an active volcano) and Mt. Terror (a dormant one). On February 1 they encountered a barrier in latitude 78°4'S that, in Ross's words, "was about 160 feet high, and extended as far to the east and west as the eye could discern." In fact, the impenetrable Ross Ice Shelf runs for about 1,000 miles and, as one member of the expedition put it, "we might with equal chance of success try to sail through the Cliffs of Dover." *Erebus* and *Terror* remained in the Ross Sea until the end of February and returned to Hobart in April for a three-month refit.

En route to their second visit to Antarctica, the ships visited Sydney and the Bay of Islands, New Zealand, where Ross obtained a chart of Jules S.-C. Dumont d'Urville's recent Antarctic voyages in ASTROLABE and *Zélée*. On December 18, they entered the pack ice in about 60°50'S, 147°25'W. Held fast, they drifted south at the mercy of the ice. On January 19, 1842, the ships' rudders were destroyed by ice in a furious gale, and it was not until February 1 that they were in open water again. After three weeks the expedition reached the Ross Ice Shelf in 78°9'30"S; no ship would sail farther south for nearly sixty years. On March 13, the ships were approaching a heavy ice formation when *Erebus* collided with *Terror*. As the latter ship's bowsprit was swept away, the two ships drifted toward two icebergs separated by 60 feet (200 meters) of open water. *Terror* passed through first, followed by *Erebus*, whose yards struck the iceberg repeatedly before Ross sailed her through the gap "by the hazardous expedient of the sternboard," that is, stern first with the sails aback — "which nothing could justify during such a gale with so high a sea running, but to avert the danger which every moment threatened us of being dashed to pieces."

▲ François Etienne Musin's **"HMS Erebus** in the Ice, 1846" depicts Sir John Franklin's flagship one year after the two-ship expedition disappeared into the Arctic wastes while searching for the Northwest Passage. *Courtesy National Maritime Museum, Greenwich.*

The ships returned to the Falkland Islands, made a visit to Tierra del Fuego in September, and then in December sailed south again, this time to the islands of the Antarctic Peninsula. Turning east, the ice prevented them from sailing through the Weddell Sea and they got no farther than 71°30′S, 14°51′W before turning for home. After several stops, they arrived at Folkestone on September 4, 1843, after a voyage of four years, five months. In addition to studies in magnetism, they had also brought back oceanographic data and extensive collections of botanical and ornithological specimens.

The next year, *Erebus* and *Terror* were fitted out with 20-hp engines and single-screw propellers for a new voyage in search of the Northwest Passage. Ross declined command, which went to his old friend Sir John Franklin, who had surveyed Australia in HMS INVESTIGATOR, sailed to Spitzbergen, and made a three-year trek to the Coppermine River in the Canadian Arctic. With Crozier still in command of *Terror,* the two ships sailed from Greenhithe on May 19, 1845. *Erebus* and *Terror* each carried stores for two years, and another two years' worth were carried to the Whalefish Islands in the Davis Strait by the supply ship *Barretto Junior. Erebus* and *Terror* were last seen in Baffin Bay near the entrance of Lancaster Sound in August 1845.

The ships sailed through Lancaster Sound and after trying to sail north through Wellington Channel, turned south around Cornwallis Island

and headed into Peel Strait and Franklin Strait, to the west of Somerset Island and the Boothia Peninsula. Continuing southwest, the ships became icebound in Victoria Strait between King William Island and Victoria Island. Franklin died of natural causes aboard *Erebus* on June 11, 1847, and by the following spring, twenty-three other members of the crew were dead of starvation or scurvy. On April 22, 1848, the 105 survivors abandoned the ships and attempted to march to Fort Resolution, a Hudson's Bay Company outpost on Great Slave Lake more than 600 miles (965 kilometers) to the southwest. Over the next twelve years, more than a dozen expeditions were launched to search for survivors, including both military and civilian groups from Britain and the United States.

The ships' fate was revealed only by the discovery of human remains, diaries, and relics of the expedition found in the course of scores of land and sea searches, sent out starting in 1848 and culminating in the 1859 expedition of Captain Francis L. M'Clintock in *Fox*.

Beattie and Geiger, *Frozen in Time*. Dodge, *Polar Rosses*. Owen, *Fate of Franklin*. J. C. Ross, *Voyage of Discovery and Research in the Southern and Antarctic Regions*. M. J. Ross, *Ross in the Antarctic*.

# L'Espérance

(ex-*Truite*) Frigate (3m). *Hull:* wood. *Comp.:* 113. *Built:* France; 1791.

By the beginning of 1789, France had learned that La Pérouse's ships ASTROLABE and BOUSSOLE were overdue at the Ile de France. Even as the French Revolution gathered headway, there was widespread concern among both the nobility and revolutionaries for the fate of the expedition, and plans were put in place for the dispatch of a search party. On September 29, 1791, three months after the arrest of Louis XVI, two converted storeships — *L'Espérance* (ex-*Truite*) and *La Recherche* (ex-*Durance*) — sailed from Brest under command of A. R. J. de Bruni, Chevalier d'Entrecasteaux. The crew of *Recherche* numbered 106, under J. M. Huon de Kermadec. Although the chief object of the voyage was to search for La Pérouse, the expedition carried a full complement of scientists — five naturalists, two hydrographers, two draughtsman, and a botanist.

Orders called for d'Entrecasteaux to sail for New Holland (Australia), but at Cape Town he heard a report that people dressed in French uniforms had been seen in the Admiralty Islands, and he altered his plans accordingly. The ships' progress towards the Moluccas was so slow, however, that he decided instead to make for Van Diemen's Land (Tasmania), arriving on April 21, 1792. The French spent five weeks charting and exploring the southeast coast before striking northeast across the Tasman Sea toward New Caledonia. Reefs prevented a landing there, so they continued northeast past the Solomon Islands to land on New Ireland for a week. July 26 brought the ships to the Admiralty Islands, but there was no sign of La Pérouse.

After provisioning at the Dutch entrepôt of Amboina, on October 13 *L'Espérance* and *Recherche* were bound for Van Diemen's Land. Rounding Cape Leeuwin, on the southwest corner of Australia, they came to the Recherche Islands and then explored the barren shore of Nuyts Land in the Great Australian Bight. On January 21, 1793 — the day of Louis XVI's execution — the ships anchored at Van Diemen's Land. From there they headed to Tongatapu, where La Pérouse was known to have sailed after leaving Botany Bay in 1788. Although they were well received by the Tongans, from whom they bought hundreds of pigs, birds, and breadfruit trees, there was no sign of La Pérouse, and they made for New Caledonia, where Huon de Kermadec died on May 6. Thirteen days later, they came to a previously unknown island south of Santa Cruz — Vanikoro, the very island on which *Astrolabe* and *Boussole* had wrecked. The inhabitants were hostile, and the French sailed without learning anything of the fate of their countrymen.

Sailing through the Solomons and the Louisiades in May and June, the crews became increasingly ill with scurvy and dysentery. On July 20 d'Entrecasteaux died, and command of the expedition fell to the ailing A. Hesmivy d'Auribeau.

The French sailed through Torres Strait and on October 19 reached Surabaya, only to learn that France was at war with the Dutch. News of the French Revolution also divided the officers and crew, and the expedition dissolved. The officers were pro-monarchy and had many of the republican crew arrested by the Dutch. The scientists made their way back to France as best they could, but the officers had sent their collections and manuscripts to England, from which they were returned to France only after intervention by Sir Joseph Banks — and after all the charts had been copied by the Admiralty.

Brosse, *Great Voyages of Discovery.* Dunmore, *French Explorers in the Pacific.*

# F

## FLIP

Nonpropelled research platform. *L/B/D:* 354.3′ × 25.9′ × 12.5′/300′ (108m × 7.9m × 3.8m/91.4m). *Tons:* 700 long tons. *Hull:* steel. *Comp.:* 16. *Mach.:* generators. *Des.:* Fred Speiss, Fred Fisher. *Built:* Gunderson Brothers Engineering Co., Portland, Oreg.; 1963.

One of the more curious research vessels ever built is the U.S. Navy's *FLIP*. Designed by researchers at the Scripps Institute of Oceanography as a vehicle for studying the targeting accuracy of submarine-launched missiles, the vessel's name is an acronym for *FLoating Instrument Platform*. It also describes the vessel's most obvious characteristic: when on station, it flips from a horizontal to a vertical position, leaving only 85 percent of its hull visible above the waterline. This makes the station far more stable than a conventional hull. The hull has three primary divisions. The forward (lower) 150 feet (46 meters) consist of a series of ballast tanks that are flooded to bring the ship to the vertical; compressors and air tanks needed to blow the ballast tanks occupy the next 150 feet; and living and research spaces occupy the after (upper) 55 feet (17 meters) of the ship.

*FLIP* has no propulsion system of its own, and must be towed in the horizontal position. Once on station, it takes about twenty minutes to change the orientation of the vessel from the horizontal to the vertical. Research stations and accommodations such as galley fixtures, bunks, and toilets must be reoriented manually. Once on station, *FLIP* can be left to drift or anchored via a three-point mooring in waters as deep as 5 kilometers (3 miles). At anchor, *FLIP* is extremely stable. Vertical movement is about 10 percent of the average wave height, so that in a 10-meter (33-foot) swell *FLIP* rises and falls only 1 meter. (Designed to work in

waves as high as 9 meters, *FLIP* has survived 24-meter seas.) The watch circle diameter is usually no more than 200 meters.

This stability has made *FLIP* an invaluable tool for the study of such phenomena as low-frequency and ambient noise propagation with large arrays of hydrophones. Although *FLIP* is owned by the U.S. Navy, it is operated by the Marine Physical Laboratory at the Scripps Institution of Oceanography in La Jolla, north of San Diego. In addition to military research, the station has been employed in a variety of other scientific research projects, including geophysics, meteorology, physical oceanography, wave studies, and global climate change. Despite its age, there are no plans to retire the vessel in the foreseeable future.

Markell, "Built to Flood."

## FNRS-2

(later *FNRS-3*) Bathyscaph. *L:* 6.5′ dia. *Tons:* 12.5 tons. *Hull:* nickel-chrome molybdenum. *Comp.:* 2. *Built:* Emile Henricot Works, Court Etienne, Belgium; 1948.

The world's first bathyscaph was the creation of the Swiss physicist and oceanographer Auguste Piccard. The principle of the bathyscaph — the word was Piccard's coinage, derived from the Greek words meaning "deep boat" — was simple. Piccard wanted a manned vessel fitted with observation portholes yet strong enough to withstand the enormous stresses created at great depths — as much as 8 tons per square inch — and able to descend and rise on its own, without being tethered to a mother ship.

Piccard was already well known for his ascent in

a balloon to 50,000 feet (15,240 meters) in order to study cosmic rays, in 1931. The impetus for the bathyscaph arose from a conversation with King Leopold of Belgium, whose father had founded the Fonds National de la Recherche Scientifique, the organization responsible for much of Piccard's research. Asked how his work was progressing, Piccard, who had long been interested in oceanography, found himself telling the king of his plans to build a bathyscaph for abyssal research.

The design of the first bathyscaph, *FNRS-2* (the original *FNRS* was Piccard's stratospheric balloon), was relatively straightforward. The passenger compartment was a steel sphere large enough to hold two crew and fitted with two portholes. This sphere was attached to an elongated float filled with gasoline, which is lighter than water and therefore more buoyant. (The relationship of gasoline and water is comparable to that of helium and air, and the bathyscaph has been compared to an underwater balloon.) The tank also had provisions for water and iron ballast, which could be jettisoned at the bottom of the dive in preparation for the ascent.

On November 3, 1948, *FNRS-2* made an unmanned trial descent to a record depth of 1,371 meters (4,500 feet) off Dakar, Senegal. Funding difficulties led to the bathyscaph's transfer to the French navy, and it was officially renamed *FNRS-3*. In 1954, *FNRS-3* descended to a record 4,049 meters (13,284 feet) off Dakar, a depth not exceeded until 1959, during TRIESTE's workup for its assault on the 10,912-meter (35,800-foot) Challenger Deep. In the 1960s, *FNRS-3* was replaced by the French navy's *FNRS-4*.

Houot and Willm, *2000 Fathoms Down*. Piccard, *Earth, Sky, and Sea*. Piccard and Ditez, *Seven Miles Down*.

# Fox

Steam yacht (1f/3m). *Tons:* 170 burthen. *Hull:* wood. *Comp.:* 26. *Mach.:* steam; 1 screw. *Built:* Alexander Hall & Co., Aberdeen, Scotland; <1857.

Built as a yacht for Sir Richard Sutton, who made one voyage in her to Norway, *Fox* was purchased from his estate by Sir John Franklin's widow, Lady Jane Franklin, who put the ship under command of Arctic veteran Captain Francis Leopold M'Clintock, to search for the remains of her husband's HMS EREBUS and TERROR, which had been missing since 1848. *Fox* sailed from Aberdeen on July 1, 1857, and became icebound in Melville Bay in northwest Greenland. During the winter she was pushed south through Davis Strait to Cumberland Sound in southern Baffin Island. In April 1858, she resumed her journey, calling at Godthåb and Beechey Island. From there, M'Clintock intended to descend through Peel Sound, between the Boothia Peninsula and Prince of Wales Island, but ice conditions forced him south into Prince Regent Inlet (between Baffin Island and Somerset Island), and then west through Bellot Strait, between Somerset Island and the Boothia Peninsula. From winter quarters at Port Kennedy, sledging expeditions traced the southern shore of Prince of Wales Island from Franklin Strait in the east to McClintock Channel in the west, as well as the western shore of the Boothia Peninsula and King William Island.

In May 1859, M'Clintock's expedition found remnants of the Franklin expedition at Victory Point, in northwest King William Island. A dispatch from Graham Gore dated May 28, 1847, indicated that *Erebus* and *Terror* had attempted to sail across what became known as McClintock Channel but were frozen in off Cape Felix at the entrance to Victoria Strait, in 70°5′N, 98°23′W. A

▼ This handsome portrait by an anonymous English painter shows **Fox** in Arctic waters during the yacht's successful attempt to find the remains of Sir John Franklin's ill-fated voyage in **HMS Erebus** and **Terror** (1857–59). *Courtesy National Maritime Museum, Greenwich.*

▲ The quintessential polar research vessel **Fram,** photographed in Antarctica during Roald Amundsen's expedition of 1910–12, when he and four companions became the first people to reach the South Pole. *Courtesy Norsk Sjøfartsmuseum, Oslo.*

year later, Commander James Fitzjames annotated the report. The ships had been frozen in from September 12, 1846; Franklin, 8 other officers (Gore among them), and 15 men had died; the ships were abandoned on April 22, 1848; and the remaining 105 men under Captain Crozier "start on tomorrow the 26th for Back's Fish River." None survived.

With this expedition, from which *Fox* returned to England in September 1859 laden with geological and biological specimens and extensive meteorological data, the search for Franklin was officially over. Although the cost of discovery had been high, as Ernest Dodge wrote, "No doubt remained that the Northwest Passage existed. It had yet to be navigated." That would wait until Roald Amundsen and Gjøa in 1906.

Dodge, *Northwest by Sea.* M'Clintock, *Voyage of the "Fox" in the Arctic Seas.*

# Fram

Topsail schooner (1f/3m). *L/B/D:* 127.8′ × 34′ × 15′ (39m × 11m × 4.8m). *Tons:* 402 grt; 307 net. *Hull:* wood. *Comp.:* 16. *Mach.:* triple expansion, 220 ihp, 1 screw; 7 kts. *Des.:* Colin Archer. *Built:* Colin Archer, Larvik, Norway; 1892.

In 1879, George W. De Long's attempt to reach the North Pole ended in failure when his ship, Jeannette, became lodged in the ice for seventeen months. However, the ship's 600-mile (965-kilometer) drift in the ice from Wrangel Island north and west almost to the New Siberian Islands suggested to the Norwegian zoologist and explorer Fridtjof Nansen "that a current passes across or very near the Pole into the sea between Greenland and Spitzbergen." Nansen determined to use the current to bring him as far north as possible before setting out across the ice to reach the North Pole. To do this, he wrote,

> I propose to have a ship built as small and as strong as possible — just big enough to contain supplies of coal and provisions for twelve men for five years. . . . The main point in this vessel is that it be built on such principles as to enable it to withstand the pressure of the ice. The sides must slope sufficiently to prevent the ice, when it presses together, from getting firm hold of the hull, as was the case with the *Jeannette* and other vessels. Instead of nipping the ship, the ice must raise it up out of the water.

Nansen turned to the naval architect Colin Archer, who designed a ship that differed "essentially from any other previously known vessel." *Fram* ("Forward") was a massively built, smooth-sided, double-ended vessel shaped like a pilot boat but without a keel or sharp garboard strakes — "able to slip like an eel out of the embraces of the ice." The stem had an aggregate thickness of 4 feet (1.2 meters), the frames were 21 inches (53 centimeters) wide, and the hull planking — of thirty-year-old oak — had a maximum thickness of 13 inches (33 centimeters). The beams were reinforced with balks, stanchions, braces, and stays. Rigged as a three-masted schooner and fitted with an auxiliary engine, *Fram* carried enough coal for four months' steaming.

*Fram* sailed from the northern port of Vardö on July 21, 1893. Heading east across the Barents Sea, she passed south of Novaya Zemlya into the Kara Sea and hugged the Eurasian coast until about 135°E, when she turned north. On September 22, 1893, *Fram* lodged in the ice in about 78°43′N. As predicted, the ship was carried to the northwest until November 1895, when her course shifted to the southwest. All the while, her crew took extensive magnetic, astronomical, hydrographic, and meteorological observations, from which they determined, among other things, that the Arctic was covered not with a solid, immobile mass of ice but a continually breaking and shifting expanse of drift ice. *Fram* finally emerged from the ice on August 13, 1896, off the northwest coast of Spitzbergen, just as Nansen had predicted.

In the meantime, Nansen and Frederik Johansen had left *Fram* on March 14, 1895, when the ship lay in about 84°4′N, 102°27′E, in an effort to reach the North Pole with sleds and kayaks. By April 9 they had reached as far as 86°14′N, 95°E before their way was blocked by uneven ice and they turned south for Franz Jozef Land. Here they wintered in a cave on Frederick Jackson Island (81°30′N, 55°E) from August 1895 until May 19, 1896. On June 17, they arrived at an English camp at Cape Flora, Northbrook Island, from which they returned to Vardö in the supply schooner *Windward*. Several weeks later, the two men reunited with *Fram* and her crew at Tromsø. Despite the lack of fresh food, the extensive periods of perpetual light and dark, and the unrelenting cold — the highest monthly average temperature was about 32°F, and the lowest −35°F — the members of the Norwegian Polar Expedition remained in excellent physical and mental health. Nansen cheerfully reported how upon his arrival at Cape Flora he discovered that he had gained 22 pounds, and Johansen 13 pounds, since leaving *Fram*.

In 1898, Otto Sverdrup, who commanded the ship after Nansen left for the North Pole, took *Fram* on a three-year expedition in northwest Greenland. After exploring the west coast of Ellesmere Island and other islands, he returned to Norway with a large collection of natural history specimens.

In 1910, *Fram* was brought out of retirement by Roald Amundsen, who wanted to emulate Nansen's attempt to reach the Pole by putting his ship in the ice in the Bering Sea. When he learned that Robert Peary (based aboard the ROOSEVELT) had beaten him to the Pole, Amundsen secretly decided to make for the South Pole, a plan he revealed to his crew only when the ship was at Madeira. *Fram* arrived in the Ross Sea in January 1911, reaching 78°38′S, 163°37′W, about 870 miles from the Pole. Averaging 17 to 23 miles per day, Amundsen, Oscar Wisting, Helmer Hanssen, Sverre Hassel, and Olav Bjaaland set out across the Ross Ice Shelf with four sledges and forty-two dogs. Crossing the Queen Maud Mountains, the Norwegians became the first people to reach the South Pole, on December 16, 1911 — thirty-one days before Robert Scott's ill-fated expedition from TERRA NOVA. They returned to Framheim, their base camp, on January 25, 1912, and sailed for home five days later.

The intrepid *Fram* was later acquired by the Norsk Sjøfartsmuseum in Oslo, where she is on public display.

Amundsen, *South Pole*. Nansen, *Farthest North*. Smith, *Fram*. Sverdrup, *New Land*.

# G

## Gabriel

Bark (3m). *Tons:* 20 tons. *Hull:* wood. *Comp.:* 18. *Built:* 1576.

Following John Cabot's ill-fated second voyage to North America in 1498, European interest in a northwesterly route to the Orient was abandoned in favor of the pursuit of the Northeast Passage. But by the 1570s, there was such a mass of hearsay evidence and hypothesis that people began to think again that a Northwest Passage might exist. For the English, the primary motive for finding such a route was to capture part of the lucrative oriental spice trade from the Spanish and Portuguese. But there were those, such as Sir Humphrey Gilbert, who sought to inhabit

> part of those countries, and settle there such needy people of our country which now trouble the commonwealth and through want here at home are enforced to commit outrageous offenses, whereby they are daily consumed with the gallows.

One of the most fervent believers in the Northwest Passage was Martin Frobisher. With backing from the Muscovy Company, on June 12, 1576, he embarked in the bark *Gabriel* and sailed from Gravesend in company with the 25-ton *Michael* and a pinnace of 10 tons. A storm sank the pinnace and forced *Michael* back to England. *Gabriel* carried on and, after nearly capsizing off Greenland, sailed northwest into Davis Strait and by July 20 was off Resolution Island, between Labrador and Baffin Island. On August 11, *Gabriel* sailed into Frobisher's Bay, which, after covering 150 miles (241 kilometers) in fifteen days, Frobisher and his companions believed was a strait separating America and Asia. They noted that the people "be like to Tartars, with long black haire, broad faces, and flatte noses, and tawnie in color." Unfortunately, five of the English were kidnapped by Eskimos, and in retaliation Frobisher seized an Eskimo, who was taken back to England.

The crew also returned with iron pyrites mistakenly thought to be gold. This discovery was more than enough incentive for a second voyage, sponsored by the newly formed Adventurers to the North-West for the Discovery of the North-West Passage, or the Companye of Kathai. In 1577, *Gabriel*, now under Robert Fenton, sailed with *Michael*, Queen Elizabeth's own AID, and a company of about 155 men. Departing in mid-May, the ships arrived at Baffin Island on July 17. They returned home at the end of the summer with three Eskimos — a man, a woman, and her child, all of whom died after a month in England — and 200 tons of ore assayed (again incorrectly) as containing gold and silver. In 1578, *Gabriel* was one of fifteen ships in Frobisher's third expedition, during which his ships sailed partway into Hudson Strait. The Company of Cathay spent five years trying to smelt precious metals from iron and eventually went bankrupt; Frobisher took the blame. Creditors seized *Gabriel*, and her ultimate fate is unknown.

Hakluyt, *Principal Navigations.* Stefansson, ed., *Three Voyages of Martin Frobisher.*

## La Géographe

Corvette (3m). *Tons:* 350. *Hull:* wood. *Arm.:* 30 guns. *Built:* France; <1800.

In 1800, a French voyage of exploration was proposed, the goal of which was "to make a detailed exploration of the coasts of the southwest, the west, the northwest, and the north of New Holland [Australia], some of which are still unknown and others imperfectly known." The project was endorsed by First Consul Napoleon Bonaparte and carried the imprimatur of the veteran explorer Louis Antoine de Bougainville. Commanded by Captain Nicolas Baudin, a veteran of three other scientific voyages, the expedition included the most impressive array of scientific talent ever sent to sea — twenty-four astronomers, botanists, zoologists, mineralogists, gardeners, and draftsmen. Leaving Le Havre on October 19, 1800, La Géographe and her storeship, Naturaliste, sailed along the coast of Africa, rather than the normal, faster route, which ran southwest toward Brazil and then turned southeast for the Cape of Good Hope. As a result, it took 145 days to reach Ile de France, where forty of the crew, officers, and scientists quit the expedition, some because of illness, others because they refused to continue with the authoritarian Baudin.

Considerably behind schedule, on June 1, 1801, the ships came to Géographe Bay (which they named), near Cape Leeuwin, Australia. Turning north, the ships became separated in a storm, but Géographe landed at various points along the western coast of Australia — including Shark Bay — before heading to the Dutch settlement at Kupang, Timor, in August. (Naturaliste spent considerable time exploring the Swan River, Australia, and didn't reach Kupang until September 21.) The ships sailed on November 13, but their crews had been further depleted by scurvy, which was cured at Kupang, and dysentery, which was contracted there. The ships headed south again, and then sailed for Van Diemen's Land, arriving on January 13, 1802. Despite the recurrence of scurvy, Baudin pushed west toward Nuyts Land, though as before he was separated from Naturaliste. By the end of March, Géographe had reached the inhospitable south coast of New Holland, which the French called Terre Napoleon. On April 8, 1802, Géographe encountered Matthew Flinders's ship, HMS INVESTIGATOR, in Encounter Bay. Although Flinders gave Baudin a copy of the chart he had just completed, the French captain continued to drive his exhausted crew westward and only put about when the ship was out of fuel and water. (Flinders was later arrested at Ile de France, and before his release in 1810 the French took credit for his discoveries.) Géographe finally arrived at the British settlement at Port Jackson (Sydney) a month later.

The French were not, for the moment, at war with England. They were well cared for at the former penal colony where they were soon joined by Naturaliste. Baudin also hired a 30-ton schooner, La Casuarina, which was put under command of Lieutenant Louis de Freycinet. On November 18, 1802, the three ships sailed south again. From the Bass Strait, Naturaliste sailed direct for France with a large number of scientific specimens. Géographe and Casuarina continued a slow and deliberate survey of the south, west, and north coasts of Australia as far as Joseph Bonaparte Gulf (the name remains today) before putting in once again at Timor from May 6 to June 3. Although the crew continued to succumb to death and disease, the ships sailed with a large collection of exotic animals. After a quick sweep of the Gulf of Carpentaria, they sailed for home via Ile de France. Here Baudin himself died on September 16. Casuarina was sold and Géographe continued under Captain Pierre Milius, returning to L'Orient on March 25, 1804.

Initially condemned as a failure because of the human toll, in scientific terms the expedition was anything but. In three and a half years, they had collected "more than 100,000 samples of animals both great and small, . . . and the number of new species is more than 2,500," including two black emus that survived in captivity until 1822, at which point they were extinct in the wild. Five narratives of the voyage were published, the most important being the five-volume work by zoologist François Péron and, following his death, Freycinet.

Brosse, Great Voyages of Discovery. Dunmore, French Explorers in the Pacific.

◀ Roald Amundsen's converted fishing vessel **Gjøa** was the first vessel to transit the Northwest Passage, albeit in stages. Here she is seen at Gjøahaven, on Prince William Island in the Canadian Arctic, where she remained fast in the ice from September 12, 1903, to August 13, 1905. *Courtesy Norsk Sjøfartsmuseum, Oslo.*

## Gjøa

Sloop. *L/B/D:* 70′ × 20.6′ × 7.7′ (21.3m × 6.3m × 2.3m). *Tons:* 67 grt. *Mach.:* "Dan" engine, 13 hp, 1 screw. *Built:* Kurt Johannesson Skaale, Rosendal, Hardanger, Norway; 1872.

Under the explorer Roald Amundsen, *Gjøa* was the first ship to transit the Northwest Passage. Named for the fighting Valkyrie of the Vikings, she was built for the fishing trades, in which she worked for twenty-eight years under Captain Asbjørn Sexe of Hangesund and, from the mid-1880s, Captain H. C. Johanneson of Tromsø. Amundsen bought the shallow-draft *Gjøa* for his intended Arctic voyage in 1900 and spent the following year on trials between Norway and Greenland, after which he gave her 3-inch oak sheathing, iron strapping on the bow, and a small kerosene-fueled internal combustion engine.

On June 16, 1903, *Gjøa* sailed from Christiania (Oslo) with Amundsen and a crew of six. They anchored first at Godhavn on the west side of Greenland, where they embarked sleds, dogs, and kayaks. Crossing Melville Bay, they transited Lan-caster Sound, and descended south into Peel Sound between Somerset and Prince William Islands before anchoring at King William Island on September 12, 1903. They spent two years at Gjøahaven (68°39′N, 96°08′W) taking observations in an effort to determine the location and movement of the North Magnetic Pole. On August 13, 1905, they sailed west between continental Canada and the south shore of Victoria Island, and on August 26, off Banks Island (in what is now Amundsen Gulf), they encountered the U.S. whaler *Charles Hanson,* which had sailed from the Pacific. At this point they knew that they had transited the elusive Northwest Passage. They wintered again off King Point, during which one of the crew died. From here Amundsen trekked up the Porcupine and Yukon Rivers to Eagle, Alaska, where he telegraphed the news of his success to the world. *Gjøa* arrived in Nome on August 31, 1906, pausing briefly before pushing on to San Francisco. *Gjøa* passed through the Golden Gate on October 19 and was given a hero's welcome by the city, still recovering from the calamitous earthquake in April.

Despite an invitation to be the first ship to pass through the Panama Canal, at the instigation of the Norwegian community in San Francisco, *Gjøa* was turned over to the city and put on exhibit in Golden Gate Park. She remained there for thirty years, admired but slowly deteriorating. A reconstruction of the ship was attempted in 1939, but World War II intervened, and the work was only completed in 1949. *Gjøa* remained in San Francisco until 1974, when she was returned to Norway and exhibited at the Norsk Sjøfartsmuseum, Bigdøy, Oslo.

Amundsen, *My Life as an Explorer; Northwest Passage.* Baker, "*Gjøa.*"

# Glomar Challenger

Drill ship (1f/3m). *L/B/D:* 399.9′ × 65.3′ × 20′ (121.9m × 19.9m × 6.1m). *Tons:* 6,281 grt. *Hull:* steel. *Comp.:* 70. *Mach.:* diesel-electric, 5,100 bhp, 2 screws; 11 kts. *Built:* Levingston Shipbuilding Co., Orange, Texas; 1968.

Named in honor of the oceanographic survey vessel HMS Challenger (Glomar was an acronym for her owner, Global Marine, Inc.), the distinctive-looking *Glomar Challenger* resembled a floating oil rig, with a 45-meter-high (148-foot) lattice drill derrick situated amidships. The idea for *Glomar Challenger* arose out of the need for a way to extract core samples from the ocean floor to study the climatological and geological evolution of Earth. In the words of Cesare Emiliani, a hole bored on the seabed was necessary because

> geographical, geochemical, micropaleontological, and mineralogical analysis of the cores will yield information of great importance on the conditions prevailing on the ocean floor in the water column above, at the ocean surface, in the atmosphere, in neighboring continents, and even in outer space and in the sun, during the time of sediment deposition, that is during the past 100 × 10⁶ [100 million] years or so.

Emiliani's idea was adopted by the Joint Oceanographic Institutions for Deep Earth Sampling (JOIDES), whose members comprised the Lamont Geological Observatory, the Scripps Institution of Oceanography, the Woods Hole Oceanographic Institute, and the University of Miami, which used *Glomar Challenger* first in the Deep Sea Drilling Project, or DSDP.

The technology used in her work was that of the deep-sea drill. Rather than anchoring — an impossibility over the great depths in which she operated — *Glomar Challenger* was kept in position by a "dynamic positioning system" using sonar beacons on the ocean floor that relayed data to hydrophones aboard ship, which in turn activated bow and stern thrusters. Her complement comprised twenty-four scientists and technicians, a twelveman drilling team, and the ship's crew. The roughnecks operated the drill, which could bore a 1,000-meter-deep (3,280-foot) hole in the surface of a

4,000-meter (13,100-foot) seabed. The drill string consisted of lengths of drill pipe of between 9.5 and 28.5 meters (31.2 and 93.5 feet) in length, with a tungsten carbide tip at the working end. The only major accident occurred when about 4,000 meters of drill pipe were lost during operations in 6-meter (20-foot) seas and 50-knot winds about 150 kilometers (93 miles) south of Cape Horn, in April 1974. To compound the crew's problems, three days later the ship was seized by an Argentine gunboat whose captain suspected *Glomar Challenger* of being an illegal oil-prospecting ship.

*Glomar Challenger*'s contributions to scientific understanding were of enormous significance. From core samples retrieved on her earliest voyages — which JOIDES called "legs" — geologists were able to establish that Alfred Wegener's theory of continental drift, first advanced in about 1915 and subsequently debunked by U.S. geologists, was in fact correct. Researchers were also able to prove the theory of seafloor spreading and determine the age of the seafloor, which was put at about 38 million years. Later voyages also demonstrated that Earth's Magnetic Poles have reversed themselves repeatedly over time. During fifteen years of operation, *Glomar Challenger* operated in all the major seas of the world from the Arctic Ocean to the Ross Sea and the Mediterranean and Black Seas. After her ninety-sixth leg, in the Gulf of Mexico, *Glomar Challenger* was scrapped at Mobile in 1983.

Hsu, *Challenger at Sea*.

# Glomar Explorer (AG-193)

(ex-*Hughes Glomar Explorer*) Heavy lift ship (3m). *L/B/D:* 618.8′ × 115.7′ × 46.7′ (188.8m × 35.3m × 14.2m). *Tons:* 63,300 disp. *Hull:* steel. *Comp.:* 180. *Mach.:* diesel-electric, 13,200 bhp, 2 screws; 11 kts. *Built:* Sun Shipbuilding & Dry Dock, Chester, Pa.; 1973.

Shortly after a Soviet Golf 2-class ballistic missile submarine sank in mid-Pacific about 750 miles (1,200 kilometers) northwest of Hawaii, the Central Intelligence Agency initiated Operation Jennifer, a secret program to raise the wreck from a depth of 4,000 meters (13,100 feet). Built ostensibly for Global Marine Development, Inc., a subsidiary of Howard Hughes's Summa Corp., *Hughes Glomar Explorer* arrived at the site on July 4, 1974. Over the next month she managed to raise the forward portion of the submarine, including, it was believed, nuclear-tipped torpedoes. The main body of the submarine, which held SSN-5 ballistic missiles, was left in place. The bodies of six of the submarine's eighty-six crew were also recovered, and buried with full military honors. The project was estimated to have cost about $550 million, including the ship, personnel, and salvage equipment.

The U.S. Navy purchased and renamed *Glomar Explorer* the next year. The ship was of little use to the Navy, except for a two-year lease to Global Marine for seafloor mining, which proved unprofitable. When the survey ship GLOMAR CHALLENGER was broken up in 1983, it was thought that *Glomar Explorer* might be converted to carry on her work. The effort failed and she remained in the National Defense Reserve Fleet until 1996, when she was again converted for use as an oil-drilling rig for Global Marine.

Burleson, *Jennifer Project*. Polmar, *Ships and Aircraft of the U.S. Fleet*. Varner, *Matter of Risk*.

## Golden Hind

(ex-*Pelican*) Galleon (3m). *L/B/D:* ca. 70′ bp x 19′ × 9′ (21.3m × 5.8m × 2.7m). *Tons:* ca. 150 burden. *Hull:* wood. *Comp.:* 80–85. *Arm.:* 18 guns. *Built:* Plymouth, Eng.; 1576.

Destined to become one of the greatest seamen of all time, Francis Drake made two voyages to the Spanish Main between 1566 and 1568 in company with his kinsman John Hawkins. Although lured by the profitable slave trade and South American silver, the Protestant Drake was further motivated by a fervent anti-Catholicism. His hatred increased after the loss of *Jesus of Lübeck* to Spanish duplicity at San Juan d'Ulua in 1568. In 1576, Queen Elizabeth approved, albeit secretly, Drake's captaincy of a mission with a threefold aim: to pass through the Strait of Magellan, reconnoiter the Pacific coast of South America, and, if possible, return via the Northwest Passage; to establish relations with people not yet subject to European princes; and to plunder Spanish shipping.

Drake's command consisted of about 180 men in five ships. The flagship, *Pelican,* carried courses, topsails, and topgallants on her main- and foremasts, and a lateen-rigged mizzen. The other ships were *Elizabeth* (80 tons, 16 guns) under John Winter; *Marigold* (30 tons, 16 guns) under John Thomas; *Swan* (50 tons, 5 guns) under John Chester; and *Christopher* (15 tons, 1 gun) under Tom Moone. After a false start in November, the expedition cleared Plymouth on December 13, 1577. After stopping at Mogador, Morocco, the crew sailed for the Cape Verde Islands, capturing half a dozen Spanish ships and, more important, the Portuguese pilot Nuño da Silva. His *Santa Maria* was renamed *Mary* and put under command first of Thomas Doughty, one of several "gentlemen adventurers" on the voyage, and then of Drake himself, who exchanged *Pelican*'s command with Doughty. The latter proved a troublemaker and Drake soon relieved him of command altogether.

The ships reached the coast of southern Brazil on April 5, proceeded from there to the River Plate, and then on to Puerto San Julian where they landed on June 20. The fleet remained at anchor for a month, during which the crisis with the mutinous Doughty came to a head. Tried on the spot, Doughty was found guilty and executed in the same place that Ferdinand Magellan had executed the treasonous Gaspar de Quesada in 1520. It was here, too, that Drake delivered his celebrated sermon enjoining the "gentlemen to haul and draw with the mariner, and the mariner with the gentlemen," in order to ensure their mutual success.

After abandoning the other three ships, *Pelican, Marigold,* and *Elizabeth* put to sea on August 17. Three days later, they rounded the Cape of Virgins at the entrance to the Strait of Magellan, where Drake rechristened his ship *Golden Hind.* The choice of name was political, for the golden hind was found on the coat of arms of Sir Christopher Hatton, one of the voyage's principal backers and a friend of the late Thomas Doughty. After only fourteen days in the strait, the English flag first flew in the Pacific on September 6, 1578. The ships' luck failed when a furious storm drove them southward, costing the expedition two ships. *Marigold* was lost with her twenty-nine crew, and John Winter turned back to England. Drake, however, established that the Strait of Magellan did not separate South America from Terra Incognita Australis, as was then believed, but that its southern shore was made up of islands to the south of which lay open ocean, now known as Drake Passage.

When the storm abated, the English struck north along the unsuspecting west coast of Spanish America. Looting the small port of Valparaiso on December 5, they pressed on to Arica, where silver from the mines of Potosí was shipped to Panama. When *Golden Hind* arrived at Callao on February 15, 1579, word of the English presence had preceded them, although there was little the Spanish could do to detain them. Learning that a treasure ship had sailed only three days before, Drake took off in pursuit and on March 1 captured *Nuestra Señora de la Concepción* — nicknamed the *Cacafuego* — off Cape Francisco, Colombia. Sailing out of the main coastal shipping lane, the English transshipped 80 pounds of gold and 26 tons of silver bars with a value of about £126,000 — or about half the English Crown's revenues for a year. Although chiefly interested in returning home with their treasure intact, the English captured a few more ships, and their crews were almost unanimous in their respect for Drake's gentility and fairness. Their greatest concern was over his drawings of the coastline, which seemed to suggest that more English would follow, "for everything is depicted so naturally that anyone who uses these paintings as a guide cannot possibly go astray."

In searching for the Strait of Anian, or Northwest Passage, Drake sailed as far as 48°N — just south of the Strait of Juan de Fuca — before turning south. On June 17, 1579, *Golden Hind* anchored in 38°30′N at a "convenient and fit harbor" generally thought to be Drake's Bay, on Point Reyes, California, just north of San Francisco Bay. Drake's dealings with the natives were characteristically evenhanded, and the English found "a goodly countrye, and fruitfull soyle, stored with

▲ A replica of the **Golden Hind,** the galleon in which Sir Francis Drake encompassed the world on the first circumnavigation by an English ship. *Photo by Beken of Cowes.*

many blessings fit for the use of man" — fit even to be called New Albion and claimed for her majesty.

On July 25, *Golden Hind* sailed west across the Pacific, making no landfall until September 30, when she landed in either the Palau or Ladrones Islands. By October 16 she was off Mindanao Island in the Philippines, from where she turned south for the Moluccas. The king of Ternate had recently thrown out the Portuguese, but he allowed Drake to load spices and refit his ship. After a month preparing for the last leg of their journey home, the expedition sailed on December 12 but spent a month in the maze of islands and shoals in the Indonesian archipelago. On January 9, 1580, *Golden Hind* struck a coral reef and was held fast for a day before the wind shifted and she slid into deep water. After watering his ship at Tjilatjap on the south coast of Java (previously thought to be connected to Terra Australis), Drake weighed anchor on March 26. A nonstop journey of over 9,700 miles — remarkable for its lack of incident — brought *Golden Hind* to Sierra Leone on July 22. The first English circumnavigation of the globe ended on September 26, 1580, when *Golden Hind* sailed into Plymouth after a voyage of two years, ten months, and eighteen days with fifty-nine of her crew aboard, a great achievement given the record of many later voyages.

Cautioned to lie low while the diplomatic consequences of his voyage were considered at London, Drake was finally received by Queen Elizabeth. On April 4, 1581, Drake was knighted on the decks of *Golden Hind* at Deptford. Elizabeth also ordered the ship displayed in dry dock, and the intrepid ship remained on public view until the 1660s.

Hampden, *Francis Drake Privateer.* Sugden, *Sir Francis Drake.*

# La Grande Hermine

Ship (3m). *L/B/D:* 78.8′ × 25′ × 12′ dph (24m × 7.6m × 3.7m). *Tons:* 120 tons. *Hull:* wood. *Built:* France; <1535.

French fishermen reached the Grand Banks off Newfoundland early in the sixteenth century, but the first French voyage of exploration was dispatched in 1524. In a commission for François I, Giovanni da Verrazzano sailed LA DAUPHINE along the coast of North America from North Carolina to Newfoundland. The French did not follow up on this pioneering effort for another decade. In 1534, François I commissioned Jacques Cartier to sail with two ships (their names are not known) on a voyage that took him along the coast of Newfoundland, through the Strait of Belle Isle, to the northern coast of New Brunswick, where he embarked two sons of the Indian chief Donna-

conna for the return to France. So promising were the results of this voyage that the king renewed his commission and Cartier was given three ships to make a second voyage "to explore beyond *les Terres Neufves* [and] to discover certain far-off countries." The latter referred specifically to Cathay, which, it was hoped, could be reached via the Northwest Passage.

Cartier's ships on this voyage were *La Grande Hermine* (120 tons), *La Petite Hermine* (60 tons), and the pinnace *L'Emerillon* (40 tons). They sailed from Saint Malo in May 1535 and on August 10 put into a small bay on the southern coast of Labrador that Cartier named for Saint Lawrence, whose feast day it was. This name eventually applied to the Gulf of St. Lawrence and the river that flows from Lake Ontario past Montreal and Quebec, but Cartier simply called it La Grande Rivière. Lured by descriptions of the riches of the mythical kingdom of Saguenay, Cartier sailed up the St. Lawrence and eventually reached Donnaconna's village near present-day Quebec City. From there he continued west with *L'Emerillon* as far as Lac Saint-Pierre, and with his longboats touched the village of Hochalega under the hill he called Mont Royal (Montreal). His way barred by rapids, he returned to Quebec for the winter. The following spring, Cartier kidnapped Donnaconna and several of his tribesmen so that they could relate their tales of Saguenay directly to the French king.

War with Spain postponed the launch of a new expedition until 1541. On May 23, Cartier sailed with *La Grande Hermine* (which François I had given to him), *L'Emerillon,* and three other ships as part of an ambitious attempt to establish a French colony in Canada and reach Saguenay. Donnaconna had died in France and Cartier's reception was not as warm as it had been previously. The French established a fort at Charlesbourg-Royal, and during the winter thirty-five of their company were killed in Indian attacks. A second fleet, under Sieur de Roberval, was supposed to have joined them, but in May Cartier's group sailed alone for France. They met up with Roberval at St. John's, Newfoundland, but Cartier refused to turn back, and continued to France. The riches of Saguenay with which they returned proved to be nothing more than iron ore and quartz.

Although the lack of material success and a half century of civil war prevented France from mounting further expeditions to Canada, fishermen and trappers continued to visit the area throughout the sixteenth century. The next French voyages of political significance would be those in which Samuel de Champlain took part between 1603 and 1635. Although few details of *La Grande Hermine* survive, a full-size model was made for Canada's Expo '67. The dimensions given here are based on that model, which is on display at the Cartier-Brebeuf Park in Quebec.

Morison, *European Discovery of America: The Northern Voyages.*

## Le Griffon

Brig. *Tons:* 45–60 tons. *Hull:* wood. *Comp.:* 34. *Arm.:* 5 guns. *Built:* René-Robert Cavalier, Sieur de La Salle, New York; 1679.

Although French explorers had reached the western Great Lakes as early as 1634, they traveled in canoes or on foot. It was not until 1679 that René-Robert Cavalier, Sieur de La Salle, built the first sailing ship on the upper lakes, near the junction of Cayuga Creek and the Niagara River at the eastern end of Lake Erie in what is now New York State. Work was completed in midsummer and the brig was christened *Le Griffon,* for the heraldic device of the Comte de Frontenac, governor general of New France. On August 7, 1679, the ship set sail for the west in search of a water route to the Orient. The crew of thirty-four included La Salle and the Jesuit diarist Father Louis Hennepin. In three days *Le Griffon* crossed the length of Lake Erie and turned north into the Detroit River, Lake St. Clair, St. Clair River, and Lake Huron. After weathering a violent fall storm on Lake Huron, *Le Griffon* came to a Jesuit mission on Michilimackinac Bay, off the Straits of Mackinac, and proceeded from there to a trading post on the shores of Green Bay. There La Salle, Hennepin, and a few others left the ship, which was then loaded for the return voyage. On September 18, *Le Griffon* sailed for the east, but she was never seen again.

Braynard, *Famous American Ships.*

# H

## Halve Maen

Vlieboat (3m). *L/B/D:* 65′ lod × 17.3′ × 8′ (19.8m × 5.3m × 2.4m). *Tons:* 80 om. *Hull:* wood. *Comp.:* 17–20. *Built:* Dutch East India Company, Amsterdam; 1608.

In the early 1600s, Dutch merchants decided to consolidate their efforts to expand trade to the East by forming the Verenigde Oostindische Compagnie (VOC, or United East India Company). Eager to find a short route to the Indies, they took up the search for a Northeast Passage. Shortly after the failed Willem Barents expedition, the VOC contracted with the English explorer Henry Hudson "to search for a passage by the north around the north side of Nova Zembla, and . . . continue thus along that parallel until he shall be able to sail southward to the latitude of 60 degrees." An amendment to the contract enjoined Hudson "to think of no other route or passage, except the route around the north or northeast, above Nova Zembla. . . . If it cannot be accomplished at that time, another route will be the subject of consideration for another voyage."

The vessel chosen was the bark-rigged *Halve Maen,* a relatively flat-bottomed merchant vessel designed for the shallow waters around Vlieland and The Texel at the mouth of the Zuyder Zee. The ship sailed on March 25, 1609, and after rounding the North Cape on May 5, she entered the Barents Sea. Two weeks later, Hudson abandoned his eastward search. Turning west, on the twenty-first the ship redoubled the North Cape. Rather than return to Holland, Hudson sailed for the Faeroe Islands, where he watered his ship before continuing west. In early July *Halve Maen* encountered a fleet of French fishing boats on the Grand Banks off Newfoundland. On July 12 she was off Nova Scotia and

a week later the crew landed at the southern end of Penobscot Bay, where they cut and stepped a new foremast. Turning south, they stopped at Cape Cod, which Bartholomew Gosnold had named during his 1602 visit in CONCORD. Continuing south and southwest, they arrived off the mouth of Chesapeake Bay on August 18. Although the Jamestown settlement — founded two years before on the James River — was known to Hudson, he did not enter the bay.

On August 27 they were at the mouth of the Delaware (or South) River and seven days later anchored off Sandy Hook, New Jersey. Relations with the Indians were generally good, although one of the ship's company was killed while exploring lower New York Bay on September 5. The surroundings were bountiful, and Hudson wrote that "it is as pleasant a land as one need tread upon; very abundant in all kinds of timber suitable for shipbuilding, and for making large casks or vats." On September 13, *Halve Maen* began a four-day, 147-mile (237-kilometer) ascent of the North (or Hudson) River as far as the site of present-day Albany. North of that, the river had a maximum depth of only seven feet (2.1 meters). Of the surrounding countryside Hudson observed,

> The land is the finest for cultivation that I ever in my life set foot upon, and it also abounds in trees of every description. The natives are very good people, for when they saw that I would not remain, they supposed that I was afraid of their bows, and taking the arrows, they broke them in pieces, and threw them into the fire.

Turning south on September 23, the ship's mate killed an Indian who tried to steal some clothes out of the stern cabin. A more serious incident off

▲ It was in just such lithe, small vessels as the wish-bone-sailed **Hawai'iloa** that early Polynesians peopled the widely spaced islands of the Pacific. *Courtesy Bishop Museum, Honolulu.*

Manna-hata (Manhattan) on October 2 resulted in the death of four or five Indians who attacked the ship.

On October 4, *Halve Maen* sailed out of New York Bay and after thirty-three days at sea landed at Dartmouth, England. Hudson's decision to stop in England has led some to speculate that he was actually in the pay of English merchants to whom he intended to report his findings. In the event, *Halve Maen* was kept at Dartmouth until after Hudson had sailed on his next and last expedition in search of the Northwest Passage in DISCOVERY. In 1610, *Halve Maen* was returned to the VOC, together with the ship's papers, though the Dutch crews' reports had already spurred Holland to establish trading posts in the Great River of the Mountains, as Hudson's mate Robert Juet described the Hudson River.

In 1611, *Halve Maen* was dispatched to the East Indies under command of Captain Laureus Reale. Her subsequent fate is not known with certainty, and various reports indicate that she was wrecked off Mauritius in the same year, that she was lost off Sumatra in 1616, or that she was burned at Sumatra by the British in 1618. Two important replicas of *Halve Maen* have been built. The first was built in the Netherlands for the Hudson-Fulton Celebration in New York in 1909, and the second by the New York–based New Netherland festival.

Asher, *Henry Hudson the Navigator.* Hendricks, "Construction of the 1988 *Half Moon*." Johnson, *Charting the Sea of Darkness.*

## Hawai'iloa

Polynesian voyaging canoe (2m). *L/B:* 57' × 19' (17.4m × 5.8m). *Tons:* 17,725 pounds. *Hull:* wood. *Comp.:* 12. *Des.:* Dick Rhodes, Rudy and Barry Choy. *Built:* Wright Bowman, Jr., Honolulu; 1993.

Named for the legendary Polynesian voyager who first discovered the Hawaiian Islands some 2,000 years ago and who is the ancestor to all native Hawaiians, *Hawai'iloa* is a replica of the traditional voyaging canoes used by Polynesian islanders in their settlement of Oceania. The largest such canoe built in the twentieth century, *Hawai'iloa* has two hulls shaped from Alaskan spruce logs. (Larger Hawaiian canoes were often made of drift logs that washed ashore on the islands.) The hulls are joined by seven crossbeams fashioned from 'Ohio logs and each hull is built up of koa wood. The sole source of power is two V-shaped, or wishbone, sails. Built to reenact the long-distance voyages of the Polynesians, *Hawai'iloa* is navigated by the traditional practice of "wayfinding." This is based on an intimate knowledge of such natural phenomena as the movements of the sun and stars, wind and wave patterns, the color of the sky, and seamarks, including birds or fish with particular attributes.

On February 6, 1995, *Hawai'iloa* embarked on her first major voyage from Hawaii to Papeete, Tahiti, a distance of 2,400 miles (3,860 kilometers) covered in less than twenty-two days. The voyage out was made in company with the Polynesian Voyaging Society's first vessel, the 62-foot (100-meter) *Hokule'a* ("Star of Gladness," the Hawaiian name for the star Arcturus), built in 1976. They then sailed to Raiatea, 150 miles (240 kilometers) east of Tahiti, for a gathering of traditional craft; the other vessels were the Hawaiian *Makali'i*, the Maori *Te 'Aurere*, and the Cook Islanders' *Te 'Au o Tonga* and *Takitumu*. Following a rededication of the temple of Taputapuatea, a primary center of Polynesian voyaging 600 years ago, the canoes sailed from the Society Islands northeast to Nuku Hiva in the Marquesas Islands (thought to be where Hawai'iloa originally came from) and then back to Hawaii. *Hawai'iloa*'s second major voyage came in the summer of 1995, when, again in company with *Hokule'a*, she sailed to the Pacific Northwest for a reunion with the Tlingit and Haida of southern Alaska, who donated the spruce logs for *Hawai'iloa*'s hull.

Finney, *Voyage of Rediscovery*.

# HMS Hecla

*Hecla*-class bomb vessel (3m). *L/B/D:* 105' × 28.5' × 13.8' (32m × 8.7m × 4.2m). *Tons:* 372 bm. *Hull:* wood. *Comp.:* 67. *Arm.:* 1 × 13" mortar, 1 × 10" mortar, 8 × 24pdr, 2 × 6pdr. *Des.:* Sir Henry Peake. *Built:* Barkworth & Hawkes, North Barton, Hull, Eng.; 1815.

Launched one week after the surrender of Napoleon Bonaparte at Waterloo, Belgium, on July 15, 1815, HMS *Hecla* was designed for war but was born at the start of the near-century-long Pax Britannica. Although there were few opportunities for men or ships in the peacetime navy, such heavily constructed bomb vessels (her sister ships included HMS EREBUS, *Sulphur,* and *Fury*) were ideally suited for voyages of exploration. In 1819 *Hecla* was fitted out for an Arctic expedition under William Edward Parry, who had sailed as second-in-command to John Ross's expedition with ISABELLA and *Alexander* the year before. Chief among his assignments was to determine whether Lancaster Sound was open, of which Parry was certain, or only an inlet, as Ross believed. Parry sailed from Yarmouth on May 11, 1819, with the ships *Hecla* and *Griper* on the first of his three voyages to the Arctic. By August 1, the two ships were completely through Lancaster Sound, which separates Baffin and Devon Islands, and after a detour south into Prince Regent Inlet, they continued through and named Barrow Strait and Melville Strait as far as 112°51'W. They backtracked a little to Winter Harbour, at the southern end of Melville Island, and on September 22 settled in for the winter. Parry's men suffered no unusual hardship, and in the spring Parry led a two-week expedition to Melville Island, north to the shore of Hecla and Griper Bay, and then south again via the head of Liddon Gulf. On August 1, 1820, they left Winter Harbour and continued west as far as 113°46'W (August 15) and named the land to the southwest in honor of Sir Joseph Banks. The ships returned to England at the end of October and Parry was lionized for having traversed half of the Northwest Passage. The next ship to make it so far west in one season would be the 940-foot (287-meter) icebreaker-tanker MANHATTAN, in 1969.

Parry was adamant in his belief that "should another Expedition be determined on, the attempt must be made in a lower latitude; perhaps about Hudson's or Cumberland Straits." He further cautioned that "*because* so great has been our late success, . . . nothing short of the entire accomplishment of the North-West Passage in to the Pacific will satisfy the Public." Nonetheless, in May 1821 *Hecla* and her sister ship *Fury* sailed for Hudson Bay, annually visited by ships of the Hudson's Bay Company, but seldom explored. The ships traversed Hudson Strait and turned northwest along the coast of Baffin Island and across Foxe Channel to the southern end of Melville Peninsula (nearly 600 miles southeast of Melville Island of the year before). After exploring around Southampton Island, they wintered at Winter Island. The next spring, Parry resumed the search for the Northwest Passage, bringing his ships to the northern end of Foxe Basin, where the perennially frozen Hecla and Fury Strait leads west into the Gulf of Boothia. A second winter near an Eskimo settlement on Melville Peninsula brought the English into close contact with the Eskimos, from whom they learned the use of sled dogs and Arctic survival techniques, and who were also able to draw rough maps of the region. Parry's men also conducted scientific observations. The persistence of ice in Hecla and Fury Strait and the onset of scurvy persuaded Parry to return to England in 1823, and the ships arrived in the Shetland Islands in October.

No sooner had he returned than plans were forwarded for a third expedition. Before sailing, Parry was made Acting Hydrographer of the Navy, and more than 6,000 people visited *Hecla* when she was open to the public at Deptford until her next departure, on May 8, 1824. Parry's third expedition returned him to Lancaster Sound, but rather than continue due west, once past the Brodeur Peninsula (the western arm of Baffin Island), they were to turn south into Prince Regent Inlet. This was a bad year for ice, however, and the ships were beset for two months before they entered Lancaster Sound. They resumed their westward progress again only to be caught in the ice at the head of Prince Regent Inlet and driven back almost to the mouth of Lancaster Sound. This ice broke up, too, and the ships sailed as far as Port Bowen, on the western shore of the inlet. During the winter there, they concentrated on the problem of magnetic variation. On August 1, 1825, the ships searched in vain for westward leads in the Gulf of Boothia and were driven ashore by the ice. The badly damaged *Fury* was unloaded and hove down for repairs. Before these could be finished, the ship was further damaged by ice and was abandoned on August 25, at which point *Hecla* turned for England.

Though this was the last of *Hecla*'s voyages to the Canadian Arctic, in March 1827 Parry took her north again in an attempt to reach the North Pole. Anchoring *Hecla* at Sorgfjord in northern West Spitsbergen, on June 21 he set out with twenty-four men in two boats with provisions for seventy-one days. The ice conditions, heavy loads, and spartan diet prevented them from making much progress, and the drifting ice was also pushing them south. On July 21, having reached 82°43'N, 19°21'E, they decided to abandon the effort about 500 miles from the Pole. They returned to *Hecla* and turned for home in August.

Over Parry's objections, *Hecla* was withdrawn from Arctic service and dispatched as a survey vessel to the coast of West Africa. She remained in service there through 1831, when she was sold.

Parry, *Journal of a Voyage for the Discovery of a North-West Passage . . . ; Journal of a Second Voyage . . . ; Journal of a Third Voyage . . . ; Narrative of an Attempt to Reach the North Pole. . . .* Parry, *Parry of the Arctic.*

# Heemskerck

Jacht (3m). *Tons:* 120 tons (60 lasts). *Hull:* wood. *Comp.:* 60. *Built:* Dutch East India Company, Netherlands; <1638.

In August 1642, the expansionist Governor General of the Indies, Anthonie Van Diemen, ordered Abel Jansen Tasman and Franchoys Jacobsen Visscher "to discover the partly known and still unreached South and Easternland" (that is, Australia), not for the sake of geography or science, but specifically "for the improvement, and increase of the [Dutch East India] Comp[an]y's general welfare." Two primary aims were to determine whether there was a passage from the Indian Ocean to the Pacific Ocean — which would allow for an increase in trade with Peru and Chile — and to search for the elusive passage to the Pacific south of New Guinea. To undertake this mission, Tasman was given two vessels, the war jacht *Heemskerck* (named for a Dutch explorer and naval hero), which had sailed out to the Indies in 1638, and the *fluit*, or transport, *Zeehaen.*

On August 14, 1642, the ships left Batavia (Djakarta) for Mauritius, where they spent a month repairing *Zeehaen*'s rotten spars and rigging. On October 8, they sailed south to about 50°S before heading east. On November 17, they arrived off "Anthonie Van Diemensland" — later Tasmania — where they landed several times and saw smoke, but no people, and claimed the land for the Netherlands and the Dutch East India Company (Verenigde Oostindische Compagnie, or VOC). Unable to sail west through the Bass Strait, they turned east again and after eight days in the Tasman Sea came to the South Island of New Zealand, which Tasman thought a continuation of Staten Island off Cape Horn, some 5,000 to 6,000 miles (8,000 to 9,600 kilometers) to the east. Accordingly, they named it Statenland. Heading north, on December 18 four of the crew were killed by Maoris in Murderer's Bay. From here they sailed east and almost passed through Cook Strait, but adverse weather and seas prevented them from making this singular discovery of the Pacific. They tried but were unable to land near Cape Maria Van Diemen (which they named for the wife of the Governor General). They then headed northeast, believing themselves to have entered the Pacific — as indeed they had — at last. But Van Diemen later disagreed, and wrote to the VOC that "whether on this longitude there now exists a passage through to Chile and Peru, as the discoverers are firmly convinced, is not so sure. . . . This is conjecture and should not be deduced from unfounded evidence."

On January 21, 1643, they provisioned at Tongatapu in the Tonga Archipelago. On February 1, they turned north and then west, when they narrowly missed losing their ships among the reefs of the Fiji Archipelago. Over the next seven weeks they sailed only 300 miles, but on March 22 they spotted Onthong Java. From here they followed Schouten and Le Maire's 1616 route in EENDRACHT. The voyage ended at Batavia on June 15, 1643. Although Tasman had established that the "Southland" — Australia — was an island, he had discovered nothing of the land per se, which was disappointing to the merchant directors of the VOC, who were eager for new markets.

Sharp, *Voyages of Abel Janszoon Tasman.* Tasman, *Abel Janszoon Tasman's Journal.*

# L'Hérétique

Raft (1m). *L/B/D:* 15.4' × 6.2' × 1.6' (4.7m × 1.9m × 0.5m). *Hull:* rubber. *Comp.:* 1. *Built:* M. Debroutelle, France; 1953.

In the early 1950s, the French surgeon Dr. Alain Bombard became interested in the problems associated with survival at sea. Despair, he believed, is "a far more ruthless and efficient killer than any physical factor." Conversely, the morale of the shipwreck victim is as vital to survival as is the need for food and water. Analyzing the nutritional composition of seawater, plankton, and pelagic fish, Bombard determined that as a last resort, seawater can be drunk in small quantities for short periods, that plankton is a source of vitamin C, and that potable water — as well as protein — can be extracted from fish. Taking his experiments outside the laboratory, he set out on a transatlantic voyage in a rubber raft fitted with a single sail and named, in honor of his unorthodox methods, *L'Hérétique.*

Starting in southern France, he made a number of short passages before reaching the Canary Islands, which he departed from on October 18, 1952. Subsisting on raw fish, plankton caught in a fine net, and rainwater, Bombard confirmed that his biggest obstacle was not physical but mental. His body adjusted to its new diet, but to combat his solitude, he maintained a rigorous daily routine that included checking the raft for potential leaks, exercising, and writing up his log and a record of his pulse and blood pressure. Because of a colossal navigation error, Bombard underestimated the time needed to reach the West Indies by several weeks, which he only realized after a chance encounter with a British freighter when he was fifty-three days out from the Canaries and 600 miles east of Barbados. After ninety minutes aboard the *Arakaka*, during which he had a shower and a light meal (at which his body later revolted), he resumed his voyage. On December 22, he fetched up at Barbados.

After sixty-five days at sea, Bombard had lost 55 pounds, he was anemic, and he suffered from a variety of minor ailments, from which he quickly recovered. He suffered from neither dehydration nor scurvy, the latter having been prevented by his intake of vitamin C in plankton. Bombard's voyage revolutionized the study of survival techniques worldwide, and he continued his research into the physiopathology of sailors. In recognition of Bombard's achievement, *L'Hérétique* was exhibited at the Musée de la Marine in Paris.

Bombard, *Voyage of the "Hérétique."*

# Hero

Sloop (1m). *L/B/D:* 47.3′ × 16.8′ × 6.3′ (14.4m × 5.1m × 1.9m). *Tons:* 44 om. *Hull:* wood. *Built:* Groton, Conn.; 1800.

In 1819, the British sealer William Smith discovered the South Shetland Islands and their abundant rookeries of seals, whose pelts fetched high prices in China. Reports of the discovery spread quickly, and in the same year the first U.S. sealers sailed from Stonington, Connecticut. In 1820, the Americans returned with a fleet of five ships, including Captain Nathaniel B. Palmer's *Hero,* whose crew included the discoverer and author Edmund Fanning. The ships were based at Deception Island, and after hearing reports of mountains to the south, the expedition leader Captain Benjamin Pendleton sent Palmer to investigate further. In November 1820, *Hero* sailed south and west until he approached what he took to be a continuous, snow-capped landmass. There were no seals on the nearby islands, which made their further investigation unprofitable, and Palmer sailed for the South Shetlands. On his return he encountered the Rus-

sian navigator Baron Fabian Gottlieb von Bellingshausen, who was exploring the Southern Ocean in Vostok and *Mirny*. Bellingshausen later reported Palmer's discovery and gave Palmer's name to the land now known as the Antarctic Peninsula. *Hero* made a second voyage to the South Shetland sealing grounds in 1821–22, after which she was sold at Coquimbo, Chile.

Fanning, *Voyages around the World*. Stackpole, *Voyage of the Huron and the Huntress.*

# Hokule'a

Voyaging canoe (2m). *L:* 62′ (18.9m). Hull: wood and fiberglass. Comp.: 13–15. *Built:* Hawaii; 1976.

In 1976, the Polynesian Voyaging Society was founded to study how Polynesian seafarers colonized the Pacific islands. One of three culturally distinct island groups of Oceania, Polynesia covers a triangular area of more than 7 million square miles (18.1 million square kilometers). The region is described by a line drawn from Hawaii in the north to New Zealand in the southwest (approximately 4,500 miles or 7,200 kilometers) to Easter Island — Rapa Nui — in the east (4,000 miles or 6,400 kilometers) and back to Hawaii (4,000 miles). The westernmost islands of Polynesia — Samoa and Tonga — were settled in about 1000 BCE. About 500 years later, Tahiti was colonized, and over the course of the next 1,000 years, Polynesians spread out to Easter Island in the east and Hawaii in the north. By about the year 1000, New Zealand had also been reached.

This sequence was established through a complex study of oral traditions, a fragmentary archaeological record, and plant and animal migration (ethnobotany and ethnozoology). That the islanders were accomplished navigators has long been an established fact. During Captain James Cook's first voyage of exploration, in HMS Endeavour, Joseph Banks recorded that the Tahitian Tupia could locate scores of remote islands and that journeys of twenty days were not uncommon. Europeans also described in words and pictures the types of boats they encountered all over the Pacific. Whereas slender outrigger canoes were used for fishing and short trips, longer voyages were made in double-hulled voyaging canoes capable of carrying large numbers of people and provisions. What was less well understood was how Polynesians navigated without instruments.

In order to gain a better understanding of how the first people came to Hawai'i, the Polynesian Voyaging Society built a voyaging canoe rigged in traditional fashion with two V-shaped "wishbone" sails. Their first voyage using traditional "way-finding" navigation was from Hawai'i to Tahiti. Wayfinding is based on the systematic observation of the ocean environment, meteorology, and astronomy. Factors to be considered in navigation include the rising and setting of the stars and planets at the horizon, the shape of sea swells, the direction of waves and currents, where certain species of fish or sea mammals are found, and the flight paths of birds.

These skills had all but died out in Polynesia, and for the first voyage the Society had to enlist the services of Mau Piailug, a wayfinder from the atoll of Satawal in the Caroline Islands, which is part of Micronesia. The first voyage, conducted as part of the celebration of the United States Bicentennial, was from Hawai'i to Tahiti, a distance of about 2,400 miles (3,900 kilometers).

Departing from Honolua Bay, Maui, on May 1, 1976, after weeks of calms and head winds in the Northeast Trades, Hokule'a crossed the Equator and, riding the Southeast Trades, made the atoll of Mata'iva in the Tuamotu Archipelago thirty-one days out from Hawaii. After two days on the island, they put out again and reached Tahiti on June 3, thirty-four days after departing from Maui. Although the completion of the voyage without recourse to modern navigational techniques and instruments, the trip was marred by differences between the native Hawaiians in the crew, for whom the voyage had enormous symbolic significance, and the non-Polynesians, for whom the exercise was little more than a scientific experiment. As a result of these tensions, Mau Piailug returned home directly, and the Hokule'a returned to Hawaii with a crew using modern navigation techniques. Nonetheless, the trip from Hawaii to Tahiti

signaled the start of a renaissance in Polynesian seafaring.

In 1980, Hokule'a sailed again to Tahiti, this time under the navigator Nainoa Thompson, who had studied under May Piailug. Hawaiian contact with the rest of Polynesia is believed to have stopped about five centuries ago, so Thompson is probably the first Hawaiian to captain a voyaging canoe using wayfinding in the past 500 years. Five years later, Hokule'a embarked on a two-year "Voyage of Rediscovery," during which she sailed 16,000 miles (26,000 kilometers) along various routes within the Polynesian Triangle and called in at the Society and Cook Islands, New Zealand, Tonga, Samoa, Tahiti, and the Tuamotus. This voyage showed that it was possible for Polynesian canoes to sail from west to east in the Pacific when the prevailing easterly trade winds were replaced by seasonal westerlies.

A large number of voyaging canoes representing different traditions have been built throughout Polynesia, and Hokule'a was one of sixteen canoes that sailed to Rarotonga to participate in the Sixth Pacific Arts Festival in 1992. The next year, the voyaging canoe HAWAI'ILOA was built entirely of wood, and after a voyage to the Marquesas, from which Hawaii is believed to have been settled in about 500, in 1995 the two canoes were shipped to Seattle. Hawai'iloa sailed to Alaska, for a voyage of thanks to the Tlingit, Haida, and Tshimshian Indians who had contributed the wood for her construction, while Hokule'a sailed down the coast to San Diego. On June 15, 1999, Hokule'a embarked on its most difficult voyage to date, a 14,000-mile (22,500-kilometer) trip from Hawaii to Easter Island — Rapa Nui — and back. Sailing from Hawaii, they reached Nukahiva in the Marquesas on July 13, Mangareva (sailing August 2 and arriving August 29) and Rapa Nui (September 21–October 9). En route home they sailed via Tahiti (November 9–December 3), and left there February 5 to reach Hawaii on February 29.

Finney, "Hokule'a"; Voyage of Rediscovery. Polynesian Voyaging Society.

# I

## HMS Investigator

(ex-*Xenophon*) Ship-sloop (3m). *L/B:* 100.5′ × 28.5′ (30.6m × 8.7m). *Tons:* 334 bm. *Hull:* wood. *Built:* Sunderland, Eng.; 1795.

In 1798, Matthew Flinders served as lieutenant of HMS *Norfolk* during George Bass's expedition along the southeast coast of Australia, during which the ship passed through Bass Strait to confirm that Tasmania was an island. Three years later, Flinders applied to Sir Joseph Banks for support in mounting a voyage around Australia. The Admiralty endorsed the plan and Flinders was supplied with *Xenophon,* a stout North Country ship that "in form resembled the description of vessels recommended by Captain Cook as best calculated for voyages of discovery."

Departing Spithead on July 18, 1801, the renamed HMS *Investigator* called at the Cape of Good Hope before setting out across the Indian Ocean. *Investigator* arrived off Cape Leeuwin at the southwest corner of Australia on December 6. After putting into King George Sound, the expedition began a running survey of the Great Australian Bight, which stretched 3,200 kilometers (2,000 miles) to Spencer Gulf. Among the other objects of their search was a passage that led north to the Gulf of Carpentaria, for Australia was then believed to be divided by a strait. At the entrance to Spencer Gulf, seven of the ship's company were lost when a small boat capsized. Flinders surveyed Port Lincoln, which he named for his home county. Working their way east, *Investigator*'s crew next charted Kangaroo Island, Yorke Peninsula, and St. Vincent Gulf. On April 8, at Encounter Bay, they were surprised to meet LA GÉOGRAPHE under Nicolas Baudin, with whom Flinders had several

cordial meetings, despite the fact that their two countries were then at war. Sailing eastward through Bass Strait, Flinders visited King Island and Port Philip (Melbourne) before arriving at Port Jackson (Sydney) on May 9.

*Investigator* took aboard twelve new men, including an aborigine named Bongaree, with whom Flinders had sailed previously and who served as an intermediary with other aborigines encountered on the voyage. The expedition was also joined by *Lady Nelson,* a centerboard brig designed for surveying in shallow water; she proved a sluggish sailor and eventually returned to Port Jackson. Following in the wake of Cook's ENDEAVOUR, *Investigator* hugged the east coast of Australia before passing through the Great Barrier Reef and then transiting Torres Strait, which Flinders had previously sailed through with Captain William Bligh in HMS *Providence.* While surveying the Gulf of Carpentaria, *Investigator*'s timbers were found to be in a dismal state, and the ship's carpenter reported that the ship would not last much more than six months. Flinders sailed to the Dutch settlement on Timor, but as there was no prospect of obtaining another ship, he decided to sail westabout around Australia for Port Jackson, setting "all possible sail day and night" and reluctantly abandoning his survey of the north and west coasts.

*Investigator* reached Port Jackson in June 1803 and Flinders sailed for home in the storeship *Porpoise,* only to be shipwrecked on the Great Barrier Reef. Placed in command of *Cumberland,* he was forced to put into Ile de France, not knowing that England and France were again at war. Detained until 1810, he returned to England broken in health and lived barely long enough to see his memoirs in print. Meanwhile, *Investigator* had been repaired and returned to England; she was hulked in 1810.

Flinders, *Voyage to Terra Australis.* Ritchie, *Admiralty Chart.*

## HMS Investigator

Ship (3m). *L/B/D:* 118' × 28.3' × 18.9' (36m × 8.6m × 5.8m). *Tons:* 422 bm. *Hull:* wood. *Comp.:* 66. *Built:* Charles Scott & Co., Greenock, Scotland; 1848.

On May 12, 1848, Sir James Clark Ross led the Admiralty's first expedition in search of HMS EREBUS and TERROR. The very same ships with which he had spent four years exploring Antarctica were now lost in the Canadian Arctic under command of Sir John Franklin. HMS *Investigator* and *Enterprise* sailed through Lancaster Sound and Barrow Strait to Somerset Island; from here sledges were dispatched in search of Franklin. On one of them, Ross and Francis L. M'Clintock descended Peel Sound to within 70 miles (115 kilometers) of *Erebus* and *Terror* before they were forced to turn back. After only one winter, *Investigator* and *Enterprise* returned to England in 1849.

On January 31, 1850, Captain Richard Collinson, in *Enterprise,* and Lieutenant Robert McClure, in *Investigator,* sailed from England in an attempt to discover whether Franklin's ships had actually completed the Northwest Passage. The ships rounded Cape Horn and were separated in the Pacific. Rather than wait for Collinson at Bering Strait, McClure sailed *Investigator* east into the Beaufort Sea and then northeast into the Prince of Wales Strait between Banks Island and Victoria Island, but by September *Investigator* was fast in the ice. In October, McClure set out by sledge up the strait to the shore of Viscount Melville Sound, to which William E. Parry had sailed in HMS HECLA in 1819–20, and thereby confirmed the existence of a Northwest Passage, however choked with ice.

The next season, McClure worked *Investigator* south and around the western and northern shores of Banks Island, through McClure Strait toward Melville Sound. Heavy ice prevented their making for Winter Harbour, about 175 miles (280 kilometers) to the east, and on September 23, 1851, *Investigator* put into Mercy Bay on northeast Banks Island. In 1852, a sledging expedition visited Winter Harbour and left a note describing the desperate situation at Mercy Bay, where the ship's crew was subsisting on daily rations of a half pound of beef and twelve ounces of flour. The note was discovered by the crew of HMS RESOLUTE, then thirty-five miles (56 kilometers) east of Winter Harbour, and on April 6, 1853, a sledge party reached Mercy Bay. McClure reluctantly abandoned *Investigator* in late May, and her surviving crew marched east to *Resolute.* They did not return to England until 1854.

Dodge, *Northwest by Sea; Polar Rosses.* McClure, *Discovery of the North-West Passage by H.M.S. "Investigator."*

## Isabella

Ship (3m). *L/B:* 110' × 28' (33.5m × 8.5m). *Tons:* 383 bm. *Hull:* wood. *Comp.:* 57. *Built:* Hull, Eng.; 1786.

With the end of the Napoleonic Wars, British interest in scientific exploration began to widen and in 1818, the Admiralty launched two expeditions to take up the long-dormant search for northern routes to the Pacific. Bound for the waters around Spitzbergen in search of the Northeast Passage were Captain John Buchan in the hired whaleship, *Dorothea,* and Lieutenant John Franklin in *Trent.* The more notable expedition, for the Northwest Passage, was under Commander John Ross in *Isabella,* sailing in company with *Alexander,* under William Parry. The two converted whaleships rounded the southern tip of Greenland and then sailed into Davis Strait. These waters were well known to the whalers from Hull and other British whaling ports, though only as far as Disco Island, and Ross's two ships were in company with forty-five of them around Hare Island. Ross pressed on past 75°N through the Davis Strait and Baffin Bay as far as Melville Bay on Greenland's west coast —

the first ships to do so since William Baffin in DIS-COVERY in 1616. The expedition then crossed to the southern end of Ellesmere Island and sailed south past the eastern entrances to Jones Sound and Lancaster Sound. Ross decided that neither provided an outlet to the west. In particular, he believed that Lancaster Sound was blocked by a range of mountains, the "Croker Mountains." This mirage vanished the next year when Parry sailed through Lancaster Sound and about halfway through the Northwest Passage in HECLA and *Griper.* In the twentieth century, Lancaster Sound was the preferred eastern channel of the Northwest Passage.

*Isabella* returned to the Hull whaling fleet in 1819 and continued whaling for many seasons, bringing home as much as 250 tons of oil in a good year. On August 26, 1833, the ship was in Lancaster Sound just west of Navy Board Inlet when she was approached by three long boats. In these were none other than the survivors from Captain John Ross's exploration ship VICTORY, which had left England in 1829 and wrecked in 1831. The next year, on May 12, 1833, *Isabella* was lost on the Greenland coast.

Dodge, *Polar Rosses.* Lubbock, *Arctic Whalers.* Ross, *Voyage of Discovery; Narrative of a Second Voyage in Search of a North-West Passage.*

# J

## Jeannette

(ex-*Pandora*) *Philomel*-class gun vessel (1f/3m). *L/B/D:* 145′ × 25.5′ × 15′ (44.2m × 78m × 4.6m). *Tons:* 244 grt. *Hull:* wood. *Comp.:* 33. *Mach.:* steam, 200 hp, 1 screw. *Built:* Pembroke Dockyard, Wales; 1861.

After fourteen years as a Royal Navy gunboat, HMS *Pandora* was sold to Sir Allen Young, who made two voyages in her in search of the Northwest Passage via Peel Sound. In 1876, Young sold *Pandora* to Lieutenant George W. De Long, USN, acting on behalf of the flamboyant New York newspaper publisher James Gordon Bennett, who wanted to sponsor an expedition to reach the North Pole. Congress passed legislation to put the expedition under the U.S. Navy's jurisdiction while Bennett footed the bill and generated publicity. The premise of the expedition was that beyond the Arctic ice so far encountered by explorers, the north polar region comprised a warm, open sea fed by the Gulf Stream in the Atlantic and the Kuro Shio Current in the North Pacific. For this reason, the rechristened *Jeannette*, named for Bennett's sister, was to sail through the Bering Strait, the first polar expedition to use that route since Lieutenant Robert McClure in HMS INVESTIGATOR in 1850–51.

Strengthened for work in the ice, *Jeannette* departed San Francisco on July 8, 1879. After stops at Unalaska, St. Michael, where the crew took aboard sleds and forty sled dogs and two Inuit drivers, and Lavrentia, Siberia, where they recoaled for the last time, they sailed through the Bering Strait on August 28. They made several stops along the Siberian coast and made for Wrangell Island. Nine days later, *Jeannette* was stuck fast, even as the U.S. Coast and Geodetic Survey published a report on Bering Sea currents, concluding that "nothing in the

least tends to support the widely spread but unphilosophical notion that in any part of the Polar Sea we may look for large areas free from ice."

The course of *Jeannette*'s drift in the ice took her well west of Wrangell Island, but it was erratic. By January 1881 the ship had meandered 1,300 miles (2,100 kilometers) but was only 250 miles (400 kilometers) northwest of her position when originally beset. Few of the experimental devices worked as they should, the hull leaked badly, and navigator John Danenhower required repeated operations for an eye condition brought about by syphilis. In May 1881, the ship was within sight of Henrietta Island, where a team led by Engineer George W. Melville deposited an account of the voyage thus far. (The precaution of placing written accounts of an expedition's progress in various locations was common among Arctic explorers intent on securing credit for their discoveries, or directing parties sent out to search for them. Melville's account was recovered by Soviet scientists in 1938.) Shortly thereafter, the ice bore down on the ship, and on the morning of June 12, 1881, *Jeannette* was crushed in position 77°08′N, 153°25′E, about 250 miles from Siberia.

The crew managed to take off two cutters, a whaleboat, eight sleds, and sled dogs. At first, the drift of the ice carried them 3 miles northwest for every mile they made southwest, but by July 29 they were in the New Siberian Islands. Setting out again, they encountered more open water. On September 12, about 100 miles from the Siberian coast, the boats were separated in a gale. Lieutenant Charles Chipp and his seven crew disappeared, but the boats commanded by De Long and Melville landed about 125 miles apart in the Lena River delta. Melville's party of eleven reached safety at a Tungus village and later dispatched search parties to look for the others. According to De Long's diary, by October 30, 140 days after the loss of the *Jeannette*, De Long and all his men were dead. The scientific failure of the expedition and heavy loss of life led to a congressional hearing. At a time when the United States was beginning to emerge as a world power, the prestige of the navy was on trial, and the hearing became a forum for the rehabilitation of the *Jeannette*'s officers and crew.

Gutteridge, *Icebound*.

## Joliba

Schooner. *L/B/D:* 40′ × 6′ × 1′ (12.2m × 1.8m × 0.3m). *Hull:* wood. *Comp.:* 6. *Built:* Sansanding, Bambara (Mali); 1805.

In 1805, the Scottish explorer Mungo Park set out to travel the length of the Niger River to the sea, a feat not yet accomplished by any European. Although the source of the Niger was known, the location of the river's mouth had been a mystery to Europeans as long ago as Herodotus in the fifth century BCE. The Niger was variously believed to drain into the Sahara, descend under the desert to emerge in the Mediterranean, flow into the Nile or Congo Rivers, or empty into the Atlantic — as in fact it does, at the end of its 2,600-mile (4,200-kilometer) course to the Gulf of Guinea. On his first expedition to West Africa (1794–97), Park had seen the Niger near Ségou (in what is now Mali), where the river flows east. Eight years later, now aged thirty-four, Park embarked on his second journey. Ascending the Gambia River with forty-four men at the start of the rainy season in April, he reached Ségou in September with only three men left. There King Mansong gave him two canoes that he cobbled together into what he hopefully called "His Majesty's Schooner *Joliba*." On November 20, 1805, Park, his surviving companions, and three servants set out down the Niger. After passing Tombouctou, they had traveled to within 600 miles (965 kilometers) of the river mouth when they were killed at Bussa, in what is now Nigeria. The journey was completed in 1830 by John and Richard Lander.

de Gramont, *Strong Brown God*.

# K

## Kon-Tiki

Raft (1m). *L/B:* 45′ × 18′ (13.7m × 5.5m). *Hull:* balsa wood. *Comp.:* 6. *Des.:* traditional. *Built:* Callao, Peru; 1947.

In 1937, Norwegian zoologist Thor Heyerdahl went to live on the island of Fatu Hiva in the Marquesas Islands. Heyerdahl was intrigued by the presence in Polynesia of plants indigenous to South America, and especially by legends on Easter Island that echoed those of the Inca tradition in Peru: Tiki, the son of the sun, who was ancestor of the Easter Islanders, seemed to be the same as Kon-Tiki, the mythical head of a white race who, expelled by the Incas from around Lake Titicaca, sailed west across the Pacific. After World War II, Heyerdahl tried to circulate his theory of American colonization of the Pacific, but he was snubbed by the scholarly community. The basis for his rejection was the certainty that "none of the peoples of South America got over to the islands in the Pacific [because] they couldn't get there. They had no boats." Heyerdahl determined to demonstrate the feasibility of crossing thousands of miles of open water using pre-Columbian raft-building techniques.

The balsa logs were felled in the mountain jungles of Ecuador, floated downriver to Guayaquil, and shipped from there to the naval dockyard at Callao, Peru. The design of the vessel was based on Spanish descriptions of Inca rafts at the time of the Conquest. The longest of the nine logs, which formed the center of the raft, was 45 feet (13.7 meters); progressively shorter logs were laid symmetrically on either side so that the sides were only 30 feet (9 meters) long. These were lashed together with 1¼-inch-thick (3.2-centimeter) hemp, and fir planks driven between big gaps in the logs acted as centerboards to prevent the raft from drifting to leeward. The mast consisted of two mangrove poles angled toward each other and lashed at the top; from this was set a square sail on a bamboo yard. A 19-foot (6-meter) steering oar rested between two thole pins on a large block astern. Lighter bamboo logs were laid crossways on the raft and covered with a bamboo decking. Aft there was a bamboo cabin.

On April 28, 1947, *Kon-Tiki* was towed 50 miles (80 kilometers) northwest of Callao by a tug and cast adrift. After a day of calms, the crew encountered sixty hours of rough weather in the Humboldt Current, which pushed them far to the northwest. They struggled with the unwieldy steering oar for several weeks before they discovered that the most effective way to regulate the direction of the raft was with the centerboards, which the Incas, according to a Spanish account, "pushed down into the chinks between the timbers." Another concern was the rate at which the balsa wood initially absorbed water, leading each crew member in turn to wonder whether the raft would sink before reaching land. Early on in the planning of the expedition, Heyerdahl had estimated that it would take at least ninety-seven days to reach land, but on July 30 — only ninety-three days from Callao — the company sighted the island of Puka Puka in the Tuamotus. They were unable to close with the land, but four days later they were off Angatau, though again prevented from landing. Four days after that, *Kon-Tiki* was washed onto the Raroia reef. After a week on an uninhabited island, they were visited by islanders from across the lagoon and through them began the slow return to civilization. The schooner *Tamara* was dispatched from Tahiti to bring the raft and crew to Papeete, whence they proceeded to the United States aboard the Norwegian freighter *Thor-I.*

The raft returned to Oslo and was made the centerpiece of the Kon-Tiki Museum, devoted to the story of the voyage itself and related aspects of American and Polynesian ethnography. As Heyerdahl himself acknowledged:

> My migration theory, as such, was not necessarily proved by the successful outcome of the Kon-Tiki expedition. What we *did* prove was that the South American balsa raft possessed qualities not previously known to scientists of our time, and that the Pacific islands are located well inside the range of prehistoric craft from Peru.

The *Kon-Tiki* expedition proved to be the first of several similar ventures Heyerdahl would undertake to demonstrate the abilities of prehistoric navigators, chief among them being the transatlantic RA II expedition in 1970, and the TIGRIS expedition from the Persian Gulf to the Red Sea in 1978.

Heyerdahl, *Kon-Tiki.*

# L

## Lenin

Icebreaker (2m). *L/B/D:* 439.7′ × 90.7′ × 34.1′ (134m × 27.6m × 10.4m). *Tons:* 13,366 grt. *Hull:* steel. *Comp.:* 220. *Mach.:* nuclear reactors, steam turbines, 30,200 shp, 3 screws; 18 kts. *Built:* Baltic Shipbuilding and Engineering Works, Leningrad, USSR; 1957.

Although Russia borders on four major seas — the Pacific and Arctic Oceans and the Baltic and Black Seas — internal maritime trade has long been complicated by the fact that except for the eastern Arctic and northern Pacific, none of these is contiguous to any other. The only ice-free sea routes between European and Asiatic Russia are around Africa and Asia via the Suez Canal (11,574 miles, or 18,606 kilometers) from St. Petersburg to Vladivostok), via the Cape of Good Hope (15,902 miles, or 25,586 kilometers) to Vladivostok, or via Cape Horn (18,624 miles, or 29,966 kilometers). Of even greater significance to the Soviet Union in the midtwentieth century was its growing reliance on maritime transportation to the remote but resource-rich territories of northern Siberia, where land transport was inadequate.

The Russians began to invest in icebreaking technology in the late nineteenth century in an effort to open the Northeast Passage — pioneered by Adolf Nordenskiöld's Vega in the 1870s — to maritime trade. The Russians' single greatest innovation came in 1959, when they commissioned the *Lenin,* the world's first nuclear-powered surface ship. Nuclear power is theoretically an ideal technology for vessels operating in such remote and inaccessible places because it obviates the need for regular supplies of fuel. *Lenin* escorted her first convoy of merchant ships in 1960, and she made it possible for freighters to service the ports of Dikson and Dudinka on a regular basis. With a service speed of 18 knots in open water, she could make 2 knots through ice 1.4 meters (4.6 feet) thick.

During the 1966–67 season, a nuclear accident resulted in the deaths of thirty of her crew. Abandoned for a year, she was towed to Murmansk for repairs and reentered service with a new nuclear plant rated at 44,000 shp in 1972. Despite the inherent hazards, the Soviets built eight more nuclear-powered icebreakers, including Arktika, which became the first surface ship to reach the geographic North Pole. The *Lenin* was decommissioned in 1989 to serve as a stationary power station.

Brigham, "Arctic Icebreakers." Gardiner and Greenway, eds., *Golden Age of Shipping.* Polmar, *Naval Institute Guide to the Soviet Navy.*

## Limmen

Jacht (3m). *Tons:* 120 gross. *Hull:* wood. *Comp.:* 56. *Built:* Dutch East India Company, Netherlands; <1639.

Although Abel Tasman's first voyage around Australia with Heemskerck and *Zeehaen* in 1642–43 confirmed his ability as a navigator, the councilors of the United East India Company (Verenigde Oostindische Compagnie, or VOC) observed, rightly, that "no riches or things of profit but only the said lands and apparently good passage [toward Chile] were discovered." They could not immediately pursue the route to the Americas, but instead they sent Tasman to southern New Guinea "in order to find out whether the known Southland [Australia's Cape York Peninsula] is continuous with it, or in fact separated." If there was a passage, he was then to circumnavigate Australia clockwise and find out whether Van Diemen's Land (Tasmania) was separate from Australia, and look for the wreck of the retour ship BATAVIA.

To fulfill this goal, Tasman was given the jachts *Limmen* (a place name) and *Zeemeeuw* ("Seagull," 100 tons, forty-one crew) and the galiot *Bracq* (fourteen crew), to be used for inshore exploration. Sailing from Banda in February 1644, Tasman failed utterly — perhaps inexcusably — to find Torres Strait (as it would later be known, for the Spaniard who had first traversed it, in SAN PEDRO in 1605). He then skirted lightly along the western Cape York Peninsula and across the Gulf of Carpentaria to follow the coast of Australia as far as Port Hedland (about 120°E), where he turned north. Although Tasman failed the VOC in the particulars, he established that the Southland was a vast landmass, and as Governor General Anthonie Van Diemen wrote to the VOC, "That such a big country, covering different climates — i.e., that southeast at 43½ degrees S. Lat. going down to 2½ degrees — should not have anything of advantage, is hardly plausible. Compare the big Northern areas of America." But with Van Diemen's death the next year, organized Dutch exploration of Australia came to a close.

Sharp, *Voyages of Abel Janszoon Tasman.*

# Lindblad Explorer

Passenger ship (1f/1m). *L/B/D:* 250′ × 46′ × 15′ (76.2m × 14.0m × 4.6m). *Tons:* 2,500 grt. *Hull:* steel. *Comp.:* 100 pass.; 60 crew. *Mach.:* twin diesels, 3,800 hp, 1 screw; 14 kts. *Built:* Nystad Varv Shipyard, Helsinki, Finland; 1969.

Built specifically for "expedition cruising," to take small groups of adventurous travelers to remote or inaccessible places, *Lindblad Explorer* was named for her creator, Lars-Eric Lindblad. She was commissioned in 1969; her maiden voyage was marred by a shipboard fire off Senegal, and she later grounded twice in the Antarctic. Although these were unwelcome accidents, the ship, commonly known as "the Little Red Boat," was built to sustain much of the punishment of the seas of the world, having been constructed to the most stringent U.S. Coast Guard requirements, with a view especially to cruising in polar waters. Her staff of academics and scientists varies depending on the itinerary. Although best known for her cruises to Antarctica and the islands of the Southern Ocean, in 1984 *Lindblad Explorer* became the first passenger ship to traverse the Northwest Passage, and she has reached farther north (82°12′N) and south than any other passenger vessel. Her voyages have also taken her to remote islands of the Pacific from the Galápagos to the East Indies, as well as up the Amazon River.

Shackleton, *Wildlife and Wilderness.* Snyder and Shackleton, *Ship in the Wilderness.*

# Los Reyes

Galleon (3m). *Tons:* 250 bm. *Hull:* wood. *Built:* <1567.

Although Ferdinand Magellan's VICTORIA crossed the Pacific Ocean east to west in 1521, subsequent transpacific voyages were few and far between. In 1565, the Spanish founded a settlement in the Philippines, and in the same year the seaman-friar Fray Andres de Urdaneta, sailing in SAN PABLO, pioneered the first west–east transpacific route. At the same time, in Peru, Pedro Sarmiento was planning a westward voyage in search of lands rich in gold and silver. Two arguments favored the existence of such a land. European geographers had long postulated a huge southern Terra Australis to counterbalance the earth's northern landmasses. According to Inca tradition, Tupac Yupanqui had sailed to the west and returned with gold, silver, and slaves. Sarmiento received permission for such an expedition, and *Los Reyes* ("The Kings") and *Todos Los Santos* ("All Saints") were outfitted for the voyage. Unfortunately, the fabled land was thought to lie only 600 leagues (1,800 miles, or 2,900 kilometers) from Peru, and the ships were provisioned accordingly, although the 150 crew were bound on a voyage that would take them 7,000 miles (11,260 kilometers) across the Pacific.

On November 22, 1567, the expedition sailed from Callao "for islands to the west, called Solomon," under the command of twenty-five-year-old Alvaro Mendaña, a nephew of the viceroy. The crew first sailed west southwest to 15°S and then turned to the northwest until latitude 6°S. They made their first landfall in the Ellice Islands on January 15, 1568, but were swept past the islands by the current. Seventeen days brought them to Ongtong Java in the northern Solomon Islands. Blown southward in a storm for six days, on February 7 they came into Bahía de Estrella on Ysabel Island, which they first took to be a continent. Mendaña's men immediately began to build a brigantine in order to explore the surrounding coasts.

On April 7, the brigantine began its first voyage of exploration with thirty men under the senior pilot, Hernan Gallego. Sailing east along Santa Isabel, they crossed to Guadalcanal, then returned to Santa Isabel and completed a tour of the coast. Relations with the islanders deteriorated as Spanish demands for food grew, so Mendaña moved his ships to Guadalcanal on May 12. It was no better with the cannibals of Guadalcanal, and on one watering trip, nine Spaniards were killed and mutilated. Reprisals left forty natives dead or wounded before June 13, when Mendaña moved again, to San Cristobal Island, which had been found on the brigantine's second trip when the explorers also visited the islands of Malaita and Ulawa. On San Cristobal, the Spanish stole food, burned villages, and killed and kidnapped locals. Though most of the prisoners escaped when the ships were careened for three weeks, six sailed with the ships on August 11.

Although Mendaña was supposed to colonize his islands, he was overruled by Gallego and the others, who urged him to return to Peru. Sailing north of the Equator, they made landfall in the Marshall Islands, but they could find nothing useful on them. With food and water in short supply, they passed waterless Midway Island on October 2, and on October 16 the ships were separated just before a storm hit "with such fury as I had never before seen," wrote Gallego, "although I have been forty-five years at sea, and thirty of them a pilot." Both ships were dismasted, and *Los Reyes* only reached Sebastián Vizcaíno Bay in Baja California on December 20, 1568. A few weeks later, at Santiago de Colima (19°5′N), *Todos Los Santos* appeared. By the time they reached Callao on July 26, 1569, only 100 of those who set out were still alive. Despite the exertions of the best navigators, the existence of Mendaña's Solomon Islands would not be confirmed until D'Entrecasteaux visited them in *Recherche* and L'Espérance in 1792.

Amherst and Thomson, *Discovery of the Solomon Islands by Alvaro de Mendaña in 1568.*

# M

## Manhattan

Icebreaker-tanker (1f/3m). *L/B/D:* 940′ × 132′ × 52′ (286.5m × 40.2m × 15.8m). *Tons:* 115,000 dwt. *Hull:* steel. *Comp.:* 60–126. *Mach.:* steam turbine, 43,000 shp, 2 screws; 17 kts. *Built:* Bethlehem Steel Co., Quincy, Mass.; 1962.

Prompted by the discovery of oil in Prudhoe Bay on the North Slope of Alaska in 1968, the Humble Oil & Refining Company and Atlantic Richfield Company decided to test the feasibility of transporting oil via ship through the Northwest Passage. They chartered the tanker *Manhattan* and sent her to the Sun Shipyard at Chester, Pennsylvania, for conversion to an icebreaker. The world's largest commercial ship when commissioned, *Manhattan* had had a checkered career as a tanker because her deep draft forced her either to sail light or to transship her cargoes outside of port. In preparation for her Arctic voyage, *Manhattan* was cut into four sections, each of which was modified for work in the ice. When reassembled, the ship had grown 65 feet (20 meters) in length and 16 feet (5 meters) in beam.

On August 24, 1969 (exactly one month after *Apollo 11* returned to Earth from the first manned lunar landing), *Manhattan* sailed from Chester with 112 crew, scientists, and journalists. Escorted by the Canadian icebreaker *John A. Macdonald,* on September 5 she sailed west across the top of Baffin Island into Lancaster Sound. Stopped by the ice about 50 miles into McClure Strait between Melville and Banks islands, on September 10, *Manhattan's* Captain Arthur W. Smith executed a U-turn and headed south to pass through Prince of Wales Strait between Banks and Victoria islands and entered Amundsen Sound on September 14. Turning west along the coast of continental Can-

ada, *Manhattan* arrived five days later at Prudhoe Bay, where she took aboard a symbolic cargo of one barrel of oil. On the twenty-first, she reached Point Barrow, her western terminus. During the return voyage, engineers conducted tests to determine the machinery requirements needed for commercial navigation through the ice. Exiting Lancaster Sound on October 30, *Manhattan* returned to New York on November 12. Although her success showed that the voyage was physically possible, the route was neither environmentally nor economically sound, and it was decided to build a trans-Alaska pipeline to Valdez on Prince William Sound. *Manhattan* resumed regular service again until 1987. Laid up off Yosu, South Korea, she was scrapped after grounding in a typhoon.

Guravich, Keating, and Olson, *North West Passage*. Smith, *Northwest Passage*.

## Ma-Robert

Steamboat (1f/2m). *L/B:* 75′ × 8′ (22.9m × 2.4m). *Hull:* steel. *Comp.:* 17. *Mach.:* steam, sidewheels. *Built:* MacGregor Laird, Birkenhead, Eng.; 1858.

Following the appointment of the missionary-explorer David Livingstone as consul for East Africa at Quelimane, Mozambique, the British government ordered a paddle steamer to be built for his use on the Zambesi River. The first steam vessel built of steel, she was called *Ma-Robert,* the name by which the Makalolo people called Mrs. Livingstone after the birth of her first son. The vessel was sent out to Africa in sections and assembled at the mouth of the Zambesi River in the summer of 1858. *Ma-Robert* sailed up the Zambesi to Tete, but proved inadequate for the task. Livingstone condemned her as "a wretched sham vessel" and deplored especially her engines, which were, he wrote, "evidently made to grind coffee in a shop window." Worse yet, her draft was too deep for good river work, and her poor-quality steel hull rusted out and had to be caulked with mud. In 1859, Livingstone steamed 200 miles (322 kilometers) up the Shire River, and with his staff and porters trekked overland to the source of the Shire, becoming, in September, the first Europeans to view Lake Nyasa. In December 1860, Livingstone took *Ma-Robert* up the Kongoni River, where on the twenty-first she grounded and sank. In the meantime two new vessels, *Pioneer* and *Lady Nyasa,* had been sent out. Nonetheless, in May 1863 Livingstone hoped to salvage *Ma-Robert,* only to find that she had been burned three months before.

Jeal, *Livingstone.*

## Matahorua

Voyaging canoe. *Comp.*: 67. *Built:* Tahiti; ca. 1000.

According to tradition, the first Polynesian expedition to New Zealand was led by Kupe, a seafaring fisherman from Hawaiki (Tahiti). The story relates that the fishermen of Hawaiki kept losing their bait to a school of octopuses whose leader belonged to Muturangi, "an enemy of Kupe." When Kupe and his companions attempted to kill the octopus he headed out to sea, so Kupe decided to follow him in his canoe, *Matahorua,* accompanied by Ngake in his canoe, *Tahirirangi.* Kupe evidently anticipated a long voyage, and *Matahorua* carried a total of sixty-seven people, including Kupe's wife, their five children, and sixty crew. The chase led them to what is now the North Island of New Zealand, down the east coast as far as Cook Strait. There they surrounded and killed the octopus. Kupe named several islands in the strait for his daughters, visited South Island, and then returned to Hawaiki from a peninsula near modern Auckland called Hokianga nui a Kupe, "Great returning place of Kupe," stopping at Rarotonga en route home.

Kupe reported the islands as having been uninhabited, but other traditions, and archaeological evidence, suggest that when the first permanent Polynesian settlers arrived, the islands were inhabited by people different from themselves. It is believed that these might have been Melanesians, possibly from Fiji, whose canoes were called *Kahutuara, Taikoria,* and *Okoki.*

Much of the oral tradition in which these stories were preserved died out after the arrival of Europeans in the eighteenth and nineteenth centuries. Elements have been corroborated by archaeological and linguistic finds in New Zealand and by a careful examination of the course of Polynesian voyaging and exploration in general. Although New Zealand lies only 2,000 miles from the Solomon Islands, which many accept as the starting place of Polynesian seafaring, it is relatively more inaccessible to navigators of voyaging canoes than are the more distant Marquesas, which lie about 3,500 miles farther east but which were reached several centuries before. The reason for New Zealand's comparatively late discovery — perhaps as early as the eighth century for the original hunter-gatherer Melanesians, and about the tenth century for the farmer-warrior Maoris who succeeded them — is that it is separated from central Polynesia by a belt of variable winds across which it is difficult to sail with any reliable expectation of safe return. New Zealand also lies in a higher (and colder) latitude, 900 miles farther from the Equator than Hawaii, in an area more subject to inclement weather. These conditions are thought to explain why the Maori eventually abandoned the sea road, or *ara moana,* back to Polynesia.

The navigational elements of the Kupe/*Matahorua* story are consistent with what is known about wayfinding, as Polynesian navigation is called. Upon his return to Hawaiki, Kupe explained his course in relation to the setting sun. The island was first located by his wife, who saw a cloud. Distinct clouds often rise above land on the open ocean and their presence is an important element of Polynesian navigation. (The Maori name for the North Island of New Zealand is Aotea, "White

Cloud.") As Polynesian women did not as a rule accompany fishing expeditions, from the presence of Kupe's family on this voyage it would seem that it was intended as an expedition to colonize a new land. Maori tradition disdains the original inhabitants of New Zealand and ascribes their presence to their having been blown off course to the island. Although some islands in Oceania were discovered as the result of "accidental drift," most of the region was explored intentionally.

Buck, *Coming of the Maori.* Irwin, *Prehistoric Exploration and Colonisation of the Pacific.*

# Mathew

Caravel (3m). *L/B/D:* 73′ × 20.5′ × 7′ (22.3m × 6.2m ×2.1m). *Tons:* 85 disp. *Hull:* wood. *Comp.:* 18. *Built:* <1493.

Identified as a *navicula,* or small ship, England's first ship of exploration was probably a caravel no larger than NIÑA, the smallest ship to sail with Christopher Columbus on his first transatlantic voyage in 1492. *Mathew*'s captain, John Cabot, was of Italian (perhaps even Genoese) birth and possibly an acquaintance of Columbus's. A veteran of the spice trade in the eastern Mediterranean — he lived in Venice and traded to Mecca — sometime after the return of Columbus's first expedition, Cabot began seeking sponsorship for a northerly voyage to the Orient. (At this point, no one realized that Columbus's voyage had brought him not to Asia but to a previously unknown continent.) Rebuffed by Spain and Portugal, Cabot turned to England's Henry VII, who in 1496 granted him letters patent

> to seeke out, discover, and finde, whatsoever iles, countreyes, regions or provinces of the heathen and infidelis, whatsoever they bee, and in what part of the world soever they be, whiche before this time have beene unbeknowen to all Christians.

Though Cabot was granted permission to sail with five ships, only one could be had for the expedition, and on May 20, 1497, the solitary *Mathew* sailed from Bristol. Particulars of the voyage are not known with certainty. According to Samuel Eliot Morison, the ship rounded the south of Ireland and took departure from Dursey Head to sail due west on about latitude 51°N. After thirty-five days at sea, she was in soundings and on June 24 fetched up off Cape Dégrat at the northern end of Newfoundland. (Other conjectured landfalls include Cape Bonavista, Newfoundland, and Cape Breton, Nova Scotia.) Probably deterred by ice from sailing north or west, Cabot turned south and, after one landing, followed the east coast of Newfoundland, exploring Trinity Bay, rounding Cape Race, and sailing into Placentia Bay before doubling back to Cape Dégrat. From there, *Mathew* turned for home on July 20 and arrived at Bristol on August 6.

Cabot brought no objects of trade with him, but on the basis of his report, Henry VII granted him additional patents, and in May 1498 Cabot sailed from Bristol with five ships. One of these put back, but the other four and their crews disappeared. *Mathew* was apparently not among these. *Mathew*'s ultimate fate is not known. In 1504 a ship of that name was listed in the Bristol records. She sailed to Ireland under Edmund Griffeth and made separate trips to Bordeaux and Spain under William Claron. In 1996, a replica of *Mathew* designed by Colin Mudie was launched in Bristol and sailed to North America for the five hundreth anniversary of Cabot's voyage. (The dimensions given are those of the replica, the design of which was based on careful analysis of the best contemporary evidence available.)

Firstbrook, *Voyage of the "Mathew."* Morison, *European Discovery of America: The Northern Voyages.* Williamson, *Cabot Voyages.*

# Maud

(later *Baymaud*) Barkentine (3m). *L/B/D:* 106.8′ lod × 40′ × 16′ dph (32.6m × 12.2m × 4.7m). *Tons:* 380 grt. *Hull:* wood. *Built:* Christian Jensen, Vollen, Asker, Norway; 1917.

*Maud* was the last, and least successful, ship used by Roald Amundsen for polar exploration. Amundsen was intent on reaching the North Pole by letting his ship become locked in the Arctic Sea ice and letting the polar current carry it over the Pole, a voyage modeled on that of Fridtjof Nansen in the FRAM. Amundsen originally intended to embark in *Fram,* which he had sailed on his successful quest for the South Pole in 1911. Because of her poor condition, Amundsen built *Maud,* which he named for the wife of Norway's Haakon VII.

*Maud* sailed from Christiana (Oslo) on June 24, 1918, and headed north and east into the Northeast Passage, the route pioneered by Adolf Nordenskiöld in the VEGA expedition. She made good progress past Cape Chelyuskin in Northern Siberia, but on September 17 *Maud* became trapped in the ice, remaining there until September 12, 1919. In the interval, two of the crew died trying to sledge home through Russia. Free of the ice for only eleven days, *Maud* was again icebound near the Kolyma River, still 500 miles (800 kilometers) shy of the Bering Strait. On July 27, 1920, more than two years after leaving Norway, *Maud* finally reached Nome, Alaska, the terminus of Amundsen's first transit of the Northwest Passage in GJØA in 1906. Returning to the Bering Sea, *Maud* was trapped for a third winter off Cape Serdze Kamen. When she finally broke free on July 1, 1921, Amundsen sailed for Seattle for much needed repairs to the ship.

Conditions had thus far prevented *Maud* from drifting with the ice, so Amundsen decided to use *Maud* as a base of operations for aerial reconnaissance and what he hoped would be the first flight over the North Pole. This effort ended in the loss of both planes. In 1925, Amundsen made one last attempt to drift in the polar ice, but *Maud* only attained 76°51′N, far short of the 84°04′N latitude Nansen reached with *Fram* in 1895. Upon his return to Seattle in September 1925, Amundsen was forced to file for bankruptcy, and *Maud* was sold to the Hudson's Bay Company as a supply vessel for its northern outposts.

The renamed *Baymaud* left Vancouver on June 21, 1926, under the command of Captain Gus Foellmer. Sailing through the Bering Strait, she called at Herschell and Baillie islands, and then sailed into Coronation Gulf for stops at Bernard Harbor, Tree River, and the Kent Peninsula. Her crew erected a new Hudson's Bay Company outpost at Fort Harmon on the southwest coast of Victoria Island. After wintering at Bernard Harbor, *Baymaud* sailed to Kent River, where the company outpost there was dismantled and taken to Cambridge Bay. The ship's deep draft made her unfit for service in coastal Arctic waters, and the company moored *Baymaud* at Cambridge Bay for use as a floating machine shop, warehouse, and radio station, in which capacity she broadcast "the first regular winter reports by radio from Canada's Arctic coast." Although kept in good repair, in 1930 *Baymaud* developed a leak around her propeller shaft and sank at her moorings in about 8 meters (26 feet) of water. Over the years, *Maud* was dismantled piecemeal, and, in 1935, Henry Larsen of the ST. ROCH dynamited the stern to get to the fuel tanks, which were leaking oil.

In 1990, the town of Asker, Norway, bought *Baymaud* from the Hudson's Bay Company with the intent of moving the ship to Norway for preservation; ownership later passed to the city of Tromsø. As late as 1996, the Norwegian ship classification society Det Norsk Veritas considered the removal and restoration of the ship technically feasible. Canadian historians have also expressed interest in preserving the vessel at Cambridge Bay.

Amundsen, *My Life as an Explorer.* Delgado, *Made for the Ice.*

## Mayflower

Galleon (3m). *L/B/D:* ca. 90′ × 26′ × 11′ dph (27.4m × 7.9m × 3.4m). *Tons:* 180 burden. *Hull:* wood. *Comp.:* 101 pass.; 20–30 crew. *Built:* Leigh, England; 1606(?).

Although the little ship that brought the Pilgrims to Plymouth Rock in 1620 is one of the most celebrated vessels in U.S. history, facts concerning her origins and end are obscure. The vessel may be the same *Mayflower* as one mentioned in London port documents of 1606 belonging to Robert Bonner of Leigh, and the record becomes clearer in 1609, when there is mention of a *Mayflower* of London, Christopher Jones master and part owner. This ship plied the seas chiefly between England and the

◀ A replica of the Pilgrims' **Mayflower** built in England in 1956 and sailed to the United States. *Courtesy Plimoth Plantation, Plymouth, Massachusetts.*

French Biscay ports of La Rochelle and Bordeaux. Outbound she carried such items as cloth and rabbit skins, returning with her hold filled with wine and brandy. She is also recorded as having shipped furs from Norway and silks from Hamburg.

While this doughty trader and hundreds like her etched their wakes in the sea lanes of northern Europe, the still young Church of England had seen the development of various schismatic groups who considered Anglicanism more Popish than Protestant. Puritans believed Anglicanism could be reformed from within, while Separatists believed in neither the authority of the Church of England nor, in spiritual matters, the monarch as head of the church. In 1607, several groups of Separatists managed to move their "unlawful religious gatherings" to the Netherlands, but ten years later they were eager to settle in the New World, under English Crown, if not religious, authority.

Direct appeals to the Company for Virginia, which had established the Jamestown colony in 1607, came to nothing. *Mayflower's* charter was eventually arranged through the Merchant Adventurers, which included representatives of the Virginia Company, the London Company, and the Plymouth Company, all of which could make land grants in the Americas. The dissenters worked most closely with Thomas Weston and John Pierce, who had secured a patent from the Virginia Company to settle within its domains, in "the neighborhood of Hudsons River in the northern part of Virginia."

The Separatists sailed from Leyden in *Speedwell* for a rendezvous with *Mayflower* at Southampton toward the end of July 1620, and the ships sailed in company on August 5, with ninety Pilgrims aboard *Mayflower* and thirty more in *Speedwell*. The latter was in no condition to make a transatlantic passage, and after her leaks forced the two ships into first Dartmouth and then Plymouth, the crews realized they could use only Captain Jones's larger

ship. Overcrowding was alleviated somewhat when about eighteen or twenty of the company decided to stay in England, and *Mayflower* finally sailed from Plymouth on September 6 with fifty men, twenty women, and thirty-four children, about half of them Separatists and the others members of the Church of England. (William Bradford was the first person to refer to the Separatists as Pilgrims, in 1630, by which he meant only that they had traveled in and to foreign lands. The first child born to a woman in the group after landing at Cape Cod was named Peregrine, or "pilgrim.")

The first half of the passage was rough, but thereafter the weather was good, and on November 9 they saw land at Truro, Cape Cod, 200 miles north of the Virginia Company's domains, which extended about as far north as New York. Jones attempted to sail south, but contrary winds and the approach of winter forced the ship back around the tip of Cape Cod, and on November 11, 1620, they anchored at Provincetown Harbor. In sixty-seven days at sea one of the group had died, and one child was born, named Oceanus Hopkins. Before going ashore, forty-one of the company signed the "Mayflower Compact," the document by which all members of the ship's company would be ruled.

On November 15, Miles Standish led a small group of Pilgrims on their first foray along the neck of Cape Cod. At the end of the month, they made a second expedition, by shallop (which was assembled after *Mayflower's* arrival), to the Pamet River, near Truro, and a third expedition took them across Massachusetts Bay. Here was a good place for wintering, and on December 16 *Mayflower* arrived at "the harbour . . . which is apparently, by Captain John Smith's chart of 1614, no other than the place he calls 'Plimouth' thereon."

Although the first winter was hard, in the spring they met an English-speaking Indian. Squanto had been to England and had been sold into the slave market in Spain in 1614. Somehow he made his way back to England and enlisted as an interpreter on a ship bound for Newfoundland. Now living with Massasoit, Great Chief of the Wampanoags, Squanto provided inestimable help to the fledgling Pilgrim settlement. By April the weather had moderated, but half of the *Mayflower*'s crew had died. She took her departure on April 5, 1621, and arrived in the Thames estuary after a run of only thirty-one days.

*Mayflower*'s history after that point becomes something of a mystery. She is last mentioned in connection with Jones's name on December 18, 1621, unloading at London the last of a cargo from La Rochelle that included 1,930 pounds of cotton yarn, "yards of Turkey grograine," and twelve hundredweight of currants. In 1624, a vessel of the same name, in which Josian Jones, the captain's widow, was a part owner, was surveyed at Rotherhithe and valued at £128 8s 4d. What happened thereafter is unknown.

In 1956, naval architect William A. Baker designed a replica of *Mayflower* based on scholarly interpretation of the few facts known about the Pilgrims' *Mayflower* and the design of other contemporary ships. With a lateen mizzen, she sets courses and single topsails on the main and foremasts, and in place of fore-and-aft headsails (a later development), she sets a single square spritsail from the bowsprit. In 1957, a crew of thirty-three under square-rigger veteran Alan Villiers sailed the replica from Plymouth, England, to Plymouth, Massachusetts, in fifty-three days. She has been on exhibit at Plimoth Plantation ever since.

Baker, *"Mayflower" and Other Colonial Vessels; New "Mayflower."* Caffrey, *"Mayflower."* Hackney, *"Mayflower."* Villiers, *"How We Sailed Mayflower II to America."*

# Meteor

(later *Ekvator*) Survey ship (1f/2m). *L/B/D:* 233.2′ × 33.5′ × 13.1′ (71.1m × 10.2m × 4m). *Tons:* 1,504 disp. *Hull:* steel. *Comp.:* 138. *Mach.:* triple expansion, 1,550 ihp, 2 screws; 11.5 kts. *Built:* Reichsmarinewerft, Wilhelmshaven, Germany; 1924.

One of the most important oceanographic expeditions of the twentieth century was that undertaken in the survey ship *Meteor*. Laid down as an *Iltis*-class gunboat and launched in 1915, *Meteor* remained incomplete at the end of World War I. With vigorous naval backing, Dr. Alfred Merz developed a program for a systematic description of the meteorological, chemical, and topographic attributes of the Atlantic Ocean. Fitted with a brigantine rig to reduce the reliance on fuel, *Meteor* was complete in 1925, and the expedition departed in April 1925. Unfortunately, Dr. Merz had to be landed in Buenos Aires, where he later died of a lung condition. Thereafter, the ship traversed the Atlantic Ocean fourteen times to generate profiles of the ocean between 20°N and 55°S. Working at 310 hydrographic stations, her scientists used 67,400 echo soundings to map the topography of the ocean floor and made 9,400 measurements of temperature, salinity, and chemical content at varying depths. Analysis of the latter established the pattern of ocean water circulation, nutrient dispersal, and plankton growth. The expedition was also the first to make extensive studies of surface evaporation.

After her return to Germany in 1927, *Meteor* was used for research and fisheries protection. After World War II, she was taken over by the Soviet Union and renamed *Ekvator*. As late as 1972, she was still in service as a barracks ship in the Baltic.

Gröner, *German Warships.* Spiess, *"Meteor" Expedition.*

# Nadezhda

Ship (3m). *Tons:* 450 bm. *Hull:* wood. *Comp.:* 85. *Built:* England; <1803.

Although the Russian-American Company first established a presence in the Alaskan fur trade in 1799, because of the inadequacy of Russia's maritime industry, all supplies had to be shipped overland across Siberia and then across the North Pacific from Petropavlovsk, with pelts returning the same way. The one-way journey could often take as long as two years. The English-trained Russian naval officer Lieutenant Adam Johann von Krusenstern had long agitated for the opening of a sea route to Alaska, and in 1803 he was given command of the English-built ships *Nadezhda* ("Hope") and *Neva* (named for the St. Petersburg river) to carry supplies to the North Pacific. His crew included Lieutenant Baron Fabian Gottfried von Bellingshausen and Cadet Otto von Kotzebue, who would go on to lead their own expeditions in Vostok and Rurik, respectively. Before he left, his mission was expanded to include the delivery of the first Russian embassy to the Japanese court. The mission was further elaborated by the addition of an astronomer and two naturalists to the ship's company.

On August 7, 1803, the ships sailed via Copenhagen for Falmouth, where they took on last-minute supplies. En route from the Canary Islands to St. Catherine's, Krusenstern recorded:

On the 26th November, we crossed the equator at about eleven in the morning in 24° 20′ W. longitude, after a passage of thirty days from Santa Cruz. Under a salute of eleven guns we drank the health of the Emperor, in whose glorious reign the Russian flag first waved in the southern hemisphere. The usual farce with Neptune could not well be represented, as there was nobody on board the ship, except myself, who had crossed the equator.

After calling at St. Catherine's, where they replaced *Neva*'s rotten fore and mainmasts, the ships rounded Cape Horn and entered the Pacific in late February. Because of the delays, Krusenstern was forced to abandon his exploration of the South Seas and proceed as quickly as possible for Kamchatka. The ships were separated, and *Neva*, under Yuri Lisianski, called briefly at Easter Island before rendezvousing at Nukahiva, in the Marquesas Islands, in early April. From there they headed to Hawaii, where they split up, *Neva* heading for the Russian factory at Kodiak and *Nadezhda* proceeding to Petropavlovsk on the Kamchatka Peninsula. *Nadezhda* spent July 2 to August 27 offloading supplies at Petropavlovsk, and repairing and reprovisioning the ship.

The second phase of the voyage, the delivery of the Russian embassy to Japan, was a diplomatic fiasco. After weathering a typhoon when they were nearly within sight of Japan, *Nadezhda* put into Nagasaki on September 26. Although it was the Japanese who had first suggested the establishment of more formal relations with Russia ten years before, much had changed in the interval. The ship's crew and diplomatic staff alike were kept at arm's length by petty officials for five months, at the end of which the Emperor declined not only to receive the emissaries but even to receive the gifts from Emperor Alexander I.

On April 5, 1805, *Nadezhda* sailed round Kyushu Island and proceeded up the Sea of Japan to further the hydrographic research conducted by Jean-François Galaups, Comte de La Pérouse, aboard L'ASTROLABE and LA BOUSSOLE in 1787. Sailing through La Pérouse Strait, the ship skirted the eastern edge of Sakhalin Island (which Krusenstern still took to be a peninsula), before crossing the Sea of Okhotsk and rounding up to Petropavlovsk on June 5. Here the emissary and his retinue left the ship to make their way overland to St. Petersburg, and on June 23 *Nadezhda* sailed again for further exploration of the Sea of Okhotsk and Sakhalin.

Returning to Petropavlovsk for the last time on August 19, the ship was prepared for the return to Europe, and on September 23, *Nadezhda* sailed. Her first port of call was Canton, on November 6, two days before *Neva*'s arrival with a cargo of furs from the Russian settlements at Kodiak and Novo Arkhangelsk (Sitka). After considerable delays only terminated through the intervention of the English commercial representative in Canton, *Nadezhda* and *Neva* sailed on February 9, 1806, passing through the Straits of Sunda. Midway across the Indian Ocean, on April 3, they were separated by a fog and proceeded independently for home. Alerted to the renewed hostilities between France and Russia, Krusenstern sailed west and north of the British Isles and in late July called at Copenhagen. *Nadezhda* finally dropped anchor at St. Petersburg on August 7, 1806, after a voyage of three years and twelve days, during which not a single man of the ship's company died.

Ivashintsov, *Russian Round-the-World Voyages.* Krusenstern, *Voyage Round the World.*

submarine Division 1 based at Coco Solo, Panama, before being placed in reserve. Slated to be scrapped under the terms of the London Naval Treaty of 1930, she was given a reprieve when Australian polar explorer Captain George Hubert Wilkins secured her for an attempt to travel under the ice cap to the North Pole. Modifications included sealing the torpedo tubes and reinforcing the bow, fitting the conning with an augur to drill through the ice, and attaching a wooden "sled deck" to the hull to enable the submarine to glide along the underside of the ice.

After fitting out at New York, the submarine was christened *Nautilus,* in honor of the submarine of the same name in Jules Verne's novel *Twenty Thousand Leagues under the Sea.* On July 4, 1931, *Nautilus* sailed from New York for Spitsbergen where, after considerable engine problems, she arrived in August. She sailed again on August 19 and on September 1 disappeared under the ice, sailing to within 500 miles of the Pole. Much of the equipment designed for the voyage didn't work and some was badly maintained; crew members reluctant to travel beneath the ice sabotaged the diving planes. Nonetheless, scientists aboard the submarine conducted valuable underwater surveys between Greenland and Norway. No other submarine sailed beneath the ice until the nuclear-powered USS NAUTILUS reached the North Pole in 1955. At the end of the expedition, Wilkins's *Nautilus* was sunk in Bergenfjord in accord with the disarmament treaty.

Cross, *Challengers of the Deep.* Wilkins, *Under the North Pole.*

# Nautilus

(ex-*O-12*) *O*-class submarine. *L/B/D:* 175′ × 16.5′ × 14′ (53.3m × 5m × 4.3m). *Tons:* 491/566 disp. *Hull:* steel. *Comp.:* 29. *Mach.:* 14/11 kts. *Built:* Lake Torpedo Boat Co., Bridgeport, Conn.; 1918.

One of sixteen *O*-class submarines commissioned by the U.S. Navy during World War I, *O-12* was originally armed with four 18-inch torpedo tubes and a 3-inch deck gun. She spent six years with

# USS Nautilus (SSN-571)

*Nautilus*-class submarine. *L/B/D:* 323.8′ × 27.7′ × 22′ (98.7m × 8.4m × 6.7m). *Tons:* 3,533/4,092 disp. *Hull:* steel; 700′dd. *Comp.:* 116. *Arm.:* 6 × 21″TT. *Mach.:* nuclear reactor, steam turbine, 13,200 shp, 2 screws; 23 kts. *Built:* Electric Boat Co., Groton, Conn.; 1955.

The brainchild of Hyman G. Rickover, who eventually rose to the rank of Admiral, USS *Nautilus* was the world's first nuclear-powered submarine and the first vessel of any description to cross the North Pole — 90°N. A veteran of the Bureau of Ships, Rickover first considered nuclear propulsion for ships while on assignment to the Atomic Energy Commission's reactor complex at Oak Ridge, Tennessee, in 1946. Later assigned to head the Bureau of Ships' Nuclear Power Division, and concurrently the Naval Reactors Branch of the Atomic Energy Commission, Rickover quickly developed plans for what became USS *Nautilus,* the fourth vessel of the name. The chief advantage of atomic power over traditional diesel power is that it produces heat to create steam through fission rather than fire; without the need for external sources of air or oxygen, a nuclear-powered submarine can stay submerged almost indefinitely. The space required to store the uranium — *Nautilus* carried about a pound — is much less than that needed for diesel fuel, which means there is more room for weapons and crew.

Laid down by President Harry S. Truman in 1955, the world's first nuclear submarine was launched two years later by First Lady Mamie Eisenhower. On January 17, 1955, under Commander E. P. Wilkinson, USS *Nautilus* cast off her lines from Groton and signaled "under way on nuclear power." On her first voyage, to Puerto Rico, she sailed 1,381 miles in 89.8 hours, the longest submerged distance covered by a submarine to that time, and achieved the highest underwater speed. By the following year, plans were being developed to send *Nautilus* under the polar ice. In purely military terms, the endurance of nuclear submarines made them ideal candidates to hide beneath the ice in anticipation of a missile attack against the Soviet Union. As a public relations exercise, sending a submarine to the North Pole would confirm American technological superiority. In 1957 *Nautilus* made her first forays under the ice cap under Commander William R. Anderson. Sailing from New London in company with USS *Trigger,* she probed under the ice north of Jan Mayen Island

▼ One of sixteen *O*-class submarines built during World War I, the **O-12** is seen here in more peaceful pursuits, threading her way through ice during her unsuccessful bid to sail under the ice pack to the North Pole in 1931.

during the first week of September. Just before reaching 86°N, a gyroscope fuse failed and she had to turn back. After participating in NATO war games in the North Atlantic, she returned to duty along the East Coast.

The following spring she was sent to the Pacific in preparation for Operation Sunshine, a top-secret voyage from the Pacific to the Atlantic via the North Pole. Departing Seattle on June 9, 1958, *Nautilus* first attempted to enter the Bering Sea via the western passage running between St. Lawrence Island and Siberia. When that proved too shallow, she doubled back around St. Lawrence Island and headed through the Bering Strait. Just shy of 70°N, *Nautilus* encountered ice more than 60 feet (18 meters) deep, in water that was barely deep enough to allow the sail to pass beneath. Reluctantly, the mission was aborted and the ship returned to Pearl Harbor, still with top-secret clearance.

After a month of shuttling between Washington, New London, Alaska, and Hawaii by key members of the crew, *Nautilus* resumed Operation Sunshine on July 22. By this time, the ice had shifted significantly and *Nautilus* was able to approach the Bering Strait via the western door. Passing the point at which she had been forced to turn back the previous month, *Nautilus* sailed for the deep Barrow Sea Valley and on August 1, laid a course for the Pole. She passed over the top of the world at 1115 EDT, cruising about 120 meters (400 feet) below the surface. Two days later, after traveling 1,830 miles (2,944 kilometers) under the ice, *Nautilus* surfaced near Spitsbergen Island and broadcast the message confirming her successful transpolar passage: "Nautilus 90° North." In recognition of this achievement, she became the first ship to receive a Presidential Unit Citation in peacetime.

*Nautilus*'s subsequent career included assignment as the first submarine with the Sixth Fleet in the Mediterranean, and she was used extensively in the development of new antisubmarine warfare techniques, the old procedures having been rendered all but obsolete by the advances afforded by nuclear propulsion. In 1962 she took part in the naval blockade during the Cuban Missile Crisis and later she operated with the Second Fleet. During her operational lifetime, *Nautilus* had three nuclear cores that drove her more than 300,000 miles (483,000 kilometers). She was not decommissioned until 1980. Five years later she was opened to the public as part of the Nautilus Memorial and Submarine Force Library and Museum in Groton, Connecticut.

Anderson, *"Nautilus" — 90 North*. U.S. Navy, *DANFS*.

# Nimrod

Barkentine (1f/3m). *L/B/D*: 136′ × 26.9′ × 16′ (41.5m × 8.2m × 4.9m). *Tons*: 334 grt. *Hull*: wood. *Comp.*: 14. *Mach.*: compound engine, 60 hp, 1 screw. *Built*: Alexander Stephens & Sons, Ltd., Dundee, Scotland; 1865.

Built for rugged work in the Arctic and Antarctic, the sealer *Nimrod* was purchased by Ernest Henry Shackleton for his British Imperial Antarctic Expedition. *Nimrod* sailed from Torquay on August 7, 1907, and reached the Ross Sea via New Zealand in January 1908. After searching in vain for a landing site on King Edward Land, *Nimrod* was forced to go to Ross Island at McMurdo Sound, despite a promise to his old captain and rival, Robert Falcon Scott (with whom he had sailed in DISCOVERY), that he would stay west of 170°E. Establishing a base at Hut Point, where *Discovery* had previously lain from 1901 to 1904, Shackleton attempted to reach the geographic South Pole 1,725 miles (2,775 kilometers) away. Crossing the Ross Ice Shelf, his team ascended to the 10,000-foot-high (3,050-meter) Polar Plateau but had to turn back at 88°23′S, 162°E — a new farthest south, yet still 97 miles (156 kilometers) from their goal. In the meantime, Douglas Mawson, T. W. Edgeworth David, and A. F. Mackay reached the South Magnetic Pole, then located at 72°25′S, 155°16′E, about 190 miles (306 kilometers) west of the Ross Sea. *Nimrod* returned to England in June 1909 and Shackleton used her as a floating museum of his voyage before selling her for funds in 1910. Shackleton's most famous Antarctic expedition was his third, in EN-DURANCE.

Shackleton, *Heart of the Antarctic*.

# Niña

*(Santa Clara)* Caravel (3m). *L/B/D:* 50′–70′ × 16′–20′ × 7′ dph (15–21m × 5–6m × 2m dph). *Tons:* 55–94. *Hull:* wood. *Comp.:* 24. *Arm.:* 9cm lombard, 4.5cm falconets. *Built:* Palos, Spain(?); <1492.

One of the three ships in Christopher Columbus's first voyage of discovery that would take him to the Caribbean islands, *Niña* was a *caravela latina* — that is, lateen-rigged on three masts, the largest sail and foremost sail being set nearly amidships. Owned by Juan Niño de Moguer and officially named *Santa Clara,* she is known to history as *Niña* because it was Spanish custom to give ships the feminine form of the owner's surname. Requisitioned by Columbus in satisfaction of a fine owed by the citizens of Los Palos to Ferdinand and Isabella, *Niña* was put under command of Captain Vicente Yáñez Pinzón, whose brother Martín Alonso was master of PINTA. *Niña* sailed from Palos in company with SANTA MARÍA and *Pinta* on August 3, 1492. The latter experienced rudder trouble, so the other two ships sailed as far as the island of Gomera to wait for their consort. When she did not arrive, they sailed back to Las Palmas. There, Captain Pinzón took advantage of the delay (it had taken *Pinta* two weeks to make port) to alter *Niña's* rig from that of a *caravela latina* to a *caravela redonda.* With her new rig, she retained her lateen-rigged mizzen, set a square sail on her mainmast (the old foremast), and set a square foresail on a new mast stepped near the bow. This made her much better suited to running before the trade winds that would carry her across the Atlantic, and she became Columbus's fastest ship, as well as his favorite.

Resuming the voyage on September 6, the ships met favorable winds for the first two weeks of the voyage, followed by several days of adverse winds and calms between September 20 and 30. On the twenty-fifth, Martín Alonso Pinzón claimed to have sighted land, though the ships were barely halfway across the Atlantic. By the second week of October, there was increasing evidence that land was near — flocks of migrating birds and flotsam in the form of a piece of carved wood and tree branches. Land was finally sighted at about 0200

on October 12, and they landed later that morning. Though it is not absolutely certain what the island was, it was definitely located in what is now the Bahamas, probably San Salvador or Samana Cay; the Taino inhabitants called it Guanahaní.

Convinced that he was very near Cipango or Cathay (Japan or China), whose gold was the chief object of his voyage, Columbus led his three ships through the Bahamas and south to Cuba, the northeast coast of which he explored for about six weeks. On November 22, *Pinta* departed from the other two ships to explore Great Inagua Island. Vicente Yáñez Pinzón remained with Columbus, and a few days later, at Puerto Cayo Moa, *Niña* received a new mizzen mast. The two ships crossed the Windward Channel to Hispaniola on December 6, sailed along its northwest coast, and skirted the south coast of Tortuga. Early Christmas morning *Santa María* grounded on a coral reef. After her crew of forty salvaged what they could from the ship, it was clear that they could not possibly embark in *Niña* for the return voyage, so a fort was erected from *Santa María's* timbers and thirty-nine men volunteered to stay at a settlement they called La Navidad.

Columbus transferred his flag to *Niña* and proceeded east along the coast on January 4, 1493. Two days later, he was making his way to open water when a lookout saw *Pinta* in the distance. Putting about, the ships rendezvoused at Isle Cabra. On January 8, they began working their way down the coast, getting as far as Cape Samana in what is now the Dominican Republic. Abandoning plans to visit additional islands of which he had heard from various Arawaks — ten of whom he had picked up along the way either to serve as interpreters, to convert them to Christianity, or to furnish certain proof that he had visited a distant land — on January 16 he turned the ships for Spain.

The first month was smooth sailing, but on February 12, *Niña* and *Pinta* were separated in a three-day storm (the first of the voyage) near the Azores, which belonged to Portugal. Although they were in sight of Santa Maria Island on the fifteenth, it took them three more days to reach the island, which had no secure anchorage. There, while offering penitential prayers for their deliverance from the storm in a chapel at Anjos, half the crew were arrested on suspicion of having plundered Portuguese possessions on the Guinea Coast. Columbus had received his early seafaring education from Portuguese mariners and his wife was Portuguese, and within a few days he had won his crew's release and they sailed again on February 21. Five days out they were overcome by another storm, possibly of hurricane force, which lasted five days. On the night of March 3, they were perilously close to land, which turned out to be just down the coast from the Tagus River. The next morning they sailed into Lisbon. While there, Columbus was summoned to the court of João II, the Portuguese king who had declined his request for sponsorship for his planned voyage as early as 1484–85. When the King, Dom João, heard Columbus's account of his voyage, complete with presentations by the Caribbean natives, he was more than a little chagrined to realize what he had lost in not sponsoring the Genoese captain himself.

Lisbon was only a two-day sail from Los Palos, and *Niña* nosed into the Rio Tinto on March 15, only hours before *Pinta* — thirty-two weeks from port to port. Within three weeks, he had exchanged correspondence with Ferdinand and Isabella, then holding court 700 miles (1,125 kilometers) away at Barcelona, receiving from them confirmation that he was now Admiral of the Ocean Sea. This was among the honors he had been promised, as well as support for a second voyage, preparation for which got under way almost immediately.

*Niña* was too small to sail as Columbus's flagship, which honor was reserved for a new *Santa María*, nicknamed *Mariagalante*. The new fleet consisted of seventeen ships and more than 1,200 sailors, colonists, and other supernumeraries. Sailing from Cadiz on September 25, the fleet called again at the Canaries, remaining there for about a week before leaving sometime between October 7 and 10. The voyage over was uneventful, and on Sunday, November 3, they made their first landfall, at Dominica. For the next three weeks, they sailed north along the Leeward Islands, giving names to many of the islands that endure today. On November 23, they were back on the north coast of Hispaniola, where they learned that the entire thirty-nine-man garrison left at La Navidad had been killed. On January 2, 1494, Columbus and his ships decided to establish a base at Isabela, Hispaniola, to be near the gold at Cibao, in the interior.

On April 24, Columbus chose the caravels *Niña* (of which he now owned half), *San Juan,* and *Cardera* for an exploring expedition. This took them first to the southeast coast of Cuba (including Guantánamo Bay and Santiago), then across to northern Jamaica, back to Cuba as far as Bahia Cortez, and then again along the southern shores of Jamaica and Hispaniola. The ships returned to Isabela on September 24, after an absence of four months. Columbus remained at the ill-managed colony for another eighteen months, during which he worked to establish a trade in Taino slaves. On March 10, 1496, *Niña* and *Santa Cruz* sailed for Spain, embarking between them about 255 people. (*Santa Cruz* had been built at Hispaniola after a hurricane in June 1495 destroyed all Columbus's remaining ships save *Niña*.) A month later they were still in the Caribbean, calling at Guadeloupe in April, where they attempted to reprovision in the face of hostile Caribs. On April 20, 1496, they weighed anchor again, but it was not until June 11 that they fetched up again in the Bay of Cadiz.

Traffic between Spain and the Caribbean was not confined only to Columbus's fleets, and several ships had arrived at Hispaniola while Columbus was there and before his return. While Columbus made preparations for his third voyage to the New World, *Niña*'s Captain Alonso Medel decided to do some trading to Rome on the side, only to be captured by Sardinian pirates. The ship was recaptured by her crew, and returned to Cadiz in time to sail from Sanlúcar on January 23, 1498, under Captain Pedro Francés, shortly before Columbus's main fleet sailed on his third voyage. Her subsequent career in the Caribbean is not known, and the last written record of her is in 1501.

Fernández-Armesto, *Columbus*. Gardiner and Unger, *Cogs, Caravels and Galleons*. Morison, *Admiral of the Ocean Sea*. Pastor, *Ships of Christopher Columbus*. Phillips, "Evolution of Spanish Ship Design."

# Nonsuch

Ketch. *L/B:* 50′ × 15′ (11m × 4.3m). *Tons:* 43 bm. *Hull:* wood. *Comp.:* 12–24. *Arm.:* 8 guns. *Built:* Wivenhoe, Essex, Eng.; 1650.

An eight-gun navy ketch from 1654 to 1667, when she was sold to Sir William Warren, the diminutive *Nonsuch* was the vehicle responsible for the founding of the Hudson's Bay Company. Prior to that she had a varied career, being built as a merchant trader and purchased by the navy in 1654. Captured by two Dutch privateers while escorting a merchant ketch through the English Channel on February 3, 1659, she was retaken two months later. In the meantime, the Huron allies of the French fur traders Médard Chouart, Sieur des Grosselliers, and his brother-in-law Pierre Esprit Radisson had been defeated by the Iroquois (allied with the English), and thus their trade via the St. Lawrence River and Great Lakes was jeopardized. To make up for this, Chouart and Radisson proposed to open direct trade with the "fur belt" via Hudson Bay. Angered by the high rates at which their furs were taxed and denied any redress from France, they went to England, where they were introduced to the court of Charles II by the chemist Robert Boyle.

By 1667, the nucleus of the Hudson's Bay Company had formed around these two men, and on June 5, 1668, the vessels *Nonsuch* and *Eaglet* (loaned for the venture by Charles II) sailed from London. The ships' primary cargo was "wampumpeage," small marine shell beads widely used as a medium of exchange among eastern Indians. *Eaglet* was damaged in midatlantic and returned to England with Radisson, but *Nonsuch* sailed into Hudson Bay and south to the shores of James Bay. On September 29, 1668, the adventurers landed and began to build Charles Fort (later named Rupert's House) on the Rupert River. After almost a year of trading with the Indians, Grosselliers returned to England in October 1669 with a cargo of furs. The following year the Hudson's Bay Company was formally incorporated and given by king's grant an area equivalent to nearly 40 percent of modern Canada. The later fate of the *Nonsuch* is unknown. A near replica of the vessel, designed by Alan Hinks in 1968, is on exhibit at the Manitoba Museum of Man and Nature in Winnipeg.

Rich, *History of the Hudson's Bay Company*.

# P

## HMS Paramore

Pink (3m). *L/B/D:* 64′ od (52′ keel) × 18′ × 9.6′ (19.5m (15.8m) × 5.5m × 2.9m). *Tons:* 89 bm. *Hull:* wood. *Comp.:* 24. *Built:* Fisher Harding, Deptford Dockyard, Eng.; 1694.

Edmund Halley, who would later have a comet named after him, was the first master and commander of HMS *Paramore,* the first ship built specifically for surveying. The first of Halley's two expeditions "to improve the knowledge of the Longitude and the [magnetic] variations of the Compasse" left Portsmouth on November 29, 1698. The ship visited Madeira, Fernando de Noronha, Brazil, Barbados, and Anguilla, and returned to England on June 22, 1699. After cashiering his refractory lieutenant, Halley sailed again on September 16. The second voyage ventured as far south as 52°24′S, which was reached on February 1, 1700. There they encountered "great islands of ice, of so incredible a height and magnitude that I scarce dare write my thoughts about it." After sighting Tristan da Cunha, the expedition made a landing at St. Helena (where Halley had spent from February 1677 to January 1678 cataloguing stars of the southern skies). They then sailed to Trinidad Island off Brazil (which Halley tried to claim for Britain), Pernambuco, and from there northward through the Caribbean and the North Atlantic to Newfoundland. *Paramore* returned to England on September 7, 1700. Halley's third voyage, in 1701, was a four-month cruise crisscrossing the English Channel to observe tidal currents. The same year he published the first magnetic charts of the Atlantic and Pacific Oceans. Refitted as a bomb ketch, HMS *Paramore* sailed under Captain Robert Stevens in Sir George Rooke's Mediterranean squadron in the 1702 war against France. She was sold to Captain John Constable in 1706.

Thrower, *Three Voyages of Edmund Halley.*

## Pinta

Caravel (3m). *L/B/D:* 55′–74′ × 18′–21′ × 7′ dph (17–23m × 5–7m × 2m dph). *Tons:* 75–116 toneladas. *Hull:* wood. *Comp.:* 26. *Arm.:* 9cm lombard, 4.5cm falconets. *Built:* Los Palos, Spain(?); <1492.

The smallest and least known of Christopher Columbus's three ships on his first voyage to the Americas in 1492–93, *Pinta* was a *caravela redonda,* a trading vessel setting a single square sail on the fore- and mainmasts, and a single lateen sail on the mizzen. As was the case with NIÑA, Columbus requisitioned the ship for the voyage in satisfaction of a fine levied by Spain's Ferdinand and Isabella. Acquired from Cristóbal Quintero, who sailed as a seaman on the voyage, she was put under the command of Martín Alonso Pinzón and sailed from Los Palos in company with SANTA MARÍA and *Niña* on August 3, 1492. Three days out, *Pinta* had trouble with her rudder, which could not be permanently repaired until Pinzón put into Las Palmas, on Grand Canary Island. Columbus pressed on to Gomera, in hopes of finding a replacement vessel, and when they returned to Las Palmas on August 25, two weeks later, *Pinta* had been there barely a day. With repairs to *Pinta* complete, and *Niña* sporting a new rig, the little fleet sailed on September 1, and after two days at Gomera, they resumed their westward voyage on September 6.

Martín Alonso Pinzón, one of the leading seamen of Los Palos, whose brother Vicente Yáñez Pinzón commanded *Niña,* was in large part responsible for Columbus's success in recruiting crew and outfitting his ships, and he seems to have chafed somewhat at being second-in-command. The Genoese Columbus was, after all, a foreigner, and his Enterprise of the Indies was not one to which people thronged, even though it had royal backing. On September 25, Martín Alonso Pinzón claimed a landfall, which proved false — they were in mid-Atlantic — and on October 6, he advised Columbus that he thought they had already overshot Cipango (Japan), their intended destination. By the second week of October, flotsam indicated that land was near. At about 0200 on October 12, *Pinta's* lookout, Rodrigo de Triana, made the first verifiable sighting of land. Nonetheless, on the basis of having seen a light some hours before (when they were probably 30 miles, 48 kilometers, from land), Columbus claimed the first sighting — and the 10,000 *maravedís* promised by Ferdinand and Isabella — for himself.

The island, which Columbus named San Salvador, was the Taino island of Guanahaní, in what is now the Bahamas. (Though the exact landing place is unknown, the leading candidates for the island are San Salvador and, about 60 miles (100 kilometers) southwest, Samana Cay.) The three ships explored the Bahamas between October 12 and 26, and then headed south to the northeast coast of Cuba.

On November 20, the three ships made a tentative foray in the direction of the Bahamas, but while trying to return to Cuba, Pinzón took off in *Pinta* to investigate Babeque (now Great Inagua Island) in hopes of finding gold, and probably to assert his independence from Columbus. The effort proved fruitless, and he sailed south to the northern coast of Hispaniola, spending about three weeks in a harbor to the east of where *Santa María* and *Niña* were exploring. From his base (possibly Puerto Blanco), Pinzón explored the interior and, he later claimed, visited the gold-rich region of Cibao. Hearing of the wreck of *Santa María* on Christmas Day, he attempted to rejoin Columbus,

and he did so at Isla Cabra on January 6, 1493, just as Columbus was beginning his voyage home in *Niña.*

After two days of repairs and provisioning, the two ships sailed for Spain. They remained in company until February 13, when they were separated in a storm. *Pinta* made her way to Bayona, north of the Portuguese border, probably by the end of February. While there, Pinzón sent letters to Ferdinand and Isabella requesting permission to report to them in person on the successful completion of the voyage. Rebuffed, he was forced to return to Los Palos, where he arrived only hours after Columbus. Ill and despondent at being bested by Columbus, Martín Alonso Pinzón made his way home and died soon thereafter. *Pinta's* subsequent fate is unknown.

Fernández-Armesto, *Columbus.* Morison, *Admiral of the Ocean Sea.* Pastor, *Ships of Christopher Columbus.* Philips, "Evolution of Spanish Ship Design."

## USS Polaris

(ex-*Periwinkle, America*) Schooner-rigged screw tug (1f/2m). *L/B/D:* 140' × 28' × 10.5' (42.7m × 8.5m × 3.2m). *Tons:* 387 burden. *Hull:* wood. *Comp.:* 16–37. *Arm.:* 2 × 24pdr. *Mach.:* steam, 1 screw. *Built:* Neafie & Levy, Philadelphia; 1864.

Originally named *America,* the screw tug USS *Periwinkle* first saw duty on Chesapeake Bay and the Rappahannock River with the U.S. Navy. She was laid up at the Norfolk Navy Yard from 1867 to 1870, when the Navy loaned her to Charles Francis Hall's North Polar Expedition. Renamed *Polaris* (for the North Star), after being fitted out for work in the Arctic ice, she sailed from the New York Navy Yard in July 1871. That season, the northern reaches of Baffin Strait were remarkably clear of ice, and by August 30, *Polaris* was on the edge of the Lincoln Sea at 82°11′N, a record farthest north. *Polaris* was stopped by the ice and pushed south while Hall established winter quarters at Thank God Harbour, Greenland, on September 10. On November 8, Hall died following a suspicious illness. (A 1968 autopsy found high levels of arsenic, although whether he was poisoned deliberately or accidentally — patent medicines of the day were rich in arsenic — was never determined.) Command of the expedition devolved on Sidney O. Budington, who dispatched an expedition to try for the Pole in June 1872. This was unsuccessful and *Polaris* turned south. On October 12, the ship was beset by ice in Smith Sound and was on the verge of being crushed. Nineteen of the crew and Eskimo guides abandoned ship for the surrounding ice and fourteen crew remained on the ship. The latter ran *Polaris* aground near Etah and she was crushed on October 24. After wintering ashore, the crew sailed south in two boats; they were rescued by a whaler and returned home via Scotland. Miraculously, the nineteen icebound castaways, including Eskimo women and children, drifted 1,500 miles, migrating from floe to floe as their temporary homes threatened to break up, and were rescued by the whaler *Tigress* on April 30, 1873.

Loomis, *Weird and Tragic Shores*. Silverstone, *Warships of the Civil War Navies*.

## Pourquoi Pas?

Screw bark (1f/3m). *L/B/D:* 139.7′ × 31.2′ × 15.4′ dph (77.4m × 13.7m × 5.6m). *Tons:* 449 reg. *Hull:* wood. *Comp.:* 42. *Mach.:* compound engine, 1 screw. *Built:* Ed Gautier, St. Malo, France; 1908.

The whimsical name Jean-Baptiste Charcot, France's foremost Antarctic explorer, gave his *Pourquoi Pas?* translates simply as "Why not?" The veteran leader of France's first Antarctic expedition in *Français* (1903–1905), Charcot departed Le Havre on his second expedition on August 23, 1908. After calling in various South American ports, he sailed from the Norwegian sealing port at Deception Island, South Shetland Islands, on Christmas Day. Charcot was disappointed in his ambitious expectation of sailing farther south than anyone before him, and *Pourquoi Pas?* wintered at Point Circumcision, on Petermann Island, until

November. Despite a cursory survey at Deception Island that revealed damage to the stem, *Pourquoi Pas?* sailed for a second winter in the Antarctic. On this trip, she sailed between 69°S and 70°S, as far west as 122°W. Among other achievements, the Charcot expedition surveyed 1,250 miles (2,010 kilometers) of Antarctic coastline and made extensive hydrographic surveys — including a 225-day study of tides — meteorological studies, bacteriological experiments, and magnetic observations. On January 7, 1910, the expedition also discovered Charcot Land, which Charcot named for his father, an esteemed physician.

Returning to France in June 1910, *Pourquoi Pas?* was handed over to the École Pratique des Hautes Études for use as a training ship in northern latitudes. Laid up at the beginning of World War I, in 1916 she was requisitioned by the French navy for work as a training ship stationed at L'Orient. Following the war, Charcot resumed command of his ship, sailing her to Iceland and the Faeroe Islands nearly every summer. In 1925, she made her first visit to Greenland's Scoresby Sound, and the next year she carried ninety Eskimos from Angmagssalik to Rosenvinge Bay to establish an Eskimo colony at Scoresby Sound.

In 1928, *Pourquoi Pas?* was dispatched in a vain search for Roald Amundsen, the Arctic explorer whose plane had disappeared during a search for Umberto Nobile's airship, *Italia*. In 1931, she was back at Scoresby Sound to establish an observation post at Rosenvinge Bay, and she returned there every year until 1936, the last year in which the sixty-nine-year-old Charcot would be eligible to sail. Departing Saint Servan on July 16, *Pourquoi Pas?* spent a month in the remarkably ice-free waters of Greenland, her crew engaged primarily in correcting charts. On August 30, a coal dust explosion forced her to accept a tow into Reykjavik. Following repairs, *Pourquoi Pas?* sailed for France on September 15. Despite the fine weather that day, a storm of unusual violence came up that night and *Pourquoi Pas?* narrowly missed going ashore on Akranes Point. An hour and forty minutes later, the mizzen mast went by the boards, and at 0515 she hit a submerged rock off Bargafjord, north of Reykjavik. There was only one survivor, a seaman named Gonidec, among the forty-two officers and crew.

Charcot, *Voyage of the "Pourquoi Pas?"* Oulié, *Charcot and the Antarctic.*

# Predpriyatiye

Sloop-of-war (3m). *Hull:* wood. *Comp.:* 122. *Arm.:* 24 × 6pdr. *Built:* St. Petersburg; 1823.

Built specifically for service between Kamchatka and Russia's North American colonies in what is now Alaska, *Predpriyatiye* ("Enterprise") sailed from Kronstadt on July 28, 1823, under command of Otto von Kotzebue, a veteran of circumnavigations in NADEZHDA (1803–6) and RURIK (1815–18). Although the purpose of the voyage out was to deliver goods to Kamchatka, Kotzebue was also under orders to confirm old discoveries — or make new ones — along his route. After rounding Cape Horn, with a stop in Valparaiso, *Predpriyatiye* sailed through the Tuamotu Archipelago, where Kotzebue found several previously unseen islands, one of which he named for his ship. The Russians continued first to Tahiti and then Samoa before turning northwest to sail through the Radak Chain to Petropavlovsk, where they arrived on June 9, 1824. Arriving in Novoarkhangelsk (Sitka, Alaska) in October, Kotzebue learned that his ship was not needed on station until the following spring, so he sailed for Yerba Buena (now San Francisco), where the Russians spent a month before sailing for the Sandwich (Hawaiian) Islands. *Predpriyatiye* returned to Novoarkhangelsk on February 24, 1825, and remained in Alaskan waters for five months conducting extensive surveys of the approaches and surrounding waters. The return voyage via Hawaii and the Radaks resulted in the discovery of Bikini Island (initially named for Johann F. Eschscholtz, one of two naturalists aboard). After two months at Manila, *Predpriyatiye* sailed for Kronstadt, where she arrived on July 10, 1826, after several stops en route.

Ivashintsov, *Russian Round-the-World Voyages.* Kotzebue, *New Voyage Round the World.*

# R

## Ra II

Reed raft (1m). *L/B/D:* 39′ × 16′ × 6′ deep (11.9m × 4.9m × 1.8m). *Hull:* papyrus reed. *Comp.:* 8. *Des.:* traditional. *Built:* Safi, Morocco; 1970.

Intrigued by the strong resemblance between various aspects of ancient Egyptian and pre-Columbian culture, Thor Heyerdahl set out to demonstrate that the sources of New World technology and belief could have come from across the Atlantic. A crucial point of similarity was the design of reed boats shown in Egyptian tombs and found on Lake Chad, the Andean Lake Titicaca, and Easter Island in the Pacific, to which he had sailed in the balsa raft KON-TIKI in 1947. Heyerdahl hired a Chadian reed-boat builder, Abdullah Djibrine, and two Buruma colleagues to build a *kaday* from papyrus cut on Lake Tana, the source of the Blue Nile in Ethiopia. The design was worked out in consultation between Djibrine and Björn Langström, a Swedish authority on ancient Egyptian boat design.

The finished *Ra* — named for the Egyptian sun god — made entirely of papyrus and rope was taken by truck and ship to the Moroccan port of Safi, where she was launched. The polyglot crew consisted of Heyerdahl, Djibrine, Yuri Alexandrovich Senkevich (Soviet Union), Norman Baker (United States), Carlo Mauri (Italy), Santiago Genoves (Mexico), and Georges Sourial (Egypt). Provisions for the voyage were carried in 160 amphorae modeled on a 5,000-year-old example in the Cairo Museum. The voyage began on May 25, 1969. Although *Ra* made it most of the way across the Atlantic, covering about 60 miles (97 kilometers) a day (averaging 2.5 knots), the crew were forced to abandon *Ra* near Barbados, because much of the stern had sagged and the raft was breaking up.

Convinced only that he had chosen the wrong design, Heyerdahl arranged to build *Ra II*, a Moroccan *madia* whose design more closely resembled that of the reed rafts on Lake Titicaca. Four Aymara reed-boat builders from Bolivia were brought to Morocco for the project, which again used reeds from Lake Tana. Though 10 feet (3 meters) shorter than *Ra*, *Ra II* carried eight crew, Madanni Ait Ouhanni (Morocco) and Kei Ohara (Japan) sailing in place of Djibrine. The second attempt, in 1970, was a success, the voyage from Morocco to Barbados being completed in only fifty-seven days.

Heyerdahl, *"Ra" Expeditions.*

## USS Ramapo (AO-12)

*Pataka*-class oiler (1f/2m). *L/B/D:* 477.8′ × 62.2′ × 26.2′ (145.6m × 18.9m × 8m). *Tons:* 16,800 disp. *Hull:* steel. *Comp.:* 90. *Arm.:* 2 × 5″. *Mach.:* 11.6 kts. *Built:* Newport News Shipbuilding & Dry Dock Co., Newport News, Va.; 1919.

Owing to its transpacific commitment to its far-flung colonial holdings in the Philippines, the U.S. Navy was one of the first navies to convert to fuel oil. By 1916, the switch to oil was widespread enough to warrant the construction of "fuel ships," or oilers, as they came to be known. The first attempts to transfer oil while under way were conducted in calm seas in 1913, but little notice was taken at the time. In April 1917, just after the United States entered World War I, Lieutenant

Chester W. Nimitz, in command of *Maumee* (AO-2), used his ship to fuel six destroyers bound for Britain in mid Atlantic.

After service between the Gulf of Mexico and ports in the Caribbean, the East Coast, and Europe, in 1928 *Ramapo* transferred to the Pacific, where she would spend the remainder of her career. She worked nine years on the run between San Pedro and U.S. bases in the Philippines and China, averaging about four round-trips annually. In addition to the work for which she was intended, *Ramapo* was also requisitioned from time to time by the U.S. Hydrographic Office to conduct oceanographic surveys in the western Pacific.

In early 1933, *Ramapo* was en route from Manila to San Diego when she encountered a week of storms. The gale reached its peak on February 6, when wind gusts, reaching 68 knots (Force 12), helped churn up tremendous, fast-moving seas. The period of the waves — the time it takes two successive wave crests to pass the same point — was calculated at about fifteen seconds, with a wavelength of 335 meters and a speed of 55 knots. They also attained enormous size, rising successively 24, 27, 30, and 33 meters. Then, as the scientist and author Rachel L. Carson explained:

> While standing watch on the bridge during the early hours of that day, one of the officers of the *Ramapo* saw, in the moonlight, a great sea rising astern to a level above an iron strap on the crow's nest of the mainmast. The *Ramapo* was on even keel and her stern was in the trough of the sea. These circumstances made possible an exact line of sight from the bridge to the crest of the wave, and simple mathematical calculations based on the dimensions of the ship gave the height of the wave. It was 112 feet [34 meters].

Although many ships have been overwhelmed in smaller seas, *Ramapo* rode out this storm. The extreme wave encountered on February 6, 1933, remains the highest wave reliably recorded.

*Ramapo*, which was named for a serene river in New Jersey, was shifted to the Hawaiian run in early 1941, and she was at Pearl Harbor during

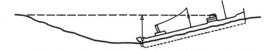

A schematic drawing showing how the **Ramapo**'s mate calculated the height of the 112-foot (34-meter) wave that passed under the ship. Looking astern, the mate saw that the crow's nest aligned with the crest of the wave and the horizon beyond. The stern of the ship was in the trough (bottom) of the wave. From F. G. Walton Smith, *The Seas in Motion.*

the Japanese attack on December 7. The next year she entered service between the West Coast and American bases in the Aleutian Islands, and she remained in that work for the duration of the war. She was decommissioned in January 1946.

Carson, *Sea Around Us.* Smith, *Seas in Motion.* Wildenberg, *Gray Steel and Black Oil.*

## HMS Resolute

(ex-*Refuge, Ptarmigan*) Bark (3m). *L/B/D:* 115′ × 28.3′ × 11.5′ (35.1m × 8.6m × 3.5m). *Tons:* 424 bm. *Comp.:* 61. *Hull:* wood. *Built:* Smith(?), Shields, Eng.; 1849.

Built as the merchant ship *Ptarmigan* and purchased by the Royal Navy in 1850, HM Discovery Ship *Resolute* was one of six vessels sent out that year under command of Captain Henry Austin in search of Sir John Franklin's HMS EREBUS and TERROR. The expedition also included the Royal Navy's bark *Assistance*, the steamers *Intrepid* and *Pioneer*, and the privately owned brigs *Lady Franklin* and *Sophia*. The ships wintered in Lancaster Sound and returned to England in the fall of 1851, having found no trace of Franklin's ships.

The four Navy ships sailed again for the Arctic in April 1852. The expedition was led by Sir Edward Belcher in *Assistance*, with Captain Henry Kellett in *Resolute*, Captain Sherard Osborn in *Pioneer*, and Captain Francis L. McClintock in *Intrepid*. Leaving the supply ship *North Star* at

Beechey Island in Lancaster Sound, *Assistance* and *Pioneer* turned north into Wellington Sound (between Devon and Cornwallis islands), where they were iced in off Griffith Island. *Resolute* and *Intrepid* sailed west toward Melville Island and reached Winter Harbour on September 5 before withdrawing to Dealy Island, 35 miles (56 kilometers) east. From there, various sledging expeditions set out in search of both the Franklin expedition and that of Leopold McClure's HMS INVESTIGATOR and Richard Collinson's *Enterprise* — the "search for the searchers." Returning to Winter Harbour, a sledge party found a note from McClure's party indicating that *Investigator* was at Banks Island, 175 miles southwest across Melville Sound. The following April, a rescue party was sent out and the survivors of the *Investigator* returned to *Resolute.*

Having exhausted any hope of finding Franklin's expedition in Barrow Strait or Melville Sound, Kellett decided to return to Beechey Island. The ice was impenetrable, and *Resolute* and *Intrepid* wintered off the southeast of Bathurst Island. In the summer of 1854, Belcher sent orders for Kellett to abandon his ships and march his men to Beechey Island. Kellett reluctantly complied. On August 26, 1854, *North Star* turned for home with a total complement of 263 men — the crews of six ships, including her own. The same day, she fell in with the supply ships *Phoenix* and *Talbot,* and the men were divided between the three ships for the return to England.

Though acquitted for his poor handling of his ships, none of which was at risk of sinking when abandoned, Belcher was publicly disgraced. A year after his return to England, the American whaler *George Henry* came upon *Resolute* drifting in the Davis Strait 1,100 miles (1,800 kilometers) east of where she had been abandoned. Captain James Buddington took the ship in tow to New London, Connecticut. The U.S. government purchased the vessel and after a refit presented her to the British government. The ship was eventually laid up at Chatham, but before she was broken up in 1879, Queen Victoria ordered a table made from her timbers and presented to President Rutherford B. Hayes. In 1961, John F. Kennedy became the first president to use the table in the Oval Office of the White House.

de Bray, *Frenchman in Search of Franklin.* M'Dougall, *Eventful Voyage of H.M. Discovery Ship "Resolute."*

## HMS Resolution

(ex-*Drake, Marquis of Granby*) Ship-sloop (3m). *L/B/D:* 110.7′ × 30.5′ × 13.2′ dph (33.7m × 9.3m × 4m). *Tons:* 461 tons. *Hull:* wood. *Comp.:* 112; 12 civilians. *Arm.:* 12 × 6pdr, 12 swivels. *Built:* Fishburn, Whitby, Eng.; 1770.

Shortly after returning to England from his first voyage of discovery in ENDEAVOUR, Commander James Cook was given two ships for a voyage to determine the existence of a great southern continent. Cook's flagship was *Resolution,* and Commander Tobias Furneaux was the senior officer aboard HMS ADVENTURE; originally bark-rigged North Sea colliers, the two were rerigged as ships. The ships departed Plymouth on July 13, 1772. After a stay at Cape Town, in November they sailed south to become the first ships known to have crossed the Antarctic Circle, on January 17, 1773, ultimately reaching 67°15′S. The two ships were separated by fog on February 8, and after failing to find *Adventure,* Cook continued exploring the fringes of the southern ice pack until March 17, when he turned for New Zealand. *Resolution* arrived at Dusky Sound on South Island on March 25 and rendezvoused with *Adventure* at Ship Cove in Queen Charlotte Sound on the south side of Cook Strait on May 18.

A month later they sailed east, looking for land, then turned for Tahiti, staying there from August 15 to September 7. Sailing west, the two ships called in the Tonga Islands, which Cook named "the Friendly Archipelago as a lasting friendship seems to subsist among the Inhabitants and their Courtesy to Strangers intitles them to that Name," before heading again for New Zealand, where they arrived at the end of October. *Resolution* and *Adventure* were separated in a storm, and after waiting at Cook Strait until November 26, *Resolution* headed south. The ship crossed the Antarctic Circle for the second time and ultimately reached as far as 71°10′S, 106°30′W (east of the Palmer Peninsula). After stopping at Easter Island, she continued east through the Marquesas, to Tahiti, where Cook and his crew were warmly entertained for six weeks. *Resolution* sailed again on June 4, 1774, and after exploring Espiritu Santo (Vanuatu), New Caledonia, and Norfolk Island, she arrived again at the Cook Strait.

A month later, *Resolution* shaped a course for Cape Horn on November 9. Cook explored Tierra del Fuego and Staten Island from December 17 to January 3, 1775, and then sailed east, discovering uninhabited South Georgia Island on January 14 and the South Sandwich Islands a few days later. Having sailed the length of the Southern Ocean, but "having failed to find a southern continent" — as Cook explained to the Admiralty — "because it does not lie in a navigable sea," she sailed for Cape Town. After several Atlantic stops, *Resolution* arrived at Spithead on July 29.

No less remarkable than this expedition's extraordinary contribution to geographic knowledge is the fact that, thanks to Cook's strict regimen for cleaning and airing the ship and the antiscorbutic diet (including "sour krout") he insisted on to prevent scurvy, in the course of a 70,000-mile (113,000-kilometer) voyage lasting three years and eighteen days, only four of *Resolution*'s crew died, and only one of them was lost to sickness.

Promoted to the rank of Post Captain, Cook was soon off again on a voyage to find the Northwest Passage, for the discovery of which the British Parliament had pledged £20,000. *Resolution* was retained for the purpose, this time paired with DISCOVERY under Captain Charles Clerke. Among *Resolution*'s crew on this voyage were Lieutenant John Gore and William Bligh, who sailed as master, and Omai, who was returning to Tahiti after two years in London, where he had traveled in *Adventure*. *Resolution* sailed on July 14, 1776, and was joined by *Discovery* at Cape Town on November 10.

The ships continued eastward, stopping at new and familiar lands, including three months in Van Diemen's Land, the Tonga Islands, and Tahiti. The expedition left the South Pacific and headed north. After stopping in the Sandwich (Hawaiian) Islands in January 1778, they sailed northwest, arriving on the coast of North America on March 7 and at Nootka Sound on the twenty-ninth. There *Resolution* received a major overhaul, including a new mizzen, fore topmast, and foremast. Departing again on April 26, the ships sailed northwest along the Alaska coast, anchoring in Prince William Sound on May 12 — "520 leagues to the westward of any part of Baffins or Hudsons bay" — and, two weeks later, Cook Inlet. Rounding the Alaska Peninsula, they sailed into the Bering Sea, calling along the coast before passing Cape Prince of Wales, the east side of the Bering Strait, and then north and west as far as Icy Cape, 126 miles southwest of Point Barrow, on August 18. The ships made the coast of the Chukotski Peninsula on August 29, and then spent from October 3 to 26 at the Russian settlement at Unalaska before proceeding back to the Sandwich Islands. Anchoring at Hawaii, they remained through the winter, Cook being venerated as a chief (or, as some people believe, a divinity called Orono). The ships sailed again on February 4, 1779, but a sprung foremast in *Resolution* forced them back a week later. On the fourteenth, an argument between a group of Hawaiians and a shore party led to a skirmish in which four marines and Cook himself were killed. So died "one of the most celebrated Navigators that this or former ages can boast of."

Command of the expedition, and *Resolution,* fell to Captain Clerke; *Discovery* was under command of Lieutenant John Gore. The ships sailed from the Sandwich Islands on March 23 bound for Petropavlovsk on the Kamchatka Peninsula. After a second foray past Icy Cape to 71°56′N, the crew abandoned their effort to find a northern passage to the Atlantic. Captain Clerke died on August 22 and was buried at Petropavlovsk, where the ships landed two days later. Command of the expedition now fell to Gore, a veteran of two expeditions in HMS DOLPHIN as well as Cook's first, in HMS ENDEAVOUR. James King was promoted to command the *Discovery.* The ship sailed southwest to trace the coast of Japan (though storms hindered them greatly) and called in at Macao. She then sailed for Cape Town, avoiding Batavia (Djakarta). Forced north about Ireland, the ships landed at Stromness in the Orkneys on August 22, 1780, and were back in The Nore on October 4, after a voyage of four years, two months, and twenty-two days.

Resolution subsequently became a Royal Navy transport and sailed for the East Indies in March 1781. On June 10, 1782, she was captured by the French ships Annibal and Sphinx northwest of Trincomalee, Sri Lanka. Admiral Suffren later intimated that she either sank or was recaptured by the British, but her ultimate fate is unknown.

F. S., "Cook's Resolution." Freeston, "His Majesty's Sloop Resolution, 1772." McGowan, "Captain Cook's Ships."

# Resolution

Ship (3m). L/B: 100.3' × 26.2' (30.6m × 8m). Tons: 291. Hull: wood. Built: Fishburne & Broderick, Whitby, Eng.; 1803.

Among the most influential families in the history of Arctic exploration was the Scoresby family. William Scoresby, father and son, hailed from Whitby, North Yorkshire, one of the premier English fishing and whaling ports. In 1803, the elder Scoresby took command of the whaleship Resolution; in this ship his son rose from apprentice to first mate and, in 1810, captain. English whalers in this period routinely made annual voyages to Arctic waters, and collectively they had contributed more to the scientific understanding of the region than anyone else. On May 25, 1806, the Scoresbys sailed Resolution to a record high latitude of 81°30′N. Eleven years later, the younger Scoresby would relay to Sir Joseph Banks the fact that Arctic conditions were moderating — the sea was "perfectly devoid of ice" as high as 80°N and the Greenland shore was ice-free. This information set in motion the parade of government-sponsored voyages in search of the Northwest Passage. Although Scoresby sought to command the first expedition, and was backed by Banks (a veteran of Captain James Cook's first voyage in HMS ENDEAVOUR), the command fell to Captain John Ross, with ISABELLA and Alexander.

Scoresby sold his interest in Resolution in 1813, but the ship remained under Whitby ownership until 1829, when she was sold to Peterhead interests.

Berton, Arctic Grail. Lubbock, Arctic Whalers.

# HMS Roebuck

5th rate, 26 (3m). L/B/D: 96' × 25.5' × 9.8' (29.3m × 6.9m × 3m). Tons: 292 bm. Hull: wood. Comp.: 50–125. Arm.: 12 guns. Built: Snelgrove, Wapping, Eng.; 1690.

Originally commissioned as a fireship, HMS Roebuck, the seventh ship of the name, is best known for her part in the exploration of Australia and New Guinea under the journal-keeping buccaneer and explorer William Dampier. In 1688, Dampier had sailed from Mexico to the Philippines in Cygnet, subsequently landing on the coast of Australia for repairs. Although he returned to England penniless, the competence of his New Voyage around the World in 1697 impressed the Admiralty, and he was given command of Roebuck for a voyage to New Holland (Australia). Departing The Downs on January 14, 1699, he called at Bahia, Brazil, and from there proceeded east to arrive on August 7 at Shark Bay, near where Dirck Hartog had landed in EENDRACHT in 1616. A week later he sailed north, following the coast as far as Roebuck Bay (near Broome) before quitting the coast of New Holland on September 5. After calling at Timor on September 15, Roebuck was off the New Guinea coast by December. Dampier rounded north of New Britain, which he named after determining that it "does not join to the main Land of New Guinea, but is an Island, as I have described it in my Map."

Returning to Batavia (Djakarta), Roebuck was fitted out for the passage to England and sailed on October 17 via the Cape of Good Hope and "Santa Hellena." On February 21, 1700, about a mile from Ascension Island, the ship sprang "a Leak which could not be stopped, [and] foundered at Sea." The crew landed on Ascension and were rescued five weeks later by a British convoy.

Beaglehole, Exploration of the Pacific. Dampier, Voyages.

# Roosevelt

Steam schooner (3m). *L/B/D:* 185′ × 35.6′ × 16′ (56.4m × 10.8m × 4.9m). *Tons:* 1,600 disp. *Hull:* wood. *Comp.:* 20. *Des.:* Robert E. Peary. *Built:* McKay & Dix Shipyard, Bucksport, Me.; 1905.

Designed specifically for Arctic expeditions, the auxiliary schooner *Roosevelt* was named for President Theodore Roosevelt, who helped Commander Robert Peary obtain leave from the U.S. Navy to pursue his ambition of being the first man to reach the North Pole. Built along the lines of Roald Amundsen's FRAM, *Roosevelt*'s rounded hull enabled her to be pushed up by the encroaching ice rather than be crushed by it. On the first voyage, *Roosevelt* departed New York in July 1905 and sailed through the Davis Strait and on to Cape Sheridan at the northern end of Ellesmere Island on the Arctic Ocean. Peary attempted to reach the Pole over the ice, but he only reached 87°6′N before being forced to turn back on April 21, 1906. Meanwhile, *Roosevelt* had been badly damaged in the ice. Captain Bob Bartlett wrestled her back to New York, where she underwent extensive repairs that meant postponing Peary's next expedition by a year.

On July 8, 1908, Peary began his most famous expedition. At Etah, Greenland, *Roosevelt* embarked sixty-nine Eskimos and 246 sled dogs for the final push north to Cape Sheridan, Ellesmere Island, where the ship arrived on September 5. After setting up supply depots along their prospective route north, on March 1, 1909, Peary set out from Cape Columbia, 90 miles (145 kilometers) northwest of Cape Sheridan. A total of twenty-four men blazed the trail north, but the final assault on the Pole was left to Peary, Matthew Henson, and the Eskimos Egingwah, Seeglo, Ootah, and Ooqueah. It is doubtful that they reached the Pole, as Peary claimed (April 6), but they returned to the ship without serious incident on April 23. Peary's return to the United States was met with great acclaim, and Congress made him a rear admiral.

In 1910, the Peary Arctic Club sold *Roosevelt* to John Arbuckle, who sold her to the U.S. Fisheries Commission in 1915. Employed by the Navy on the West Coast during World War I, she was later bought for use as a tug, first by the West Coast Tug Company and, from 1924, the Washington Tug & Barge Company. She was abandoned in 1942.

Peary, *Nearest the Pole; North Pole.*

# Rurik

Brig. *Tons:* 180 bm. *Hull:* wood. *Arm.:* 8 guns. *Comp.:* 32–34. *Built:* Abo, Finland; 1815.

Named for the ninth-century founder of the Rurik dynasty, which ruled Russia for eight centuries, *Rurik* was built for an expedition proposed by Count Nikolai P. Romanzof to sail through the Bering Strait and search for the Northeast Passage. Lieutenant Otto von Kotzebue, who had circumnavigated the globe in Adam Johann von Krusenstern's NADEZHDA in 1803, commanded the expedition, whose members included the naturalists Adelbert von Chamisso and Johann Friedrich Eschscholtz. Sailing from Kronstadt on July 30, 1815, after stops at Copenhagen and Portsmouth *Rurik* entered the Atlantic on October 5, 1815. While rounding Cape Horn in January 1816, Kotzebue sustained a chest injury that would plague him for the rest of the voyage, and storm damage to the ship forced him to put into Talcahuano, Chile.

Heading west in March, *Rurik*'s next Pacific landfall was at Easter Island on March 28. Sailing via the Tuamotus and the Marshall Islands, the Russian ship arrived at Petropavlovsk, Kamchatka, on June 3. Over the course of the next twelve days, *Rurik* was sheathed in copper taken from the hull of Vasilii M. Golovnin's sloop DIANA. On July 30, *Rurik* sailed through the Bering Strait and, hugging the northern coast of the Seward Peninsula, she sailed into Kotzebue Sound, which at first Kotzebue believed might be an arm of the Northeast Passage. Heading east to Cape Dezhnev, the easternmost part of Asia, on August 19 *Rurik* turned back from St. Lawrence Bay. Stopping at Yerba Buena (now San Francisco) for supplies in October, she sailed for the Sandwich (Hawaiian) Islands in November and thence on to the Marshall and Caroline islands, which the expedition surveyed through March 1817.

On April 13, *Rurik* was pooped and lost her bowsprit; several sailors were also badly injured, including Kotzebue. A few days later, the ship was almost lost on Unimak Island, but after two months of repairs at Unalaska, she put to sea again on June 29, with fifteen Aleuts and equipped with *baidarkas* (skin boats) for coastal survey work. Greatly weakened by his Cape Horn injury, Kotzebue was forced to abandon the effort and return to Unalaska. By October 1, *Rurik* was back at Honolulu, where the Russians gathered plants for transplantation in the Radak Island chain of the Marshall Islands, en route to Manila. En route home, at the end of March 1818, the Russians met the French ship URANIE at the Cape of Good Hope. After stops at Portsmouth and Copenhagen, *Rurik* arrived at the Neva on August 3, 1818. Kotzebue's account of the voyage was one of several. Chamisso and Eschscholtz published studies of marine and animal life as well as ethnographic studies of the Siberian Chuchkis, California mission society, and the Sandwich Islands. (Eschscholtz sailed again with Kotzebue on the PREDPRIYATIYE expedition of 1823–26.)

*Rurik* was later purchased by the Russian-American Company and in 1821–22 made a second voyage under Navigator Klochov, in company with the ship *Elisaveta*, in what was intended to be a second circumnavigation. The latter ship had to be sold at Cape Town, and *Rurik* proceeded alone to Novoarkhangelsk (Sitka) where she was put into colonial service, in which she ended her days. Her officers and crew returned home via Okhotsk and thence overland.

Ivashintsov, *Russian Round-the-World Voyages.* Kotzebue, *Voyage of Discovery.*

# S

Saint (see also *San, São, Sviatoi*)

## St. Jean-Baptiste

Ship (3m). *Tons:* 650 bm. *Hull:* wood. *Comp.:* 172. *Arm.:* 26 × 12pdr, 10 × 6pdr. *Built:* Nantes, France; 1767.

*St. Jean-Baptiste* was a merchant ship built for trade between France and India following the effective demise of the French East India Company (Compagnie des Indes), which followed the loss of Pondicherry to the British in 1761. Jean-François-Marie de Surville was captain and part owner. On June 3, 1767, she sailed for the Ganges River on the Bay of Bengal and arrived in November 1768. The next spring, she traded between French-Indian ports at Madras, Chandernagore, and Binganapali before Surville began to ready her for a voyage east. Surville and his partners hoped to find a land rumored to have been discovered by the English during Captain Samuel Wallis's cruise in HMS DOLPHIN, reports of which had been conflated with the century-old rumor of Davis Land, off the coast of Chile. Surville was also to "open trade with the Dutch and share it with the Dutch." If these plans failed, the enterprise might at least break even by selling off trade goods at Manila.

*St. Jean-Baptiste* sailed from the Hooghly River on March 3, 1769. After calling at Pondicherry, she crossed to Malacca and Trengganu, and then sailed north to the Philippines and the Bashi Islands between Luzon and Formosa (Taiwan). From here she entered the Pacific and sailed southwest until, on October 8, she came to Choiseul Island, east-ernmost of the Solomon Islands (first identified by Alvaro Mendaña in 1568, though the French did not recognize them as such). Surville and his crew anchored at what they named De Surville Island, east of Santa Isabel. On October 22, they sailed south through the Coral Sea and into the Tasman Sea in search of new lands. They narrowly missed New Caledonia, and after two months, during which scurvy ravaged the crew, they turned hopefully east to seek shelter on New Zealand, then known only from Tasman's 1642 voyage in HEEMSKERCK.

On December 12, they fell in with the land off Hokianga Harbor, about 100 miles below Cape Maria Van Diemen. Doubling the cape, they came to anchor in what Captain James Cook had six days before named Doubtless Bay. One estimate suggests that *St. Jean-Baptiste* and Cook's ENDEAVOUR missed each other by as little as 30 miles, and certainly not more than a few days at Doubtless Bay. The Maoris proved helpful and the surviving crew soon regained their strength. After discussing the available options, Surville decided it was safer to run down the 5,000 miles to Chile before the prevailing westerlies than to risk the fickle winds and island-studded waters back to the Indies. Having kidnapped a Maori named Ranginui to retaliate for the theft of a yawl boat, the French sailed on New Year's Eve, 1769.

*St. Jean-Baptiste* crossed the Pacific in about 35°S, a higher southern latitude than any ship to that time, and thereby removed any lingering doubts about the existence of a Davis Land or Terra Australis in the central South Pacific. Nonetheless the journey took its toll, and many of the

▲ The Royal Canadian Mounted Police auxiliary schooner **St. Roch,** on patrol in loose Arctic ice in northern Canada. *Courtesy Vancouver Maritime Museum.*

crew died, including Ranginui. The men were so enfeebled that Surville could not put ashore at Más Afuera, on March 24, 1770. Continuing to the Peruvian coast, on April 7 they made a landfall at Chilca, where Surville drowned in the surf when his boat capsized as he went ashore. First Officer Guillaume Labé took the ship to Callao, Peru, where the French were arrested and held for three years. With a crew that included sixty-three Spaniards recruited to make up for the seventy-nine deaths and twenty-three desertions from the original crew, *St. Jean-Baptiste* sailed on April 7, 1773, and arrived back at Port-Louis, Brittany, on August 20. The voyage was a commercial disaster, and the ship and what cargo remained were auctioned.

Dunmore, *Expedition of the "St. Jean-Baptiste."*

# St. Roch

Auxiliary schooner (1f/2m). *L/B/D:* 104.3′ bp × 24.8′ × 13′ (31.8m × 7.5m × 4m). *Tons:* 323 disp. *Hull:* wood. *Comp.:* 9. *Mach.:* diesel, 150 hp. *Built:* Burrard Dry Dock Co., Ltd., North Vancouver, B.C.; 1928.

Built for the Royal Canadian Mounted Police service in the Arctic, the patrol vessel *St. Roch* was named for the fourteenth-century French saint celebrated for his gift of healing. Norwegian-born RCMP Staff Sergeant Henry Larsen joined the ship on her first voyage and became master in August 1928. The first ten years of *St. Roch*'s career were spent patrolling the Eskimo communities of the western Arctic, returning to Vancouver via the Bering Strait for fresh supplies and crew every summer. In 1940, concerned about establishing uncontested sovereignty over the islands of the Canadian Arctic, the government ordered Larsen "to proceed, if possible, from Vancouver, British Columbia, on patrol to Halifax, Nova Scotia, via the Canadian Arctic, if there was sufficient time left after . . . duties in the Western Arctic."

On June 23, 1940, *St. Roch* sailed north through the Bering Strait into the Arctic Sea fully expecting to attempt the passage that year, but made it only as far as Victoria Island. The next spring, the wartime shipping shortage obliged Larsen to return to Vancouver to load more supplies for the northern communities. Setting out from Cambridge Bay in August 1941, *St. Roch* made it as far as the Boothia Peninsula, where the crew wintered in Pasley Bay. One of the crew, Albert Chartrand, died of a heart attack, and Larsen and two of the crew walked 1,140 miles (1,835 kilometers) to fetch a Catholic priest to conduct a funeral for him the following spring. When the ice broke up in August, they proceeded through Bellot Strait, a narrow defile measuring 18 miles (29 kilometers) long and 1 mile wide. From there they made for Lancaster Sound, south into the Davis Strait, and put into Halifax, Nova Scotia, on October 11, 1942. *St. Roch* was the first ship to make the Northwest Passage from east to west, and after Roald Amundsen's GJØA only the second ship to make the passage in either direction.

In 1943, *St. Roch* was employed in servicing communities in the eastern Arctic for a season before being fitted with a new 300-horsepower engine and rerigged as a ketch. In 1944, Larsen was ordered to return to Vancouver. Rather than go back by Amundsen's route, the way he had come, he decided to sail north around Victoria Island via the McClure and Prince of Wales straits. From Holman Island, he raced the encroaching ice in a successful effort to avoid wintering in the Arctic. He sailed through the Bering Strait in September and was back in Vancouver on October 16. Having covered 7,295 miles in eighty-six days, *St. Roch* was the first ship to make the Northwest Passage in a single season. After two more voyages to the western Arctic in 1945–46 and 1947–48, she returned to Halifax. Upon her arrival, it was decided that she was no longer fit for Arctic voyaging and she was laid up. In Vancouver, public sentiment for the ship was strong, and in 1954 funds were raised to return the ship to her homeport. Today the Arctic veteran is preserved in a tent-shaped building erected by the Vancouver Maritime Museum.

Delgado, *Dauntless "St. Roch."* Larsen, *The Big Ship.*

# San Jerónimo

*Tons:* 150 tons. *Built:* Guayaquil, Ecuador(?); <1605.

Although Alvaro Mendaña sought to establish a colony in the Solomon Islands, which he discovered on his heroic but fruitless voyage of 1567–69 in LOS REYES and *Todos Los Santos*, it was not until 1574 that he secured in Spain authorization to take 500 men (50 of them with their wives and children), as well as cattle, horses, goats, sheep, and pigs for breeding, to fortify three cities within six years. No sooner was this done than Mendaña was arrested on a trumped-up charge. By the time he was free, Francis Drake had entered the Pacific in GOLDEN HIND, "whereupon commandment was given that [the Solomons] should not be inhabited; that the English, or others who pass the Straits of Magalhanes to go to the Malucas, might have no succour there but such as they got of the Indians."

Mendaña languished in Peru for the next fifteen years, but on April 5, 1595, he set sail with four ships — *San Jerónimo* (purchased from Sebastian de Goite y Figueroa), *Santa Ysabel,* the frigate *Santa Catalina,* and the galliot *San Felipe* — and 386 emigrants, including his wife, Doña Ysabel de Barreto, and her three brothers. The chief pilot was Pedro Fernández de Quirós. The ships first sailed through the Marquesas Islands, which Mendaña named for the Viceroy Marquesas de Mendoza. Mendaña's lack of leadership plagued the expedition and contributed to the murder of 200 Marquesans, most of whom were killed with little or no provocation.

Running west in about 10°S, the ships next passed between the Ellice and Cook islands, but before they reached the Solomons, they came to Santa Cruz Island, 6° east of San Cristóbal. At the same time, *Santa Ysabel* disappeared, possibly sinking during an eruption of Tinakula volcano, 15 miles (24 kilometers) away. After making a start at founding a colony, the soldiers — who treated the inhabitants ruthlessly — grew restive and decided they wanted to leave. Mendaña killed the camp master in an effort to restore order and allegiance to himself, but he was ailing and died a few days later, on October 18, leaving command of the expedition to his wife. Sickness descended on the camp, and it was not until November 18 that the three remaining ships sailed. On December 10, near the Equator, *San Felipe* disappeared, only to arrive independently at Mindanao. Though those aboard *San Jerónimo* and *Santa Catalina* were starving or dying of thirst at the rate of more than one person a day, Mendaña's widow refused to share her provisions with the ship's company, and even used the scarce water to wash her clothes. On December 19, Quirós asked to bring the few survivors from *Santa Catalina* aboard his ship, but the governess refused and the frigate disappeared.

On December 23, the Spanish sighted Ponape, in the Carolines, but were unable to land here or, on January 1, 1596, at either Guam or Rota in the Marianas. Finally, on January 12, *San Jerónimo* reached the Philippines, where the crew found food. On February 11, Quirós's ship arrived at Manila; fifty of her complement had died en route.

> There was not a yard that was not bent downward owing to parted lifts, the topsail ties were gone, and perhaps for three days at a time the sail was flapping in the waist because no one cared to hoist it with a rope that had been spliced thirty-three times.

Mendaña's widow remarried and, with her new husband, refitted the ship for the return to Mexico on August 10, 1596; they arrived at Acapulco on December 11. *San Felipe* eventually reached Mindanao, but neither the frigate *Santa Catalina* nor *Santa Ysabel* was ever heard from again, except for a vague report that the latter was run ashore on some unknown island and seen rotting with her crew.

Quirós, *Voyages of Fernández de Quirós.*

## San Pablo

Nao (3m). *Tons:* 300. *Hull:* wood. *Comp.:* 211. *Built:* La Navidad, Mexico; 1564.

*San Pablo* was the ship in which Spanish navigators first unlocked the key to transpacific navigation from Asia to America. Although Christopher Columbus had sailed across the Atlantic to establish a direct route to Asia, Spain's subsequent efforts to establish a foothold in the Orient were hampered by the provisions of the Treaty of Tordesillas (1494), which gave the East Indies to Portugal. There was also the seemingly insoluble problem of how to sail across the Pacific from west to east. In 1520, Ferdinand Magellan became the first European to cross the Pacific, east to west, landing in the Philippines — which he named for Saint Lazarus, and where he was killed. The expedition's survivors, under Juan Sebastian de Elcano, sailed south to the Moluccas (the Spice Islands). The Portuguese were established in the spice trade there, and several members of the expedition were held at Tidore. In 1525, Charles V of Spain ordered an expedition to rescue them. About 330 of the 450 people who sailed from Mexico died before the ships reached the Spice Islands, including Juan García Jofre de Loaisa and his second-in-command, Elcano. A second fleet was dispatched in 1528 under Álvaro de Saavedra, but the survivors of this expedition suffered the same fate as their compatriots: the Portuguese allowed the survivors of these two expeditions to return to Spain only in 1536. Although several ships had tried, none had succeeded in finding a way around the winds that had carried them west across the Pacific to the Spice Islands.

In 1529, Spain renounced its claim to the Moluccas by the Treaty of Zaragosa, but thirteen years later Ruy Lopéz de Villalobos was sent from Mexico on a mission for the "discovery, conquest and colonization of the islands and provinces of the South Sea towards the west." He reached the Philippines, which he renamed for the Infante, later Philip II, but the expedition ended badly, with Villalobos dying in the care of the Jesuit missionary, and later saint, Francis Xavier. Again, the survivors returned to Europe in Portuguese ships via the Cape of Good Hope.

The second phase of Spanish interest in the East began in 1559, when Philip II issued plans for a new undertaking, the most important aim of which "after service given to God our Lord is to establish a route to New Spain from the Islands of the West." Five years later, on November 21, 1564, a fleet of five ships carrying 350 men sailed from La Navidad, Mexico. The pilot in fact, though not in name, was Friar Andrés de Urdaneta, a veteran of Loaisa's 1525 expedition. He had since become an Augustinian missionary and was ineligible to serve as captain-major; but he was asked to name the leader of the expedition, and chose Miguel López de Legazpi. The expedition's ships included the galleons *San Pedro* (*capitana,* 500 tons), *San Pablo* (*almiranta,* 300 tons), the pinnaces *San Lucas* (40 tons) and *San Juan* (80 tons), and a small *fragata.* The fleet sailed west at a latitude of about 9°–13°N, stopping at Guam from January 23 to February 3, 1565, and reaching the island of Samar on February 13. From there they sailed northeast through Surigao Strait south of Samar to the island of Cebu, in the heart of the Philippine archipelago, where they established Spain's first colony in the East on April 27. (Legazpi moved the capital to Manila six years later.)

On June 1, 1565, at the start of the southwest monsoon, *San Pablo* began the return voyage east, with Urdaneta serving as the pilot under Legazpi's seventeen-year-old grandson, Felipe de Salcado. Sailing via the San Bernardino Strait north of Samar, Urdaneta maintained a northeasterly course until the ships found the westerlies in about 39°N. They continued east keeping between 30° and 39°N latitude, dropping south as they reached North America to make their first landfall at San Miguel Island (33°N), just off Los Angeles, on September 18. They did not land, but continued south via Acapulco to La Navidad, where they arrived on October 8.

Here they learned that *San Lucas,* which had separated from the fleet early on November 29, 1564, also had made it to the Philippines. Her captain, Don Alonso de Arellano, her pilot, Lope Martin (who had planned to seize the ship for himself), and about eighteen others had then sailed the ship back at an even higher latitude than *San Pablo,* to reach California on July 18. It is likely that Arellano was following a course Urdaneta had recommended earlier. Moreover, Urdaneta's chart was so thoroughly annotated and revised that it became the standard chart of the Pacific for 200 years, and it is Urdaneta who is credited with the discovery of the west-to-east route. Arellano and Martin were also under suspicion for desertion, although the following year Martin was named pilot of *San Jerónimo* to carry supplies to Legazpi. Again he attempted to seize the ship, but he was outwitted and marooned on an island with twenty-six of his followers, and never heard from again.

The significance of these west-to-east Pacific voyages was enormous. Between 1520 and 1564, only five expeditions had crossed the Pacific east to west, from the Americas to Asia, and none had made the return passage. After, the *San Pablo*'s 1564 voyage, at least one Manila galleon would make the same voyage almost every year for 250 years. The initial prospects were not so bright, and much depended on the merchant junks of China, "whence come silk, porcelain, benzoin, musk, and other articles," as Legazpi wrote. In 1571, Spanish sailors rescued the crew of a junk near Mindoro, a gesture that reaped handsome dividends. The next year, Chinese traders returned to Manila and, in the words of the historian Padre Martin de Zuñiga, "With this the foundation of a lucrative commerce was laid." In 1573, two Spanish ships sailed from Manila with a cargo that included 712 pieces of silk and 22,300 pieces of "fine gilt china and other porcelain wares." The Manila galleons sailed annually until 1815. Although dozens were lost to the perils of the sea, only four were taken by the enemies of Spain: the unarmed *Santa Ana* fell to Thomas Cavendish in *Desire* and *Constant* in 1587; *Nuestra Señora de la Encarnación Disenganio* to Woodes Rogers's *Duke* in 1709; *Nuestra Señora de la Covadonga* to Commodore George Anson's HMS *Centurion* in 1743; and *Santisima Trinidad* to HMS *Panther* and *Argo,* under Captain Hyde Parker, in 1762.

Mairin, *Friar Andrés de Urdaneta.* Schurz, *Manila Galleon.*

## San Pedro

Nao (3m). *Tons:* 100 tons. *Hull:* wood. *Comp.:* 47. *Arm.:* 6 × 3pdr. *Built:* Peru(?); <1597.

In 1597, Pedro Fernández de Quirós, a veteran of Alvaro Mendaña's SAN JERÓNIMO, began planning an expedition to find Terra Australis. Seven years later he assembled three ships at Callao, Peru: the 100-tonners SAN PEDRO Y SAN PABLO and *San Pedro* (commanded by Luis Vaéz de Torres and nicknamed *San Pedrico*), and the 20-ton *Los Tres Reyes*. The fleet sailed on December 21, 1605, and headed west along 26°S for thirteen weeks, when the ships arrived at the Duff Group (Taumaco Island). After nine days they turned south for the New Hebrides and Espiritu Santo, where they stayed six weeks. Here, on June 11, 1606, Quirós secretly withdrew from the expedition and returned to Mexico in *San Pedro y San Pablo*.

Command of the expedition fell to Torres, and on June 26, *San Pedro* and *Los Tres Reyes* sailed into the Coral Sea. Ten days later they turned north and on July 14 arrived in the Louisiade Archipelago. From here they made their way west along southern New Guinea, anchoring about August 28 off Port Moresby. Three days later they began threading their way across what Torres called "*el placel*," the shallow, coral-strewn waters of the Gulf of Papua, and about October 2, they sailed through the strait separating New Guinea from Australia's Cape York Peninsula. This transit established that New Guinea was not the "mainland of the summit of the antarctic pole," as had been thought. Unfortunately, Torres's official reports were filed in Spain to prevent any intelligence from the voyage falling into the wrong hands. They were not rediscovered until 1770, the same year that Cook passed through Torres Strait — as it became known after about 1775 — in HMS ENDEAVOUR.

Once safely through, *San Pedro* and *Los Tres Reyes* sailed along southwestern New Guinea. On November 9, 1606, they arrived at Kepulauan Fam, between New Guinea and the Moluccas Islands. Here they met a Portuguese-speaking local who told them they were only five days from Ternate, which Philippines-based Spaniards had seized seven months before. Torres remained at Ternate from January 6 to May 1, 1607, before sailing for Manila, where *San Pedro* arrived on May 22; *Los Tres Reyes* had been left at Ternate. Remarkably, none of the crew had died from disease in the seventeen-month voyage. The ship also carried twenty New Guineans, one of whom is believed to have traveled to Spain and been painted by Velázquez. The subsequent careers of Torres and *San Pedro* are unknown.

Hilder, *Voyage of Torres.*

## San Pedro y Pablo

Nao (3m). *Tons:* 100. *Hull:* wood. *Built:* Peru; <1605.

The chief pilot and savior of Alvaro Mendaña's ill-fated expedition to the Santa Cruz Islands, Pedro Fernández de Quirós, concluded that those islands, Mendaña's Solomons, and New Guinea must lie near one another, and that Terra Australis must be nearby as well. Backed by Pope Clement VIII and Philip III of Spain, the pious Quirós was given a fleet of three ships, *San Pedro y Pablo*, SAN PEDRO (under Luis Vaéz de Torres), and the *zabra*, or launch, *Los Tres Reyes Magos*. Embarking 300 sailors, soldiers, and friars and sufficient provisions to establish a colony, the fleet sailed from Callao, Peru, on December 21, 1605. Quirós first sailed west-southwest to 26°S, then on January 22 turned west-northwest. Four days later he sighted Ducie Island (near Pitcairn), and on February 10 the ships landed briefly on Hao Island in the Tuamotus. Pressing on, in 10°40′S Quirós turned west, sailing through the Cook Islands in search of Santa Cruz, where he knew he could get food and water for his restless crew. It was not until April that the ships anchored at Taumako atoll, where they learned they were five days from Santa Cruz (60 miles, or 100 kilometers, to the southwest). With his crews freshly provisioned, Quirós resumed his search for Terra Australis, heading first southeast then southwest, until on May 3 the ships came to what he believed to be the southern continent. He named it Austrialia (for King Philip's House of Austria) del Espiritu Santo; it was actually the largest island in Vanuatu. Despite his initial enthusiasm, Quirós decided to leave after only three weeks. Once at sea, he changed his mind again, but foul weather prevented *San Pedro y Pablo* from regaining the land, and Torres was left with *San Pedro* and *Los Tres Reyes Magos* to fend for themselves.

Quirós tried again to find Santa Cruz, but gave up and sailed north to the Marshall Islands. The inadequacies of seventeenth-century navigation and geographical knowledge can be judged from the fact that on July 23 Quirós and his pilots believed themselves about 2,700 miles from Mexico and 2,400 miles from the Philippines, which left about 4,000 miles of the Pacific unaccounted for. Nonetheless, they climbed into the high northern latitudes and turned for Mexico with the westerlies at their backs and arrived at Acapulco on November 23, 1606. Quirós had neither located Terra Australis nor founded a new settlement, and it was Torres who made the most significant — if not immediately appreciated — contribution to geography, by finding the passage between New Guinea and Australia. Quirós turned over *San Pedro y Pablo* to the Viceroy of Mexico, and the next year the ship was sent to the Philippines.

Beaglehole, *Exploration of the Pacific.* Kelly, *Austrialia del Espiritu Santo.* Quirós, *Voyages of Pedro Fernández de Quirós.*

# Santa María

Nao (3m). *L/B/D:* 58′–86′ × 19′–26′ × 10′–11′ dph (18–27m × 6–8m × 3m). *Tons:* 108–239. *Hull:* wood. *Comp.:* 40. *Arm.:* 9cm lombard, 4.5cm falconets. *Built:* Galicia, Spain; 1492.

One of the single most important voyages in history was the first of Christopher Columbus's four voyages from Spain to the Americas between 1492 and 1502. Columbus had no intention of discovering anything other than a direct route to the Orient, "the land of India and the great island of Cipango [Japan] and the realms of the Great Khan," that is, Cathay, or China. His estimates of the distances involved — 2,400 miles, or 3,900 kilometers, from the Canary Islands to Japan and 3,550 miles, or 5,700 kilometers, to China — were wide of the mark. The actual distances form Spain to Japan and China are 10,600 miles (17,055 kilometers) and 11,766 miles (18,930 kilometers), as the crow flies. Nonetheless, although Columbus landed in South America and Central America on

his last voyage, he died in the belief that the Orient was only ten days from Honduras.

Columbus first approached João II of Portugal, but João declined to sponsor him, although Portugal had been funding exploratory expeditions down the coast of Africa for about fifty years. In 1485, Columbus moved to Los Palos de la Frontera, Spain, with a view to interesting Ferdinand and Isabella of Castile in the same venture, and in this he was ultimately successful. When Columbus received his commission, the citizens of Palos furnished him with two caravels, NIÑA and PINTA, in satisfaction of a fine levied against the town by Ferdinand and Isabella. Columbus also hired the nao *Santa María,* a merchant ship from Galicia whose owner, Juan de la Cosa, sailed as pilot.

Although a nao was larger than a caravel, and *Santa María* was large enough for Columbus to make her his *capitana,* or flagship, she was not an especially large ship for her day. Sometimes called *La Gallega,* an epithet referring to her Galician origins, she had three masts. The mizzen carried a single fore-and-aft lateen sail, the mainmast two square sails, a course, and a topsail, and the foremast a single square sail. There was also a spritsail, a square sail carried forward, on the bowsprit. In good weather, the area of the mainsail could be increased by the addition of two bonnets, additional lengths of canvas that could be laced to the foot of the course. The helmsman steered with a tiller that led to a rudder. With one deck and a year's provisions, there were few creature comforts, and sleeping quarters were fairly rude. (Crew accommodations in European ships improved after Columbus's crew adopted the hammocks they found in the Caribbean.) For auxiliary power, the ship could be pulled by a heavy yawl boat or rowed by wooden sweeps. Columbus found *Santa María* a dull sailer, and he complained that her draft was too deep to make her useful for exploration.

Sailing from Los Palos on August 3, 1492, *Santa María* and *Niña* arrived at the island of Gomera in the Canary Islands on August 12. *Pinta's* rudder trouble had forced her into Las Palmas, on Grand Canary Island, where *Santa María* and *Niña* put back to on August 25. The trio sailed for Gomera and finally resumed their westward voyage on September 6. Light airs kept them in sight of the Canaries until the ninth. Thereafter they met favorable winds. They reached the Sargasso Sea (about 32°W longitude) on the sixteenth, and three days later they were out of the tradewinds. There followed about a week of light and variable winds. On September 25, *Pinta*'s Martín Alonso Pinzón made the first false landfall. Conditions improved considerably between October 2 and 6, when they made 710 miles, including their best run of 182 miles in twenty-four hours. The next day they made their second false landfall while still about 400 miles east of the Bahamas, but they were close enough to land to follow the path of birds heading southwest. Nonetheless, by the tenth the crew of *Santa María* were near mutiny and Columbus apparently agreed to put about within a few days if they did not sight land. The next day, the appearance of manmade artifacts and tree branches confirmed that land must be near.

All eyes strained to be the first to see the new shore (Ferdinand and Isabella had promised a reward of 10,000 maravedís, the equivalent of ten months' pay for a seaman); at about 2200 that night Columbus believed he saw a light in the distance. Four hours later, at about 0200 on October 12, *Pinta*'s lookout, Rodrigo de Triana, saw the Taino Indian island of Guanahaní, in what is now the Bahamas, where they landed later that morning. Columbus gave this island the name San Salvador, although the English later renamed it Watlings Island. When it was realized that Watlings had a strong claim to a historical pedigree, they renamed it San Salvador. Most important, the Tainos wore jewelry made of gold — a chief object of the Spaniards' adventure.

Sailing through the Bahamas for two weeks, the little fleet crossed south to Cuba on October 27. They explored the north coast of that island for six weeks, sailing as far west as Puerto Padre. At the beginning of November, Columbus dispatched an embassy to the inland village of Holguín, hopeful that it would prove to be a major Asiatic capital. He was disappointed to learn that his interpreter, Luis de Torres — whose languages included Hebrew, Aramaic, and Arabic — could make no headway with the local people. On November 20, the three ships made a tentative foray in the direction of the Bahamas, but, while trying to return to Cuba, Martín Alonso Pinzón in *Pinta* split off from the others to investigate Great Inagua Island, and he was gone until the New Year.

After completing their investigation of northeast Cuba, on December 5 *Santa María* and *Niña* sailed east to Cape St. Nicholas, the northwestern tip of Hispaniola in what is now Haiti. On December 12 at Moustique Bay, they took possession of the land in the name of Ferdinand and Isabella. The presence of more gold artifacts and the friendliness of the local cacique, Guacanagarí, encouraged the explorers. But while working their way eastward, tragedy struck on Christmas Eve. The only man awake aboard the ship seems to have been a ship's boy at the tiller, for the master of midwatch, Juan de la Cosa, and the helmsman had fallen asleep. Shortly after midnight, *Santa María* grounded on a coral reef. No one was killed, but the ship was ruined and Christmas Day was spent salvaging what could be saved from the flagship. It would have been virtually impossible to cross the Atlantic with more than sixty men in *Niña*, so thirty-nine crew from *Santa María* and *Niña* volunteered to remain on the island in a fort fashioned from the flagship's timbers and named La Navidad. *Niña* sailed on January 4, 1493, rejoining *Pinta* at Isla Cabra two days later for the voyage home. As fate would have it, none of the men who stayed in Hispaniola would survive to greet Columbus on his return in November 1493.

A number of replicas of Columbus's ships have been built since the four hundredth anniversary of the first voyage. As there are neither detailed descriptions nor plans of any of the ships — or their contemporaries — the dimensions have varied significantly. José Martínez-Hidalgo's designs for the 1992 replicas, based in part on the *Mataró* ship (a votive model hung from the ceiling of a church near Barcelona and dated to 1450), are described in Xavier Pastor's *Ships of Christopher Columbus*.

Fernández-Armesto, *Columbus*. Morison, *Admiral of the Ocean Sea*. Pastor, *Ships of Christopher Columbus*. Philips, "Evolution of Spanish Ship Design." Smith, *Vanguard of Empire*.

# São Gabriel

Nao (3m). *Tons:* 100. *Hull:* wood. *Comp.:* ca. 60. *Arm.:* 20 guns. *Des.:* Batolomeu Dias. *Built:* Lisbon; <1497.

Although Christopher Columbus's transatlantic voyage of 1492 had incomparable consequences for world history, of more immediate significance to world trade of that time was the voyage of Vasco da Gama, who sailed with four ships from Portugal around the Cape of Good Hope to India five years later. In the fifteenth century, Portugal had taken the lead among European countries in the systematic compilation of geographic knowledge and voyages of discovery down the coast of Africa and among the islands of the near Atlantic. Portuguese ships pushed south beyond the Canary Islands and Cape Bojador — the "Bulging Cape," in what is now Mauretania — to reach Madeira by 1420, Cape Bianco in 1441, and the Cape Verde Islands in 1445. The next year, they arrived at the Gambia River and thereafter developed a brisk West African trade in slaves, gold, and ivory.

During the reign of João II, Bartolomeu Dias sailed with three ships on a voyage that first brought Europeans around the southern tip of Africa, to land, on February 3, 1488, at Mossel Bay, 200 miles (320 kilometers) east of the Cape of Good Hope. Dias returned in December 1488 after an absence of more than sixteen months. At the same time, João had sent Pero da Covilhã eastward in search of the rumored Ethiopian Christian king known as Prester John. (Several Ethiopian embassies visited Europe during the fifteenth century, including one to Lisbon in 1452.) Covilhã reached Calicut and Goa on India's west coast before returning to the court of Alexander of Ethiopia, "Lion of the Tribe of Judah, and King of Kings." Letters back to Portugal revealed

> how he discovered cinnamon and pepper in the city of Calicut, and that cloves came from beyond, but that all might be had . . . in the said cities of Cananor and Calicut and Goa, all on the coast, and that to this one could navigate by the coast and seas of Guinea [that is, from the west coast of Africa].

Domestic problems prevented the Portuguese from following up immediately on Dias's monumental achievement, but João ordered Dias to build two 100-ton, square-rigged naos, *São Gabriel* and *São Rafael,* for a new voyage. In 1497, João's successor, Manoel, named the courtier Vasco da Gama to lead a four-ship expedition, including these two ships, the 50-ton caravel *Bérrio,* and an anonymous storeship of perhaps 120 tons. Gama appointed his brother Paulo captain of *São Rafael* and Nicolau Coelho captain of *Bérrio.* Provisioned for three years, the ships had a total complement of between 140 and 170 crew, including pilots, interpreters, and ten exiles (*degredados*) for hazardous undertakings ashore.

On July 8, 1497, the fleet set out from the Tagus River village of Restelo, later named for the church of St. Mary of Bethlehem, or Belém. Sailing via the Canary and Cape Verde islands, they came to Sierra Leone. To avoid the northerly Benguela Current, Gama turned west until he reached the southerly Brazil current. They next steered southeast until, after three months at sea, the ships anchored in the Bay of St. Helena, South Africa, on November 8. The fleet doubled the Cape of Good Hope on November 22, landed at Mossel Bay three days later, and remained there two weeks. On Christmas they were at Natal, farther east than Dias had gone. The Portuguese first saw evidence of trade with the east at the Quelimane River, where they stayed in January and February 1498 making repairs to the ships. Their next stop was at the island of Moçambique, where friction with Arabs of the town erupted into violence, as it would again at Mombasa, much of it instigated by the Portuguese. Unaccountably, the expedition's planners had provided Gama with only second-rate goods, and the Arab traders disdained the meager offerings of cotton, beads, tin ornaments, trousers, and hats.

The Portuguese were better received at Malindi, a rival to Mombasa. Here they hired a pilot to guide them to India, known to the Portuguese as Malemo Cana, or Canaqua; these may be functional titles rather than personal names. Canaqua has been erroneously identified with Ahmed ibn Majid, author of several books on piloting and esteemed as "one of the most trustworthy of the many pilots and mariners of the west coast of India." After four months of almost daily contact with Arab traders in East Africa, the Portuguese departed Malindi on April 24. Whoever their pilot was, he guided Gama's fleet across the Indian Ocean from Malindi to Calicut, a distance of 2,300 miles (3,700 kilometers), in only twenty-two days. At long last, the Portuguese had opened the much sought after sea route to the Indies.

Calicut was the most important and cosmopolitan trading center on the Malabar coast of India, midway along the flourishing trade route between Asia and the Middle East. The Portuguese referred to the ruler of Calicut as "samorin," their corruption of Samudri Raja, king of the sea. Gama met the Samorin of Calicut on May 28. Although he was initially well disposed toward the Portuguese, his opinion was tempered by their paltry offerings and overbearing manner, together with the antagonism of the Muslim traders already established at Calicut. On August 9, Gama decided it was time to leave, but the Samorin insisted that they pay a customs charge for the meager amounts of cinnamon, cloves, and precious stones they had managed to acquire. When the unsold Portuguese goods were seized and members of the crew detained ashore, Gama took eighteen hostages. The crisis was resolved a week later and on August 29 Gama sailed with his three ships. (He also kept a number of hostages, five of whom returned to India with Pero Álvares Cabral in 1500.) The Portuguese stopped for several weeks in the Angediva (Anjidiv) Islands, south of Goa, where they embarked a Venetian-speaking Jewish merchant-pirate, who returned with them to Portugal and was baptized en route as Gaspar da Gama. They turned west on October 2 for a torturous three-month crossing of the Arabian Sea, during which thirty of the crew died. Skirting the African coast, they came to Malindi on January 7, 1499. After only four days, they resumed their voyage, but by this time there were so few crew that Gama decided to burn *São Rafael* off Mombasa and continued the voyage with only *São Gabriel* and *Bérrio*. After stopping briefly near Moçambique, they doubled the Cape of Good Hope on March 20 and reached the Cape Verde Islands in mid-April. From here, *Bérrio* sailed di-

rectly to Lisbon, where she arrived on July 12; *São Gabriel* arrived some time later. Gama had left his ship at Cape Verde to race for home in a hired caravel with his ailing brother, Paulo, who died and was buried at Madeira. Gama finally returned to Lisbon about September 1, 1499.

Gama's voyage was the culmination of the Portuguese age of discovery, and in one stroke it altered the pattern of European trade forever. Having broken the Arab-Venetian monopoly of the spice trade — the Venetians would have to "become fishermen," exulted one correspondent, somewhat optimistically — Lisbon became, briefly, the most important entrepôt in Europe. Whether by good luck or design, Gama had also pioneered the standard sailing ship route from Europe to the Indian Ocean. Although the Portuguese maintained colonies in India, Africa, and Asia well into the twentieth century — Macao was ceded to China in 1999 — their prosperity was undermined by ruthlessness toward their hosts and rivals. (On his second voyage in 1502, Gama showed uncommon savagery in the burning of a pilgrim ship from Mecca.) However brief, Portugal's golden age was well deserved, owing as it did not to luck but perseverance.

Hart, *Sea Road to the Indies.* Subrahmanyam. *Career and Legend of Vasco da Gama.* Velho, *Journal of the First Voyage of Vasco da Gama.*

## Sea Venture

*L:* 50′–80′ (15–25m). *Tons:* ca. 240 burden. *Hull:* wood. *Comp.:* 150. *Arm.:* 8 sakers, 8 minions. *Built:* East Anglia(?); 1603.

One of the best-known shipwrecks in literature is that of the merchantman *Sea Venture* (sometimes called *Sea Adventure, Seaventure,* or *Seaventer*), whose loss on a Bermudan reef in 1609 was the inspiration for William Shakespeare's *Tempest.* Her early history is not known with certainty, but it is believed that she is the same *Sea Venture* owned by members of the Company of Merchant Adventurers, for whom she traded between London, the Elbe River port of Stade, and the Dutch market at

Middelburg, carrying mostly wool and cloth. In 1609 she was purchased or chartered by the Virginia Company to sail as flagship of the second supply mission sent out to the fledgling Jamestown colony since its establishment in 1607.

The ship sailed from Plymouth on June 2, 1609, as flagship of the "Third Supply" (as it was known), which comprised six full-rigged ships and two pinnaces. On July 23, they were caught in a hurricane and *Sea Venture* became separated from the rest of the ships. After four days in midocean, when the ship "was growne five feet suddenly deepe with water above her ballast," Admiral of the flotilla Sir George Somers saw land. Soon thereafter, the ship lodged fast between two reefs about three quarters of a mile from land, and the entire company of 150 rowed ashore on Bermuda, a place dreaded by mariners who knew it as "the Island of Devils." The ship remained afloat long enough for the crew to salvage most of her equipment and stores. They also built the pinnaces *Deliverance* and *Patience,* in which all but two of the company continued their passage to Jamestown, arriving on May 10, 1610. The two men who remained at Bermuda were the first permanent settlers in what officially became an English settlement in 1612.

In 1610, William Strachey published an eyewitness account entitled "A True Repertory of the Wreck and Redemption of Sir Thomas Gates, Knight," and Silvester Jourdain published *A Discovery of the Barmudas otherwise Called the "Isle of Devils."* It is believed that Shakespeare read both of these accounts in the course of writing his celebrated romantic drama *The Tempest* (1611), the last of his complete plays.

The wreck remained undisturbed until 1959, when the American diver and amateur historian Edmund Dowling found it at a depth of 9.1 meters (30 feet). The artifacts he retrieved suggested that the wreck was that of *Sea Venture*, until experts at the Tower of London misidentified one of the ship's guns as a saker dating from the eighteenth century, rather than a minion from the early seventeenth. Work on the site ceased and was not resumed until 1978, when divers working under the auspices of the Bermuda Maritime Museum Association resumed operations. The site yielded relatively few artifacts: some cannon shot and smaller weapons, fragments of ceramic plates, and vessels of English, Rhenish, Spanish, and Chinese origin, and pewter spoons. Little of the hull remains, apart from a 15-meter (50-foot) section of keel (which originally may have been as long as 25 meters, or 82 feet), a few ceilings and outer planks, and some floors.

Jourdain, *Discovery of the Barmudas.* Peterson, "*Sea Venture.*" Strachey, "*True Repertory.*" Winwood, "*Sea Venture.*"

# Senyavin

Sloop of war (3m). *L/B/D:* 90' bp × 29' × 12.8' (27.4m × 8.8m × 3.9m). *Hull:* wood. *Comp.:* 62. *Arm.:* 16 carronades. *Built:* Okhta Shipyard, St. Petersburg, Russia; 1826.

In the early 1820s, relations between Russia and the United States were strained over the extent of czarist holdings in North America. Russia planned to send two warships to patrol its claims, but agreement on 54°40′N as the southern limit of its American territory in 1824 obviated the need for such a military presence, and the ships were ordered to explore the coasts of Russian America and Asia. Otto von Kotzebue returned to Kronstadt from his circumnavigation in Predpriyatiye on July 10, 1826, and on August 16 *Senyavin,* under Captain Lieutenant Fedor Petrovich Litke, sailed in company with *Möller,* under Captain Lieutenant M. N. Staniukovich. Litke's orders were to

> reconnoiter, and describe, the coasts of Kamchatka, the land of the Chuchkis and the Koriaks (the coasts of which have not yet been described by anyone, and which are unknown except by the voyage of Captain Bering); the coasts of the Okhotsk Sea, and the Shantar Islands, which although they are known to us, have not been sufficiently described.

During the winter they were to cruise the western Caroline Islands as far south as the Equator. (Staniukovich was to explore along the Alaskan coast but was lackluster in pursuit of his objectives.)

The vessels proceeded in company to Portsmouth, but they were separated soon after sailing from England. After rounding Cape Horn on February 24, 1827, *Senyavin* called at Concepción, Chile, in March before proceeding to Novoarkhangelsk (Sitka), where the Russians remained from June 11 to July 19. After calling at Unalaska, they arrived at Petropavlovsk, Kamchatka, in mid-September. From November 1827 through April 1828, they cruised in the Caroline Islands and the Bonin-Jima group before returning to Kamchatka in May. That summer they surveyed the Kamchatka coast from Avacha Bay to Karaginskii Island and then sailed through the Bering Strait for a survey of the Chuchki coast from the East Cape to the Anadyr River. The ships left Petropavlovsk for the last time in October and rejoined *Möller* at Manila on January 1, 1830, before sailing for Europe via the Cape of Good Hope. *Senyavin* returned to Kronstadt on September 16, 1829.

Litke's voyage in *Senyavin* was among the most productive voyages of discovery sent out by any country in the nineteenth century. In addition to the survey work on the Asian coast, the expedition discovered twelve island groups and described another twenty-six in the Carolines. Experiments with an invariable pendulum enabled the company to determine the degree to which the earth flattens at the poles. The naturalist Karl Heinrich Mertens, the ornithologist Baron von Kittlitz, and the mineralogist Alexander Postels described over 1,000 new species of insects, fish, birds, and other animals, and more than 2,500 different types of plants, algae, and rocks. In addition, they also collected ethnographic artifacts and made more than 1,250 sketches of their findings.

Shortly after the conclusion of the voyage, *Senyavin* was dispatched on a second scientific expedition to Iceland, again under Litke. The expedition's chief scientist, Mertens, died two weeks after the ship's return to Kronstadt in September 1830.

Ivashintsov, *Russian Round-the-World Voyages*. Litke, *Voyage Round the World: 1826–1829*.

# HMS Sirius

(ex-*Berwick*) 6th rate, 10 (3m). *L/B/D:* 110.4′ × 32.8′ × 12.9′ (33.7m × 10m × 3.9m). *Tons:* 512 bm. *Hull:* wood. *Comp.:* 50–160. *Arm.:* 4 × 6pdr, 6 × 18pdr. *Built:* Christopher Watson, Rotherhithe, Eng.; 1781.

The merchant ship *Berwick* was built for the Baltic trade, but while still on the stocks, she was purchased by the Royal Navy for use as an armed transport. After five years in service between Britain and North America, she was renamed HMS *Sirius* and fitted out for service as flagship of the "First Fleet" sent out to Botany Bay to establish a European settlement in Australia. Though the expedition has often been derided as nothing more than an expedient measure to rid England of criminals, in fact it was part of a well-considered plan to establish a firm British presence in the Pacific as a counterweight to the Spanish in the Americas and the Philippines, and the Dutch in the East Indies. Nor was the idea of "transportation" of convicts new. Sir Humphrey Gilbert proposed the idea in the sixteenth century, and it became official policy in 1717. Previous destinations included Africa and the American colonies.

On May 13, 1787, the sixth rate *Sirius* sailed from Portsmouth at the head of a fleet of eleven ships and a total complement of 1,350 people under Commander-in-Chief and Governor Arthur Phillip. These included the convict transports *Scarborough* (with 208 male convicts), *Alexander* (195 men), *Lady Penrhyn* (101 female convicts), *Charlotte* (88 men, 22 women), *Friendship* (76 men, 21 women), and *Prince of Wales* (1 man, 49 women). There were also the storeships *Fishburn, Golden Grove,* and *Borrowdale,* and the replenishment ship *Supply.* The convicts were given a certain amount of freedom in the ships, which the majority of them seem not to have abused. However, there was trouble not only from some of the prisoners but from the crew and guards, some of whom were disciplined for mutiny, disobedience, or sleeping with the women prisoners. The ships sailed via Tenerife, Rio de Janeiro (where they remained a month), and Cape Town. Shortly before their arrival at the latter port, convicts and members of *Alexander's* crew conspired to seize the ship but were thwarted at the last minute, and the ships arrived without further incident on October 13.

Departing Cape Town on November 12, the fleet broke into three separate squadrons. *Supply* and the faster transports would arrive early and make preparations for the arrival of the others. Bad weather slowed *Supply*'s progress, and she arrived at Botany Bay on January 18, 1788, only two days before the rest of the fleet, and eight months and one week since leaving Portsmouth. Dissatisfied with the situation at Botany Bay, Phillip reconnoitered Port Jackson (Sydney) ten miles to the north, which he found more suitable for a colony, with a better anchorage and more fertile land. The first ships arrived on January 26 at Sydney Cove, named for Lord Sydney, Secretary of the Home Office, under whose auspices the First Fleet sailed. On the same day, *Sirius* and the nine remaining ships were attempting to leave Botany Bay when they encountered Jean-François de La Pérouse's L'ASTROLABE and LA BOUSSOLE. The French explorers remained at Port Jackson for several weeks before sailing to their doom.

The last convicts were finally landed on February 6, and after a night of debauchery among the newly released convicts, Phillip established a colonial government on the following day. Despite the rough material with which he had to work, he was inordinately optimistic about the potential for success. He wrote:

> We have come today to take possession of this fifth great continental division of the earth, on behalf of the British people, and have founded here a State which we hope will not only occupy and rule this great country, but also will become a shining light among all the nations of the Southern Hemisphere. How grand is the prospect which lies before this youthful nation.

A short time later, *Supply* sailed for Norfolk Island, about 1,500 miles northeast of Sydney, to establish another penal colony. In May, three ships sailed for China to load tea for London. By September, the colony was dangerously short of supplies, and under Captain John Hunter, *Sirius* sailed

via Cape Horn for Cape Town, and arrived back at Port Jackson on May 9, 1789. After four months of repairs, Phillip ordered *Sirius* and *Supply* to carry additional convicts to Norfolk Island to relieve the strain on the Port Jackson settlement. Forced by the weather to stand off the island for four days, on March 19, *Sirius* approached the settlement on Sydney Bay. The strong current and a sudden wind shift pushed her onto a reef. As her lieutenant related, "An Anchor was let go on Her first striking / in Less than 10 Minutes the Masts were all over the side, the Ship an intire Wreck."

Everything that could be salvaged was taken ashore, but the loss of the ship and her supplies, together with the addition of the survivors to the population, tested the island's resources to the limit. It was not until August 1791 that the next relief ships arrived. The location of the wreck of *Sirius* remained unknown. It was not until the 1980s that the Sirius Project excavated the site in anticipation of Australia's bicentennial. The ship has yielded hundreds of diverse artifacts, including iron and copper fastenings, navigational instruments, a pantograph (used for copying maps to scale), medical supplies, two carronades, personal effects, and an aboriginal stone ax, probably obtained as a souvenir at Port Jackson.

Henderson and Henderson, "Sirius." Phillip, *Voyage of Governor Phillip to Botany Bay*. Stanbury, *HMS "Sirius."*

# USS Skate (SSN-578)

*Skate*-class nuclear submarine. *L/B/D:* 267.7′ × 25′ × 20′ (81.6m × 7.6m × 6.1m). *Tons:* 2,570/2,861 disp. *Hull:* steel; 700′ dd. *Comp.:* 93. *Arm.:* 6 × 21″TT. *Mach.:* 18+ kts. *Built:* Electric Boat Division, General Dynamics Corp., Groton, Conn.; 1957.

Named for a type of ray, USS *Skate* was the second submarine of the name. Assigned to the Atlantic for her entire career, on July 30, 1958, she began a voyage to the Arctic Circle under Commander James F. Calvert. Over the course of ten days during which she sailed 2,400 miles and surfaced through the ice nine times, she became the second ship, after USS NAUTILUS, to reach the North Pole. In March 1959 she headed to the Arctic for a second time to develop operational capabilities for submarines at periods of extreme cold and ice thickness. On March 17, *Skate* surfaced at the North Pole — the first ship to be on the surface at the Pole. There her crew committed to the sea the ashes of the Arctic explorer Sir Hubert Wilkins, who had led the first submarine expedition under the ice pack in *Nautilus* in 1931. Three years later, she undertook a third Arctic mission, this time rendezvousing with USS *Seadragon*. The submarines surfaced together at the North Pole on August 2, 1962.

In addition to normal operations with the Atlantic Fleet, *Skate* made three more voyages to the Arctic between 1969 and 1971. She was decommissioned in 1986 and held for disposal through the nuclear-powered ship and submarine recycling program in Bremerton, Washington.

Calvert, *Surface at the Pole*. U.S. Navy, *DANFS*.

# Sohar

Dhow (2m). *L:* 87' (26.5m). *Hull:* wood. *Comp.:* 19. *Des.:* Colin Mudie. *Built:* Sur, Oman; 1980.

Inspired by the tale of Sinbad the Sailor, in *The Thousand and One Nights* (a collection of ancient Persian-Indian-Arabian stories), who was probably a mythic amalgam of Arab seafarers from the eighth to eleventh centuries, Tim Severin decided to sail a dhow on a 6,000-mile voyage from the Persian Gulf to China. The design of *Sohar* (named for an ancient port said to have been the birthplace of the legendary Sinbad) was based on a drawing of a *boom*, a type of dhow pictured in a sixteenth-century Portuguese manuscript. The vessel's hull was built of *aini* wood from India sewn together with 400 miles of hand-laid coconut cord from Agatti in the Lakshadweep Islands (Laccadives) off southwest India. The 20,000 holes through which the coir (rope made from coconut husks) passed were plugged with coconut husks and a mixture of lime

and tree gum, and the hull's interior was preserved with vegetable oil.

*Sohar*'s building and fitting out — paid for by Oman's Sultan Qaboos bin Said — took eleven months. When she sailed from Muscat on November 23, 1980, her crew included nine Omanis and ten Europeans, including Trondur Patursson, a veteran of Severin's BRENDAN voyage. The timing of the voyage was dictated by the availability of favorable winds, and *Sohar* ran off before the northwest monsoon, averaging 4 knots, or 80 miles (130 kilometers) per day, and arriving at Chetlat in the Lakshadweep Islands in mid-December. From there she sailed to the Indian mainland, stopping at Calicut and Beypore, where the ship was careened. The next port of call was at Galle, Sri Lanka, where she arrived on January 21, 1981. Severin had hoped to catch the southwest monsoon, but the winds were late and he was fifty-five days at sea before arriving at Sabang at the northern entrance to the Strait of Malacca on April 18. From there, he continued on to Singapore. Pressing on to avoid the typhoon season, in mid-June *Sohar* was hit by five days of vicious squalls in the South China Sea. She arrived off the Pearl River on June 28, and was greeted at Guangzhou (Canton) by Chinese and Omani officials. *Sohar* was later shipped back to Oman for display as a museum ship at Muscat.

Severin, *Sinbad Voyage*.

# Southern Cross

(ex-*Pollux*) Bark (3m). *L/B/D:* 146.5' × 30.5' × 0.0' (44.7m × 9.3m × 0.0m). *Tons:* 522 grt. *Hull:* wood. *Comp.:* <175. *Mach.:* triple-expansion, 100 hp, 1 screw. *Des.:* Colin Archer. *Built:* Arendal, Norway; 1886.

The *Pollux* was designed and built by the Norwegian naval architect Colin Archer, who would later design FRAM, which carried Fridtjof Nansen and Roald Amundsen to polar regions. After twelve years as a sealer, *Pollux* was purchased by the Norwegian explorer Carsten Egeberg Borchgrevink. As part of a whaling expedition aboard a ship named *Antarctica*, on January 23, 1895, Borchgrevink was a member of the first party known to have set foot on the southern continent, going ashore with other members of the crew in Victoria Land on the shore of the Ross Sea. Three years later, Borchgrevink — a longtime friend of Amundsen's — purchased *Pollux* with the intention of leading the first expedition ever to winter over intentionally on the Antarctic continent, which he named the South Polar Expedition. He eventually obtained funding for the venture from the British magazine publisher George Newnes.

The renamed *Southern Cross* sailed from England in August 1898 and after stops at Madeira and St. Vincent landed in Hobart, Tasmania, in late November. On December 19, *Southern Cross* sailed for the Antarctic, and after forty-three days in the ice, the party reached Cape Adare, Victoria Land (71°S, 170°E), on February 17, 1899. Borchgrevink and nine companions established a camp, and *Southern Cross* sailed for Australia on March 1. Over the course of the next eleven months, the expedition took magnetic and meteorological readings, collected geological and faunal samples, and undertook several overland expeditions, in the course of which they attained 78°50′S. Tragically, the zoologist Nicolai Hanson died at Cape Adare, apparently of beriberi.

*Southern Cross* returned to Antarctica on January 28, 1900, and after collecting Borchgrevink and his men, sailed along the Ross Ice Barrier for 400 miles (645 kilometers) before turning north for Australia. *Southern Cross* reached Melbourne in April, and the expedition members returned to England aboard RMS *Ortona*. *Southern Cross* was subsequently acquired by the Newfoundland Sealing Company, and was lost with all hands off the Newfoundland coast in early April 1914.

Bernacchi, *To the South Polar Regions.* Borchgrevink, *First on the Antarctic Continent;* "Southern Cross" Expedition." Crawford, *That First Antarctic Night.* Hocking, *Dictionary of Disasters at Sea.*

# Stella Polare

(ex-*Jason*) Bark (1f/3m). *L/B/D:* 147.0′ × 30.6′ × 17.1′ (44.8m × 9.3m × 5.2m). *Tons:* 495 reg. *Hull:* wood. *Comp.:* 20. *Mach.:* compound engine, 1 screw; 7 kts. *Built:* Actieselskabet Oceania, Arendal, Norway; 1881.

*Jason* spent eleven years in Norway's Arctic whale fishery before being purchased by Fridtjof Nansen for his exploration of southern Greenland in 1888. Ten years later, Nansen was approached by Luigi Amadeo di Savoia, Duke of the Abruzzi, one of the foremost Italian explorers of the late nineteenth and twentieth centuries. After making the first ascent of Mount St. Elias, in Alaska, Abruzzi was keen to lead an expedition to the North Pole. He particularly admired Nansen's methods and the success of his polar expedition in the FRAM in 1893–96; he bought Nansen's old ship, which he renamed *Stella Polare* ("Pole star"). Abruzzi also followed Nansen's lead in choosing a civilian crew of proven mettle; the expedition was made up of twelve Italians and eight Norwegians. (Applicants for the expedition were many, and varied. Among those not chosen was the mountaineering priest Father Achille Ratti, later Pope Pius XI.)

*Stella Polare* sailed from Christiania (Oslo) on June 12, 1899. At the end of the month, they were in Archangel, where they embarked 121 sled dogs. From here, *Stella Polare* sailed for Franz Josef Land, a group of islands lying north of the 80th parallel. On August 16, the ship put into Teplitz Bay on Rudolph Island (80°47′N) to prepare for the winter. Abruzzi had decided to use *Stella Polare* herself as the winter quarters rather than establish a camp on the ice. Unfortunately, on September 7, a pressure ridge in the ice pitched the ship over 20° and threatened to sink her. It took three months to repair the ship, which was in any case uninhabitable at such an angle, and the party established a base on the ice.

Frostbite forced Abruzzi to turn over command of the expedition to Assistant Captain Umberto Cagni, and on February 21, 1900, Cagni set off for the Pole with twelve men. The first attempt was aborted after three days, but they set out again, with only ten men, on March 11. Progress was slower than anticipated, and ten days and 45 miles (72 kilometers) out from Rudolph Island, Cagni sent back three men to *Stella Polare.* The men became lost in the changing topography of the constantly shifting ice, and a search party failed to find them. By March 30, Cagni's team had reached 83°16′N, and another detachment of three men was sent back. It took them sixteen days to travel 89 miles (143 kilometers), but they arrived safely.

In the meantime, Cagni pressed on to 86°34′N, 60°E, farther north even than Nansen had reached. The return journey took a month longer than planned, and Cagni's team did not reach Rudolph Island until June 23, having covered 637 miles (1,025 kilometers) in 104 days. The next few months were spent making *Stella Polare* seaworthy and trying to get to open water, which they did by dynamiting the ice. On August 6, she sailed for Norway, arriving at Hammerfest on September 5.

Abruzzi, *On the "Polar Star."* Tenderini and Shandrick, *Duke of the Abruzzi.*


# Sunneshine

Bark (3m). *Tons:* 50 tons. *Hull:* wood. *Comp.:* 16–23. *Built:* England; <1585.

John Davis in 1584 organized an expedition to search for the Northwest Passage. His supporters constituted the North-West Company and included Sir Humphrey Gilbert, Sir Francis Walsingham, and William Sanderson. The next year he sailed from Dartmouth with the ships *Sunneshine* and *Mooneshine,* the latter having a crew of nineteen. Adverse winds held them in the Scilly Islands until June 28. The ships rounded southern Greenland on July 20 and sailed up the west coast, which Davis called the Land of Desolation. On July 28 they landed in about 64°15′N, the area of modern Godthåb, then named Gilbert Sound. Here they encountered their first Eskimos, for whom the *Sunneshine*'s four musicians played their instruments and with whom they traded for furs, kayaks, and other items. On July 31, the English resumed their search to the northwest, reaching Baffin Island on August 6 in 66°40′N and studding their

map of the region with the names of patrons and familiars such as Mt. Raleigh, Exeter Sound, and Cape Walsingham. Turning south, they took their departure from Cape of God's Mercy and sailed across the opening of Cumberland Gulf, which Davis thought might be the Northwest Passage and which he named for George Clifford, Earl of Cumberland. The onset of winter forced their return before he could explore further, and the ships arrived in England in September.

The following year Davis undertook a second expedition, sailing on May 7 with the ships *Mermaid* (120 tons) and *North Star* (10 tons). Davis went with *Mermaid* and *Mooneshine* to explore again the shores of Davis Strait, while *Sunneshine* and *North Star* sailed north to Iceland in search of a strait between there and Greenland. This route was blocked by ice after only two days, but the two vessels followed the ice eastward back to Iceland, then westward again for a rendezvous with Davis at Gilbert Sound — but Davis had chosen another route. The two ships sailed for home at the end of August, but *North Star* and her crew were lost at sea. In the meantime, Davis sailed up the coast to about 66°33′N before crossing Davis Strait and sailing into Cumberland Gulf, where "we plainely perceived a great current striking to the West. This land is nothing in sight but Isles, which increaseth our hope" of the existence of a passage west. They then sailed south along the Labrador coast before turning for home.

The next spring, Davis sailed with three ships, *Sunneshine, Elizabeth,* and *Helen.* After sailing to Greenland, *Sunneshine* and *Elizabeth* sailed for the Newfoundland fisheries — an easy way to earn back the expenses of the voyage. Davis resumed his exploring in *Helen,* sailing north through the Davis Strait to a point he called Hope Sanderson (72°46′N), arriving on June 30. From there he shaped a southerly course, passing the Cumberland Islands, Lumley's Inlet (Frobisher's Strait), and Cape Chidley in northern Labrador. *Helen* returned to Dartmouth in September; the fate of *Sunneshine* is unknown.

Hakluyt, *Principal Navigations.* Morison, *European Discovery of America: The Northern Voyages.*

## Susan Constant

Bark (3m). *L/B/D:* approx. 55.2′ × 22.8′ × 9.5′ (16.8m × 6.9m × 2.9m). *Tons:* 120. *Hull:* wood. *Comp.:* 85. *Arm.:* 4 minions, 4 falcons. *Built:* London; ca. 1605.

▲ A replica of **Susan Constant,** flagship of the first English fleet to plant a successful colony in what became the United States. She and he companion replicas *Godspeed* and **Discovery** are homeported at the Jamestown Settlement, Williamsburg, Virginia. *Courtesy Jamestown-Yorktown Foundation.*

Originally owned by the merchant firm of Colthurst, Dapper and Wheatley, *Susan Constant* was probably built in or near London on the Thames River in about 1605. She is known to have made at least one voyage to Spain in 1606, and around the same time she was in collision with a 100-ton merchant ship, *Phillip and Francis,* a case that was settled by the courts.

It was also in 1606 that the *Susan Constant* was purchased by the Virginia Company to sail as flagship of a colonizing expedition to North America. James I granted a charter for the Virginia Company on April 10, 1606. The company was composed "of two severall Colonies." Influenced by an

exploratory tradition that began with Sir Walter Raleigh's ill-fated settlement at Roanoke, North Carolina, in 1585–86, London courtiers and merchants were granted the lands between 34° and 41°N. West Countrymen — "sondrie Knightes Gentlemen merchauntes and other Adventurers of our Cities of Bristoll and Exeter and of our town of Plymouthe" — were to settle the lands between 38° and 45°N. In so doing they were following in the wake of Bartholomew Gosnold, who had explored the area around Cape Cod in the CONCORD in 1602, Martin Pring's exploration of the Maine coast in *Speedwell* and *Discoverer* in 1603, and George Waymouth, also to Maine, in the *Archangell* in 1605. The lands between 38° and 41°N were to be administered by whichever of the two groups was best able to take on the work.

With Christopher Newport as captain of the expedition, *Susan Constant* embarked seventy-one colonists; her consorts *Godspeed* and *Discovery* carried fifty-two and twenty-one, respectively. "On Saturday, the twentieth of December in the yeere 1606, the fleet fell from London." So wrote George Percy, one of the colonists. Stormbound in the English Channel for nearly a month, they did not reach the Canary Islands until February 21. From there they headed west to the West Indies, where they landed to take on water and other provisions. Heading north, the ships entered Chesapeake Bay in mid-April and finally landed at Jamestown Island — named in honor of their king — on May 13, 1607. Although the colony's early years were marked by illness and dissension, it weathered a succession of crises to become the first permanent English establishment in North America.

In the meantime, the northern group's settlement on the Kennebec River in Maine (known as the "Second Colonie") had failed, and many of its backers joined the Londoners. In this way, the London group also acquired the 30-ton pinnace VIRGINIA, the first European ship built in North America. *Virginia* was one of two pinnaces included in the "Third Supply," which sailed for Jamestown in 1609. It was during this passage also that the SEA VENTURE was lost on Bermuda, an adventure that probably inspired William Shakespeare's play *The Tempest.*

*Susan Constant* returned to England in May 1607 and, as the Virginia Company had no further use for her, resumed general trade. Her ultimate fate is not known, but there are records of her sailing from Bristol to Marseilles as late as 1615. The Jamestown-Yorktown Foundation at Williamsburg, Virginia, built replicas of the three ships in the 1980s. (The dimensions for the replica *Susan Constant* differ somewhat from those estimated by Brian Lavery, in *The Colonial Merchantman Susan Constant 1605.*) Today these are used as living history exhibits and to teach people how seventeenth-century sailors made their way in the oceans.

Barbour, ed., *Jamestown Voyages Under the First Charter.* Lavery, *The Colonial Merchantman Susan Constant 1605.*

## Sutil

Brig. *L/B/D:* 45.8′ × 11.8′ × 4.6′ (14m × 3.6m × 1.4m). *Tons:* 33 toneladas. *Hull:* wood. *Comp.:* 20. *Arm.:* 4 arrobas. *Built:* San Blas de California, Mexico; 1791.

In 1791, following his voyage of exploration in the corvettes DESCUBIERTA and *Atrevida,* Don Alejandro Malaspina dispatched his hydrographer, Frigate Captain Dionisio Alcalá Galiano, on a voyage to the Pacific Northwest. His primary objective was to sail through the Strait of Juan de Fuca "to decide once and for all the excessively confused and complicated questions" of whether a Northwest Passage existed from Hudson Bay in the east to somewhere near Vancouver on the west coast. This last Spanish voyage of discovery in the Pacific sailed from Acapulco on March 8, 1792, and the expedition arrived at the Spanish settlement at Nootka on May 12. In early June, *Sutil* and *Mexicana* entered the Strait of Juan de Fuca and proceeded north through the islands of the Strait of Georgia. Near the Fraser River, the Spanish encountered Captain George Vancouver's HMS DISCOVERY and *Chatham,* with whom they exchanged information about their respective discoveries. Continuing around Vancouver Island, Galiano sailed west into Queen Charlotte Strait and back to Nootka, where the Spanish caught up with Vancouver's ships before returning to San Blas on November 25. Although the Galiano expedition was less significant than its immediate predecessor, because Malaspina was in disgrace, it received greater publicity.

Kendrick, *Voyage of "Sutil" and "Mexicana," 1792.*

## Sviatoi Gavriil

(*St. Gabriel*) (1m). *L/B/D:* 60' × 20' × 7.5' dph (18.3m × 6.1m × 2.3m). *Hull:* wood. *Comp.:* 44. *Built:* Nizhnekamchatsk, Russia; 1728.

In the early 1700s, Czar Peter I conceived an expedition to find North America from Asia and determine the eastward extent of Asiatic Russia. The vessels were to be built on the Kamchatka Peninsula from where they would sail north. (That Asia and North America were not a contiguous landmass had been determined in a forgotten 1648 expedition by Semen Dezhnev; he explored in seven unnamed *koches,* a type of Siberian single-masted vessel well suited to sailing in ice-strewn waters.) As the commander for the First Kamchatka Expedition, Peter chose Vitus Bering, Danish born but in Russian service since 1703, with Alexei Chirikov as his second-in-command. They left St. Petersburg on January 25, 1725, to start a three-year overland journey that brought them to the Pacific shore. Reaching Okhotsk in October 1726, they built a small vessel named *Fortuna* in which they crossed the Sea of Okhotsk to the Kamchatka Peninsula. From there, supplies were carried by land and river to Nizhnekamchatsk at the mouth of the Kamchatka River on the Pacific in January 1728.

Here Bering built *Sviatoi Gavriil,* which put to sea for the first time on July 13. Hugging the Asian coast, on August 1 Bering landed in Kresta Bay, at the base of the Chukotski Peninsula. Bering continued around the peninsula and sailed north through the Bering Strait to reach 67°18′N, 166°53′W, on August 16, when he turned back, having never seen the American continent. Retracing his course along the Asian shore, he returned to Nizhnekamchatsk on September 2. On June 5, 1729, Bering sailed about 130 miles (209 kilometers) east of Kamchatka in hopes of finding land — North America is about 1,500 miles (2,400 kilometers) away on that parallel — but as the boat was not designed for deep-sea voyaging, he turned back to Okhotsk. From here he returned to St. Petersburg.

In 1732, *Sviatoi Gavriil* undertook a second mission to explore the islands and "Big Land" known to lie east of the Chukotski Peninsula.

Sailing on July 23 under Ivan Fedorov and Mikhail Gvozdev, the brig hugged the coast for two weeks before sailing east to Big Diomede Island, reached on August 17. Little Diomede Island came three days later, and on the following day the brig arrived at what is now called Cape Prince of Wales, Alaska. Although Bering and his crew did not land on the Big Land, before returning to Nizhnekamchatsk they learned from Eskimos of its extensive forests and fur-bearing animals.

In 1738 and 1739, *Sviatoi Gavriil* was employed in two more expeditions to the south. The first, including three ships, resulted in the discovery of nearly thirty new islands in the Kurile chain between Kamchatka and Japan. On the second, the ships sailed over the area where a sixteenth-century explorer believed he had seen "Juan de Gama Land," before turning south and sailing to Matsmai Island, where they traded with the Japanese. *Sviatoi Gavriil*'s fate is unknown. Russian support for exploration stopped after Bering's ill-fated expedition in Sviatoi Petr and Sviatoi Pavel in 1740.

Divin, *Great Russian Navigator, A. I. Chirikov.* Fisher, *Bering's Voyages.* Frost, *Bering and Chirikov.*

## Sviatoi Pavel

(*St. Paul*) Brig. *L/B/D:* 80' × 22.5' × 12' dph (24.4m × 6.9m × 3.7m). *Tons:* 360 dwt. *Hull:* wood. *Comp.:* 76. *Arm.:* 14 guns, 3 falconets. *Built:* Andrei Kuzmin, Okhotsk, Russia; 1737–40.

The sister ship of Vitus Bering's flagship, *Sviatoi Petr,* after sailing from Petropavlovsk, Kamchatka (June 4, 1741), under command of Aleksei Chirikov, *Sviatoi Pavel* was separated from the flagship on June 20 in about latitude 48°49′N. Steering east, on July 15 *Sviatoi Pavel* reached the coast of North America near Dixon Entrance, in 54°25′N, 132°30′W on the Alaska-Canada border. There Chirikov followed the coastline north, and three days later he sent ashore a party of eleven men near Lisianskii Strait to get water and interview any natives about the surrounding country. Five days later another boat was sent out to search for the men, but it too disappeared without trace. Forced to return to Kamchatka, Chirikov sailed through the Aleutian Islands and arrived at Petropavlovsk on October 12.

The following May Chirikov once more sailed for North America, to return to St. Theodore (Attu) Island, which he had seen the previous year. However, his crew were too weak to make the voyage and they returned to Okhotsk in August. Hereafter, government interest in the North Pacific waned, and *Sviatoi Pavel* was laid up at Okhotsk. Chirikov and his officers returned to St. Petersburg.

Divin, *Great Russian Navigator, A. I. Chirikov.* Fisher, *Bering's Voyages.* Frost, *Bering and Chirikov.*

## Sviatoi Petr

Brig. *L/B/D:* 80′ × 22.5′ × 12′ dph (24.2m × 6.9m × 3.7m). *Tons:* 360 dwt. *Hull:* wood. *Comp.:* 76. *Arm.:* 14 guns, 3 falconets. *Built:* Andrei Kuzmin, Okhotsk; 1740.

In 1730, fresh from his voyage in Sviatoi Gavriil through the Bering Strait between Asia and North America, Vitus Bering wrote the Russian senate that "America is not far from Kamchatka, perhaps at a distance of 150 or 200 [German] miles. It is possible to arrange trade with people in America; so it is necessary to build a small cargo vessel in Kamchatka." Two years later he was authorized to build two vessels for an expedition "for the profit of the state and the enhancement of our interests." It was hoped that the core of this prosperity would be new sources of fur and gold. After recruiting master shipwright Andrei Kuzmin and mineralogist Georg W. Steller from St. Petersburg, Bering proceeded overland to Okhotsk, where the ships *Sviatoi Petr* and Sviatoi Pavel were built over the course of four years. In the fall of 1740, the ships departed Okhotsk and in October established winter quarters at Petropavlovsk — which takes its name from the two ships — on the Pacific coast of Kamchatka.

On June 4, 1741, the ships sailed east-southeast as far as 46°N in search of the rumored Juan de Gama Land, which turned out to be nonexistent. Separated in a fog on June 13, *Sviatori Petr* headed northeast, and on July 20 the Russians landed on Saint Elias (Kayak) Island. Although short of water, Bering was eager to return to Kamchatka and weighed anchor the next day. At the end of August, he was forced to stop again in the Shumagin Islands, but in his haste, he loaded brackish water, which further debilitated the weakened crew. Winter storms forced them to land on Bering Island in November, 6,400 miles from Petropavlovsk. Wracked with scurvy, by the summer the crew had lost thirty men, including Bering, who died on December 8. *Sviatoi Petr* was all but ruined, and the survivors broke her up and fashioned a smaller *Sviatoi Petr* (40 feet on the keel, 13 feet on the beam) in which they returned to Petropavlovsk on August 27 with 600 fur pelts.

Divin, *Great Russian Navigator, A. I. Chirikov.* Fisher, *Bering's Voyages.* Frost, *Bering and Chirikov.*

## HMS Swallow

Sloop 14 (3m). *L/B:* 92′ × 26.5′ (28m × 8.1m). *Tons:* 278 bm. *Hull:* wood. *Comp.:* 86. *Arm.:* 14 × 6pdr. *Built:* Rotherhithe, Eng.; 1745.

HMS *Swallow* spent her first twenty years' service lying in ordinary in the Medway. Surveyed in 1763, she was found in need of repairs, which were only carried out when it was decided that she sail as a consort to HMS Dolphin on that ship's second circumnavigation, under Captain Samuel Wallis. The ship was small and much slower than the copper-bottomed *Dolphin,* and Commander Philip Carteret described his new command as "a miserable tool" and "one of the worst if not the very worst of her kind; in his majesty's Navy." The ships left Plymouth on August 21, 1766. *Swallow's* dull handling made progress down the Atlantic slow going, and she barely survived the agonizing four-month transit of the Strait of Magellan. As the two ships entered the Pacific on April 11, 1767, *Dolphin* vanished from sight, leaving Carteret and *Swallow* to carry on alone.

Contending with unseasonable gales, Carteret

made first for the Juan Fernández Islands and then sailed west in latitude 28°S, "in as high, if not higher South latitude then Any men, before which have gon across this Ocean." In about 130°W longitude, Carteret headed north and on July 2 discovered an island that he named for Midshipman Robert Pitcairn. (Three decades later, the uninhabited island, "scarce better than a large rock," would shelter the BOUNTY mutineers.) Heading west in about 10°S, Carteret hoped to find Alvaro Mendaña's Solomon Islands, but running short of water, he gave up and continued west until coming to Egmont Island (named for John Perceval, Earl of Egmont, First Lord of the Admiralty) in the group he called the Queen Charlotte Islands. Only later did he realize that Egmont Island was the Santa Cruz Island of Mendaña and Pedro Fernández de Quirós's voyage in SAN JERÓNIMO in 1595. Unfortunately, eight of *Swallow*'s crew were wounded in a skirmish with the islanders, and four later died, including the master.

Although he had hoped to turn south to explore the eastern part of New Holland (Australia), with scurvy debilitating his crew Carteret was forced northwest. On August 20, *Swallow* was off Gower's, Carteret's, and Simpson's Islands, which he all but ignored, little realizing that they comprise the northern limit of the Solomon Islands. On August 26, *Swallow* came to New Britain, where Carteret's crew was refreshed and the ship repaired, and which Carteret claimed for England. Sailing again on September 7, they passed through St. George Channel, identified by Carteret as a strait between New Britain and New Ireland and not a gulf, as previously believed. *Swallow* reached the Dutch settlement at Macassar on December 27, 1767, and she remained there until the following May, when favorable winds allowed for the passage to Batavia.

After repairs to the ship, she sailed for England in September, stopping at Table Bay (Cape Town) from November 28 to January 6, 1769. Three weeks north of Ascension Island, *Swallow* was hailed by the French ship LA BOUDEUSE, under Louis Antoine de Bougainville, who was returning from his own expedition and, having followed in *Swallow*'s wake since New Ireland, was well acquainted with Carteret's voyage. Bougainville's appreciation for Carteret was heartfelt, and as he sailed away he wrote, "His ship was very small, went very ill, and when we took leave of him, he remained as it were at anchor. How much he must have suffered in so bad a vessel may well be conceived." *Swallow* finally straggled into Spithead on March 20, 1769, after a voyage whose results could be attributed only to Carteret's determination. *Swallow* had more than outlived her usefulness, and as she was "a leeward sloop, and bad sailor, merchant built and 24 years of age," she was sold on June 20.

Wallis, *Carteret's Voyage Round the World.*

# T

## Tegetthoff

*Barkentine (3m). Tons:* 220 burden. *Hull:* wood. *Comp.:* 24. *Mach.:* steam, 100 hp. *Built:* Bremerhaven, Germany; <1871.

As late as the second half of the nineteenth century, there was still a vestigial belief that north of the Arctic ice lay a warm "Polar Sea." In 1871, the Austrian government dispatched veteran Arctic explorers Julius von Payer and Karl Weyprecht to investigate this possibility. As Payer wrote, "Our ideal aim was the north-east passage, our immediate and definite object was the exploration of the seas and lands on the north-east of Novaya Zemlya." The ship chosen was *Tegetthoff,* a wooden steamship sheathed in iron and named for the late Vice Admiral Wilhelm von Tegetthoff (1827–71). With provisions for three years, the ship sailed from Bremerhaven on June 13, 1872. Having rounded Norway and sailing into the Barents Sea, on August 20 she became icebound off Novaya Zemlya in 76°22′N, 63°3′E. By August 1873 she had drifted northwest to 79°43′E, 59°33′, near the previously unknown Franz Josef Land, a group of islands about 275 miles (440 kilometers) northeast of Novaya Zemlya and the northernmost extension of the Eurasian continent. After exploring the islands, which they named for the Austrian emperor, and advancing as far north as 82°5′N, on May 20, 1874, Payer and Weyprecht decided to abandon *Tegetthoff* and sledge back to Novaya Zemlya with the ship's boats. Three months of sledging brought them to the edge of the ice pack in 77°40′N. Taking to their boats, they were rescued by the Russian whaleship *Nicholas* off Novaya Zemlya.

Payer, *New Lands Within the Arctic Circle.* Sondhaus, *Naval Policy of Austria-Hungary.*

## Terra Nova

*Bark (1f/3m). L/B/D:* 187′ × 31.4′ × 19′ (57m × 9.6m × 5.8m). *Tons:* 744 grt. *Hull:* wood. *Comp.:* 65. *Mach.:* compound steam engine, 140 nhp, 1 screw. *Built:* Alexander Stephen & Sons Ltd., Dundee, Scotland; 1884.

Built for the Dundee whaling and sealing fleet, *Terra Nova* (Latin for Newfoundland) was ideally suited for work in the polar regions. Her first voyage in the cause of science was as a relief ship for the Jackson-Harmsworth Arctic Expedition of 1894–97. In 1903, she sailed in company with the fellow Dundee whaler *Morning* to assist in freeing from McMurdo Sound the National Antarctic Expedition's DISCOVERY, under Commander Robert Falcon Scott.

In 1909 she was purchased from Messrs. C. T. Bowring & Company for the British Antarctic Expedition, known also as the Terra Nova Expedition. Reinforced from bow to stern with seven feet of oak to protect against the Antarctic ice pack, she sailed from England in June 1910 under overall command of now Captain Scott, who described her as "a wonderfully fine ice ship. . . . As she bumped the floes with mighty shocks, crushing and grinding a way through some, twisting and turning to avoid others, she seemed like a living thing fighting a great fight."

Although the twenty-four officers and scientific staff made valuable observations in biology, geology, glaciology, meteorology, and geophysics along the coast of Victoria Land and on the Ross Ice Shelf, Scott's last expedition is best remembered for the death of Scott and four companions. After wintering at Cape Evans, on Ross Island, Scott, Henry Robertson Owers, Edgar Evans, Lawrence Edward Grace Oates, and Edward Adrian Wilson set out on a race against Roald Amundsen to be the first men

▲ Although best known for their tragic end in the Arctic wastes under Sir John Franklin, **HMS Terror** and **Erebus** also spent time in the South Pacific during James Clark Ross's expedition to Antarctica. This painting by John Wilson shows the two ships surrounded by native craft in New Zealand in the early 1840s. *Courtesy National Maritime Museum, Greenwich.*

at the South Pole. They started with tractors and Mongolian ponies, but the final 800 miles (1,290 kilometers) had to be covered by man-hauling alone. Reaching the South Pole on January 17, 1912, they found that Roald Amundsen's expedition (based on FRAM) had beaten them by thirty-three days. Worse was to come, as all five men died on the return journey. Spurred by national pride, Edwardian propagandists romanticized the expedition and made Scott a hero. As Amundsen's success clearly showed, however, his planning and logistics were inadequate and the loss of the explorers was avoidable.

After returning from the Antarctic in 1913, *Terra Nova* was purchased by her former owners and resumed work in the Newfoundland seal fishery. Her end came on September 13, 1943, when she foundered off Greenland; her crew were saved by a U.S. Coast Guard cutter.

Cherry-Garrard, *Worst Journey in the World*. Debenham, *Quiet Land*. Lubbock, *Arctic Whalers*. Taylor, *With Scott — The Silver Lining*. Wilson, *Diary of the "Terra Nova" Expedition to the Antarctic.*

## HMS Terror

*Vesuvius*-class bomb vessel (3m). *L/B/D:* 102′ × 27′ × 12.5′ (31.1m × 8.2m × 3.8m). *Tons:* 325 bm. *Hull:* wood. *Comp.:* 67. *Arm.:* 1 × 13″ mortar, 1 × 10″ mortar, 2 × 6″, 8 × 24″. *Des.:* Sir Henry Peake. *Built:* Davy, Topsham, Eng.; 1813.

Best known for two expeditions in company with HMS EREBUS, HMS *Terror* was a bomb vessel designed primarily for shore bombardment. *Terror* saw service during the War of 1812, but she was then laid up until 1828. Recommissioned for duty in the Mediterranean, she was damaged near Lisbon and withdrawn from service after repairs. To withstand the tremendous recoil of their 3-ton mortars, such ships were powerfully built and therefore suitable for Arctic service. In 1836, *Terror*, under command of George Back, sailed to Hudson Bay with a view to entering Repulse Bay, from where shore parties were to be sent out to determine whether the Boothia Peninsula was an island or a peninsula. *Terror* failed to reach Repulse Bay and barely survived the winter off Southampton Island; at one point she was pushed 40 feet up the side of a cliff before the ice subsided. After ten months in the ice, Back extricated his leaking command and limped to Ireland, where she was beached.

Following repairs, *Terror* sailed with James Clark Ross's expedition to Antarctica, under command of Francis Crozier. On a voyage lasting from September 1839 to September 1843, *Terror* and *Erebus* made three forays into the waters of Antarctica, crossing the Ross Sea south of New Zealand twice, and sailing once through the Weddell Sea southeast of the Falkland Islands. The next year, the two ships were fitted with 20-horsepower engines and single-screw propellers in preparation for a voyage in search of the Northwest Passage under command of Sir John Franklin. The expedition sailed from Greenhithe on May 19, 1845, and it was last seen in Baffin Bay near the entrance to Lancaster Sound in August 1845.

Search parties later learned that the ships sailed through Lancaster Sound, and after going north through Wellington Channel and around Cornwallis Island, they headed into Peel Sound and Franklin Strait, which lie west of Somerset Island and the Boothia Peninsula. Continuing southwest, the ships became icebound in Victoria Strait, between King William Island and Victoria Island. Franklin died on June 11, 1847, and command of the expedition fell to Crozier. By the following spring, twenty-three more men had died, and on April 22, 1848, the 105 survivors abandoned the ships and attempted to march to Fort Resolution, a Hudson's Bay Company outpost more than 600 miles (965 kilometers) to the southwest. None survived, and their fate was not learned until 1859, when notes and other artifacts from the expedition were found on King William Island by search parties from Francis M'Clintock's *Fox*.

Back, *Narrative of an Expedition in HMS "Terror."* Beattie and Geiger, *Frozen in Time*. Dodge, *Polar Rosses*. Owen, *Fate of Franklin*. Ross, *Ross in the Antarctic*.

# Tigris

Reed ship (1m). *L:* 60′ (18.3m). *Hull:* Berdi reed bundles. *Comp.:* 11. *Built:* Thor Heyerdahl, al-Qurna, Iraq; 1977.

Named for the Mesopotamian river along whose course Sumerian civilization flourished about 3000 BCE, *Tigris* was built by Norwegian explorer Thor Heyerdahl, who intended to prove that Sumerians and their contemporaries could have navigated such craft over long distances. Heyerdahl had made previous similar investigations in KON-TIKI and RA II. Modeled on early renderings of seagoing craft from the Persian Gulf and Egypt, *Tigris* was built by so-called Marsh Arabs, of Iraq's Shatt al-Arab, who bundled the reeds, and Aymara Indians from the Lake Titicaca region of Peru, who turned the reed bundles into "a sickle-shaped ship that would neither capsize nor lose its shape in the ocean waves." She carried a single mast, from which were set two square sails.

Launched in November 1977, and flying the flag of the United Nations, *Tigris* had difficulty navigating through the Persian Gulf owing to unseasonably adverse winds and the tremendous amount of tanker traffic and offshore oil wells that had to be avoided. The first port of call was the island country of Bahrain, which many archaeologists have identified as Dilmun, the great seaport of the Gilgamesh epic. From there she sailed south and east out of the Strait of Hormuz before heading west along the coast of Oman. When they landed at Muscat, the *Tigris* crew were among the first westerners to visit the remains of the ancient copper-mining center at Shohar. After they headed for Africa, a change in the wind enabled them to sail for Pakistan's Indus Valley, the site of the ancient civilization centered on the cities of Mohenjo Daro and Harappa, which evidently traded with Sumer. From there they sailed west until they passed through the strait called Bab al-Mandeb, at the mouth of the Red Sea, and on to Djibouti, where they arrived in March 1978.

At Djibouti, on April 3, 1978, they burned *Tigris* to protest the conflicts that had prevented them from landing in North or South Yemen on the Arabian Peninsula, or in war-torn Somalia or Ethiopia. Their five-month, 4,200-mile (6,760-kilometer). voyage through the Persian Gulf and across the Indian Ocean had proved both the navigability and extreme seaworthiness of such reed craft and had "shown that the ancient people in Mesopotamia, the Indus Valley and Egypt could have built man's earliest civilizations through the benefit of mutual contact with the primitive vessels at their disposal five thousand years ago."

Heyerdahl, *"Tigris" Expedition.*

## Trieste

Bathyscaph. *L/B/D:* 59.5′ × 11.5′ × 18′ (18.1m × 3.5m × 5.5m). *Tons:* 50 disp. *Hull:* steel. *Comp.:* 2. *Mach.:* electric motors, 2 hp; 1 kt. *Des.:* Auguste Piccard. *Built:* Navelmeccanica, Naples, Italy; 1953.

The creation of Swiss physicist and oceanographer Auguste Piccard, and a successor to his *FNRS-2* and *FNRS-3*, the bathyscaph *Trieste* was built in 1953. The vessel is named for the Adriatic port whose citizens supported Piccard's endeavors after disagreements with the French navy arose over the fate of *FNRS-3.* (At the time the Free Territory of Trieste was administered by Yugoslavia, the United States, and Britain; it passed to Italy in 1954.)

*Trieste* has two distinct components. The larger is a compartmentalized steel float with a capacity of 28,000 gallons (106 cubic meters) of gasoline used to provide buoyancy. Originally 50 feet (15 meters) long, it was lengthened to 59.5 feet (18 kilometers); its diameter is 11.5 feet (3.5 meters). The two end compartments are used for water bal-

last. In addition, the float holds solid ballast in the form of iron pellets; originally 9 tons, this was later increased to 16 tons. Attached to the bottom of the float is a steel passenger sphere. The original sphere, built by the Industrial and Electrical Company of Terni, Italy, was made of an alloy of nickel, chromium, and molybdenum. It had an exterior diameter of 7.2 feet (2.2 meters) and an interior diameter of 6.6 feet. There were two cone-shaped Plexiglas windows, 4 inches (10 centimeters) wide on the inside and 16 inches (40 centimeters) on the outside, and 6 inches (15 centimeters) thick. This sphere was later replaced by a Krupp-built sphere constructed especially for the U.S. Navy's Project Nekton. This had an interior diameter of 6.4 feet (1.9 meters). The windows were 2.5 inches (6 centimeters) on the inside and 16 inches (40 centimeters) on the outside. Designed for vertical, not horizontal, movement, *Trieste*'s two electric motors generated 2 horsepower and could move the bathyscaph at about 1 knot. External light was provided by 500 mercury vapor lights.

*Trieste* first took the water in August 1953. After three shallow test dives around Castellamare, Piccard and his son Jacques took her down to 3,540 feet (1,080 meters), south of Capri, and then, on September 30, to a depth of 10,300 feet (3,150 meters) off Ponza Island. *Trieste* made a further eight dives in 1954, but a lack of funding forced her layup the following year. In 1956, she resumed oceanographic explorations and achieved a depth of 12,110 feet (3,691 meters), south of Ponza Island in 40°37′N, 12°49′E.

By 1957, *Trieste*'s viability as a research vehicle had been firmly established and she was used in a number of experiments, including oceanographic and biological observation, underwater high- and low-frequency sound experiments, and light penetration measurements. The same year she was also chartered by the U.S. Navy, which was so pleased with the results that it purchased her from Piccard in 1958 and moved her to the Naval Electronics Laboratory in San Diego.

In anticipation of Operation Nekton, the Navy ordered the new passenger sphere from Krupp and lengthened the float by nine feet. In November

1959, *Trieste* was transferred to Guam in preparation for an attempt to descend to the bottom of the Mariana Trench. Jacques Piccard and Lieutenant Don Walsh piloted her on a succession of ever deeper dives that culminated in a descent to the bottom of the Nero Deep (23,000 feet, or 7,010 meters), and fifteen days later, on January 23, 1960, to the bottom of the Challenger Deep — 35,800 feet (10,912 meters) — in position 11°18'N, 142°15'E, about 200 miles southwest of Guam — then the deepest known place on the planet. The deepest point on Earth is now believed to be 37,808 feet (11,524 meters), in the Mindanao Trench, off the Philippines.

Subsequently used for oceanographic research off San Diego, in 1963 *Trieste* was sent to the East Coast to take part in the search for the lost submarine USS *Thresher*. After ten dives under Commander Donald A. Keach, *Trieste* located wreckage from the ill-fated submarine, including the sail, in about 8,400 feet (2,560 meters) of water, 200 miles southeast of Boston. Retired after the commissioning of *Trieste II*, *Trieste* was put on exhibit at the Washington Navy Yard in 1980.

Piccard, *Earth, Sky, and Sea*. Piccard and Dietz, *Seven Miles Down*. U.S. Navy, *DANFS*.


# Trieste II (DSV-1)

Bathyscaph. *L/B/D:* 67' × 15' × 12.4' (20.4m × 4.6m × 3.8m). *Tons:* 46 long tons. *Hull:* steel. *Comp.:* 2. *Mach.:* electric motors. *Des.:* Auguste Piccard. *Built:* Mare Island Navy Yard, Vallejo, Calif.; 1964.

Designed as a successor to the first bathyscaph to hold the name, *Trieste II* was built by the U.S. Navy and incorporated the original sphere built for her predecessor, combined with a longer but more maneuverable external float. Her first assignment was to investigate the area in which the submarine USS *Thresher* sank in April 1963. (The original *Trieste* had already located parts of the submarine in 1963.) *Trieste II* was taken over by the Navy in 1966 and employed in a variety of deep-submergence operations. In 1971 she was reclassified as a deep-submergence vehicle. Experiments with *Trieste*

have contributed especially to the design and construction of submarine rescue and comparable vessels. Taken out of service in 1984, she was put on display at the Naval Undersea Museum in Keyport, Washington.

U.S. Navy, *DANFS*.


# USS Triton (SSRN-586)

*Triton*-class submarine. *L/B/D:* 447.5' × 37' × 24' (136.4m × 11.3m × 7.3m). *Tons:* 5,940/7,780 disp. *Hull:* steel; 985' dd. *Comp.:* 183. *Arm.:* 6"TT. *Built:* Electric Boat Division, General Dynamics, Groton, Conn.; 1959.

The fifth U.S. Navy vessel of the name, USS *Triton* was named for a Greek demigod, the son of Poseidon and Amphitrite. *Triton* sailed into history on her maiden voyage when, in lieu of a shakedown cruise, she embarked on Operation Sandblast, the first underwater circumnavigation of the globe. Leaving New London, Connecticut, on February 15, 1960, under command of Captain Edward L. "Ned" Beach, *Triton* sailed south into the Atlantic, passing St. Peter and St. Paul's Rocks off Brazil on February 24. The effort was nearly jeopardized when a sailor suffering from kidney stones had to be transferred to the cruiser USS *Macon* off Montevideo on March 5. However, this was accomplished by surfacing only far enough for him to exit the sail, and *Triton*'s hull remained under water. Two days later she rounded Cape Horn, and from there she sped across the Pacific, passing Easter Island on March 13 and Guam on March 28. On April 1, *Triton* sailed into Magellan Bay off the Philippine island of Mactan, where Ferdinand Magellan was killed on April 27, 1521. After passing through Lombok Strait into the Indian Ocean, *Triton*'s next landfall was the Cape of Good Hope on Easter Sunday, April 17. Seven days later she was once again off St. Peter and St. Paul's Rocks, having sailed 27,723 miles in sixty days, twenty-one hours.

Although this landfall marked the official beginning and end of the circumnavigation, *Triton* had been submerged since departing New London,

and would remain so until reaching her homeport on May 10. Her sail broke the surface only to take on a doctor off the Canary Islands, and again off the Virginia Capes so that Captain Beach could be flown to the White House for a ceremony with President Dwight D. Eisenhower. Although the voyage had been conceived as a way for Eisenhower to impress Soviet General Secretary Nikita Khrushchev at the Paris Summit, this conference was canceled after U-2 pilot Francis Gary Powers was shot down over the Soviet Union on May 1. But coming less than two years after the transpolar expedition of USS NAUTILUS, *Triton*'s accomplishment was a clear reaffirmation of U.S. technological supremacy.

*Triton* next deployed as a radar picket vessel

▲ The bathyscaph **Trieste** being hoisted out of the water at a tropical port in 1958–59, shortly after her purchase by the U.S. Navy. The scientist passengers are confined to the sphere below the larger gasoline-filled cylinder. *Courtesy U.S. Naval Historical Center, Washington, D.C.*

with NATO forces. In 1962 she was converted to an attack submarine, and from 1964 to 1967 she served as flagship of the Submarine Force, Atlantic Fleet, based at Norfolk. Decommissioned in 1969, in 1986 she entered the nuclear-powered ship and submarine recycling program in Bremerton, Washington.

Beach, *Around the World Submerged.*

# U

## L'Uranie

(ex-*La Ciotat*) Corvette (3m). *Hull:* wood. *Comp.:* 126. *Arm.:* 20 guns.
*Built:* France; <1816.

The last decade of the Napoleonic Wars forestalled all attempts by the French to dispatch any voyages of exploration, but in 1816, Captain Louis de Freycinet was appointed to command a one-ship scientific expedition in *L'Uranie*. Among the ship's company were Rose de Freycinet, the captain's wife (who was disguised as a midshipman until the ship reached Gibraltar). *L'Uranie* departed Toulon on September 17, 1817, en route for Australia. The primary aim of the expedition was more scientific than geographic, the emphasis being on studies of terrestrial magnetism and astronomical observation. The passage out took a year, as the French conducted exhaustive pendulum observations and collected specimens of flora and fauna at Rio de Janeiro, the Cape of Good Hope, and Mauritius. At Dirk Hartog Island in Shark Bay, Australia, Freycinet found an inscribed pewter plate with which Willem de Vlamingh, in 1697, replaced one originally dedicated by Hartog, sailing in EENDRACHT in 1616. (The Vlamingh plate is now in the Western Australian Maritime Museum in Perth.)

From Australia, *L'Uranie* sailed to Dutch and Portuguese Timor and the Moluccas, where the crew were afflicted with dysentery and, despite the frequent stops, scurvy. On March 18, 1819, *L'Uranie* arrived at the Spanish outpost on Guam, in the Mariana Islands, where the crew recuperated and the young Lieutenant Louis Duperrey (who later commanded two expeditions in L'ASTROLABE), conducted surveys of the island. In May, the ship headed for Hawaii, arriving in early August to an enthusiastic welcome by the Hawaiians and the fledgling European community in Honolulu. Sailing south and southwest, *L'Uranie* arrived at Sydney, New South Wales, where the French spent six weeks as guests of the English governor, Lachlan Macquarie.

On Christmas Day, 1819, *L'Uranie* sailed for France via Cape Horn. Attempting to enter Berkeley Sound in the Falkland Islands, the ship ran aground and had to be abandoned. Assistance arrived in the form of two American vessels. The French were taken to Montevideo in *Mercury,* where they purchased the vessel and renamed her *Physicienne* before returning to Le Havre on November 13, 1820.

Brosse, *Great Voyages of Discovery.* Dunmore, *French Explorers in the Pacific.*

# Vega

Bark (1f/3m). *L/B:* 142′ × 26′ (43.3m × 7.9m). *Tons:* 357 grt. *Hull:* wood. *Comp.:* 35. *Mach.:* steam, 60 hp, 1 screw; 7 kts. *Built:* Bremerhaven, Germany; 1873.

In 1873, veteran polar explorer Adolf Nordenskiöld began studying the feasibility of a Northeast Passage from European waters across the top of Russia to the Bering Sea. His first two efforts, in 1873 and 1875, aboard *Pröven* and *Ymer,* demonstrated that the coast of the Kara Sea was relatively ice-free, and he eventually received backing from Oscar II of Norway and Sweden, among others, to undertake an expedition in the converted German whaler *Vega.* Accompanied by three support ships, *Vega* departed Tromsø, Norway, on July 21, 1878. By August 19 they had passed Cape Chelyushkin at the top of the Taimyr Peninsula, the northernmost point of continental Eurasia, and nine days later *Vega* was off the mouth of the Lena River. From here Nordenskiöld tried to explore the New Siberian Islands to the north, but forced back by the ice, *Vega* continued her way east.

On September 27, 1878, *Vega* became icebound just east of North Cape and only 120 miles from the Bering Strait. The ship remained fast in the ice for the next ten months, during which time *Vega*'s ethnographic and scientific experts studied the Chuchki culture and collected fauna and flora specimens. Addressing the problem of pack ice head-on, Nordenskiöld wrote "On the Possibility of Commercial Navigation in the Waters off Siberia," a report that anticipated by several decades the development of such a route by Soviet planners. On July 18, 1879, *Vega* was free of the ice and resumed her way east, and on July 20 she cleared Bering Strait. "Thus," as Nordenskiöld observed, "at

last the goal was reached that so many nations had struggled for, ever since Sir Hugh Willoughby [in EDWARD BONAVENTURE] ushered in the long series of voyages to the Northeast." Nordenskiöld continued to make scientific observations for several weeks before turning for Japan, where he arrived in September. *Vega* returned to Europe via the Suez Canal, Naples, and London, but the ship's arrival at Stockholm on April 24 was a momentous occasion.

*Vega* was sold following the voyage and returned to her work in the fisheries under the Swedish flag for two decades. She was lost off Greenland when she was trapped in the ice, and sank.

Kish, *North-east Passage.* Nordenskiöld, *Voyage of the "Vega" Round Asia and Europe.*

# Victoria

Carrack (3m). *Tons:* 85 tons. *Hull:* wood. *Comp.:* 60. *Built:* Spain(?); <1519.

By the 1490s, Spain and Portugal were the world's dominant sea powers, and it seemed reasonable for the Pope to be called upon to divide the world between the two competing kingdoms. In 1493, a papal bull drew a north-south line 100 leagues (about 300 miles) west of the Cape Verde Islands, but the following year the Treaty of Tordesillas divided the world along a north-south line drawn 370 leagues (about 1,100 miles) west of the Cape Verde Islands. This gave Portugal a foothold in what is now Brazil, but it remained to be seen whether the Spice Islands (the Moluccas), to which Portugal had established a claim, fell within Spanish territory. The enormous wealth to be made trading in pepper, cloves, and other spices was impetus enough for Magellan, but he was also determined to find a westward route to the Pacific and the Orient through the Americas — in essence, to continue the voyage upon which Christopher Columbus had embarked with NIÑA, PINTA, and SANTA MARÍA in 1492. Although such a route could easily have led to a circumnavigation of the globe, that was not Magellan's intent, as he believed that the westward route was shorter than the Portuguese route via the Cape of Good Hope.

Spurned by Manoel I, the king of his native Portugal, Magellan (his Portuguese name is Fernão de Magalhães) turned to the Spanish court, where his seven years' experience in the East Indies and well-conceived plan won him the support of Charles V, who consented to the voyage in March 1518. Despite royal backing, it was not until September 20, 1519, that Magellan sailed from Sanlúcar de Barrameda on the Guadalquivir River; he headed 237 men in a fleet of five ships provisioned for two years: San Antonio (120 tons), commanded by Juan de Cartagena; Trinidad (110 tons), in which Magellan himself sailed; Concepción (90 tons), under Gaspar de Quesada; Victoria (85 tons), under Luis de Mendoza; and Santiago (75 tons), under Juan Serrano.

Early on Magellan learned that some of the Spanish captains were plotting his overthrow, but he did not move against them at the time. Sailing from the Cape Verde Islands on October 3, the ships ran along the African coast as far as Sierra Leone, a route that his Spanish captains did not understand and that Magellan did not explain. When Cartagena protested by refusing to show the evening signal, Magellan had him arrested and put San Antonio under command of Antonio de Coca. After crossing the Equator, the ships stood south-southwest until they reached the coast of Brazil on November 29, staying two weeks in the area of what is now Rio de Janeiro. They next explored the Plate River, and from there continued south, finally putting into Puerto San Julian for the winter. Here they encountered the people they called Patagonians (Spanish for "big feet"); two were kidnapped, though both subsequently died at sea. It was here also that the Spanish conspiracy against Magellan came to a head. On April 1, Quesada, Cartagena, and Juan Sebastian de Elcano, Concepción's master, seized San Antonio. Magellan moved quickly to take Victoria, and the mutineers, outnumbered three ships to two, surrendered. Quesada was decapitated and then drawn and quartered, and when the fleet sailed, Cartagena and a priest were marooned.

On May 22, Santiago was wrecked near the mouth of the Santa Cruz River, about 70 miles (115 kilometers) south of San Julian, without loss of life, and shortly thereafter Magellan shifted winter quarters to Santa Cruz, where the expedition remained until October 18. Three days later, the ships rounded the Cape of the Eleven Thousand Virgins — named in honor of the Feast of St. Ursula — and Concepción and San Antonio were sent ahead to explore. Concepción confirmed that the passage to the west was a strait — San Antonio's disgruntled pilot, Estevão Gómez, had turned back for Spain — and the remaining ships began the arduous five-week journey through the fickle winds and currents of the strait that would later bear the name of Magellan, between Patagonia and Tierra del Fuego. On November 28, the three surviving ships passed Cape Desire (Cabo Deseado) — the thing they had so long desired — and entered the Pacific.

Magellan's route across the Pacific is unknown. The ships may have sailed north until about 20°N before turning west, or they may have sailed only to the latitude of Juan Fernández Island before heading roughly northwest. Whatever the case, it was not until March 6 — after fourteen weeks at sea — that the surviving crews, wracked with scurvy and on the brink of starvation, reached the Mariana Islands in the western Pacific. These they called the Ladrones ("Thieves") because the islanders stole from the ships. In return, the Spanish burned forty or fifty houses and killed seven islanders. A week later they reached Samar in what eventually became the Philippines. At the island of Limasawa, Magellan's Malay slave, Enrique, could make himself understood in his native language. At this point, Enrique and Magellan had effectively circled the globe, though not in a single voyage.

On April 7 the ships landed at the island of

Cebu, the Philippines. Here Magellan became a blood brother of the local ruler, a rajah who converted to Christianity together with several thousand of his kinsmen. To impress his new ally with Christian might, Magellan led a small Spanish expedition against one of the rajah's reluctant vassals. On April 27, 1521, Magellan waded ashore on the island of Mactan, where he was killed, together with seven of the forty or fifty men who accompanied him. To make matters worse, his wounded slave, Enrique, plotted with the rajah against the Spanish, and twenty-four more men were killed by Magellan's erstwhile blood brother. Retreating to the island of Bohol, the Spanish burned *Concepción* and distributed the remaining crew between *Trinidad* and *Victoria*. Command of the expedition passed to the ineffectual pilot João Carvalho. After several months aimlessly cruising the Philippines, Juan Sebastian de Elcano and Gonzalo Gómez de Espinosa took charge.

On November 8, *Victoria* and *Trinidad* arrived at Tidore in the Moluccas, called the Spice Islands. Here the Spanish were warmly received by the local ruler, and traded red cloth, hatchets, cups, linen, and other items for cloves, mace, nutmeg, cinnamon, and sandalwood. Six weeks later, the ships were prepared to return to Spain, but *Trinidad* was detained for repairs. On December 21, *Victoria* sailed with forty-seven European crew and thirteen East Indians. Stopping at Timor toward the end of January, they kidnapped a local chief's son and ransomed him for food before setting out southwest across the Indian Ocean on February 11. Their passage home was long and difficult. It took twelve weeks to double the Cape of Good Hope, and they did not reach the Cape Verde Islands until July 8. In their twenty-one weeks at sea, twenty-one crew died and they lost their foremast. Then, a watering party of thirteen men was arrested by the Portuguese at Santiago, and de Elcano was forced to continue with his reduced and enfeebled crew. On September 6, 1522, eighteen Europeans limped ashore at Sanlúcar, accompanied by three East Indians, having completed the first single-voyage circumnavigation of the globe, in two years, eleven months, and two weeks. (Espinosa attempted to sail *Trinidad* back across the Pacific but was forced

to return to Tidore; only four of her crew returned to Spain, in August 1527.)

Despite the disastrous consequences for most of the participants, *Victoria*'s voyage under Magellan was a milestone in the history of navigation. In finding a water route from the Atlantic to the Pacific through the Americas, he had proved that the American continent was not attached to a southern continent, a Terra Australis, and that the Pacific could be crossed, if as yet only by brute determination. Yet in key particulars Magellan was wrong: the westward route to the Spice Islands was not shorter than that by way of the Cape of Good Hope, and the Moluccas were eventually found to lie within the Portuguese sphere described by the Treaty of Tordesillas.

*Victoria* made two voyages to Hispaniola, but she foundered on the return from the second with the loss of all her crew. In 1524 de Elcano sailed as captain-major of a fleet of seven ships under Juan Garcia Jofre de Loaisa bound for the Spice Islands by way of the Strait of Magellan. The expedition was a disaster, and de Elcano died in mid-Pacific.

Mitchell, *Elcano*. Pigafetta et al., *Magellan's Voyage Around the World*.

# Victory

Sidewheel steamer (3m). *Tons:* 85 tons. *Hull:* wood. *Comp.:* 23. *Mach.:* steam, sidewheels. *Built:* England; <1828.

In 1828, English gin distiller Felix Booth commissioned John Ross to sail in search of the Northwest Passage. Ross had not held such a command since the return of his controversial expedition in ISA-BELLA and *Alexander* in 1819. For the expedition, he purchased the paddle steamer *Victory*, originally built for service between Liverpool, the Isle of Man, and Ireland. Ross raised her sides by 5.5 feet (1.6 meters), which increased her tonnage from 85 to 150 tons, and he ordered from John Ericsson a high-pressure boiler of new, unproven design. *Victory* sailed from England in the spring of 1829. Passing through Lancaster Sound (which Ross had once thought was blocked by a mountain range), the ship sailed south through Prince Regent Inlet between Baffin Island and the Boothia Peninsula. By October, *Victory* was icebound at Felix Harbor on the east coast of the Boothia Peninsula (both named for the expedition's patron). Ross's nephew and second-in-command, James Clark Ross, made overland expeditions in search of the North Magnetic Pole, which he located on May 31, 1831, in 70°5'N, 96°46'W.

*Victory* remained fast in the ice through the next winter, and in the spring of 1832, after 136 days of temperatures below −18°C (0°F), Ross decided to abandon the ship in Felix Harbor and seek help from the whaleships that plied Lancaster Sound. After wintering at Fury Beach, near the wreck of William E. Parry's *Fury* (abandoned in the ice in 1825), the party reached Lancaster Sound. On August 26, 1833, about 10 miles (16 kilometers) east of Navy Board Inlet, they were rescued by the crew of the whaleship *Isabella*, John Ross's command in 1818–19. Remarkably, only three of the crew had died in the course of the voyage — one of them after abandoning ship.

Dodge, *Polar Rosses.* Ross, *Narrative of a Second Voyage in Search of North-West Passage.* Ross, *Polar Pioneers.*

## USS Vincennes

Sloop-of-war (3m). *L/B/D:* 127' × 33.8' × 16.5' (38.7m × 10.3m × 5m). *Tons:* 780 reg. *Hull:* wood. *Comp.:* 80. *Arm.:* 20 × 32pdr. *Built:* New York Navy Yard, Brooklyn, N.Y.; 1826.

Named for the Indiana fort twice captured by American forces under George Rogers Clark during the American Revolution, the first USS *Vincennes* had one of the most extraordinary careers of any ship in the U.S. Navy. Dispatched to the Pacific Squadron under Master Commandant William Bolton Finch one week after her commissioning, in 1828 she was ordered to look after American merchant and whaling interests in the Marquesas, Tahiti, and Sandwich (Hawaiian) Islands. From Hawaii she sailed east, stopping at Macao, Manila, Cape Town, and St. Helena before returning to New York on June 8, 1830, the first U.S. Navy ship to circumnavigate the globe. The

following year found her on patrol in the Caribbean under Commander Edward R. Shubrick. In 1833–34 she made a second circumnavigation, under Commander Alexander S. Wadsworth, calling at Guam and Sumatra, among other places, en route.

In 1838, *Vincennes* was chosen as flagship of Lieutenant Charles Wilkes's United States South Sea Surveying and Exploring Expedition, also known as the Great United States Exploring Expedition. The origins of the Wilkes expedition can be traced to the fertile imagination of John Cleves Symmes, Jr., who believed that "the earth is hollow and habitable within . . . and that it is open at the poles twelve or sixteen degrees." This theory attained widespread currency, but Congress declined to sponsor a voyage of exploration. Symmes and his theory eventually passed into memory, but the cause of a polar expedition was taken up by his erstwhile disciple, Jeremiah Reynolds. In 1836, Congress reversed itself, and Commodore Thomas ap Catesby Jones was appointed to lead the expedition. Exhausted by the endless politics of the preparations, Jones resigned, and command eventually fell to Wilkes.

On August 18, 1838, the expedition sailed with six vessels, *Vincennes, Peacock* (under Lieutenant William Hudson), *Porpoise* (Lieutenant Cadwallader Ringgold), *Relief,* and the schooners *Flying Fish* and *Sea Gull.* After calling at Madeira, Cape Verde, Rio de Janeiro, and Rio Negro, they rounded Cape Horn and put in at Orange Harbor on Tierra del Fuego. *Vincennes* remained here while *Relief* surveyed the Strait of Magellan, and the four remaining ships sailed south on February 25, 1839. *Porpoise* and *Sea Gull* skirted the (unseen) southeast coast of the Palmer Peninsula as far as 63°10'S on March 15. *Flying Fish* knocked its way south through the ice to 70°S, 101°11'W on March 22, and *Peacock* attained 68°08'S, 97°58'W. *Sea Gull* was later lost in a storm, but the other ships rendezvoused at Valparaiso in May, before continuing to Callao, on the Peruvian coast.

The ships reached the Tuamotus group in mid-August and worked their way west toward Tahiti, arriving on September 11. A month later they con-

▲ Often attributed to Captain Charles Wilkes, this engraving of the **USS Vincennes** in Disappointment Bay, Antarctica, was probably based on a sketch by the commander of the U.S. South Sea Surveying and Exploring Expedition of 1838–42. *Courtesy Peabody Essex Museum, Salem, Massachusetts.*

tinued to Samoa and from there to Sydney, Australia. *Relief* was sent home, and the other ships were readied for their second voyage south. On January 11, 1840, they encountered an ice barrier, and five days later in 65°18′S, 157°36′E, Henry Eld and William Reynolds in *Peacock* sighted two mountains (named for them), which confirmed the existence of a continental landmass. On January 28, land was also sighted from *Vincennes,* then in 66°35′S, 140°30′E. Wilkes wrote that "it could be seen extending to the east and west of our position, and now that all were convinced of its existence, I gave the land the name of the Antarctic Continent." By the next year, the region had appeared on German maps as Wilkes Land.

After regrouping in New Zealand, the expedition sailed for Hawaii, spending six months en route surveying the Fiji Islands before arriving at Honolulu on September 23, 1841. In December, *Peacock* and *Flying Fish* left to reconnoiter islands in the central Pacific before proceeding to a rendezvous at the Columbia River. In April 1842, *Vincennes* and *Porpoise* sailed for the Pacific Northwest and surveyed the waters around Vancouver Island and the Strait of Juan de Fuca. Returning to the Columbia River in August, Wilkes learned that *Peacock* had wrecked on the bar on July 17, though without loss of life. *Vincennes* was sent to San Francisco while a party of nine men, including the geologist James Dwight Dana, botanist William Dunlop Brackenridge, and naturalist-painter Titian Peale, marched overland to San Francisco. *Peacock's* crew were put aboard a purchased vessel renamed *Oregon.* The squadron sailed for Hawaii in November, and from there the ships made their way west via Wake (where Wilkes and Peale islands were named), Manila, Singapore, Cape Town, and eventually New York, where they arrived on June 10, 1842.

Much of the expedition's collections had preceded the ships home, having been sent to Philadelphia from various ports en route. The task of conservation and display fell to the fledgling Smithsonian Institution, established with a half-million-dollar bequest from an Englishman, James Smithson. At first, the scientific achievements paled in comparison with the public enthusiasm for the various courts-martial that began shortly after the ship's return, all centering on the conduct of Lieutenant Wilkes. The choice of the relatively junior officer as expedition leader had been questioned early on, for despite his industry and scientific attainments, he was a poor commander whose conduct, in the words of William Stanton, "in one incident after another created a bond of unity [among his subordinates] that could hardly have existed under a more popular commander."

Little the worse for wear, *Vincennes* was soon assigned to the Home Squadron, and under Commander Franklin Buchanan, she cruised the West Indies and the Caribbean until 1844. The next year *Vincennes* and USS *Columbus* were sent to the Orient with orders to open trade with Japan. The squadron arrived at Edo (Tokyo) on July 21, 1846, but they were denied permission even to land, much less negotiate, and Commodore James Biddle was obliged to leave after ten days. *Vincennes* was laid up at New York from 1847 to 1849, when she sailed again for a two-year stint with the Pacific Squadron. The following year, she was named the flagship of the United States Surveying Expedition to the North Pacific Ocean. Under Commander John Rodgers, she sailed with *Porpoise* via the Cape of Good Hope to chart parts of the Indian Ocean, the Bonins and Ladrones in the South China Sea,

and the Ryukyu and Kurile islands (south and north of Japan). In 1855, the expedition sailed through the Bering Strait and 400 miles (650 kilometers) west, to 176°E, farther into the Bering Sea than any ships before them.

In 1857, *Vincennes* joined the antislavery patrol on the African station, and from June 1861 to the end of the Civil War she served with the Gulf Coast Blockading Squadron between Pensacola and the Mississippi River. She was sold at Boston in 1867.

Bartlett, "Commodore James Biddle and the First Naval Mission to Japan." Hoffman, *Voyage to the Southern Ocean.* Johnson, *Thence Round Cape Horn.* Lundeberg and Wegner, "Not for Conquest but Discovery." Stanton, *Great U.S. Exploring Expedition.* U.S. Navy, *DANFS.*

## Virginia

Pinnace (1m). *L/B/D:* ca. 50′ × 13′ × 6′ dph. *Tons:* 30. *Hull:* wood. *Built:* Digby (of London), Popham, Me.; 1607.

The 30-ton pinnace *Virginia* was the first ship built by English colonisers in New England. Although her builders abandoned their colony on the banks of Maine's Kennebec River after only a year, their discovery of pine timbers suitable for ships' masts and the launch of the *Virginia* signaled the tentative start of a shipbuilding industry that would peak in the mid-nineteenth century. In April 1606, James I chartered the Virginia Company, which reserved the lands between 34° and 41°N for a group based in London and those between 38° and 45°N for a group from England's West Country. In December, the London branch dispatched the SUSAN CONSTANT, *Godspeed,* and *Discovery,* which carried the nucleus of the Jamestown Colony in what is now Virginia.

In the meantime, Sir John Popham of the West Country group, his son Sir Francis Popham, and Sir Ferdinando Gorges were planning a voyage to the shores of New England, which had been explored by Bartholomew Gosnold in CONCORD, among others. On May 31, 1607, the ships *Gifte of God* and *Mary and John* sailed from Plymouth with a complement consisting largely of retired soldiers,

▲ A modern rendering of the pinnace **Virginia,** a contemporary of the Jamestown Settlement's **Susan Constant.** *Courtesy Maine's First Ship, Phippsburg, Maine.*

who were to establish a fort at the mouth of the Kennebec River and develop a fur trade with the Abnaki people. Sailing via Nova Scotia, they arrived at the Kennebec on August 18. Here they built a fort and a man named Digby began to build a pinnace, called *Virginia,* for exploring upriver. It was normal practice to carry the materials for such a boat on board ship for assembly at one's destination, but it seems that *Virginia* was made entirely of materials gathered on site. The only written descriptions of this vessel are that she was of 30 tons — perhaps 50 feet long. A picture-plan by John Hunt showing Fort St. George as it appeared in October 1607 includes a sketch of *Virginia,* which appears to have a flat transom and a single mast carrying a lug rig.

*Mary and John* and *Gifte of God* sailed for home during the fall, leaving forty-five colonists to struggle through the winter on the Kennebec. There are no detailed accounts of what happened for the remainder of the colony's existence. Two small ships arrived in May or June of 1608, followed by *Gifte of God* in the early fall. John Popham had died and his successor, Gilbert, was returning home to claim an inheritance. Because there were "no mynes discouered, nor hope thereof," and "the feare that all other winters would proue like this first," it was decided to abandon the colony. "Wherefore they all embarqued in that this new arrived shippe and in the new Pynnace ye *Virginia* and sett saile for England, and this was the end of the northerenn Colony yponn the Riuer of Sachadehoc."

With the failure of the "Second Colonie," as the Kennebec settlement was known, many of the backers turned to the London group, which acquired *Virginia.* She was one of two pinnaces that accompanied the "third supply" to Jamestown, Virginia, in 1609. (It was on this voyage that the SEA VENTURE was lost on Bermuda.) The ultimate fate of this veteran of at least two transatlantic voyages is not known. A group has been formed to build a reconstruction of the *Virginia* to commemorate the four hundredth anniversary of the Popham colony.

Baker, *Colonial Era Vessels.* Quinn and Quinn, *English New England Voyages.*

# Vostok

Sloop-of-war (3m). *L/B/D:* 129.8′ × 32.7′ × 9.6′ (39.6m × 10m × 2.9m). *Tons:* 900 tons. *Hull:* wood. *Comp.:* 127. *Arm.:* 28 guns. *Built:* Stoke and Kolodnin, Okhta Shipyard, St. Petersburg, Russia; 1818.

In 1819, Czar Alexander I ordered the dispatch of two expeditions for polar exploration. The first, under Captain Fabian Gottlieb von Bellingshausen (a veteran of Adam Johann von Krusenstern's NADEZHDA expedition of 1803–6), was to sail toward the South Pole with the flagship *Vostok* ("East") and the 120-foot transport-turned-navy-sloop *Mirny* ("Peaceful," ex-*Lagoda*). The other — made up of the sloops *Otkrytie* and *Blagonamerennyi* — was to sail through the Bering Strait to explore the Arctic Ocean. The primary object of Bellingshausen's two-year expedition was "to carry out a voyage of discovery in the higher southern latitudes, and to circumnavigate the ice-belt of the southern Polar Circle." During the southern winter, he was to withdraw to equatorial waters.

*Vostok* and *Mirny* departed Kronstadt on July 4, 1819, and after stops at Copenhagen and Portsmouth, they entered the Atlantic Ocean on August 29, 1819, arriving at Rio de Janeiro on November 2. From Rio, the two ships headed for the South Georgia Islands, along the way searching for several features that were indicated on charts but did not, in fact, exist. Passing South Georgia on November 16, the Russians named several nearby islands before continuing to the South Shetlands, near which they discovered the Marquis de Traversay Islands. By January 4, 1820, they had sailed to 60°25′S, 27°58′E, when heavy ice forced them eastward. Crossing the Antarctic Circle for the first time on January 15 in about 3°W, they were no more than 20 miles from the coast of what is now called Princess Martha Land. As Bellingshausen's English editor wrote, "A few hours of clear weather here on this day would have certainly antedated the discovery of land by 110 years." Though they were forced below the Antarctic Circle by heavy ice on several occasions, on February 13 the sight of shore birds indicated land was nearby, although the nearest known bodies — Prince Edward Island and the Kerguelen Islands — were 1,200 miles (1,950 kilometers) away. (It would be another eleven years before the sealer Captain John Biscoe, sailing with *Tula* and *Lively*, actually spotted and named Enderby Land.) Continuing in their circumnavigation of the as yet unseen Antarctica, the Russians encountered land birds for the second time on February 24 (in 62°32′S, 57°41′E). On March 5, *Vostok* and *Mirny* (commanded by Mikhail Petrovich Lazarev) separated for their return to Port Jackson (Sydney), Australia, so that their parallel courses would fall between those followed by Captain James Cook in HMS Resolution and Captain Tobias Furneaux in HMS Adventure during Cook's second voyage.

*Vostok* arrived at Port Jackson on March 30, and *Mirny* on April 7, both remaining in port until May 8. Intending to sail north of New Zealand, the ships were forced south by contrary winds, and they passed through Cook Strait between North and South islands. From there, they headed northeast for the Tuamotu Islands, where in early July they confirmed the position of, or put on the map for the first time, fifteen islands between 15°5′E and 17°49′E in about as many days. On the twenty-second they put into Matavai Bay, Tahiti, for five days. En route back to Port Jackson, the Russians discovered and named Lazarev (Matahiva), Vostok, and the Grand Duke Alexander Islands, among others. Repairs to the masts and rigging kept the ships in port for seven weeks, and it was not until October 31 that they resumed their cruise in Antarctic waters. Encountering ice at 62°18′S, 164°13′E, they turned east again, being forced north intermittently because of the ice. On January 10, 1821, they spotted a coast to which they could approach no closer than fourteen miles and which they named Peter I Island (now the Norwegian territory Peter I Øy), in honor of Peter the Great, the founder of the Russian navy. On January 17 they again encountered land, which they called Alexander I Land. Skirting the unseen Antarctic Peninsula, *Vostok* and *Mirny* turned northeast, sailing through the South Shetland Islands, whose extent they determined to be about 160 miles (260 kilometers).

After stops at Rio de Janeiro (to pick up the Russian ambassador) and Lisbon (to transfer him to Portugal), *Vostok* and *Mirny* returned to Kronstadt on August 28, having completed a voyage of 751 days. They had spent 224 days at anchor and 527 under sail, and had sailed more than 57,000 miles, in the course of which they discovered twenty-nine islands — two in the Antarctic — and one coral reef and a lagoon. That part of the Southern Ocean lying between the Antarctic Peninsula in the east and Thurston Island in the west was subsequently named the Bellingshausen Sea.

Bellingshausen, *Voyage of Captain Bellingshausen to the Antarctic Seas*.

# HMS Wager

6th rate 24 (3m). *L/B/D:* 123′ × 32.2′ × 14.3′ dph (37.5m × 9.8m × 4.4m). *Tons:* 559 bm. *Hull:* wood. *Comp.:* 180 crew. *Arm.:* 28 guns. *Built:* England; <1739.

HMS *Wager* was an East Indiaman purchased specifically for Commodore George Anson's ambitious but ill-fated expedition against Spanish Pacific outposts at the start of the War of Jenkins' Ear in 1739. Named for First Lord of the Admiralty Sir Charles Wager, the mission's prime mover, *Wager* was one of six warships in the squadron, which also included two victualers. When the undermanned squadron sailed from Portsmouth on September 18, 1740, the crews included invalids from Chelsea Hospital and untrained marines. The ships were forty days to Madeira and another seven weeks to St. Catherine's Island off the coast of Brazil, where they remained until January 18, 1741. Although they intended to sail directly from there for Cape Horn, the need for repairs forced them to put into the deserted Port St. Julian, where *Wager* came under command of Lieutenant David Cheap, formerly first lieutenant in George Anson's flagship, HMS CENTURION.

The ships transited the Straits of Le Maire on March 7, whereupon they were at the mercy of furious and relentless storms that kept them from rounding Cape Horn for more than six weeks. On April 24, *Wager* lost sight of the other ships, and for the next four days Cheap lay to at night despite the danger of doing so on a lee shore and despite standing orders from Anson to rendezvous at Juan Fernández Island. On May 13, *Wager* was in the Bay of Peñas, Chile, but "with only thirteen sickly hands" to work the ship, at 0430 the next morning she struck a reef and came to rest "not above a

musket shot from shore." At first the ship's company was divided between those who went ashore in the ship's boats, a cutter and a barge, and those who stayed aboard sating themselves with brandy and wine. Eventually the latter group landed, too, but the crew gradually broke into a number of factions; some were in a state of mutiny against Cheap's authority, while others simply ignored their fellow castaways and went off on their own. For five months they remained on inhospitable and barren Wager Island, until the carpenter finished enlarging the longboat so that it could accommodate all the survivors.

A major point of contention was whether they should sail north and try to overpower an unsuspecting Spanish merchantman and resume their voyage, as Cheap proposed, or return home via the Strait of Magellan, as the gunner John Bulkeley suggested. Bulkeley's view carried the day, and on October 14 most of the survivors embarked in the longboat (named *Speedwell*), the cutter, and the barge. Ten of the men volunteered to return to Wager Island in the barge to fetch extra canvas, but instead they rejoined Captain Cheap and three others who had stayed behind. Five deserters came back as well, but of these twenty, only four — including Cheap and Midshipman John Byron (later to circle the world in DOLPHIN) — would survive the seemingly endless struggle up the coast. Arriving at Santiago in January 1743, Cheap and the others were made prisoners of the Spanish, but with the freedom of the town; they remained there for more than two years. Though they sailed for England on March 1, 1745, they were not home until the following year.

In the meantime, *Speedwell* and the cutter con-

◀ The Sea Education Association's oceanographic training schooner **Westward** under press of sail. *Photo by Jennifer Rose/SEA.*

tinued south with eighty-one men. On the night of November 6, 1742, the cutter was lost and her ten crew embarked in *Speedwell*. On the fourteenth they entered the Strait of Magellan and reached Cape Virgin Mary on December 16 and Port Desire four days later. From there they sailed across Golfo San Giorgio, on whose uninhabited shores eight men were abandoned (three eventually returned to England, in 1746). After landing briefly near Montevideo, *Speedwell* sailed on to the Rio Grande in Brazil, where she arrived on January 28, 1743, with only thirty men in her crew. Most of these men eventually returned to England. Upon their return, a court-martial was convened to inquire into the loss of the ship, and the mate on duty at the time was reprimanded. Thanks to Anson's intervention, neither Bulkeley nor any of the others who left Cheap on Wager Island were tried for mutiny. There are eyewitness accounts by the *Wager*'s survivors, and Patrick O'Brian's *Unknown Shore* is a readable and accurate, though fictional, account of the voyage and its aftermath.

Bulkeley and Cummins, *Voyage to the South Seas*. Byron, *Narrative*. Shankland, *Byron of the "Wager."*

General Justo Urquiza following the siege of Buenos Aires, Page began his official assignment. *Water Witch* was the first steam vessel to ascend the Paraná, Paraguay, and Salado Rivers, and her three years of surveys showed that these rivers were navigable by large, powered vessels, a fact that had great implications for the growth of Argentina, Paraguay, and Brazil. Though the expedition was a success, on February 1, 1855, Page ignored a Paraguayan decree forbidding him to ascend the Paraná River, and one sailor was killed when the fort at Itapirú fired on the ship. *Water Witch* was back in the United States in 1856. In 1858 she returned to the Plate as part of Flag Officer W. B. Shubrick's Paraguay Expedition, one aim of which was to negotiate a treaty and compensation for the dead man's family.

At the start of the Civil War, *Water Witch* was assigned to the Gulf Blockading Squadron and operated between Pensacola, Florida, and the Mississippi River. Transferred to the South Atlantic Blockading Squadron, she operated mostly around Ossabaw Island off mainland Georgia until June 3, 1864, when she was captured near Bradley's River. Taken into the Confederate Navy, on December 19, 1864, she was burned to prevent her capture by Union forces.

Silverstone, *Warships of the Civil War Navies*. Wood, *Voyage of the "Water Witch."*

## USS Water Witch

Sidewheel sloop (1f/2m). *L/B/D:* 150′ × 23′ × 9′ (45.7m × 7m × 2.7m). *Tons:* 378 burden. *Hull:* wood. *Comp.:* 77. *Arm.:* 4 × 32pdr, 1 × 24pdr. *Mach.:* inclined condensing engine, 180 hp, 2 sidewheels; 11.5 kts. *Des.:* John Lenthall. *Built:* Washington (D.C.) Navy Yard; 1853.

The first assignment for the gunboat *Water Witch* was to undertake an extensive survey of the region around the River Plate, and in particular the Paraná River in Argentina and Paraguay. The ship sailed under command of Lieutenant Thomas Jefferson Page on February 8, 1853, and after several stops, she arrived at Buenos Aires in May. After ensuring the safety of the Argentine Confederation's

## SSV Westward

Staysail schooner (2m). *L/B/D:* 125′ × 12′6″ × 21′6″. *Tons:* 250 disp. *Hull:* steel. *Comp.:* 35. *Mach.:* Cummins diesel, 500 hp. *Built:* Abeking & Rasmussen, Lemwerder, Germany; 1961.

Originally built as a yacht, after seven years in private hands, *Westward* became the vehicle for what became one of the most innovative educational programs in the United States. From April 1968 to December 1971, she was owned by the Oceanic Foundation in Waimanalo, Hawaii, and used for oceanographic work, mainly in the Line Islands. In 1971 the veteran yachtsman, teacher, and educational administrator Corwith Cramer conceived an idea for a course of study based entirely on practical experience under sail. But, as Cramer put it, the idea was not "to teach people how to sail. What we wanted to do was to take them to sea so they would learn to love the sea." With the financial support of Edward MacArthur, Cramer founded the American Sailing Education Association and purchased *Westward*, a schooner modeled on the well-found German pilot schooners of the North Sea. Over the next few years, Cramer struggled to establish a curriculum that was both academically viable and appropriate to the unique educational environment of the ship. While Cramer sought a broad-gauge liberal arts program focused on maritime history and literature as well as nautical science, Coast Guard regulations, among other things, dictated that *Westward*'s mission emphasize oceanographic studies.

Reflecting this new direction, the parent organization was renamed the Sea Education Association, and the headquarters was moved to Woods Hole, Massachusetts, in 1975. (Founded in Chicago, SEA had moved to Boston in 1972.) Here SEA was able to take advantage of its proximity to the Woods Hole Oceanographic Institution (WHOI), the Marine Biology Lab of the U.S. Geological Service, the National Marine Fisheries Service, the Coast Guard, and other organizations dedicated to marine science and seamanship. With an increasingly professional staff of mariners and scientists, SEA developed a semester-long course of study, combining classroom academics ashore and practical sea experience aboard *Westward*. The shore component includes maritime history and literature,

seamanship, and oceanography, while the sea component emphasizes practical seamanship and practical oceanography. With a fully realized, multifaceted program, SEA and *Westward* quickly gained academic respectability, attracting students from around the country while scores of colleges and universities began awarding academic credit for work completed at SEA.

In 1987, a second vessel, named for SEA's founder (who died in 1986), was built in Spain. Shortly after the launch of the *Corwith Cramer*, *Westward* underwent a substantial overhaul and modernization. Early on, her scientific equipment consisted mostly of hand-me-downs from neighbor institutions in Woods Hole. As one staff scientist remarked, "Before I came to SEA, I had only seen a Nansen bottle in a museum." (The Nansen bottle was devised in the nineteenth century by Fridtjof Nansen for taking water samples at specific depths.) Both vessels are now equipped to make a wide range of bathymetric readings and to conduct biological and geological sampling in their normal areas of operation, which include the North Atlantic, Caribbean, and Gulf of Mexico. Within the context of the prescribed shipboard curriculum, *Westward* faculty and students have also undertaken a number of long-term studies into such topics as the water mass circulation and movement, the distribution of halobates (the only marine insect), zooplankton and photoplankton, and the density of tar balls and plastic waste in the ocean.

Helfrich, *"Sailing Ships, Science and Stonework."*

MAPS

CHRONOLOGY OF
MARITIME EXPLORATION
AND DISCOVERY

GLOSSARY

BIBLIOGRAPHY

INDEX

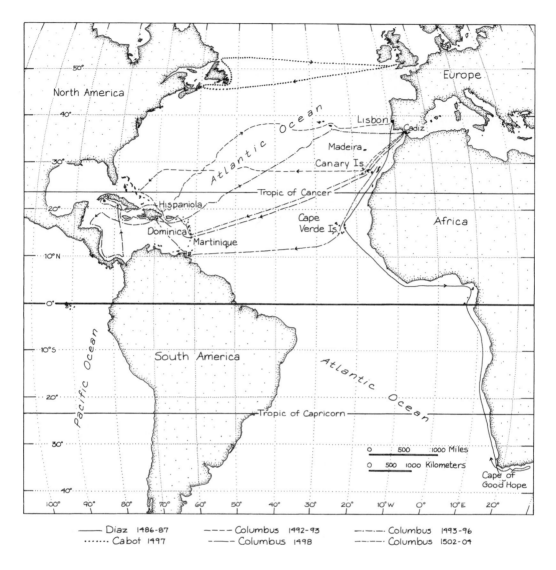

50°

North America

40°

30°

Atlantic  Ocean

Lisbon
Cadiz

Madeira

Canary Is.

Tropic of Cancer

20°

Hispaniola

Dominica

Martinique

Cape
Verde Is.

10°N

0°

10°S

20°

30°

40°

Europe

Africa

Pacific  Ocean

South America

Atlantic  Ocean

Tropic of Capricorn

0      500      1000 Miles

0    500   1000 Kilometers

Cape of
Good Hope

100°   90°   80°   70°   60°   50°   40°   30°   10°W   0°   10°E   20°

———— Diaz  1486-87        ———— Columbus  1492-93       —·—·— Columbus  1993-96
········ Cabot  1997        ——— Columbus  1998       —··—·· Columbus  1502-04

*Europe Spans the Atlantic*

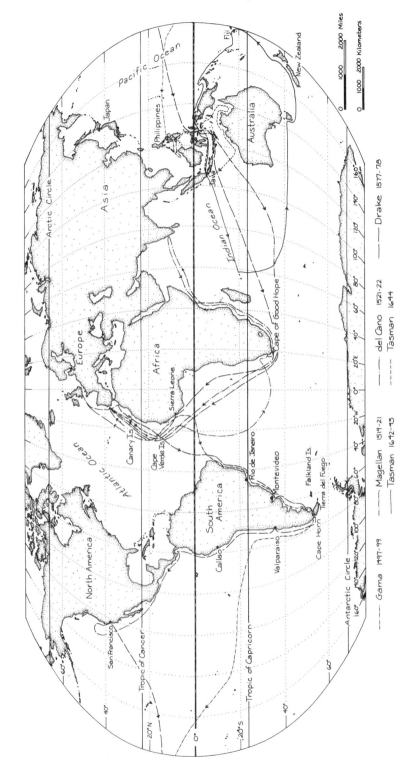

*The World Encompassed, 15th to 17th Centuries*

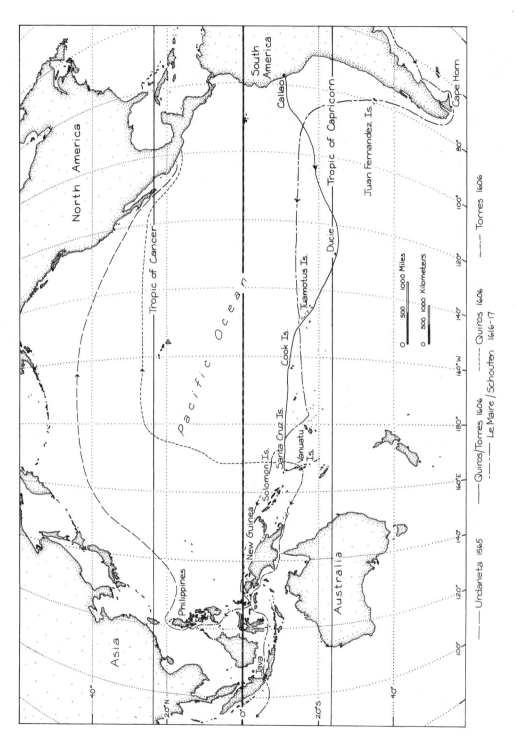

Spanish Exploration of the Pacific, 16th to 17th Centuries

Urdaneta 1565 — — — Quiros/Torres 1606 — — Quiros 1606 — — Torres 1606

Le Maire/Schouten 1616-17

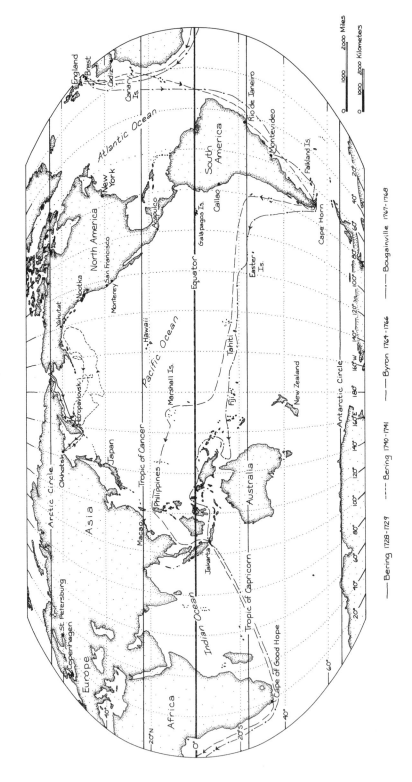

*European Exploration of the Pacific, 1728–1768*

—— Bering 1728-1729    ----- Bering 1740-1741    —— Byron 1764-1766    ——— Bougainville 1767-1768

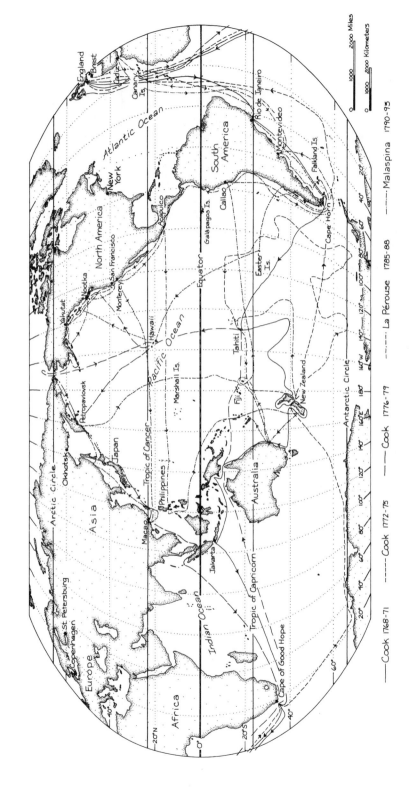

The Golden Age of European Exploration, 1768–1795

Cook 1768-71 ---- Cook 1772-75 —— Cook 1776-79 ----- La Pérouse 1785-88 ----- Malaspina 1790-95

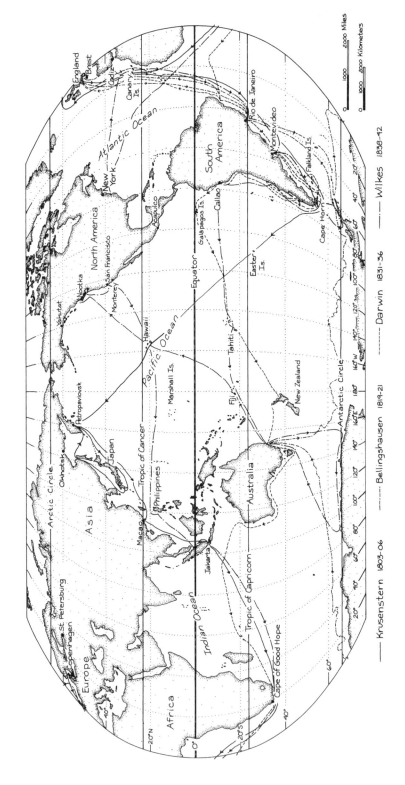

*European and American Exploration of the Pacific, 1803–1842*

——— Krusenstern 1803-06  ——— Bellingshausen 1819-21  ——— Darwin 1831-36  ——— Wilkes 1838-42

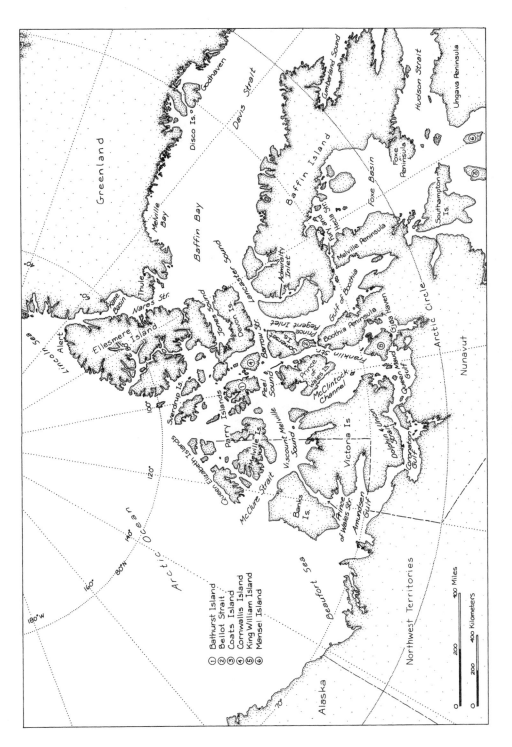

Northwest Passage

① Bathurst Island
② Bellot Strait
③ Coats Island
④ Cornwallis Island
⑤ King William Island
⑥ Mansel Island

Greenland

Baffin Island

Ellesmere Island

Nunavut

Northwest Territories

Alaska

Arctic Ocean

Beaufort Sea

Victoria Is.

Banks Is.

Baffin Bay

Davis Strait

Hudson Strait

Ungava Peninsula

Foxe Basin

Foxe Peninsula

Southampton Is.

Melville Peninsula

Boothia Peninsula

Gulf of Boothia

Prince Regent Inlet

Lancaster Sound

Jones Sound

Devon Is.

Barrow Str.

Peel Sound

McClintock Channel

Franklin Str.

Queen Maud Gulf

Gjoa Haven

Dolphin & Union Strait

Coronation Gulf

Dease Str.

Amundsen Gulf

Prince of Wales Str.

McClure Strait

Melville Is.

Viscount Melville Sound

Queen Elizabeth Islands

Parry Islands

Sverdrup Is.

Nares Str.

Thule

Kane Basin

Lincoln Sea

Lord Alert

Melville Bay

Disco Is.

Godhaven

Cumberland Sound

Admiralty Inlet

Prince of Wales Is.

Somerset Is.

Fury and Hecla Str.

Arctic Circle

400 Miles

400 Kilometers

200

200

40°

50°

60°

70°

80°N

100°

120°

140°

160°

180°W

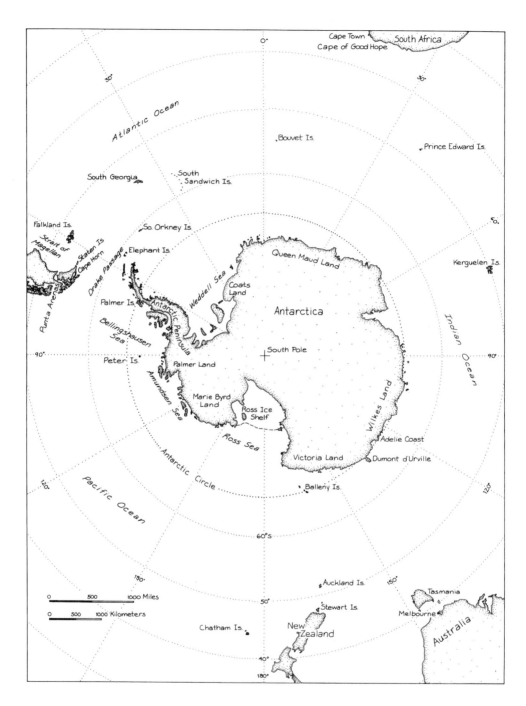

Antarctica

# Chronology of Maritime Exploration and Discovery

**ca. 2500 BCE** Sea trade between Indus Valley and Persian Gulf.

**ca. 1500 BCE** Polynesians reach Santa Cruz, Vanuatu, New Caledonia, and Fiji. Hatshepsut sends expedition to Punt.

**7th cent. BCE** Necho dispatches Phoenician expedition to circumnavigate Africa.

**500 BCE** Polynesians reach Tahiti.

**310–3060 BCE** Pytheas sails to Britain and Thule.

**146 BCE** Eudoxus of Cyzicus sails to India.

**4th cent. CE** Lateen (fore-and-aft) sails begin to predominate over square sails in Mediterranean.

**ca. 6th cent.** Polynesian voyagers reach Easter Island and Hawaii.

**790** Irish monks reach Iceland; Norse follow ca. 860.

**982** Eirik (The Red) Thorvaldsson reaches Greenland.

**ca. 1000** Leif (The Lucky) Ericsson reaches Newfoundland from Greenland. Maori reach New Zealand from Central Polynesia.

**12th cent.** Rudimentary compasses in Europe.

**13th–15th cent.** Fore-and-aft rigged caravels evolve in Mediterranean and are used extensively in voyages of exploration.

**13th cent.** Vertical hinged rudder first appears in northern Europe, eventually to replace side-mounted steering oar. Cross staff for measuring altitudes of celestial bodies invented by Jacob ben Makir in southern France.

**1291** Vivaldi brothers attempt to circumnavigate Africa.

**14th–17th cent.** Development of Mediterranean carrack, merging Mediterranean and northern European shipbuilding practices.

**1405–33** *Ch'ing Ho.* Zheng He's seven expeditions to Indian Ocean.

**15th cent.** Quadrant used by Portuguese navigators for measuring altitudes of celestial bodies.

**1445** Portuguese reach Cape Verde Islands.

**1488** Dias rounds Cape of Good Hope.

**1492** *Niña, Pinta, and Santa María.* Columbus's first voyage to Caribbean.

**1497** *Mathew.* Cabot to Newfoundland and Labrador.

**1497–99** *São Gabriel.* Gama's flagship makes first voyage around Cape of Good Hope to India.

**1500** *Anunciada* et al. Cabral's expedition lands in Brazil and inaugurates *carreira da India* between Portugal and India.

**1524** *Dauphine.* Verrazzano explores North America from North Carolina to Maine and Newfoundland.

**1519–22** *Victoria.* Magellan/de Elcano circumnavigation.

**1534, 1535–36, 1541–42** *Grande Hermine.* Cartier expeditions to Canada.

**1553** *Edward Bonaventure.* Borough/Chancellor expedition to Murmansk.

**1565–66** *San Pablo.* Urdañeta pioneers west-to-east transpacific route.

**1567–69** *Los Reyes* etc. Mendaña transpacific voyage to Solomon Islands and back.

**1576** *Gabriel.* Frobisher's first search for Northwest Passage.

**1577** *Aid, Gabriel* etc. Frobisher's second expedition.

**1577–80** *Golden Hind.* Drake's circumnavigation.

**1578** *Aid* etc. Frobisher's third expedition.

**1585** *Sunneshine* etc. Davis expedition to Greenland.

**1595–96** *San Jerónimo* etc. Mendaña's second expedition, to colonize Solomon Islands.

**1602** *Concord.* Gosnold expedition to New England.

**1602** *Discovery.* Weymouth expedition to Canada.

**1605** *Duyfken.* Jansz explores northern Australia.

**1605** *San Pedro y San Pablo, San Pedro* etc. Quiros expedition to rediscover Solomon Islands. Torres transits strait between Australia and New Guinea in *San Pedro*.

**1607** *Virginia.* First ship built by English in North America, at Popham Colony in Maine.

**1609** *Halve Maen.* Hudson ascends Hudson River.

**1610–11** *Discovery.* Hudson expedition to Hudson Bay.

**1612–13** *Discovery* etc. Exploration of Hudson Bay.

**1615–16** *Eendracht.* Schouten and Le Maire first to round Cape Horn.

**1615–16** *Discovery.* Bylot and Baffin voyages to Hudson Bay and Lancaster Sound.

**1616** *Eendracht.* Hartog lands in western Australia.

**1619–20** *Enhjørning.* Jens Munk's search for Northwest Passage in Hudson Bay.

**1621** *Mayflower.* First permanent English settlement in New England.

**1642–43** *Heemskerck* etc. Abel Tasman's exploration of Australia.

**1644** *Limmen* etc. Tasman's second expedition to Australia.

**1668–69** *Nonsuch.* Couart and Radisson's voyage to Hudson Bay lays groundwork for Hudson's Bay Company.

**1678–79** *Griffon.* La Salle's ship is first European vessel on the Great Lakes.

**1686** *Belle* et al. La Salle's expedition to the Gulf Coast.

**1698–1700** *Paramore.* Halley makes two voyages to South Atlantic for study of magnetic variation.

**1699–1701** *Roebuck.* Dampier expedition to explore Australia and New Guinea.

**1701** *Paramore.* Halley makes four-month study of tides and tidal currents in English Channel.

**1721–22** *Arend.* Roggeveen's search for southern continent.

**1725–30** *St. Gabriel.* Bering's first expedition, through Bering Strait.

**1740–41** *St. Peter* and *St. Paul.* Bering's second expedition, in Alaska.

**1740–44** HMS *Centurion, Wager* etc. Anson's circumnavigation; Byron's shipwreck.

**1757** Sextant invented in England; it is capable of measuring angles of the sun to the earth of up to 120°.

**1759** John Harrison builds first marine chronometer, enabling mariners to determine longitude at sea.

**1764–66** HMS *Dolphin.* Byron's circumnavigation.

**1766–68** *La Boudeuse* etc. Bougainville's circumnavigation.

**1766–68/69** HMS *Dolphin* and *Swallow.* Wallis's and Carteret's circumnavigations.

**1768–71** HMS *Endeavour.* Cook's first expedition to Pacific.

**1769–70** *St. Jean-Baptiste.* Surville's commercial expedition from India to Peru.

**1771–74** *Resolution* and *Adventure.* Cook's second expedition to Pacific.

**1776** James Watt develops steam engine, followed by double-acting expansion engine in 1782.

**1776–80** *Resolution* and *Discovery.* Cook's third expedition to Pacific.

**1785–88** *L'Astrolabe* and *La Boussole.* La Pérouse's ill-fated expedition.

**1788** HMS *Sirius* etc. First Fleet arrives in Australia.

**1789–93** *Descubierta.* Malaspina's exploration of the Pacific Northwest and Australia.

**1790** *Bounty.* Fletcher Christian leads mutineers to Pitcairn Island.

**1791–93** *Espérance.* Entrecasteaux's expedition to Pacific in search of La Pérouse.

**1791–95** *Discovery* etc. Vancouver circumnavigation.

**1792** *Sutil* etc. Galiano explores Pacific Northwest for Spain. *Columbia Rediviva* enters Columbia River.

**1800–4** *Géographe* etc. Baudin exploration of Australia and circumnavigation.

**1801–3** HMS *Investigator.* Flinders explores Australia.

**1803–6** *Nadezhda* etc. Krusenstern leads first Russian circumnavigation.

**1805** *Joliba.* Park's boat on the Niger River.

**1806** *Resolution.* Scoresbys attain record farthest north in Greenland Sea.

**1807–13** *Diana.* Golovnin's voyage from Russia to Northwest Pacific.

1815–18  *Rurik.* Kotzebue's circumnavigation.

1817–20  *L'Uranie.* Freycinet's circumnavigation.

1818  *Isabella* etc. John Ross's search for Northwest Passage.

1819–20  HMS *Hecla.* Parry reaches Melville Island in Northwest Passage.

1819–21  *Vostok.* Bellingshausen's expedition to Antarctica.

1820  *Hero.* American sealer under Nathaniel B. Palmer sails near Palmer (now Antarctic) Peninsula.

1821–23  *Hecla* etc. Parry explores northern Hudson Bay.

1822–25  *L'Astrolabe.* Duperrey's circumnavigation.

1823–26  *Predpriyatiye.* Kotzebue expedition to Pacific coast of North America.

1824–25  *Hecla* etc. Parry explores Prince Regent Inlet in Northwest Passage.

1825–28  *Blossom.* Beechey expedition to Pacific and Arctic.

1826–29  *Senyavin.* Litke scientific expedition to Pacific and circumnavigation.

1826–29  *L'Astrolabe.* Dumont-D'Urville circumnavigation; finds relics of La Pérouse expedition.

1827  *Hecla.* Parry attempts to reach North Pole from Spitsbergen.

1829–33  *Victory.* John Ross's second expedition in quest of Northwest Passage.

1831–36  HMS *Beagle.* Fitzroy-Darwin circumnavigation via South America and Galápagos.

1836–37  HMS *Terror.* Back expedition to Hudson Bay.

1838–42  USS *Vincennes.* Wilkes circumnavigation.

1838–43  HMS *Erebus* and *Terror.* Ross Antarctic expedition.

1845–48  HMS *Erebus* and *Terror.* Franklin's ill-fated search for Northwest Passage.

1848–49  HMS *Investigator.* Ross expedition in search of Franklin.

1848–49  HMS *Investigator* etc. McClure expedition to western Arctic.

1850–54  HMS *Investigator.* McClure establishes last link of Northwest Passage from west.

1850–53  *Advance.* De Haven Arctic expedition.

1852–54  *Resolute.* Belcher expedition to find Franklin.

1853–56  USS *Water Witch* surveys Paraná River.

1857–59  *Fox.* McClintock search for Franklin.

1858  *Ma-Robert.* Livingston explores Zambesi and Shire Rivers.

1867  *Emma Dean* etc. Powell expedition on Colorado River.

1871–1873  USS *Polaris.* Hall's third expedition in search of North Pole.

1871–74  *Tegetthoff.* Payer and Weyprecht Arctic expedition discovers Franz Josef Land.

1872–74  HMS *Challenger.* Nares oceanographic research expedition.

1875–76  *Alert* etc. Nares Arctic expedition.

1878–79  *Vega.* Nordenskiöld circumnavigates Eurasia after becoming first to traverse Northeast Passage.

1879–82  *Jeannette.* Ill-fated De Long expedition in quest of North Pole.

1883  *Albatross* first U.S. purpose-built research vessel.

1893–96  *Fram.* Nansen's drift in the Arctic Ocean.

1897–98  *Belgica.* Gerlache expedition first to winter in Antarctica.

1898–99  *Southern Cross.* Borchgrevink leads South Polar Expedition, first to winter intentionally in Antarctica.

1899–1900  *Stella Polare.* Abruzzi attempts to reach North Pole.

1901–3  *Gauss.* Drygalski leads German Antarctic Expedition.

1901–4  HMS *Discovery.* Scott leads British National Antarctic Expedition.

1903–6  *Gjøa.* Amundsen first to complete Northwest Passage.

1905–6  *Roosevelt.* Peary's fourth Arctic expedition establishes new farthest north.

1906–25  *Arctic.* Berthier's expeditions to assert Canadian sovereignty over Arctic Archipelago.

1907–9  *Nimrod.* Shackleton's British Imperial Antarctic Expedition.

1908–10  *Pourquois Pas?* Charcot's second Antarctic expedition.

1909–21  *Carnegie.* Six voyages to investigate variations in Earth's magnetic field.

1910–12  *Terra Nova.* Scott's ill-fated attempt to reach the South Pole.

1910–12  *Fram.* Amundsen first to reach South Pole.

1914–15  *Endurance.* Ship crushed in ice during Shackleton's Imperial Trans-Antarctic Expedition.

**1918** Allied Submarine Detection Investigation Committee (ASDIC) established to develop devices for determining range and bearing of submerged objects; later known as sonar (for SOund NAvigation Ranging).

**1918–19** *Maud.* Amundsen attempts to drift across North Pole.

**1921–54** *Bowdoin.* MacMillan's Arctic voyages.

**1925–27** *Meteor.* Topographic survey of Atlantic Ocean floor.

**1930s** Radar (RAdio Detection And Ranging) developed in Britain, Germany, and United States.

**1931** *Nautilus.* Wilkinson expedition first submarine under the ice pack.

**1933** *Ramapo.* Largest wave ever recorded, 34 meters (112 feet), in mid-Pacific.

**1934** *Bathysphere.* Tethered submersible descends to 923 meters (3,028 feet).

**1940–42** *St. Roch.* Larsen expedition second to traverse Northwest Passage, first from west to east.

**1943** *FNRS-3.* Bathyscaph descends to 4,049 meters (13,284 feet).

**1944** Decca hyperbolic navigation system used during D-Day invasion of Normandy.

**1945–91** *Calypso.* Cousteau's expeditions popularize oceanographic research.

**1947** *Kon-Tiki.* Heyerdahl expedition from Peru to Tuamotus in reed raft.

**1952** *L'Hérétique.* Bombard examines survival at sea in transatlantic raft voyage.

**1958** USS *Nautilus.* Anderson takes submarine to 90° North to become the first vessel at North Pole.

**1959** *Trieste* descends to 10,912 meters (35,800 feet) in Challenger Deep. USS *Skate* surfaces at North Pole. Soviet icebreaker *Lenin* is first nuclear-powered surface ship.

**1960** USS *Triton* circumnavigates the world under water.

**1963** *FLIP.* FLoating Instrument Platform launched.

**1964** *Alvin.* Launch of U.S. Navy's first deep submergence research vehicle. Locates hydrogen bomb off Spain in 1966.

**1968–83** *Glomar Challenger* used for JOIDES core-sampling expeditions.

**1969** *Manhattan.* First commercial vessel to transit Northwest Passage. *Lindblad Explorer* first cruise ship designed for expeditions to remote places.

**1970** *Ra II.* Heyerdahl transatlantic expedition from Morocco to Barbados in reed boat.

**1975** *Arktika.* First surface ship to North Pole.

**1976** *Hokule'a.* Replica voyaging canoe sails from Hawaii to Tahiti without navigational instruments.

**1976–77** *Brendan.* Severin recreates legendary transatlantic voyage of St. Brendan in curragh.

**1978** *Tigris.* Heyerdahl expedition from Persian Gulf to East Africa in reed boat.

**1980** *Sohar.* Severin expedition from Oman to China in traditional dhow.

**1984** *Argo.* Severin retraces Black Sea route of mythical Argonauts from Greece to Georgia.

**1985** U.S. Department of Defense makes Navstar global position system (GPS) satellite data available to public.

**1986** *Alvin* et al. *Titanic* located at depth of 3,780 meters (12,402 feet).

# Glossary

**almiranta** The ship carrying a fleet's second-in-command. See **capitana**.

**Antarctica** The fifth largest continent, most of which lies south of the Antarctic Circle, latitude 66°33'S. It is covered almost entirely (98 percent) by sheet ice. It has no indigenous population and apart from scientific research stations is uninhabited.

**Arctic** The regions lying north of latitude 66°33'N. The northernmost regions of Asia, Europe, and North America lie within the Arctic Circle. Most of the landmass within the Arctic is made up of islands. Sea ice covers approximately 50 percent of the Arctic Ocean — the fourth largest ocean — during summer, and 85 percent in winter.

**Atlantic Ocean** The second largest ocean, with an area of more than 82.2 million square kilometers (31.7 million square miles), lying between Europe and Africa in the east and North and South America in the west.

**bark** A three-masted vessel square rigged on fore- and mainmasts, and fore-and-aft rigged on the mizzen.

**barkentine** A vessel of three to six masts, square-rigged on the foremast, and fore-and-aft rigged on the others.

**brig** A two-masted vessel, square-rigged on both masts.

**brigantine** A two-masted vessel, square-rigged on the foremast, and fore-and-aft rigged on the main.

**capitana** The ship carrying a fleet's first-in-command or captain-major. (See also **almiranta**.)

**caravel** A relatively small Portuguese vessel of the fifteenth and sixteenth centuries setting lateen sails on two or three masts (*caravela latina*) or square sails on the fore- and mainmasts (*caravela redonda*). Highly maneuverable, caravels helped make possible the voyages of the early Portuguese and Spanish discoverers.

**carrack** A large seagoing vessel of the fourteenth century that combined northern European and Mediterranean shipbuilding techniques. Carracks resembled the northern cog, but they were constructed frame first and carried more than one mast. By the sixteenth century, they carried three masts and high stern and forecastles. Carracks were forerunners of galleons.

**carreira da India** The India Run, the yearly movement of Portuguese ships between Lisbon and Goa, and later Malacca, following Vasco da Gama's discovery of the sea route to the Indies at the end of the fifteenth century. The carreira das Índias was the Spanish term for the yearly transatlantic movement of ships between Spain and the Americas.

**chart** A map used for navigation at sea and in coastal waters. Charts contain information on land forms, landmarks, depth of water, sea marks, currents, and other information of use to navigators.

**chronometer** A device for measuring time; a clock. Before the advent of electronic navigation devices, chronometers were essential for determining longitude at sea.

**cutter** A single-masted vessel similar to a sloop but usually setting double headsails. Patrol vessels of the U.S. Coast Guard are also called cutters.

**displacement tonnage** The standard method of measuring the size of warships. Displacement tonnage is the volume of water displaced by a vessel, the weight of the water so displaced being equal to the weight of the object displacing it. (See also **tonnage**.)

**fore-and-aft sail** A sail set parallel to the centerline of a vessel. Fore-and-aft vessels are simpler to rig than square-rigged vessels, require a smaller crew, and can sail closer to the direction from which the wind is blowing.

**forecastle** Originally, a built-up structure comprising several decks in the forward part of a ship, from which archers or gunners could fire into an enemy ship. (A sterncastle aft served the same function.) In more modern usage, the forecastle (pronounced and often written "focsle") is the crew's quarters in the forward part of a ship.

**frame** A transverse rib that forms part of the skeleton of a ship's hull.

**frigate** A relatively small combatant ship. In the age of sail, frigates sailed with the fleet as reconnaissance vessels and in battle stood away from the line to relay signals from the flagship to other ships in the line whose captains could not see the flagship because of gunsmoke. Frigates were also used for convoy protection and commerce raiding.

**galleon** A full-rigged vessel that evolved in Europe in the late sixteenth and early seventeenth centuries and was the immediate ancestor of the full-rigged ship. Galleons had a higher length-to-beam ratio, lower fore- and sterncastles, and greater maneuverability than carracks. (See also **carrack.**)

**galley** A relatively narrow vessel driven primarily by oars. Galleys evolved in the ancient Mediterranean, and the galley par excellence was the Greek *trieres*, or trireme.

**hemisphere** A half a sphere. The earth is divided into a Northern Hemisphere (above the Equator) and Southern Hemisphere (below the Equator), and also into an Eastern Hemisphere (from 0° — by convention, Greenwich, England — east to 180°) and Western Hemisphere (0° west to 180°W).

**hydrography** The study of the physical characteristics of oceans, lakes, rivers, and other navigable waters: contours of surrounding and submerged land forms, bottom characteristics, tides and currents, among other things.

**Indian Ocean** The third largest ocean, with an area of more than 73.5 million square kilometers (28.4 million square miles), bounded by Africa in the west, Asia in the north, and Indonesia and Australia in the east.

**ketch** A two-masted vessel with a tall mainmast and a shorter mizzen mast.

**last** (pl. **lasten**) A unit of weight equal to about two tons (4,000 pounds).

**lateen** A triangular fore-and-aft sail set from a long spar attached to a short mast, used by mariners of the Iberian Peninsula, the Mediterranean, and the Indian Ocean.

**latitude** The angular distance north or south from the Equator. This angular distance is expressed in degrees, minutes, and seconds north or south of the Equator (0° latitude). The North Pole is 90°00′00″N, and the South Pole is 90°00′00″S.

**longitude** The angular distance east or west of the Prime Meridian — 0° longitude — which runs through Greenwich, England. Longitude is expressed in degrees, minutes, and seconds east or west of the Prime Meridian, up to 180°.

**mast** A vertical spar from which sails are set. In a square-rigged vessel, masts are often composed of separate sections: lower mast, topmast, topgallant mast, and royal mast. Masts are named, from bow to stern, foremast, mainmast, mizzen mast, and jigger mast. In some five-masted vessels, the third mast is called the middle mast. Driver and spanker masts are also found on six-masted vessels.

**nao** A generic term (from the Latin *navis*, or "ship") for the relatively large Spanish and Portuguese vessels of the fifteenth and sixteenth centuries and generally considered a forerunner of the carrack and galleon.

**Northeast Passage** The mostly icebound sea route between the Atlantic and Pacific oceans that runs across the top of Europe and Asia.

**Northwest Passage** The mostly icebound sea route between the Atlantic and Pacific oceans that runs through the Arctic Archipelago of islands lying north of North America.

**oceanography** The study of the biological, botanical, physical, chemical, and environmental characteristics of the oceans.

**Pacific Ocean** The world's largest ocean, with an area of more than 165.4 million square kilometers (63.8 million square miles). It is bounded by Asia and Australia in the west and North America in the east.

**paddle steamer** A steamboat driven by two paddle wheels mounted on either side of the hull, or a single paddle wheel in the stern.

**Poles** The points at either end of the axis around which the earth rotates. The North Pole is located at 90°N, the South Pole at 90°S.

**retour ship** A capacious, heavily armed, and well-manned merchant ship of the Dutch East India

Company (Verenigde Oostindische Compagnie, or VOC) designed for the long round-trip (*retour*) voyage from the Netherlands to the East Indies.

**schooner** A vessel of two to seven masts, all fore-and-aft rigged. A topsail schooner also sets square sails on the foremast. (See also **barkentine**.)

**ship, full-rigged** A vessel having three, four, or five masts and setting square sails on each. These are, from the deck up: course, topsail (sometimes split into lower and upper), topgallant (sometimes split), royal, and skysail. In very light airs, some clipper ship captains would rig moonrakers above the skysails.

**sloop** A single-masted vessel setting a mainsail and a single jib, or headsail.

**sloop-of-war** A three-masted, full-rigged warship, smaller than a frigate and mounting eight to twenty guns.

**sounding** Depth of water as indicated on a chart or a depth-finding device. Depths can be determined by lowering a sounding lead at the end of a line and measuring the length of the line let out. Soundings are now determined by electronic sonar devices.

**square sail** A quadrilateral sail set from a yard. Although a square rigger can carry more sail than a fore-and-aft rigged vessel of comparable size, it is more dependent on favorable (following) winds.

**staysail** A triangular fore-and-aft sail set from a stay, a piece of standing rigging leading forward from, and used to provide longitudinal support for, a mast.

**steering oar** An oar mounted on the side of a ship (usually the right-steering board, or starboard side) toward the stern and used for turning a ship. (See also **rudder**.)

**strake** A continuous row of hull planking (in a wooden ship) or plating (in an iron or steel ship) running fore and aft.

**submarine** A warship capable of operating underwater for long periods, developed in the late nineteenth century for military purposes. Since World War II, submarine technology has been used increasingly for underwater science. (See also **submersible**.)

**submersible** A vessel designed to operate below the surface of the water. The term is often used of small manned research vehicles designed to operate at extreme depths.

**thole pin** A vertical piece of wood against which a rowing oar pivots.

**tonnage** In merchant ships, tonnage is usually an expression of a ship's capacity or volume. The word has its origins in the medieval "tun," or wine cask, tunnage being the number of tuns a vessel could carry. Tonnage rules vary enormously. In the eighteenth century, tonnage was referred to as "burthen." One ton is now generally understood to equal 100 cubic feet. *Gross register tonnage* (grt) is the whole cubic capacity of all enclosed spaces of a ship. *Net register tonnage* (nrt) is the capacity under deck available for stowing cargo only. *Deadweight tonnage* (dwt) is a measure of the weight of a vessel's cargo. *Displacement tonnage* (disp.) is the volume, or weight, of water displaced by a vessel.

**yard** A spar fastened to a mast perpendicular to the centerline of a vessel from which square sails are set. In square-rigged vessels, yards run perpendicular to the centerline of the hull; in lateen-rigged vessels, yards run parallel to the centerline. The ends of a yard are called yardarms.

**yawl** A two-masted yacht similar in appearance to a ketch but with a smaller mizzen mast stepped abaft the rudder post.

# Bibliography

The Bibliography includes complete publishing information for every work cited in the article source notes.

## Nautical Bibliographies

Bridges, R. C., and P. E. H. Hair. *Compassing the Vaste Globe of the Earth: Studies in the History of the Hakluyt Society 1846–1896.* London: Hakluyt Society, 1996. Includes a list of the more than 300 titles that have appeared under the Society's imprint.

Labaree, Benjamin W. *A Supplement (1971–1986) to Robert G. Albion's Naval & Maritime History: An Annotated Bibliography.* 4th edition. Mystic, Conn.: Mystic Seaport Museum, 1988.

National Maritime Museum (Greenwich, England). *Catalogue of the Library, volume 1: Voyages and Travel.* London: Her Majesty's Stationery Office, 1968.

## On-line Resources

Hundreds of sites on the Internet are devoted to various aspects of maritime history. One that has been particularly useful is Maritime History Virtual Archives, owned and administered by Lars Bruzelius. http://pc-78-120.udac.se:8001/www/nautica/nautica.html.

In addition, there are a number of on-line discussion groups to which one may subscribe. One excellent forum is the Marine History Information Exchange Group, owned by the Marine Museum of the Great Lakes at Kingston, Ontario, and administered by Maurice D. Smith, curator of the museum. E-mail address: marhstl@post.queenscu.ca.

## Sources

Abruzzi, Luigi Amadeo di Savoia, Duke of the. *On the "Polar Star" in the Arctic Sea.* London: Hutchinson, 1903.

Alexander, Caroline. *The Endurance: Shackleton's Legendary Antarctic Expedition.* New York: Alfred A. Knopf, 1999.

Amherst, Lord, of Hackney, and Basil Thomson. *The Discovery of the Solomon Islands by Alvaro de Mendaña in 1568.* London: Hakluyt Society, 1901.

Amundsen, Roald. *My Life as an Explorer.* New York: Doubleday, Page, 1927.

———. *The Northwest Passage: The Voyage and Explorations of the Gjoa.* London: Constable, 1908.

———. *The South Pole: An Account of the Norwegian Antarctic Expedition in the "Fram" 1910–1912.* 1912. Reprint, Toronto: McClelland & Stewart, 1976.

Anderson, William R. *"Nautilus" — 90 North.* London: Hodder & Stoughton, 1959.

Anson, George. *A Voyage Round the World in the Years MDCCXL, I, II, III, IV.* Ed. Glyndwr Williams. London: Oxford University Press, 1974.

Apollonius Rhodius. *Argonautica.* Cambridge: Harvard University Press, 1967.

Asher, G. M. *Henry Hudson the Navigator — The Original Documents in which his Career is Recorded, Partly Translated, and Annotated.* London: Hakluyt Society, 1860.

Back, George. *Narrative of an Expedition in HMS "Terror" Undertaken with a View to Geographical Discovery on the Arctic Shores . . .* London: John Murray, 1838.

Baker, William A. *Colonial Vessels: Some Seventeenth-Century Sailing Craft.* Barre, Mass.: Barre Publishing Co., 1962.

———. "The *Gjoa." American Neptune* 12 (1952): 7–21.

———. "Gosnold's *Concord* and Her Shallop." *American Neptune* 34 (1974): 231–42.

———. *A Maritime History of Bath, Maine, and the Kennebec River Region.* 2 vols. Bath, Me.: Marine Research Society of Bath, 1973.

———. *"Mayflower" and Other Colonial Vessels.* London: Conway Maritime, 1983.

———. *The New Mayflower.* Barre, Mass.: Barre Gazette, 1958.

Barbour, Philip L. *The Jamestown Voyages Under the First Charter, 1606–1609. Documents Relating to the Foundation of Jamestown. . . .* 2 vols. Cambridge, England: Hakluyt Society, 1969.

Barrow, Sir John. *The Mutiny and Piratical Seizure of HMS "Bounty" its Causes and Consequences.* 1886. Reprint, London: Folio Society, 1976.

Bartlett, Merrill L. "Commodore James Biddle and the First Naval Mission to Japan, 1845–46." *American Neptune* 41 (1981): 25–35.

Basalla, George. "The Voyage of the *Beagle* Without Darwin." *Mariner's Mirror* 43 (1962): 42–48.

Beaglehole, J. C. *The Exploration of the Pacific.* 3rd ed. Stanford: Stanford University Press, 1966.

Beattie, Owen, and John Geiger. *Frozen in Time: The Fate of the Franklin Expedition.* London: Bloomsbury, 1987.

Beebe, William. *Half Mile Down.* New York: Harcourt Brace, 1934.

Beechey, Frederick William. *Narrative of a Voyage to the Pacific and Beering's Strait, to cooperate with the polar expeditions; performed in His Majesty's ship "Blossom," under the command of Captain F. W. Beechey, R. N. F. R. S. F. R. A. S. and F. R. G. S. in the years 1825, 26, 27, 28.* London: Henry Colburn & Richard Bentley, 1831.

Bellingshausen, F. G. von. *The Voyage of Captain Bellingshausen to the Antarctic Seas 1819–1821.* 2 vols. Ed. F. Debenham. London: Hakluyt Society, 1945.

Bernacchi, Louis. *To the South Polar Regions.* Bluntisham, England: Bluntisham, 1991.

Bernier, Jacques Elzéar. *The Cruise of the "Arctic," 1906–7.* Ottawa, Ont.: Government Printing Bureau, 1909.

———. *The Cruise of the "Arctic," 1908–9.* Ottawa, Ont.: Government Printing Bureau, 1910.

———. *Master Mariner and Arctic Explorer: A Narrative of Sixty Years at Sea.* Ottawa, Ont.: Le Droit, 1939.

———. *Report of the Dominion of Canada Government Expedition to the Arctic Islands and Hudson Strait on board the D. G. S. "Arctic."* Ottawa, Ont.: Government Printing Bureau, 1910.

Berton, Pierre. *The Arctic Grail: The Quest for the Northwest Passage and the North Pole, 1818–1909.* New York: Viking-Penguin, 1988.

Bixby, William. *The Track of the "Bear": 1873–1963.* New York: David McKay, 1965.

Bligh, William. *Narrative of the Mutiny on the "Bounty."* 1792. Reprint, New York: Airmont, 1965.

Bombard, Alain. *The Voyage of the "Hérétique."* New York: Simon & Schuster, 1953.

Borchgrevink, C. E. *First on the Antarctic Continent, Being an Account of the British Antarctic Expedition 1899–1900.* London: George Newnes Ltd., 1901.

———. "The *Southern Cross* Expedition to the Antarctic 1899–1900." *Geographical Journal* 16/4 (1900): 381–414.

Boroughs, Polly. *The Great Ice Ship "Bear": Eighty-Nine Years in Polar Seas.* New York: Van Nostrand Reinhold, 1970.

Bougainville, Louis de. *A Voyage round the World: Performed by Order of His Most Christian Majesty, in the Years 1766, 1767, 1768, and 1769.* London: J. Nourse & T. Davies, 1772.

———. *Louis de Bougainville's Journal, 1767–1768.* Ed. John Dunmore. London: Hakluyt Society, forthcoming.

Braynard, Frank O. *Famous American Ships.* New York: Hastings House, 1978.

Brigham, Lawson W. "Arctic Icebreakers: U.S., Canadian, and Soviet." *Oceanus* 29:1 (Spring 1986): 47–58.

Brock, P. W. "Cook's *Endeavour* and Other Ships." *Mariner's Mirror.*

———. "Dossier HMS *Blossom* 1806–1848." Victoria: Maritime Museum of British Columbia, n.d.

Brosse, Jacques. *Great Voyages of Discovery: Circumnavigators and Scientists, 1764–1843.* New York: Facts On File, 1983.

Brouwer, Norman. *International Register of Historic Ships.* 2d ed. London: Anthony Nelson, 1993.

Buchanan, J. Y., H. N. Moseley, J. Murray, T. H. Tizard. *Narrative of the Voyage.* In *The Report of the Scientific Results of the Exploring Voyage of HMS "Challenger" during the years 1873–1876,* vol. 1. London: 1885–95.

Buck, Sir Peter (Te Rangi Hiroa). *The Coming of the Maori.* Wellington: Whitcombe & Tombs, Ltd., 1950.

Bulkeley, John, and John Cummins. *A Voyage to the South Seas in His Majesty's Ship the "Wager" in the Years 1740–1741.* New York: Robert M. McBride, 1927.

Burleson, Clyde W. *Jennifer Project.* Englewood Cliffs, N.J.: Prentice Hall, 1977.

Byron, John. *Byron's Journal of His Circumnavigation, 1764–1766.* Ed. by Robert E. Gallagher. Cambridge, England: Hakluyt Society, 1946.

———. *The Narrative of . . . the Honourable John Byron . . . Containing an account of the great distresses suffered by himself and his companions on the coast of Patagonia.* 1768. Reprinted in *Voyage to the South Seas in the Years 1740–41.* London: The Folio Society, 1983.

Caffrey, Kate. *The "Mayflower."* New York: Stein & Day, 1974.

Calvert, James P. *Surface at the Pole: The Extraordinary Voyages of the USS Skate.* New York: McGraw-Hill, 1960.

Carson, Rachel L.. *The Sea Around Us.* New York: Mentor Books, 1954.

Charcot, Jean. *The Voyage of the "Why Not" in the Antarctic: The Journal of the Second French South Polar Expedition, 1908–1910.* London: Hodder & Stoughton, 1911.

Cherry-Garrard, Apsley George Benet. *The Worst Journey in the World: Antarctica 1910–1913.* 2 vols. London: Constable, 1922.

Columbus, Christopher. *The Four Voyages of Christopher Columbus.* Ed. Cecil Jane. New York: Dover, 1988.

Cook, Frederick Albert. *Through the First Antarctic Night, 1898–1899: A Narrative of the Voyage of the Belgica Among Newly Discovered Lands and Over an Unknown Sea About the South Pole.* London: C. Hurst; Canberra: Australian National Union, 1980.

Cook, James. *The Journals of James Cook on his Voyages of Discovery.* Edited by J. C. Beaglehole. 3 vols. Cambridge, England: Hakluyt Society, 1955–56.

Cooke, Alan, and Clive Holland. *The Exploration of Northern Canada, 500 to 1920.* Toronto: Arctic History Press, 1978.

Corner, George W. *Doctor Kane of the Arctic Seas.* Philadelphia: Temple University Press, 1972.

Crawford, Janet. *That First Antarctic Winter.* South Latitude Research, Ltd., 1999.

Cross, Wilbur. *Challengers of the Deep: The Story of Submarines.* New York: William Sloan Associates, 1959.

Cutter, Donald C. *Malaspina and Galiano: Spanish Voyages to the Northwest Coast 1791 and 1792.* Seattle: University of Washington Press, 1991.

Dampier, William. *Voyages.* Ed. John Masefield. London: E. Grant Richards, 1906.

Darling, Lois. "HMS *Beagle:* Further Research or Twenty Years A-Beagling." *Mariner's Mirror* 64 (1978): 315–25.

Darwin, Charles. *Diary of the Voyage of H.M.S. Beagle.* New York: Cambridge University Press, 1988.

Debenham, Frank. *The Quiet Land: The Diaries of Frank Debenham.* Ed. June Debenham Back. Bluntisham, England: Bluntisham Books, 1992.

de Bray, Emile Frédéric. *A Frenchman in Search of Franklin: De Bray's Arctic Journal 1852–54.* Toronto: University of Toronto Press, 1992.

de Gerlache, Adrien. *Voyage of the "Belgica": Fifteen Months in the Antarctic.* Banham, England: Erskine Press, 1999.

de Gramont, Sanche [Ted Morgan]. *The Strong Brown God: The Story of the Niger River.* Boston: Houghton Mifflin, 1976.

Delgado, James P. *Dauntless "St. Roch": The Mounties' Arctic Schooner.* Victoria, B.C.: Horsdal & Schubart, 1992.

———. *Made for the Ice: A Report on the Wreck of the Hudson's Bay Company Ship "Baymaud," ex-Polarskibet "Maud" (1917–30).* Vancouver: Vancouver Maritime Museum and Underwater Archaeological Society of British Columbia, 1997.

Divin, Vasilii A. *The Great Russian Navigator, A. I. Chirikov.* Fairbanks: University of Alaska Press, 1993.

Dodge, Ernest S. *Northwest By Sea.* New York: Oxford University Press, 1961.

———. *The Polar Rosses: John and James Clark Ross and Their Explorations.* London: Faber & Faber, 1973.

Drygalski, Rich von. *The German South Polar Expedition 1901–3.* Bluntisham, England: Bluntisham Books, 1989.

Dumont d'Urville, Jules-Sebastien-César. *Two Voyages to the South Seas by Captain . . . Jules S-C Dumont d'Urville.* Melbourne: Melbourne University Press, 1987.

Dunmore, John, ed. *The Expedition of the St. Jean-Baptiste to the Pacific 1769–1770.* London: Hakluyt Society, 1981.

———. *French Explorers in the Pacific,* vol. 1, *The Nineteenth Century;* vol. 2, *The Twentieth Century.* New York: Oxford University Press, 1965, 1969.

Dunnett, Harding McGregor. *Shackleton's Boat: The Story of the James Caird.* Benenden, England: Neville & Harding, Ltd., 1996.

F. S. "Cook's *Resolution." Mariner's Mirror* 17 (1931): 84.

Fanning, Edmund. *Voyages Around the World, with Selected Sketches of Voyages to the South Sea, North and South Pacific, China, etc.* 1833. Reprint, Upper Saddle River, N.J., 1970.

Fernández-Armesto, Felipe. *Columbus.* New York: Oxford University Press, 1991.

Finney, Ben R. *A Cultural Odyssey Through Polynesia.* Berkeley: University of California Press, 1994.

———. *"Hokule'a": The Way to Tahiti.* New York: Dodd, Mead, 1979.

Firstbrook, P. L. *The Voyage of the "Matthew": John Cabot and the Discovery of Newfoundland.* Toronto, Ont.: McClelland & Stewart, 1997.

Fisher, Raymond H. *Bering's Voyages: Whither and Why.* London: C. Hurst, 1977.

Fisher, Robin. *Vancouver's Charting the Northwest Coast, 1791–1795.* Vancouver: Douglas & McIntyre, 1992.

FitzRoy, R., and P. P. King. *Narrative of the Surveying Voyages of Her Majesty's Ships "Adventure" and "Beagle" between the Years 1826 and 1838, Describing Their Examination of the Southern Shores of South America and the Beagle's Circumnavigation of the Globe.* 3 vols. London: Henry Colburn, 1839.

Flinders, Matthew. *A Voyage to Terra Australis in 1801–3 in HMS "Investigator."* London: W. Bulmer and W. Nicol, 1814.

Freeston, Ewart C. "His Majesty's Sloop *Resolution,* 1772." *Mariner's Mirror* 58 (1972): 337–38.

Frost, O. W., ed. *Bering and Chirikov: The American Voyages and Their Impact.* Anchorage: Alaska Historical Society, 1992.

Fryer, John. *The Voyage of the "Bounty" Launch.* Guildford, England: Genesis, 1979.

Gardiner, Robert, and Alistair Couper, eds. *The Shipping Revolution: The Modern Merchant Ship*. Annapolis: Naval Institute Press, 1992.

Gardiner, Robert, and Ambrose Greenway, eds. *The Golden Age of Shipping: The Classic Merchant Ship, 1900–1960*. Annapolis: Naval Institute Press, 1994.

Gardiner, Robert, and Richard W. Unger, eds. *Cogs, Caravels and Galleons: The Sailing Ship 1000–1650*. Annapolis: Naval Institute Press, 1994.

Golovnin, V. M. *Detained in Simon's Bay: The Story of the Detention of the Imperial Russian Sloop Diana April 1808–May 1809*. Cape Town: Friends of the South African Library, 1964.

———. *Memoirs of a Captivity in Japan during the Years 1811, 1812, and 1813; with Observations on the Country and the People*. 3 vols. London: Henry Colburn, 1824.

Greenlee, William Brooks, ed. *The Voyage of Pedro Alvares Cabral to Brazil and India from Contemporary Documents and Narratives*. London: Hakluyt Society, 1938.

Gröner, Erich. *German Warships 1815–1945*. 2 vols. London: Conway Maritime, 1990.

Guravich, Don, Bern Keating, and John Olson. *North West Passage: Manhattan on the Tides of History*. New York: South Street Seaport Museum, 1970.

Gutteridge, Leonard F. *Icebound: The Jeannette Expedition's Quest for the North Pole*. Annapolis: Naval Institute Press, 1986.

Hackney, Noel C. L. *"Mayflower" — Classic Ships No. 2. Their History and How to Model Them*. London: Patrick Stephens, 1970.

Hakluyt, Richard. *The Principal Navigations Voyages Traffiques & Discoveries of the English Nation*. 12 vols. 1598–1600. Reprint, Glasgow: James MacLehose & Sons, 1905.

Hampden, John. *Francis Drake, Privateer: Contemporary Narratives and Documents*. University, Ala.: University of Alabama Press, 1972.

Hansen, Thorkild. *Northwest to Hudson Bay: The Life and Times of Jens Munk*. London: Collins, 1970.

Hart, Henry. *Sea Road to the Indies: An Account of the Voyages and Exploits of the Portuguese Navigators, together with the Life and Times of Dom Vasco da Gama, Capitão-Mór of India and Count of Vidigueira*. New York: Macmillan, 1950.

Helfrich, Lucy Coan. "Sailing Ships, Science and Stonework: The Stuff Dreams are Made Of." *Spritsail: A Journal of the History of Falmouth and Vicinity* 8, 2 (Summer 1994): 2–21.

Henderson, Graeme, and Kandy-Lee Henderson. *The "Sirius": Past and Present*. Sydney: Collins Australia, 1988.

Hendricks, Andrew A. "Construction of the 1988 *Half Moon*." *De Haelve Maen* 66 (1993): 42–53.

Heyerdahl, Thor. *Kon-Tiki: Across the Pacific by Raft*. Chicago: Rand McNally, 1950.

———. *The Ra Expeditions*. Garden City, N.Y.: Doubleday, 1971.

———. *The "Tigris" Expedition: In Search of Our Beginnings*. New York: Doubleday, 1981.

Hilder, Brett. *The Voyage of Torres*. St. Lucia: University of Queensland Press, 1980.

Hoffman, Anne. *Voyage to the Southern Ocean: The Letters of Lieutenant William Reynolds from the U.S. Exploring Expedition, 1838–1842*. Annapolis, Md.: Naval Institute Press, 1988.

Houot, George S., and Pierre Henri Willm. *2000 Fathoms Down*. New York: E. P. Dutton, 1955.

Howay, Frederic W., ed. *Voyages of the "Columbia" to the Northwest Coast 1787–1790 and 1790–1793*. Portland: Oregon Historical Society Press, 1990.

Hsü, Kenneth. *"Challenger" at Sea: A Ship that Revolutionized Earth Science*. Princeton: Princeton University Press, 1992.

Huntford, Roland. *Shackleton*. New York: Athenaeum, 1985.

Ibn Battuta. *The Travels of Ibn Battuta*. A.D. *1325–1354*. 5 vols. Translated and with annotations by H.A.R. Gibb and C. F. Beckingham. London: Hakluyt Society, 1958–2000.

Irwin, Geoffrey. *The Prehistoric Exploration and Colonisation of the Pacific*. New York: Cambridge University Press, 1992.

Ivashintsov, N. A. *Russian Round-the-World Voyages, 1803–1849*. Materials for the Study of Alaska History, no. 14. Kingston, Ont.: Limestone Press, 1980.

Jeal, Tim. *Livingstone*. New York: G. P. Putnam's Sons, 1973.

Johnson, Donald S. *Charting the Sea of Darkness*. Camden, Me.: International Marine, 1993.

Johnson, Robert Erwin. *Thence Round Cape Horn: The Story of United States Naval Forces on Pacific Station, 1818–1923*. Annapolis: United States Naval Institute, 1963.

Jourdain, Silvester. *A Discovery of the Barmudas*. 1610. New York: Scholars' Facsimiles and Reprints, 1940.

Jung-pang Lo. "The Decline of the Early Ming Navy." *Oriens Extremus* 5 (1958): 149–68.

Kaharl, Victoria A. *Water Baby: The Story of Alvin*. New York: Oxford University Press, 1990.

Kane, Elisha Kent. *The U.S. Grinnell Expedition in Search of Sir John Franklin: A Personal Narrative*. New York: Harper & Row, 1854.

Kelly, Celsus, ed. *La Austrialia del Espíritu Santo: The Journal of Fray Martin de Munilla, OFM, and other documents relating to the voyage of Pedro Fernández de Quirós to the South Sea . . . and the Franciscn Missionary plan.* 2 vols. Cambridge, England: Hakluyt Society, 1966.

Kendrick, John, ed. *The Voyage of "Sutil" and "Mexicana" 1792: The Last Spanish Exploration of the Northwest Coast of America.* Spokane, Wash.: Arthur H. Clark, 1991.

King, Robert J. *The Secret History of the Convict Colony: Alexandro Malaspina's Report on the British Settlement of New South Wales.* Sydney: Allen & Unwin, 1990.

Kish, George. *North-east Passage: Adolf Erik Nordenskiöld, His Life and Times.* Amsterdam: Nico Israel, 1973.

Knight, C. "H. M. Armed Vessel *Bounty.*" *Mariner's Mirror* 22 (1936): 183–99.

———. "H. M. Bark *Endeavour.*" *Mariner's Mirror* 19 (1933): 292–302.

Kotzebue, Otto von. *A New Voyage Round the World in the Years 1823–1826.* 1830. Reprint, New York: Da Capo, 1967.

———. *A Voyage of Discovery into the South Sea and Beering's Strait, for the Purpose of Exploring a North-East Passage, Undertaken in the Years 1815–1818.* 1821. Reprint, New York: Da Capo, 1967.

Krusenstern, Adam Johann von. *Voyage Round the World, in the Years 1803, 1804, 1805 & 1806 . . . on board the ships "Nadeshda" and "Neva."* London: John Murray, 1813.

La Pérouse, Jean-François de Galaup de. *The Journal of Jean-François de Galaup de La Pérouse 1785–1788.* Ed. John Dunmore. 2 vols. London: Hakluyt Society, 1994–95.

LaRoe, Lisa Moore. "La Salle's Last Voyage." *National Geographic* (May 1997): 72–83.

Larsen, Henry A. *The Big Ship.* Toronto: McClelland & Stewart, 1967.

Lavery, Brian. *The Colonial Merchantman "Susan Constant" 1605.* Annapolis: Naval Institute Press, 1988.

Levathes, Louise. *When China Ruled the Seas: The Treasure Fleet of the Dragon Throne, 1405–33.* New York: Simon & Schuster, 1994.

Linklater, Eric. *The Voyage of the "Challenger."* London: John Murray, 1972.

Litke, Frederic. *A Voyage Round the World 1826–1829,* vol. 1, *To Russian America and Siberia.* Kingston, Ont.: Limestone, 1987.

Loomis, Chauncey C. *Weird and Tragic Shores: The Story of Charles Francis Hall, Explorer.* Lincoln: University of Nebraska Press, 1991.

Lubbock, Basil. *The Arctic Whalers.* Glasgow: Brown, Son & Ferguson, 1937.

Lundeberg, Philip K., and Dana M. Wegner. "Not for

Conquest but Discovery: Rediscovering the Ships of the Wilkes Expedition." *American Neptune* 49 (1989): 151–67.

M'Clintock, Francis Leopold. *The Voyage of the "Fox" in the Arctic Seas: A Narrative of the Discovery of the Fate of Sir John Franklin and his Companions.* 1860. Reprint, Rutland, Vt.: Charles E. Tuttle, 1973.

McClure, Sir Robert John Le Mesurier. *The Discovery of the North-West Passage by H.M.S. "Investigator," Capt. R. M'Clure 1850, 1851, 1852, 1853, 1854.* Edited by Sherard Osborn. 1857. Reprint, Edmonton: Hurtig, 1969.

M'Dougall, George F. *The Eventful Voyage of H.M. Discovery Ship "Resolute" to the Arctic Regions in Search of Sir John Franklin and the Missing Crews of H.M. Discovery Ships "Erebus" and "Terror," 1852, 1853, 1854.* London: Longman, Brown, Green, Longman & Roberts, 1857.

McGowan, A. P. "Captain Cook's Ships." *Mariner's Mirror* 65 (1979): 109–118.

MacInnis, Joe. *The Land That Devours Ships.* Montreal: CBC Enterprises, 1985.

MacMillan, Donald B. *Etah and Beyond, or Life Within Twelve Degrees of the Pole.* Boston: Houghton Mifflin, 1929.

MacMillan, Miriam. *Green Seas, White Ice.* New York: Dodd, Mead, 1948.

Ma Huan. *Ying-Yai Sheng-Lang/The Overall Survey of the Ocean's Shores.* Trans. J. V. G. Mills. Cambridge, England: Hakluyt Society, 1970.

Mairin, Mitchell. *Friar Andrés de Urdaneta, O. S. A.* London: Macdonald and Graus, 1964.

Malaspina, Alejandro, ed. A. David, F. Fernandez-Armesto, C. Novi, and G. Williams. *The Journals of Malaspina.* London: Hakluyt Society, forthcoming.

Mardis, A. "*Sea Venture*": The Dowling Wreck Revisited, San Marino, Calif.: Fathom Eight, 1981.

Markell, Jeff. "Built to Flood." *Ocean Navigator* 93 (Nov.–Dec. 1998), 87–92.

Marquardt, Karl Heinz. *Captain Cook's "Endeavour."* London: Conway Maritime Press, 1995.

———. *HMS "Beagle."* London: Conway Maritime Press, 1997.

Mitchell, Mairin. *Elcano: The First Circumnavigator.* London: Herder Publications, 1958.

Morison, Samuel Eliot. *Admiral of the Ocean Sea: A Life of Christopher Columbus.* 1942. Boston: Northeastern University Press, 1983.

———. *The European Discovery of America: The Northern Voyages.* New York: Oxford University Press, 1971.

———. *The European Discovery of America: The Southern Voyages.* New York: Oxford University Press, 1971.

Murdoch, Priscilla. "*Duyfken*" *and the First Discoveries of*

*Australia.* Artarmon, N.S.W.: Antipodean Publishing, 1974.

Nansen, Fridtjof. *Farthest North: Being a Record of a Voyage of Exploration of the Ship "Fram" 1893–96 and of a Fifteen Months' Sleigh Journey by Dr. Nansen and Lieut. Johnson.* 2 vols. New York: Harper & Brothers, 1897.

Nares, George Strong. *Narrative of a Voyage to the Polar Sea During 1875–6 in HM Ships "Alert" and "Discovery."* London: Sampson Low, 1878.

Needham, Joseph. *Science and Civilization in China.* Vol. 4, part 3. Cambridge: Cambridge University Press, 1971.

Nordenskiöld, A. E. *The Voyage of the "Vega" Round Asia and Europe with A Historical Review of Previous Journeys Along the North Coast of the Old World.* 2 vols. London: Macmillan, 1881.

O'Brian, Patrick. *Joseph Banks: A Life.* London: Collins Harvill, 1988.

Oulié, Marthe. *Charcot and the Antarctic.* New York: E. P. Dutton, 1939.

Owen, Roderic. *The Fate of Franklin.* London: Hutchinson, 1978.

Parry, Ann. *Parry of the Arctic, 1790–1855.* London: Chatto & Windus, 1963.

Parry, William Edward. *Journal of a Voyage for the Discovery of a North-West Passage from the Atlantic to the Pacific; performed in the years 1819–1820, in His Majesty's ships "Hecla" and "Griper".* . . . London: John Murray, 1821.

———. *Journal of a Second Voyage for the Discovery of a North-West Passage from the Atlantic to the Pacific; performed in the years 1821–22–23 in His Majesty's Ships "Hecla" and "Fury".* . . . London: John Murray, 1824.

———. *Journal of a Third Voyage for the Discovery of a North-West Passage from the Atlantic to the Pacific; performed in the years 1824–25, in His Majesty's Ships "Hecla" and "Fury".* . . . London: John Murray, 1826.

———. *Narrative of an Attempt to Reach the North Pole in Boats Fitted for the Purpose, and Attached to his Majesty's Ship "Hecla," in the Year MDCCCXXVII.* London: John Murray, 1828.

———. *The Ships of Christopher Columbus: Santa Maria, Nina, Pinta.* Annapolis: Naval Institute Press, 1992.

Paul, J. Harland. *The Last Cruise of the "Carnegie."* Baltimore: Williams & Wilkins, 1932.

Payer, Julius. *New Lands Within the Arctic Circle: Narrative of the Discoveries of the Austrian Ship Tegetthoff in the Years 1872–1874.* London: Macmillan, 1876.

Peard, Lieutenant. *To the Pacific and Arctic with Beechy: The Journal of Lieutenant Peard of H.M.S. Blossom.* Ed. Barry M. Gough. Cambridge, England: Hakluyt Society, 1973.

Peary, R. E. *Nearest the Pole: A Narrative of the Polar Expedition of the Peary Arctic Club in the S.S. "Roosevelt," 1905–1906.* New York: Doubleday, Page, 1907.

———. *The North Pole.* London: Hodder & Stoughton, 1910.

Peterson, M. L. R. "The *Sea Venture.*" *Mariner's Mirror* 74 (1988): 37–48.

Peterson, Susan. "*Albatross:* America's First Full-Time Deep-Water Research Vessel." *Log of Mystic Seaport* 39, 4 (Winter 1988): 147–55.

Phillip, A., et al. *The Voyage of Governor Phillip to Botany Bay with an account of the establishment of the colonies of Port Jackson and Norfolk Island.* 1789. Australia: Hutchinson, Australian Facsimile Editions, 1982.

Phillips, Carla Rahn. "The Evolution of Spanish Ship Design from the 15th to 18th Centuries." *American Neptune* 53:4 (Fall 1993): 229–38.

Piccard, Auguste. *Earth, Sky, and Sea.* New York: Oxford University Press, 1956.

Piccard, Jacques, and Robert M. Dietz. *Seven Miles Down: The Story of the Bathyscaphe Trieste.* New York: G. P. Putnam's Sons, 1961.

Pigafetta, Antonio, et al. *The First Voyage Round the World, by Magellan.* London: Hakluyt Society, 1874.

Polmar, Norman. *Ships and Aircraft of the U.S. Fleet.* 14th ed. Annapolis: Naval Institute Press, 1987.

———. *The Naval Institute Guide to the Soviet Navy.* 5th ed. Annapolis: Naval Institute Press, 1991.

Powell, John Wesley. *Exploration of the Colorado River and Its Canyons.* 1875. Reprint, New York: Penguin Books, 1987.

Purchas, Samuel. *Hakluytus Posthumus, or Purchas His Pilgrims, Contayning a History of the World in Sea Voyages and Lande Travells by Englishmen and others.* 20 vols. 1625. Reprint, Glasgow: James MacLehose & Sons, 1906.

Quinn, David B., and Allison M. Quinn, eds. *The English New England Voyages, 1602–1608.* London: Hakluyt Society, 1983.

Quirós, Pedro Fernández de. *The Voyage of Fernandez de Quiros, 1593–96.* London: Hakluyt Society, 1903.

Rich, E. E. *The History of the Hudson's Bay Company, 1670–1870.* London: Hudson's Bay Record Society, 1958.

Richards, Mose. "Sis and *J-826.*" *Calypso Log* 9:2 (June 1982): 1–3.

Ritchie, G. S. *The Admiralty Chart: British Naval Hydrography in the Nineteenth Century.* London: Hollis & Carter, 1967.

Rivière, Marc Serge, trans. and ed. *Rose de Freycinet, a Woman of Courage: The Journal of Rose de Freycinet on her Voyage Around the World 1814–1820.* Canberra: National Library of Australia, 1996.

Roberts, David. "In Texas, a Ship is Found and a Grand Dream Recalled." *Smithsonian*, April 1997.

Robertson, George. *The Discovery of Tahiti: A Journal of the second voyage of HMS "Dolphin" round the world, under the command of Captain Wallis RN, in the years 1766, 1767, and 1768*. London: Hakluyt Society, 1948.

Roggeveen, Jacob. *The Journal of Jacob Roggeveen*. Ed. Andrew Sharp. Oxford: Clarendon Press, 1970.

Ross, James Clark. *A Voyage of Discovery and Research in the Southern and Antarctic Regions, During the Years 1839–43*. 2 vols. 1847. Reprint, New York: Augustus M. Kelley, 1969.

Ross, Sir John. *Narrative of a Second Voyage in Search of a North-West Passage, and of a Residence in the Arctic Regions during the Years 1829, 1830, 1831, 1832, 1833*. London: A. W. Webster, 1835.

———. *A Voyage of Discovery . . . in His Majesty's Ships "Isabella" and "Alexander" for the Purpose of Exploring Baffin's Bay, and Inquiring into the Probability of a North-West Passage*. London: John Murray, 1819.

Ross, M. J. *Polar Pioneers: John Ross and James Clark Ross*. Montreal & Kingston: McGill-Queen's University Press, 1994.

———. *Ross in the Antarctic: The Voyages of James Clark Ross in HMS Erebus and Terror, 1839–1843*. Whitby: Caedmon of Whitby, 1982.

Savours, Ann. *The Voyages of "Discovery": The Illustrated History of Scott's Ship*. London: Virgin Books, 1992.

Schurz, William Lyle. *The Manila Galleon*. New York: E. P. Dutton, 1939.

Scott, Robert Falcon. *Scott's Last Expedition: The Journals of Captain R. F. Scott*. Boston: Beacon Press, 1957.

Severin, Tim. *The "Brendan" Voyage: A Leather Boat Tracks the Discovery of America by the Irish Sailor Saints*. New York: McGraw Hill, 1978.

———. *The "Jason" Voyage: The Quest for the Golden Fleece*. London: Hutchinson, 1985.

———. *The Sinbad Voyage*. New York: G. P. Putnam's Sons, 1982.

Shackleton, Ernest Henry. *The Heart of the Antarctic: Being the Story of the British Antarctic Expedition of 1907–1909*. London: William Heinemann, 1909.

———. *South: The Story of Shackleton's Last Expedition, 1914–17*. London: Heinemann, 1919.

Shackleton, Keith. *Wildlife and Wilderness: An Artist's World*. London: Clive Holloway, 1986.

Shankland. *Byron of the "Wager."* London: Collins, 1975.

Sharp, Andrew. *The Voyages of Abel Janszoon Tasman*. Oxford: Clarendon Press, 1968.

Shelton, Russell C. *From Hudson's Bay to Botany Bay: The Lost Frigates of Laperouse*. Toronto: NC Press, 1987.

Sigmond, J. P., and L. H. Zuiderbaan. *Dutch Discoveries of Australia: Shipwrecks, Treasures and Early Voyages off the West Coast*. Adelaide: Rigby, 1976.

Silverstone, Paul H. *Warships of the Civil War Navies*. Annapolis: Naval Institute Press, 1989.

Smith, B. Webster. *The "Fram."* London: Blackie & Son, 1940.

Smith, D. Bonner. "Some Remarks About the Mutiny of the *Bounty*." *Mariner's Mirror* 22 (1936): 200–237.

Smith, F. G. Walton. *The Seas in Motion*. New York: Thomas Y. Crowell Co., 1973.

Smith, Roger C. *Vanguard of Empire: Ships of Exploration in the Age of Columbus*. New York: Oxford University Press, 1993.

Smith, William D. *Northwest Passage: The Historic Voyage of the S.S. "Manhattan."* New York: American Heritage Press, 1970.

Snyder, J., and Keith Shackleton. *Ship in the Wilderness*. London: Dent, 1986.

Sondhaus, Lawrence. *The Naval Policy of Austria-Hungary*. West Lafayette, Ind.: Purdue University Press, 1994.

Spiess, F. *The "Meteor" Expedition: Scientific Results of the German Atlantic Expedition, 1925–1927*. New Delhi: Amerind, 1985.

Stackpole, Edouard A. *The Voyage of the "Huron" and the "Huntress": The American Sealers and the Discovery of the Continent of Antarctica*. Mystic, Conn.: Marine Historical Association, 1955.

Stanbury, Myra. *HMS "Sirius": An Illustrated Catalogue of Artefacts Recovered from the Wreck Site at Norfolk Island*. Adelaide: Australian Institute for Nautical Archaeology, 1994.

Stanton, William. *The Great U.S. Exploring Expedition of 1838–1842*. Berkeley: University of California Press, 1975.

Stefansson, Vilhjalmur. *The Friendly Arctic: The Story of Five Years in Polar Regions*. New York: Macmillan, 1927.

———, ed. *The Three Voyages of Martin Frobisher*. 2 vols. London: Argonaut, 1938.

Strachey, William. "A True Repertory of the Wreck and Redemption of Sir Thomas Gates, Knight." 1610. In Samuel Purchas, *Hakluytus Posthumus, or Purchas His Pilgrims, Contayning a History of the World in Sea Voyages and Lande Travells by Englishmen and others*. 20 vols. 1625. Reprint, Glasgow: James MacLehose & Sons, 1906.

Subrahmanyam, Sanjay. *The Legend and Career of Vasco da Gama*. Cambridge: Cambridge University Press, 1997.

Sugden, John. *Sir Francis Drake*. New York: Simon & Schuster, 1990.

Sverdrup, Otto N. *New Land: Four Years in the Arctic Regions*. New York: Longmans, Green, 1904.

Swanson, Bruce. *Eighth Voyage of the Dragon: A History of China's Quest for Seapower*. Annapolis: Naval Institute Press, 1982.

Tasman, Abel. *Abel Janszoon Tasman's Journal*. Ed. J. E. Heeres. Amsterdam: Frederick Muller, 1898.

Taylor, Griffith. *With Scott — The Silver Lining*. 1916. Reprint, Banham, England: Erskine Press, 1997.

Tenderini, Mirella, and Michael Shandrick. *The Duke of the Abruzzi: An Explorer's Life*. Seattle: The Mountaineers, 1991.

Thomson, Keith S. *HMS "Beagle": The Story of Darwin's Ship*. New York: W. W. Norton, 1995.

Thorndike, Virginia. *The Arctic Schooner Bowdoin: A Biography*. Unity, Me.: North Country Press, 1995.

Thrower, Norman J. W. *The Three Voyages of Edmund Halley in the "Paramore" 1698–1701*. London: Hakluyt Society, 1981.

U.S. Navy. *Dictionary of American Naval Fighting Ships*. 8 vols. Washington, D.C.: Naval History Division, 1960–81.

Vancouver, George. *A Voyage of Discovery to the North Pacific Ocean and Round the World 1791–1795*. London: Hakluyt Society, 1984.

Varner, Roy, and Wayne Collier. *A Matter of Risk: The Incredible Inside Story of the CIA's Hughes "Glomar Explorer" Mission to Raise a Russian Submarine*. New York: Random House, 1978.

Vaughan, Thomas, E. A. P. Crowhart-Vaughan, and Mercedes Palau de Iglesias. *Voyages of Enlightenment: Malaspina on the Northwest Coast 1791/1792*. Portland: Oregon Historical Society, 1977.

Velho, Alvaro. *Journal of the First Voyage of Vasco da Gama*. Trans. E. G. Ravenstein. London: Hakluyt Society, 1898.

Villiers, Alan. "How We Sailed *Mayflower II* to America." *National Geographic* (Nov. 1957): 627–72.

Villiers, J. A. J., ed. *The East and West Indian Mirror: Being an Account of Joris Van Speilbergen's Voyage Round the World (1614–1617) and The Australian Navigations of Jacob Le Maire*. London: Hakluyt Society, 1906.

Wallis, Helen. *Carteret's Voyage Round the World 1766–1769*. Cambridge, England: Hakluyt Society, 1965.

Wead, Frank. *Gales, Ice and Men*. New York: Dodd, Mead, 1937.

Wildenberg, Thomas. *Gray Steel and Black Oil: Fast Tankers and Replenishment at Sea in the U.S. Navy, 1912–1995*. Annapolis: Naval Institute Press, 1996.

Wilkins, Sir George H. *Under the North Pole*. New York: Brewer & Putnam, 1931.

Williamson, James A. *The Cabot Voyages and Bristol Discovery under Henry VII*. Cambridge, England: Hakluyt Society, 1962.

Wilson, Edward. *Diary of the "Terra Nova" Expedition to the Antarctic 1910–1912*. Ed. H. G. R. King. London: Blandford Press, 1972.

Winwood, Allan J. "*Sea Venture*: An Interim Report on an Early 17th Century Shipwreck Lost in 1609." *IJNA* 11 (1982): 333–47.

Wood, Robert D. *The Voyage of the "Water Witch": A Scientific Expedition to Paraguay and La Plata Region (1853–1856)*. Culver City, Calif.: Labyrinthos, 1985.

Worsley, Frank. *Endurance*. London: Philip Allan, 1931.

———. *The Great Antarctic Rescue: Shackleton's Boat Journey*. London: Times Books, 1977.

Wroth, Lawrence C. *The Voyages of Giovanni da Verrazzano, 1524–1528*. New Haven: Yale University Press, 1970.

# Index